NEW YORK

KNOPF GUIDES

● Encyclopedia section

■ **NATURE** The natural heritage: species and habitats characteristic to the area covered by the guide, annotated and illustrated by naturalist authors and artists.

HISTORY AND LANGUAGE The impact of international historical events on local history, from the arrival of the first inhabitants, with key dates appearing in a timeline above the text.

LIFESTYLE Customs and traditions and their continuing role in contemporary life.

ARCHITECTURE The architectural heritage, focusing on style and topology, a look at rural and urban buildings, major civil, religious and military monuments.

AS SEEN BY PAINTERS A selection of paintings of the city or country by different artists and schools, arranged chronologically or thematically.

AS SEEN BY WRITERS An anthology of texts focusing on the city or country, taken from works of all periods and countries, arranged thematically.

▲ Itineraries

Each itinerary begins with a map of the area to be explored.

✪ **SPECIAL INTEREST** These sites are not to be missed. They are highlighted in gray boxes in the margins.

★ **EDITOR'S CHOICE** Sites singled out by the editor for special attention.

INSETS On richly illustrated double pages, these insets turn the spotlight on subjects deserving more in-depth treatment.

◆ Practical information

All the travel information you will need before you go and when you get there.

SIGHTSEEING A handy table of addresses and opening hours.

USEFUL ADDRESSES A selection of hotels and restaurants compiled by an expert.

APPENDICES Bibliography, list of illustrations and general index.

MAP SECTION Maps of areas covered by the guide, followed by an index; these maps are marked out with letters and figures making it easy for the reader to pinpoint a town, region or site.

◆ MIDTOWN

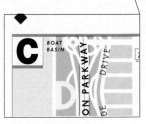

Each map in the map section is designated by a letter. In the itineraries, all the sites of interest are given a map reference (for example: **C** B2).

The mini-map pinpoints the itinerary within the wider area covered by the guide.

The itinerary map shows the main sites, the editor's choices and the places of special interest.

● ▲ ◆
The above symbols within the text provide cross-references to a place or a theme discussed elsewhere in the guide.

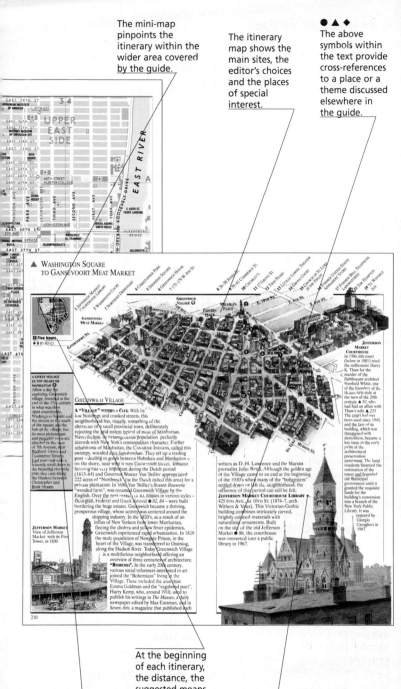

▲ WASHINGTON SQUARE TO GANSEVOORT MEAT MARKET

1 JEFFERSON MARKET COURTHOUSE LIBRARY 2 WASHINGTON COURT 3 NORTHERN DISPENSARY 4 CHRISTOPHER PARK 5 SHERIDAN SQUARE 6 GREENWICH HOUSE 7 15–19 W. 10TH ST. 8 36–40 JONES ST. 9 46–51 COMMERCE ST. 10 CHERRY ST. 11 17 GROVE ST. 12 TWO PEAKS 13 LUCILLE LORTEL THEATER 14 GROVE COURT 15 CHURCH OF ST LUKE IN THE FIELDS 16 FORMER UNITED STATES APPRAISER'S STORE 17 FORMER BELL TELEPHONE LABORATORIES 18 ST. WATERLY 19 THE HAMPTON

GREENWICH VILLAGE

A "VILLAGE" WITHIN A CITY. With its low buildings and crooked streets, this neighborhood has, visually, something of the character of a small provincial town, deliberately rejecting the grid system typical of most of Manhattan. Nevertheless, its heterogeneous population perfectly accords with New York's cosmopolitan character. Earlier inhabitants of Manhattan, the CANARSIE INDIANS, called this swampy, wooded area Sapponckanican. They set up a trading post – dealing in goods between Hoboken and Manhattan – on the shore, near what is now Gansevoort Street. Tobacco farming was very important during the Dutch period (1613–64) and Governor Wouter Van Twiller appropriated 222 acres of "Northwyck" (as the Dutch called this area) for a private plantation. In 1696, Van Twiller's Bossen Bouwerie "wooded farm", was renamed Greenwich Village by the English. Over the next century or so, houses in various styles – Georgian, Federal and Greek Revival ● 82, 84 – were built bordering the huge estates. Greenwich became a thriving, prosperous village, whose activity was centered around the shipping industry. In the 1820's, as a result of an influx of New Yorkers from lower Manhattan, fleeing the cholera and yellow fever epidemics, Greenwich experienced rapid urbanization. In 1829 the male population of Newgate Prison, in the heart of the Village, was transferred to Ossining, along the Hudson River. Today Greenwich Village is a multifarious neighborhood offering an overview of three centuries of architecture. "BOHEMIA". In the early 20th century, various social reformers interested in art joined the "Bohemians" living in the Village. These included the anarchist Emma Goldman and the "vagabond poet", Harry Kemp, who, around 1910, used to publish his writings in The Masses, a daily newspaper edited by Max Eastman, and in Seven Arts, a magazine that published such

writers as D. H. Lawrence and the Marxist journalist John Reed. Although the golden age of the Village came to an end at the beginning of the 1930's when many of the "bohemians" settled down on left the neighborhood, the influence of this period can still be felt.
JEFFERSON MARKET COURTHOUSE LIBRARY ★. 425 6TH AVE., at 10TH ST. (1874–7, arch. Withers & Vaux). This Victorian-Gothic building combines intricately carved, brightly colored materials with naturalistic ornaments. Built on the site of the old Jefferson Market ● 86, the courthouse was converted into a public library in 1967.

JEFFERSON MARKET COURTHOUSE
In 1906 this court (below in 1881) tried the millionaire Harry K. Thaw for the murder of the flamboyant architect Stanford White, one of the founders of the Beaux-Arts style at the turn of the 20th century ▲ 92, who had had an affair with Thaw's wife ▲ 233. The court had not been used since 1945, and the fate of its building, which was threatened with demolition, became a key issue in the early years of the architectural preservation movement. The local residents financed the restoration of the tower and bounded the municipal government until it granted the requisite funds for the building's conversion into a branch of the New York Public Library. It was restored by Giorgio Cavaglieri in 1967.

A LIVELY VILLAGE IN THE HEART OF MANHATTAN ✪
Allow a day for exploring Greenwich village, founded at the end of the 17th century in what was then open countryside. Washington Square and the streets to the south of the square are the hub of the village, but its most picturesque and peaceful areas are situated to the west of 7th Avenue, near Bedford, Grove and Commerce Streets. End your visit with a leisurely stroll down to the beautiful riverside path that runs along the Hudson between Christopher and Bank Streets.

JEFFERSON MARKET
View of Jefferson Market with its First Tower, in 1830.

✪ Five hours.
● B1–B2–C1

By foot

At the beginning of each itinerary, the distance, the suggested means of travel and the time it will take to cover the area are indicated beneath the maps:
🚶 By foot

✪ This symbol indicates places of special interest.

★ The star symbol signifies sites singled out by the editor for special attention.

● <u>Encyclopedia section</u>

▲ Itineraries in New York

◆ Practical information

LOWER MANHATTAN ▲135
The dynamic Financial District, home of the Stock Exchange, old colonial houses and many early and modern skyscrapers, and site of the former World Trade Center. Battery Park, where you can catch the ferry for the Statue of Liberty and New York Bay.

AROUND CITY HALL ▲167
Visit the headquarters of the mayor of New York, then explore South Street Seaport with its fish market and old riggings. Enjoy the breathtaking views afforded by a stroll across Brooklyn Bridge.

LOWER EAST SIDE ▲189
Penetrate the historic heart of New York's immigrant communities: the old Jewish neighborhood and Little Italy, which were eroded by the growth of Chinatown.

AROUND WASHINGTON SQUARE ▲197
New York at its trendiest: SoHo and TriBeCa with former warehouses converted into loft apartments, stores and galleries; Greenwich Village with its tangle of old streets, bars and jazz clubs; eclectic Chelsea, with its flea markets, galleries and old seminary.

AROUND UNION SQUARE ▲ 221
Diverse itineraries: East Village, which still exudes an arty bohemian atmosphere, Gramercy Park, a peaceful residential oasis, and the area around Madison Square with the former "Ladies' Mile", once the haunt of fashionable women.

AROUND GRAND CENTRAL TERMINAL ▲235
The heart of Manhattan, dominated by the soaring silhouette of the Empire State Building. To the west, the bright lights of Times Square and the Broadway Theater District. To the east, take a stroll toward the East River and the area around the United Nations Building.

AROUND ROCKEFELLER CENTER ▲ 273
Midtown or the business district, contemporary skyscrapers, hotels and luxury restaurants, the stylish stores of 5th Avenue and 57th Street.

AROUND CENTRAL PARK ▲ 307
Two sought-after residential neighborhoods on either side of Manhattan's "green lung": the elegant Upper East Side, home of most of the large museums, and the Upper West Side, more laid-back in character.

HARLEM AND BROOKLYN ▲ 349
Off the beaten track in Manhattan: the student enclave of Columbia University; legendary Harlem, now experiencing a new lease of life; the northernmost tip of the island with its unique Cloisters Museum; and last but not least, Brooklyn, a flourishing, working-class district.

Numerous specialists and academics have contributed to this guide.
Special thanks to: Luis R. Cancel (Commissioner, City of New York Department of Cultural Affairs), Carole Sorelle (Assistant Commissioner for Public Affairs), Seymour Durst, Gordon McCollum, Henri Peretz, Barry Bergdoll, Alain Dister

Encyclopedia section ●

NATURE
Mr. G., Sidney Horenstein, John R. Waldman, Sarah Elliott, Philippe J. Dubois

HISTORY AND LANGUAGE
Hélène Trocmé, Janette Sadik-Khan, Ed Stancik,
Nancy Green, Kim Hopper, Ken Sheppard

LIFESTYLE
Walter A. Friedman, Brooks McNamara, David Abrahamson,
Louise Kerz, Michael Kerker, Peter Watrous, Doris Hering,
Benoît Heimermann, Nina Gray, Cassie Springer

ARCHITECTURE
Isabelle Gournay, Andrew S. Dolkart

NEW YORK AS SEEN BY PAINTERS
Jonathan Weinberg

NEW YORK AS SEEN BY WRITERS
Lucinda Gane

Itineraries in New York ▲

Rod Knox, Norman Brouwer, Isabelle Gournay, Hélène Trocmé,
Catherine Hodeir, Elisa Urbanelli, Andrew S. Dolkart, Michèle de Rosset,
Edward O'Donnell, Anka Muhlstein, Seth Kamil, Sophie Body-Gendrot

We would also like to thank:

MUSEUM OF MODERN ART
Richard Oldenburg (Former Director),
Jeanne Collins (Former Director, Public Information),
Lucy O'Brien (Writer/Editor, Periodicals and Special Projects)

FRICK COLLECTION
Edgar Munhall (Former Director)

WHITNEY MUSEUM
David Ross (Former Director),
Jack Kennedy (Public Relations)

METROPOLITAN MUSEUM
Philippe de Montebello (Director), Barbara Burn (Executive Editor),
Kent Lydecker (Deputy Director for Education), Mary Doherty (Photo and Slide Library), Linda Komaroff (Assistant Museum Educator)

THE CLOISTERS
Mary Shepard

SOLOMON R. GUGGENHEIM
Thomas Krens (Director), Lisa Denison (Collections Curator),
Samar Qandil (Rights and Reproductions),
Joan Young (Administrative Curatorial Assistant)

Practical information ◆

V. Dupont, F. Hugon and Andy Young of *The New Yorker*

This is a Borzoi Book
published by Alfred A. Knopf

Completely revised and updated in 2003

Copyright © 1994 Alfred A. Knopf, New York.
All rights reserved under International and
Pan-American Copyright Conventions.
Published in the United States by Alfred
A. Knopf, a division of Random House, Inc.,
New York, and simultaneously in Canada by
Random House of Canada Limited, Toronto.
Distributed by Random House, Inc., New York.

Knopf, Borzoi Books, and the colophon are
registered trademarks of Random House, Inc

www.aaknopf.com

New York
ISBN 0-375-71026-4

Originally published in France by Nouveaux-
Loisirs, a subsidiary of Editions Gallimard,
Paris, 1994. Copyright © 1994 by Editions
Nouveaux-Loisirs

Translated by
Sue Rose

Edited and typeset by
Book Creation Services, London

Printed and bound in Italy by
Editoriale Lloyd

NEW YORK

EDITORS
Élizabeth de Farcy, Catherine Fouré, Béatrice
Viterbo, Anne-Josyanne Magniant, Frédéric
Morvan, Delphine Babelon, Cécile Dutheil,
Paule du Boucher, Cassie Springer, Christine
Silva, Sophie Lenormand, Laurence de Bélizal,
Virginia Rigot-Müller
LAYOUT
Alain Gouessant, Yann Le Duc,
PICTURE RESEARCH
Tanguy Cuzon du Rest

ILLUSTRATIONS
Nature: Gilbert Houbre, Jean Torton, Jean
Chevallier, Bernard Duhem, Jean Wilkinson,
François Desbordes, Philippe Biard, Patrick
Mérienne
Lifestyle:
Pierre-Marie Valat
Architecture: Bruno Lenormand, Claude
Quiec, Jean-Marie Guillou, Valérie Malpart
Itineraries: Bruno Lenormand, Donald Grant,
Philippe Biard, Marc Lacaze, Hubert Gauger,
Pierre-Marie Valat
Maps: Bruno Lenormand and Olivier Verdy.
Catherine Totems, Christine Adam, Claire
Cormier, Jean-Claude Senec, Stéphanie Devaux
Computer graphics: Édigraphie, Paul Coulbois

PHOTOGRAPHY
Laurence de Bélizal, Ted Hardin, John C.
Fletcher

Encyclopedia section

"Being situated on a harbor, which attracted the first Dutch settlers, made New York's fortune. Its exceptional vitality was also a contributory factor. Wealth, poverty, liberty, violence, a melting pot of races and cultures . . ."
Hélène Trocmé

"My memory of Manhattan is that of a simpler, friendlier city... There was no underground subway but, on the other hand, outings on the elevated railway represented, for a young boy, the height of enjoyment."

Mirwin Edman

"The subway often generates prolific ideas, due to the movement, the busy throng, the traveler's alert state of mind, as he clatters under streets and rivers, under the foundations of enormous buildings . . ."   Saul Bellow

ENTRANCE

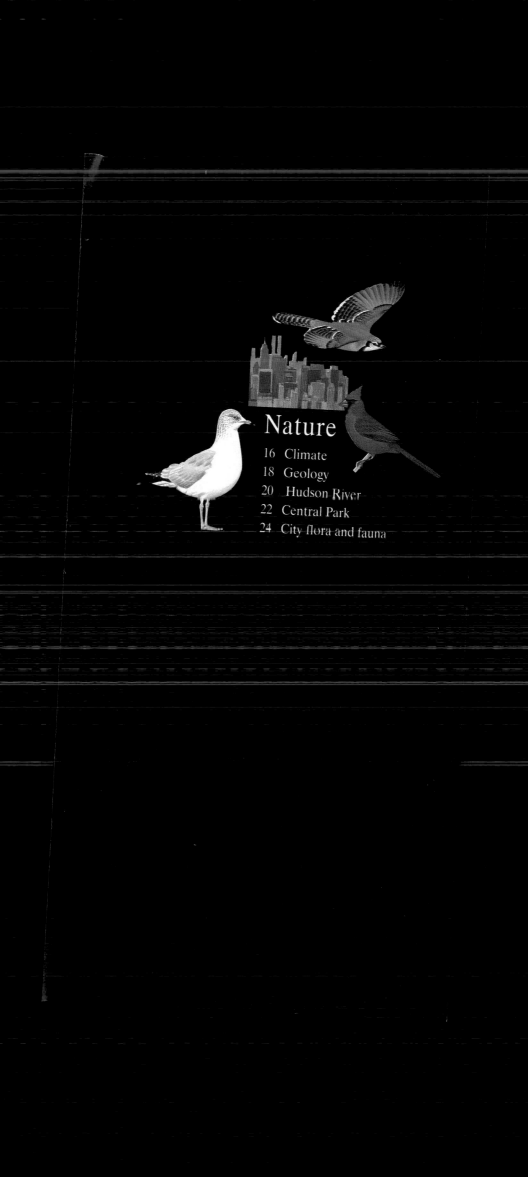

Nature

New York City's
climate resembles the
weather conditions along the northeast
coast of Asia. Frontal systems and the close proximity of the
ocean combine to accentuate great fluctuations in temperature.
Although New York is in a temperate latitude, hurricanes, heat
waves, blizzards and spectacular weather changes can occur
almost overnight. Some years the temperature can vary
considerably, from -13°F in winter to 106°F in summer, in other
words by as much as 119°F.

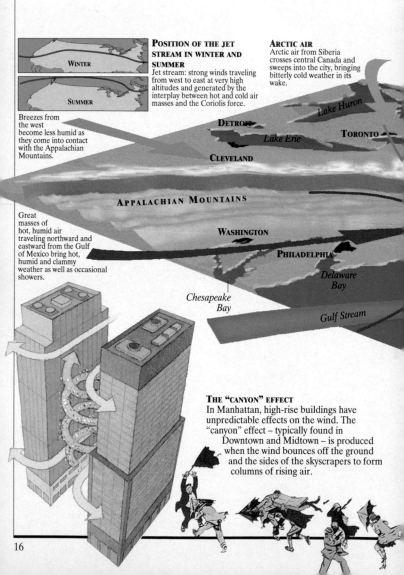

WINTER

SUMMER

POSITION OF THE JET STREAM IN WINTER AND SUMMER
Jet stream: strong winds traveling from west to east at very high altitudes and generated by the interplay between hot and cold air masses and the Coriolis force.

ARCTIC AIR
Arctic air from Siberia crosses central Canada and sweeps into the city, bringing bitterly cold weather in its wake.

Breezes from the west become less humid as they come into contact with the Appalachian Mountains.

Great masses of hot, humid air traveling northward and eastward from the Gulf of Mexico bring hot, humid and clammy weather as well as occasional showers.

Lake Huron

DETROIT

Lake Erie

TORONTO

CLEVELAND

APPALACHIAN MOUNTAINS

WASHINGTON

PHILADELPHIA

Delaware Bay

Chesapeake Bay

Gulf Stream

THE "CANYON" EFFECT
In Manhattan, high-rise buildings have unpredictable effects on the wind. The "canyon" effect – typically found in Downtown and Midtown – is produced when the wind bounces off the ground and the sides of the skyscrapers to form columns of rising air.

During extremely cold snaps, the Hudson River can become partially blocked with ice.

The ocean is responsible for violent storms in this area. At times the east coast of North America has some of the world's most changeable weather.

When temperatures soar above 100°F in the summer, hoses, fountains, even fire hydrants in certain neighborhoods, are the only solutions to cooling off.

When the city is beset by thick fog, the tops of Manhattan's highest skyscrapers disappear – like the Woolworth Building here – transforming the skyline.

In March 1993, a blizzard swept the east coast, from the Gulf of Mexico to Canada. A mass of cold air (-20°F) collided with a mass of hot air (85°F) and the difference in temperature caused snowstorms and tornados.

LAKE ONTARIO

NEW YORK

BOSTON

ATLANTIC OCEAN

Coastal regions enjoy milder weather in the winter and cooler weather in summer than areas farther inland.

THE CAUSE OF A DEPRESSION
When hot, humid air coming in from the Gulf of Mexico and cold air coming down from Canada collide, they generate a coastal storm.

■ GEOLOGY

The islands at the top of New York Bay, which form one of the
main indentations along the eastern coast of the United States,
were created by geological conditions in the region's distant
past. Because the coastline's navigable waterways are wide, deep
and fairly long, ships can be easily piloted down them and
moored. New York's location, at the mouth of the Hudson
River, on a sheltered bay that opens into several other navigable
waterways, has been a crucial factor in stimulating the city's port
growth, contributing to its status as one of the major ports in the
United States. Of the five boroughs that make up Greater New
York, only the Bronx is
connected to the
mainland.

**17,000 YEARS
AGO.** During the
Ice Age, the site of
New York was covered
with an ice sheet 1000 feet
thick and the shoreline was
600 feet farther back to
the east.

**10,000
YEARS AGO**
When the ice
melted, the glacial
debris acted as a dike
and the valleys hollowed
out by the glaciers (the Hudson,
East and Harlem rivers)
filled up.

**10,000
YEARS AGO
TO PRESENT**
The sea reached its
present level 4,000–
6,000 years ago, and the
shoreline's contours formed.

The bare face of
a marble mass,
500 million years old,
can be seen in Isham
Park, at the north end
of Manhattan.

Since building work started in Manhattan, the landscape and
shoreline have changed. Certain sites on the island were built on
landfills – among them Battery Park, South Street Seaport, the
former World Trade Center and the World Financial Center.

Hudson River

Landfills

Mudbank

Terminal moraine, composed
of boulders deposited by the
glaciers

Rocky substratum or
granite bed

The fresh waters of the Hudson
River and the salt waters of New York Bay
converge along the western shore of Manhattan. Despite being
one of the busiest ports in the world, New York harbor remains
home to many species of wildlife. Here the resident marine
fauna mingles with seasonal fauna; certain migratory fish (bass,
sturgeon) spawn farther upstream in the Hudson. Many species
are abundant here and because of the pollution they are in no
danger of being caught for mass consumption. Crabs, lobsters
and shrimp live on the sea bed, while the peregrine falcon dives
from the dizzy height of the bridges.

Many of the piers of New York Harbor, which
were in varying states of decay, have been made
into parks, but they all form extraordinary
micro-habitats.

Great black-backed gull

Herring gull

Black-necked gull

Ring-billed gull

LAUGHING GULL
This bird
migrates south in
winter anywhere
from the Carolinas
to South America.
It is a familiar sight
in the harbor in
spring and summer.

**FOUREYE
BUTTERFLY FISH**
The Gulf Stream
provides the bay with
an annual influx of
tropical fish such as
snapper, grouper and
butterfly fish.

BLUE CRAB
Large numbers of this
crab can still be found
in New York Harbor.

GULLS AND SEAGULLS
Certain species, such as the great black-
backed gull, the black-necked gull, the herring
gull and the ring-billed gull live here all year.

AMERICAN SHAD
Every spring, shad navigate the harbor on
their way to their breeding grounds farther
inland.

AMERICAN EEL
New York's waters are a
paradise for the young eels spawned
in the Sargasso Sea. They swim up the
Hudson River and its tributaries.

STRIPED BASS
Fishing for this
predator takes
place around
the Statue of
Liberty in the fall.

Aquatic fauna is plentiful around the harbor's piers, which are covered with starfish. While sea horses play hide and seek among the fronds of seaweed, predatory fish (bass, eel) come here to hunt for food.

MONARCH
This butterfly spends every fall in the park
on its way to Mexico.

For most migrating
birds New York is
between their winter
quarters and their
breeding ground.

Central Park was created in the mid-19th century,
so that New Yorkers without access to the
countryside could enjoy some of its benefits
on a small scale. The park, which extends over
840 acres, not only provides New Yorkers with
somewhere to go for a breath of fresh air but
is also important to many species of wildlife,
including birds, butterflies and dragonflies. This
lush haven in a forest of concrete is a stopover,
for several hours or several days, for various
migrating birds.

AMERICAN REDSTART
With its outspread tail, this
bird resembles a huge
butterfly. It is one of the
most common passerines
in North America.

SCARLET TANAGER
This bird, which prefers to
feed on caterpillars, leaves
South America in the spring
and nests in May in the oak
trees of Central Park.

The cardinal has extended its range northward but can be found here year round.

CARDINAL
The male has bright red plumage, the female drab brown.

BALTIMORE ORIOLE
This bird builds a ball-shaped nest suspended from a branch, occasionally using such materials as fishing twine.

BLUE JAY
The blue jay lives in the park all year round. Its name derives from its call: a very recognizable "dchay-dchay-dchay". It is fairly tame and extremely fond of corn or peanuts in the winter.

CAPE MAY WARBLER
One of the most beautiful species of its family, the striped warbler is found near spruce trees. Its migratory path takes it through Central Park.

YELLOW-RUMPED WARBLER
This is the only representative of the warbler family to spend winter in the region of New York.

MOURNING DOVE
This dove derives its name from its rather melancholy call, which is similar to that of the owl.

COMMON GRACKLE
These birds breed alone but feed in flocks in the winter.

GERMAN COCKROACH
This insect is perfectly suited to city life. In 18 months, a pair can produce 130,000 offspring.

Although it consists mainly of concrete, steel and glass, Manhattan provides a home for various animals and plants which, over time, have grown accustomed to their man-made environment. Not surprisingly, this unpromising habitat has attracted mainly adaptable species, especially those that were introduced by man, such as sparrows, starlings and pigeons. These animals and birds, some of which were brought over from the Old World, quickly multiplied in the absence of direct competition, creating fresh problems for the city's inhabitants.

STARLING
Brought over from Great Britain in 1890 and released in Central Park, this bird is now a common sight throughout the city.

NORWAY RAT
This European "immigrant" lives in Central Park, in tunnels, and in some tenements.

TREE OF HEAVEN
The ailanthus or 'tree of heaven' grows easily, and seedlings take root in cracks in the sidewalk and the façades of houses.

ROCK DOVE
Some old monuments have been ruined by this bird's droppings.

PEREGRINE FALCON
Until very recently threatened with extinction, this falcon has adapted to large American cities, where it helps to control the population of pigeons. A pair of Peregrines, Lola and Pale Male, famously nest on an 11th-story ledge of an exclusive Fifth Avenue apartment building.

History and Language

1783 CENTENNIAL 1883
EVACUATION of NEW YORK
BY THE British
November 25th 1783

● HISTORY OF NEW YORK

A scene depicting the
Algonquin way of life
(below), painted by
Théodore de Bry in the
16th century.

FROM PREHISTORY TO THE 16TH CENTURY

1000
*Viking expedition to
North America led by
Leif Eriksson.*

1492
*First voyage of
Christopher
Columbus.*

1521
*Conquest of Mexico
by Cortes.*

Giovanni da
Verrazano, the
"discoverer" of New
York in 1524.

THE INDIANS OF MANNAHATTA.
The Asian peoples who crossed the
Bering Strait are thought to have
been the first to arrive in what is now
the northeastern part of the United
States. However, it is not known
when New York was first settled.
In the 16th century the area was
occupied by Algonquin tribes who lived by fishing, hunting
and growing corn, squash and beans. The only remaining
trace of their existence in modern-day New York is the name
of the island of Manhattan ● *48* and a hotel, the Algonquin,
on West 43rd Street.

THE DISCOVERY OF NEW YORK BAY.
The French king
Francis I sent the Florentine navigator Verrazano to try
to find another route to Asia, north of the New World.
Verrazano, who sailed from Dieppe on board *La Dauphine*,
discovered and explored the bay in 1524. He immediately
noted its natural attributes ■ *20*. However, this discovery was
not followed up, and it was not until 1609, over eighty years
later, that the Englishman Henry Hudson, then employed by
the Dutch East India Company, entered the bay and sailed
up the river which was to bear his name.

17TH AND 18TH CENTURIES

1607
*Jamestown, the first
permanent British
colony, is established
in Virginia.*

Peter Minuit buys
Manhattan from
the Indians for
60 guilders.

A TRADING POST IS ESTABLISHED.
New Amsterdam, on
the island of Manhattan, was established in 1624 by the West
India Company. Peter Minuit, the settlement's first governor,
bought the island from the Canarsie Indians in 1626, and
brought in Walloon settlers. New Amsterdam grew slowly.
The colony's prosperity was based on the sale of beaver skins,
otter skins and mink, as well as on tobacco farming, on the
site of the present Greenwich Village ▲ *210* and on the
Upper East Side ▲ *308*. The first African slaves arrived
in New Amsterdam before 1630. Several Dutch farmers
established *bouweries* ● *82*
(farms) both in Manhattan
and on the city's outskirts, in
such places as Brooklyn ▲ *366*,
Harlem ▲ *350*, Yonkers and
the Bronx.

1630
*Boston is founded by
English Puritans.*

1642
*Montreal is founded
by the French.*

THE CITY IS SEIZED BY
THE ENGLISH. The struggle
between Holland and England
for supremacy at sea ended
in victory for the English. Charles II, the king of England,
presented his brother, the Duke of York, with a vast territory
including the Dutch colony of New Netherland. New
Amsterdam surrendered peacefully to the English in 1664 and
was renamed New York. The city expanded quickly; by 1700 it
numbered nearly five thousand inhabitants. Trade diversified;
and flour became one of the colony's main exports. To this
day the city's coat of arms displays two barrels of flour against
four revolving sails of a windmill.

An Algonquin Indian and a
Dutchman flanking the New
York City seal, crowned with
the American eagle.

THE STAMP ACT. In 1765, representatives from nine of the
thirteen British colonies met in New York to protest against
the imposition of a stamp duty on commodities; the act was
repealed the following year. Tradesmen played a vital role in
the initial phase of the struggle for
independence by boycotting English
produce. But the city was taken by the
English in 1776 and became a stronghold
of the Loyalists. After the end of the
hostilities, in 1783, George Washington
made a victorious entry into New York.

**NEW YORK AS CAPITAL OF THE
UNITED STATES.** This chapter in New
York's history lasted from 1789 to 1790.
The first president, George Washington, took his oath of
office on the balcony of Federal Hall ● 85 ▲ 162, which
had been reconstructed after the revolution by the French
architect Pierre Charles L'Enfant. The following year, the seat
of the federal government was moved to Philadelphia. In 1797
Albany became the capital of the state of New York, and New
York City's growth from that time onward depended purely
on its economic role.

*1776
Declaration of
Independence by the
thirteen British
colonies in America.*

Washington making a
triumphant entry into
New York in 1783.

*1783
The American
Revolution ends in
1783 with the Treaty of
Paris, which recognizes
the existence of the
United States.*

THE 19TH CENTURY

BOOM TOWN. By 1800 the city's population was more than
60,000. Over the next few decades, port activity escalated and
New York's harbor became the busiest in the country ● 42.
In 1807 on the Hudson, Robert Fulton launched the first
commercially successful steamboat. In 1818 the first regular
shipping line between New York and Liverpool was
established. Shipyards spread out along the East River, and
the food and textile industries flourished. In 1820, the Stock
Exchange replaced the open-air money market that had
operated on Wall Street since 1792 ▲ 160. In anticipation of
further growth, a commission drew up a grid street plan for
the city extending over the entire island of Manhattan ● 32.

*1803
Napoleon sells
Louisiana to the
United States.*

Warehouses and
factories, such as this
sugar refinery, were
built along the East
River.

THE OPENING OF THE ERIE CANAL. Connecting the
Great Lakes and the Atlantic, the Erie Canal consolidated
New York's supremacy as a port. By 1830 Manhattan had
more than 200,000 inhabitants. The first horse-drawn buses
appeared and a railroad running between New York and
Harlem was built ● 36.

NEW YORK TAKES THE LEAD. By 1860 the city was the
largest in the U.S. The population increased with the waves
of immigration, especially Irish and German. Brooklyn's
population had increased ten times in the space of thirty
years, while that of Manhattan quadrupled.

*1860
Election of Lincoln.*

*1861
Outbreak of the Civil
War, which ended in
1865 with victory for
the North and the
abolition of slavery.*

*1865
Lincoln is
assassinated.*

*1876
Philadelphia
Centennial Exposition.*

During the Civil War, New York remained in the Union and sent many men to fight for the North; the departure of troops leaving for the front was marked by rousing parades.

1889
Construction of the Eiffel Tower in Paris.

1898
Spanish-American War in Cuba and the Philippines. The United States annexes Hawaii.

$10,000 Reward

After years of impunity, Boss Tweed was brought to trial and convicted of theft; he died in a New York prison.

1901
Death of Queen Victoria, who had reigned over the British Empire since 1837.

1914–18
World War I. The United States enters the war in 1917.

1917
The Communists seize power in Russia.

Cast-iron structures ● *94* – office buildings with cast-iron façades – and "proto-skyscrapers" fitted with elevators, began to appear in the 1870's in downtown Manhattan, notably on Park Row. In 1856, 840 acres in the center of Manhattan were earmarked for a huge park ■ *22*, ▲ *314*. The Metropolitan Museum of Art was founded in 1870 ▲ *328*. During the Civil War, violent draft riots broke out in protest against conscription, claiming several hundred victims. In the post-war years the city government was controlled by the "Tweed Ring" under William "Boss" Tweed; he was convicted of corruption and removed from office in 1873 ● *40*.

THE CONSTRUCTION OF THE BROOKLYN BRIDGE. Completed in 1883, the bridge joined the two most densely populated areas of the city ▲ *186*. New York increasingly became the gateway to the New World, and the Statue of Liberty ▲ *144*, given to the U.S. by France in 1886, welcomed immigrants as they entered the harbor. The city grew to such an extent that there was an urgent need for improved public transportation. Streetcars dating from the beginning of the century, and the elevated railway ● *36*, built in 1867, were electrified between 1890 and 1905, and a subway system was added in 1904 ▲ *236*.

NEIGHBORING BOROUGHS ANNEXED. By 1898 the city consisted of five districts: Manhattan, a commercial and residential area with over 1.5 million inhabitants; Brooklyn, a busy borough with 900,000 inhabitants; and the less populous boroughs of the Bronx, to the north, Queens, adjacent to Brooklyn on Long Island, and Staten Island, to the south. Together, they created Greater New York, the most densely populated city in the United States, with 3.5 million inhabitants. The upper and middle classes had already started to move uptown in Manhattan, and in some cases to leave the city for the suburbs of New Jersey and Long Island.

THE 20TH CENTURY

THE SKYSCRAPER ERA. The Flatiron Building ● *96*, ▲ *233*, dating from 1902 and 312 feet high, is one of the many skyscrapers built in the heart of Manhattan at the turn of the century.

> **"This is the first sensation . . . you feel that the Americans have practically added a new dimension to space. . . When they find themselves a little crowded, they simply tip a street on end and call it a skyscraper."** William Archer

They soon threatened to overshadow the streets and in 1916 the city government drew up a "Zoning Resolution", a set of regulations controlling the design of office buildings. This ordinance required architects to design towers with setbacks, establishing the characteristic shape of the skyscraper ● *96*. By this time, Manhattan was connected to Long Island by bridges, and two new railroad stations had been built in the center: Pennsylvania Station ▲ *249*, in 1910, and Grand Central Station ▲ *236*.

THE WALL STREET CRASH. In the crash of October 24, 1929, stock prices, which had been overvalued by rash speculation, plummeted. The Depression of the 1930's hit New York hard, but this period saw the completion of major projects such as the George Washington Bridge (the first over the Hudson, the Empire State Building ▲ *242*, and the Chrysler Building ▲ *266*, as well as the start of work on Rockefeller Center ▲ *274*. Fiorello La Guardia, the high-principled mayor elected in 1933, used federal aid to mitigate the devastating effects of the Depression.

THE WORLD CAPITAL. Many intellectuals and artists (including Albert Einstein, Marc Chagall, Piet Mondrian and Artur Rubinstein) took refuge in New York from a war-stricken Europe. After World War II New York became the seat of the newly created United Nations, whose headquarters were opened in 1953 ▲ *264*. Although by 1950 New York's population had reached almost 8 million, Manhattan had already begun to see a decline in the number of its own residents: some port activities were transferred to New Jersey and some manufacturing moved out of the city. A new influx of immigrants – Germans, Italians and Greeks from Europe, and Blacks from the South – increased the city's financial burden ● *44*.

NEW LEASE OF LIFE. In 1975 New York was teetering on the brink of bankruptcy, partly because of lavish spending by its mayor, John Lindsay. Despite this, several new skyscrapers appeared on the Manhattan skyline, including the World Trade Center in 1973 ▲ *138* and the World Financial Center in 1988 in Battery Park City ▲ *103, 141*. The 1990's witnessed a return to prosperity. Under Rudy Giuliani, the city became a safer place to live and a great many construction programs were implemented: Midtown and Lower Manhattan bristled with new skyscrapers, Times Square regained its past splendor ▲ *254*, a vast redevelopment program for the banks of the Hudson was launched ▲ *141*, districts in Harlem, the Bronx and Brooklyn were rehabilitated, monuments and parks were restored with unprecedented enthusiasm and new museums were opened. The terrorist attacks of September 11, 2001 ● *46* brought this financial and social activity to a temporary standstill and left a deep emotional scar on the city, but New Yorkers are showing spirit and determination by rededicating the site of the World Trade Center as a focal point for the city's vitality and dynamism.

Panic on Wall Street (left). The Crash in October 1929 marks the start of the Great Depression.

1933
Franklin Roosevelt launches the New Deal, intended to boost the flagging American economy in the grip of recession since 1929.

1941
The Japanese attack Pearl Harbor and the United States goes to war.

1949–53
Proclamation of the People's Republic of China and war in Korea. Also the beginning of the Cold War and McCarthyism.

Fiorello La Guardia greets Albert Einstein in 1936.

1963
John F. Kennedy is assassinated in Dallas.

1969
American astronauts Armstrong and Aldrin walk on the moon.

1974
Watergate triggers Nixon's resignation.

1989
Berlin Wall falls.

1993
Bill Clinton succeeds George Bush.

2000
George W. Bush succeeds Bill Clinton.

2001
Terrorist attacks on New York and Washington D.C.

New Amsterdam was a small, prosperous, peaceful town that slowly covered the southern tip of Manhattan, a site bought from the Indians in 1626. With its windmills and brick houses, it resembled Amsterdam, its parent city. In 1650, its population numbered barely one thousand people – mainly Dutch and English settlers. New Amsterdam was annexed by the English in 1664 and renamed New York.

A TRADING POST
The Dutch who settled on the island were employed by the new West India Company, founded in Amsterdam in 1621.

FOR A HANDFUL OF GUILDERS
Some historians maintain that Peter Minuit's purchase of Manhattan from the Canarsie Indians in exchange for some glass jewelry and trinkets worth 60 guilders (the equivalent of $24) was the first case in North America of Europeans exploiting the Indians. However, it has never been determined whether Minuit intentionally took advantage of the natives' gullibility, or whether they felt at all cheated, since for several years they continued to visit the area to trade valuable skins with the Dutch.

THE SKIN TRADE
The prosperity of New Amsterdam was based on the sale of beaver skins, otter skins and mink. Between 1629 and 1635 the skin trade escalated: the number of beaver skins traded nearly doubled from 7,520 to 14,891 and the number of seal skins soared from 370 to 1,413.

A CULTURAL CENTER IN THE MAKING
In the 18th century the intellectual life of New York was not as brilliant as that of Boston or Philadelphia. However, King's College (below), the forebear of Columbia University, was founded in 1754, and a free-thinking press developed. By 1775 New York already numbered 25,000 inhabitants.

PETER STUYVESANT, GOVERNOR OF NEW NETHERLAND

This highly intelligent but difficult man, who had lost a leg during a battle at sea, was intensely disliked by the Dutch settlers, both for his authoritarian ways and for his rigorous government of New Amsterdam, which was going rapidly downhill (above, a satirical depiction of his arrival in May 1647). He decreed that the taverns should close at 9 o'clock in the evening and remain shut on Sunday mornings and, in the interest of public health, ordered that the pigs overrunning the streets be shot on sight.

IN ENGLISH HANDS

The harbor of New Amsterdam was coveted by the English. A fleet was sent from England, and on September 8, 1664, Peter Stuyvesant surrendered. In 1674, after another short-lived occupation by the Dutch, the colony reverted once and for all to the British and was renamed New York in honor of its new owner, the Duke of York, brother of King Charles II ● 26.

TOLERATION

The Dutch merchants tolerated the British, and the British respected Dutch culture and language and left people free to choose their own religion. Trinity (Episcopal) Church, as it appeared in 1737, was built for English colonists. It was replaced in 1846 by a new church in neo-Gothic style ● 86.

MELTING POT

As the city grew it became more cosmopolitan: French Huguenots took refuge in New York after the revocation of the Edict of Nantes in 1685; German Protestants joined the Dutch, English, Scottish, Irish, Jewish and African-American settlers.

New York's commercial origins made it the most heterogeneous colony in North America.

New Amsterdam's first streets were laid out by the settlers along routes already used by people and livestock. At the beginning of the 19th century, as the city continued to spread northward, a coherent town planning program became an urgent priority and the state governor appointed a commission to design a "definitive" plan for Manhattan. Between 1807 and 1811, this commission perfected the existing grid system, which makes it simple for people to find their bearings and move easily from north to south and east to west.

NEW AMSTERDAM
The earliest plan parceling out Manhattan shows the allocation of plots of land to the Dutch settlers, the fort, several streets, the swamps and pasture land ● 74.

A LOGICAL USE OF SPACE
Post Independence the city spread out in an anarchic sprawl, at the mercy of projects initiated by private property developers. The members of the 1807 commission, who were wealthy merchants, took four years to make their recommendations. Since New York was primarily a business center, the grand designs that were a feature of older European cities and which the French engineer L'Enfant had followed in designing the federal capital of Washington were deemed pointless. New York needed a simple plan that would facilitate the sale of land as well as movement around the island and, most important, from one shore to another. The darker colored area on the *Commissioner's Map* of 1811 (opposite) indicates the size of the city at that time.

CONTROVERSY
Although the grid system was efficient and fairly easy to apply, town planners began in the mid-19th century to criticize its undue inflexibility which worked against Manhattan's topography. Their dream was to achieve a perfect symbiosis between city life, with all its advantages, and a more rural setting. Frederick Law Olmsted, the "father" of Central Park ■ 22 ▲ 314 (right), designed the park that William Cullen Bryant had campaigned for, feeling that the people of New York should enjoy open spaces similar to those in European cities.

At the beginning of the 20th century the major thoroughfares devised by Olmsted and his colleagues were finally laid: Riverside Drive and the future Henry Hudson Parkway, ▲ 356 (above, a view at the turn of the century) in Manhattan, and also Eastern Parkway and Ocean Parkway in Brooklyn. Various means of locomotion were accommodated by an assortment of slip roads and footbridges. These were later replaced by highways, which were better suited to motor vehicles.

A GEOMETRIC GRID

There were to be 12 avenues running north to south, 100 feet wide, with numbering starting in the east, bisected by 155 streets running east to west, 60 feet wide, with numbering starting in the south. These blocks were then subdivided into plots all roughly the same size (25 by 100 feet). Not many public squares and open spaces were provided because, in the opinion of the Commissioners, the vast expanses of water surrounding the city made them unnecessary. A market, several squares and a huge parade ground for military drills did, however, appear on the 1811 plan. But these were soon allocated and built over, hence the campaign led by the press for a large park.

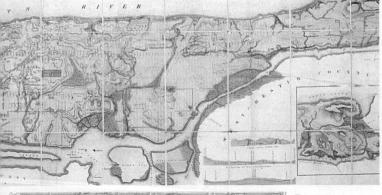

THE EXODUS NORTHWARD
The new grid system was to be applied north of Houston St. as far as 155th St. Not a tree, stream, or hill was spared (above, a topographical map). Around 1850 the grid had reached 60th St. Central Park (opposite) ■ 22, ▲ 314 was not created until 1858.

The first public services appeared at the beginning of the 19th century, when the municipal government was faced with the inevitable problems caused by the expansion of a large city. However, the authorities were not completely free to act: they were often hampered by private companies unwilling to relinquish their share of some very lucrative markets. The authorities also had difficulty persuading the state of New York to allow them to create special departments to run their public services and undertake any necessary work.

GAS AND ELECTRICITY
At the start of the 19th century, gas was the main source of power for lighting (below, a gas lamplighter in front of St. Thomas Church). In 1880 Broadway was equipped with an electric lighting system using the arc lamp. After inventing the incandescent bulb, Edison set up his own electricity company in New York in 1881. Buildings were first supplied

SUPPLY OF WATER
Although water supply was one of the most pressing problems – being vital for sanitation and fire fighting – it was not until 1837 that work began on the Croton Reservoir (above), between 5th and 6th aves. and 40th and 42nd sts., on the site now occupied by the New York Public Library and Bryant Park. Completed in 1842, the reservoir was supplied by an aqueduct from Westchester County. Private homes had running water after the 1860's.

POLICING
In 1844 a single police force of 200 men replaced the disparate units operating at the beginning of the century, which had consisted mainly of volunteers and part-time policemen. In 1853 uniforms were made compulsory, causing a great deal of dissatisfaction. From then on, the New York police force became a model for forces in other American cities.

TELEPHONE
The New York telephone system was inaugurated in 1878. Seven years later, the first long-distance trunk lines – New York–Boston, followed by New York–Chicago – were opened, the latter for the World's Columbian Exposition of 1893.

with electricity in 1882 and electric street lighting then became much more common. Below, men installing underground cabling around 1900.

The waterways of New York City.

1 : Cannonsville Reservoir
2 : Pepacton Reservoir
3 : Schoharie Reservoir
4 : Neversink Reservoir
5 : Ashokan Reservoir
6 : Rondout Reservoir
7 : West Branch Reservoir
8 : Croton Reservoir
9 : Kensico Reservoir

This underground section of New York at the corner of 6th Ave. and 50th St. was drawn in 1939. It shows the astonishing network of underground pipes that keeps the city alive. The orange cables supply power to the subway, the purple cables are for the telephone and telegraph system, the green pipes supply water, the red pipes supply steam for the district heating and the blue pipes carry gas. On the level below, the passageway to the subway can be seen, and to the left of that, the yellow sewage disposal pipe. Below that, the subway tunnels and, at the very bottom, 500–600 ft below the surface, the City Tunnel, supplying drinking water to the city.

SANITATION AND PUBLIC HEALTH

In 1866 New York reorganized its Board of Health (opposite, inside a 19th-century ambulance), establishing a team of health inspectors whose job was to enforce regulations. Some regulations were unrealistic, such as the one stipulating that every room in a building must have a window.

STATE EDUCATION

Education was mostly private in 1842, when a department run by the Board of Education (composed of thirty-four elected members), was created to distribute the city's funds among its wards. The Board was also responsible for appointing teachers, choosing textbooks and syllabi and building schools.

Free public education was begun statewide in 1849 and, by 1860, 90 percent of all elementary school students attended public school. For many years, the main priority of state schools was to teach the children of immigrants how to read and write and instill in them the values underlying democracy.

Ferries started running in the 18th century, and horse-drawn buses appeared in the 1830's. These were superseded by horse-drawn streetcars and, in 1860, by the elevated railroad (known as the "elevated" or the "El"). A solution to the problems caused by pollution and traffic congestion in the city was provided by the subway: the IRT (Interborough Rapid Transit) opened its first line in 1904. In 1955 a new agency, the New York City Transit Authority, became responsible for all the city's public transportation.

BAROUCHES AND HORSE-DRAWN BUSES
From 1831 privately owned vehicles had to share the streets with public transportation. The new horse-drawn buses created huge traffic jams, not to mention the problems caused by the horses themselves (there were 80,000 in New York around 1880). This is why

FERRIES
These were the main method of transportation to and from Manhattan until the bridges were built at the end of the 19th century ▲ 188. The first ferry started running in 1712, and many lines were opened during the steam era. In 1810 Cornelius Vanderbilt, the future railway magnate, laid the foundations of his fortune with the Richmond Turnpike Ferry, which ran between Staten Island and Manhattan. Since four of New York's five boroughs are islands, there are still ferry services (notably the Staten Island ferry which operates a 24-hour service); 75,000 people use these ferries on a daily basis.

TAXIS
It was not until 1907 that taxis were brought under regulation by the city authorities, who enforced meter inspection and set a minimum fare for each journey. The granting of licenses increased to such an extent that by 1937 the number of taxis had to be reduced from 21,000 to 14,000 (there are currently around 12,000 taxis in New York) and a badge was designed for the hood (which is the origin of the name "medallion cab"). These official taxis have been painted yellow since 1970, and although there are a great many of them in Manhattan, they are not as easy to find in the other boroughs. Since there are still not enough licensed cabs, the number of unofficial taxis has increased to some 50,000.

the "El", despite its attendant noise and pollution, was seen as a great improvement.

The "El" traces sweeping curves high above 110th St.

FROM THE "EL" TO THE SUBWAY SYSTEM

The elevated rail system had four routes which ran along 2nd, 3rd, 6th and 9th aves., making it possible to get from Harlem ▲ *350* to the Battery ▲ *142* in 40 minutes. The first pneumatic subway line, the City Hall Line, ran from City Hall ▲ *168* to 145th St., via the West Side ▲ *342*. Since then, the New York system, with 722 miles of elevated track and 469 stations, has become the largest in the world after that of Tokyo. The City Hall station (above), which has been closed for the past fifty years, is still in its original condition. On the other hand, nothing now remains of the elevated railway over the Bowery, which, with its two tracks, completely overshadowed the street (above). The last section of the 3rd Ave. line was not dismantled until 1955.

MTA NYC TRANSIT

MTA NYC Transit is the largest agency of the Metropolitan Transportation Authority, responsible for transporting 2.3 billion New Yorkers every year. As befits the city that never sleeps, its bus and subway networks provide a 24/7 service throughout the city's five boroughs.

Detail from the façade of a New York firehouse

Fire escapes have been a familiar sight on the back of many New York apartment buildings and on the front of old tenements for over a century – a legacy of several catastrophic blazes in the early 20th century which made their construction obligatory. In the past, attracted by the bells and sirens of the fire engines, onlookers used to flock to watch the raging fires. Although fires have continued to be part of the city's everyday life, no one was prepared for the sheer scale and horror of September 11, 2001.

FIRE AT THE TRIANGLE SHIRTWAIST COMPANY

On March 25, 1911, fire broke out in this factory near Washington Square, which employed 500 workers, mainly immigrant women. The garment workers' union had been asking, without success, to have additional fire escapes built and for workshop doors to be left unbolted. Women, young girls and children died from suffocation or from jumping out of the windows (above, painting by Victor Joseph Gatto). The death toll was high: 146 victims.

CONSUMED BY FIRE

In 1776 and 1778, during the American Revolution, New York was devastated by arson attacks, attributed by turns to the Loyalists and to the Patriots. In December 1835, at a time when the city was beginning to spread northward, a fire caused by a burst gas main broke out in Hanover Square ▲ 166 and in the narrow alleyways behind the docks. A strong wind carried the flames as far as South St., Broad St. and Wall St. For two days the flames raged Downtown, while the severe cold hindered the firemen; water froze in their hoses. In total, nearly seventeen blocks in the financial district were destroyed, including all the buildings from the Dutch period.

FIRE AT CRYSTAL PALACE

Built for the Exposition of 1853, this huge building, thought to be fireproof, was totally destroyed by fire in 1858. Fortunately, there were no casualties.

THE FIRE DEPARTMENT

Though impressive, with their gleaming red paint and clanging speed, fire engines could be rendered totally useless by adverse weather conditions. In March 1908, at a fire at the Equitable Building ● 97, ▲ 153 on Broadway, the water froze as it came out of the pumps.

FIREMEN

It was not until 1865 that New York City created a professional, paid fire department. Before then, as was the case everywhere, fire fighting had been left to rival groups of volunteers (it was not unusual for them to come to blows at a fire), who were proud of their shiny equipment, their badges and their traditional parades. From the end of the 19th century, the meticulous organization, efficiency and the modern equipment of the FDNY (Fire Department of New York City), were held up as a model for other cities. The department now employs more than 11,000 firefighters who deal with nearly 360,000 emergency calls per year, of which at least 100,000 are fires.

TERRORIST ATTACKS ON THE WORLD TRADE CENTER

On September 11, 2001, New York's firefighters had to face one of the biggest fires in the city's history, and probably the deadliest. Nearly 350 firefighters lost their lives in the collapse of the twin towers of the World Trade Center, after many of them had walked up countless flights of stairs for more than an hour to help with the evacuation of hundreds of people. For nearly two months after the attack, firefighters helped with rescue operations and the clearing of the site. This sacrifice by "New York's bravest" has made them permanent heroes for the city.

For lovers of "whodunits", New York is the metropolis where Ed McBain's cops use all means at their disposal to fight crime. Or there is the legendary Harlem of the 1960's policed by Ed Cercueil and Fossoyeur Johnson, the two cops created by Chester Himes. New York has acted as a magnet not only for white-collar criminals highly skilled in administration and finance, but also for mobsters, giving it a reputation for being a violent, dangerous city.

CHARLES LUCIANO
"Lucky" Luciano (above, the photos for his criminal record) became the godfather of all godfathers by arranging for the bosses of two rival gangs to be assassinated.

THE ST. SYLVESTER AT THE W. 47TH ST POLICE STATION
Drunkards, busy policemen and, in the foreground, a makeshift coffin containing the corpse of a woman who has just thrown herself out of the window of a nearby hotel. This 1939 illustration by Robert Riggs shows the police station for the area around Times Square, one of the most volatile parts of the city.

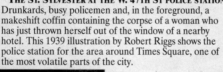

PROHIBITION
Adopted in 1920 (and repealed in 1933), this law was an unlooked-for bonus for New York's criminal elements. Instances of large quantities of contraband alcohol being destroyed by the police (below, on the docks of New York) did nothing to stop bootleggers from amassing huge illicit fortunes.

"MEAN STREETS"
In his film *Mean Streets* (1973), Martin Scorsese evoked his experiences as an adolescent in one of New York's roughest Italian neighborhoods, where crime permeated the local community to such an extent that it became a routine part of everyday life.

BOSS TWEED
In the mid-19th century, William Tweed, nicknamed "Boss" Tweed, made Tammany Hall (New York's Democratic machine) a byword for corruption. His consummate skill in electoral fraud and intimidation enabled him to control and systematically loot public funds.

AT THE SCENE OF THE CRIME
Weegee, who worked as a photographer in New York between 1930 and 1950, was always first on the scene, armed with his flash camera. He roamed the seediest parts of the city to record all that was violent and bizarre. He wrote, "Crime was my bonus, and I loved that . . . it taught me everything I know about life and photography."

THE MAFIA
This criminal organization is rumored to be involved in everything from drug rings, gambling rackets, the fish market and garbage collection to the garment industry, restaurants and the construction business. The 1980's saw the rise to power of John Gotti (above), nicknamed "Dapper Don" because of his elegant style of dress. Gotti was acquitted at three successive trials. However, in 1991, he was finally arrested and imprisoned for the murder of one of the New York mob's "made guys" in a bid to increase his power. The "King of New York" died in prison on July 10, 2002. His Brooklyn funeral looked like a scene from Francis Ford Coppola's *The Godfather*.

Blackout '77
NEW YORK'S NIGHT OF TERROR

"BLACKOUT" RIOTS
On July 13, 1977 at 9.34 pm, New York was plunged into darkness after a bolt of lightning hit electrical transmission lines in Westchester. Amid a general atmosphere of revelry mixed with chaos, there were outbreaks of looting and arson.

MURDER AT THE DAKOTA
December 1980: John Lennon, the guiding spirit of the Beatles, was murdered entering his apartment building near Central Park.

The Last Day in the Life
hn Lennon is shot to death at 40, and a bright dream fades

THE "RED MAFIA"
Traditionally, the "Red Mafia" has been thought to operate in "Little Odessa", the Russian quarter of Brooklyn, near Brighton Beach. However, during the 1990's, the American press revealed that its bosses – rich businessmen accused of corruption and embezzlement – were living in the fashionable districts of Manhattan. The enquiry also revealed that American banks were involved in money laundering for the Russian mob. One of its key figures, Vyacheslav Ivankov, nicknamed Yaponchik ("Little Japanese"), is now in prison.

THE ASIAN MAFIA
Violent Chinese and Vietnamese gang warfare has turned the spotlight on Asian crime rings. A world of secret societies and syndicates, involved in all kinds of illegal trafficking, is gradually coming to light and there is a danger that the Asian community as a whole may suffer unjustly as a result of this adverse publicity.

● THE PORT, SOURCE OF A CITY'S WEALTH

Giovanni da Verrazano, the first European to enter New York Bay, in 1524, immediately recognized its geographical advantages. The wide outer harbor (Lower Bay), itself sheltered from the ocean, opens out north of the Narrows into the magnificent Upper Bay, which also branches out into several secondary bays and channels washed by the tides. Although New York has not been the leading international port (Rotterdam having moved into the lead) since the middle of the 20th century, it is still the largest port in the United States with an average annual volume of forty million tons.

From 17th century to 1850

From 1945 onward

From 17th century to 1800

1880 to 1945

(Left) Evolution of the port activities in the New York Bay.

DOCKERS AT WORK

The completion of the Erie Canal in 1825 linked New York with the Great Lakes and the Midwest: a ton of wheat now took 6 days instead of 20 to reach New York from Buffalo and the cost of the journey plummeted from $100 to $10.

A THRIVING HARBOR

Surrounded by water, Manhattan had one of the great natural harbors. In the 17th and 18th centuries most of the shipping was concentrated around the tip of Manhattan, especially its West Side. Gradually, during the 19th century, piers built perpendicular to the shoreline extended along the East River and the Hudson River (as far as 70th St.), on the New Jersey shoreline and in Brooklyn.

SATELLITE VIEW

This shows every part of the coastline which has been developed to handle New York port traffic – that is Manhattan, Brooklyn ▲ *366*, Staten Island and New Jersey.

THE LARGE TRANSATLANTIC LINERS

In 1818, some New York shipowners created the Black Ball Line, the first regular service between New York and Liverpool. Thirty years later the British Cunard Line set an example by replacing its large

A NEW GIANT

In 2004 the Cunard Lines newest luxury liner, the *Queen Mary 2* (below), ended its maiden voyage at the piers on the west Side of Manhattan

sailing ships with steamers. Today after more than a century of heavy traffic, the New York City Passenger Ship Terminal welcomes fewer than 500,000 passengers per year.

LEADING THE FIELD

At the end of the 19th century nearly half the United States' foreign trade passed through New York. The city exported timber, meat, cereals, flour and cotton from the South and imported tropical foodstuffs and manufactured products.

THE PORT AUTHORITY

In 1921 the states of New York and New Jersey created the Port Authority of New York and New Jersey to centralize port activities and coordinate essential large-scale projects. At the end of World War II, because of cramped conditions and restricted movement, most of the shipping was transferred to Brooklyn ▲ *366*, to Newark Bay and as far as Perth Amboy, on the coast of New Jersey.

Since the foundation of the original Dutch trading post, New York has welcomed millions of immigrants from all over the world, fleeing from war, persecution or poverty – or quite simply drawn by the American dream. Each new wave of immigrants alters the face of the city and each new generation injects new life into its patchwork of communities. New York is in a constant state of ethnic flux; neighborhoods change their identity as immigrants from Russia, China, the Dominican Republic, Pakistan, India and Korea replace those who have moved into neighboring boroughs, suburbs and other states.

16TH AND 17TH CENTURIES

The first settlers to arrive in New Amsterdam were mainly Walloon, French, German and Dutch Protestants. In the late 17th century they were joined and outnumbered by the British with whom they formed the WASP (White Anglo-Saxon Protestant) majority. By 1790 Irish Catholics accounted for 25 percent of the population. The city's early inhabitants also included African slaves and Jews from southern Europe.

THE 19TH CENTURY

In 1830 Europeans accounted for 90 percent of New York's population but this had fallen to 60 percent by the end of the 19th century. In the 1890's there was a massive influx of Eastern European Jews who settled in the district of Lower East Side. A few streets further up tens of thousands of Italians recreated the atmosphere of their homeland in Little Italy, while immigrants from the Russian and Austro-Hungarian empires tended to settle in Brooklyn. In 1820 Black Americans represented 10 percent of the

city's American population but this had dropped to 2 percent by 1890. As it moved into the 20th century New York was a "white" city.

> "... this modern Eldorado, where, little European children were told, the streets were paved with gold, and the land so vast and abundant that everyone could find a place in it."
>
> Franz Kafka

1900–1950
Jews from central Europe were still flocking to New York to escape the rise in anti-Semitism. Italians represented one of the city's main "minorities", while a large Greek community was established near Astoria, Armenians settled in the

Bronx, Poles in Green Point and the Chinese began to move into Lower East Side. Around 1940 the city's Puerto Rican population registered the largest increase. At the same time the Black community also increased significantly as Black Americans left the South for the Big Apple and settled in Harlem, and a wave of immigrants from the Caribbean moved into East Harlem, the Bronx and Brooklyn.

1950 TO THE PRESENT DAY
The Cold War and the collapse of the Communist bloc led to a massive influx of Russian-speaking immigrants who transformed the districts around Coney Island into Little Odessa. In 1965 the Immigration Act relaxed immigration laws and gave rise to the influx of hundreds of thousands of Asians, mainly from China and Korea. Gradually Little Italy gave way to Chinatown and most immigrants – for example Latin Americans and Indians, Pakistanis and Bangladeshis from the Indian subcontinent – began to favor Brooklyn, Queens and the Bronx over Manhattan. The number of Black Americans and Blacks of Caribbean origin increased and by 2004 they represented 26 percent of the population, compared with 44 percent of Whites. Also by 2000, there were more Hispanic New Yorkers than Blacks for the first time in the city's history.

On September 11, 2001 the United States experienced the most serious terrorist attack in its history. Nineteen hijackers diverted four airliners, crashing two into the Twin Towers of the World Trade Center and one into the Pentagon – seen as symbols of American economic and military power. Images of the attack were broadcast live by TV stations worldwide. This act of war, claimed by the Islamic group Al-Qaeda, provoked an American military response in Afghanistan that led to the fall of the Taliban regime.

8.46 AM
American Airlines Flight 11, from Boston, is hijacked and crashes into the North Tower of the World Trade Center. It disintegrates in the intense heat and causes a massive fire.

9.02 AM
A second plane, United Airlines Flight 175, also from Boston, crashes into the South Tower of the World Trade Center (above) and the evacuation of the people working there begins. The entire district is sealed off and the New York Stock Exchange on Wall Street remains closed for an unprecedented four sessions. In the Twin Towers, there are virtually no survivors from the floors above the area of impact. Many victims, trapped by the inferno, jump in groups from the top stories.

9.40 AM
All air traffic is suspended over US territory, for the first time in American history.

Ruins of one of the World Trade Center towers (left).

survivors buried beneath the pile of metal and concrete. Hundreds of firefighters try to control the fires breaking out on the site. The death toll is high. More than 340 firefighters perish in the disaster and 3053 civilians lose their lives. Of these, 2819 are victims of the attack on the World Trade Center, 189 die in the Pentagon attack and 45 on United Airlines Flight 93. It takes eight and a half months to clear the site of the World Trade Center, and many of the victims are never identified. At Ground Zero, the Winter Garden has been restored and discussions about the new buildings continue.

9.43 AM
A third plane, American Airlines Flight 77 from Washington, crashes into the west side of the Pentagon. The building is immediately evacuated, as are all US government offices and the White House.

9.59 AM
The South Tower of the World Trade Center collapses (opposite, left) engulfing the entire area in a cloud of smoke and debris. Fires continue to burn at the site for months. The southern tip of Manhattan is shut down.

10.03 AM
A fourth hijacked plane, United Airlines Flight 93 from New York, crashes in Pennsylvania, southeast of Pittsburgh. It is later revealed that the passengers prevented the hijackers from reaching their target.

10.28 AM
The North Tower of the World Trade Center collapses, burying victims under a mountain of rubble.

5.20 PM
The 47-story building of No. 7 World Trade Center, damaged and set on fire by the Twin Towers, also gives way. Rescue workers, firefighters and workmen frantically try to rescue any

"It was a magical refuge. New York had a lingo, a language all its own."

Jerome Charyn

"THE BIG APPLE"
New York is popularly called the "Big Apple", an expression dating from at least the 1930's, when jazz musicians took the name of a Harlem nightclub and extended it to the whole neighborhood and then to the city in general. In the early 1970's, the New York Convention and Visitors Bureau used the phrase in an ad campaign to boost tourism.

English was increasingly spoken in the colony after the Duke of York succeeded the Dutch as its owner in 1664 ● 26, although as late as 1760 a Manhattan lady could still write, "The English language is beginning to be more universally understood here." Many different languages and dialects gradually entered the city, due to trade and immigration, enriching the English spoken in New York.

A POLYGLOT CITY

More than eighty languages are now spoken in New York. Spanish is the second most common language, after English, reflecting the high number of residents from Puerto Rico, the Caribbean, and Central and South America. Various other languages can be heard in daily business transactions: Yiddish in the diamond merchants' quarter (West 47th Street) ▲ 299, Moroccan Arabic, Filippino, Farsi and Bengali among newspaper vendors, Korean in fruit and vegetable stores, and Wolof between Senegalese street hawkers. Different languages can also be heard in all the ethnic enclaves scattered around the city: Cantonese in Chinatown ▲ 190, Haitian Creole on the Upper West Side ▲ 342, Ukrainian and Polish in the East Village, Hungarian in Yorkville, Armenian in Murray Hill and Spanish in East Harlem ▲ 350. It is not unusual for children to learn English simultaneously with their mother tongue.

STREET AND PLACE NAMES

Many street and place names still bear linguistic traces of New York's successive generations of settlers. Such is the case with the name "Manhattan" (formerly "Manhatta"), which owes its name to the Delaware Indians. There are many theories about the original meaning of "Manhattan", but it probably meant something like "island" or "island with hills". The Dutch legacy can be seen in the names of Harlem and Gramercy (which came from the Dutch word *krum-martsje*, meaning "crooked little swamp"). The neighborhood of Spuyten Duyvil ("the Devil's waterspout") may possibly have been named for the treacherous waters at the confluence of the Hudson ● 20 and Harlem rivers, the Bowery for *bouwerie*, ("farm" ● 82) and Brooklyn ▲ 366 for *breukelen*, ("reclaimed land"). The English names of some Lower Manhattan streets ▲ 158 are derived from the Dutch: "*De Wall*" was translated into "Wall Street", and "*Maagde Paetje*" into "Maiden Lane".

A street in Chinatown (below).

Lifestyle

In 1656 Peter Stuyvesant, the governor of New Amsterdam and a devout Protestant, tried to force the colony to embrace one religion. The West India Company was opposed to this move; it was afraid it might damage trade since New York was already a patchwork of different religions. Today New York is home to more than one hundred religious denominations. Catholicism predominates, while the Jewish community is the largest outside Israel.

ST. PATRICK'S CATHEDRAL
This cathedral, the seat of the city's Roman Catholic archbishop, is on 5th Ave., between 50th and 51st sts, and was completed in 1906 ▲ *283*. It is consecrated to the patron saint of Ireland. The number of Catholics currently living in New York is estimated at 2.5 million.

JEHOVAH'S WITNESSES
This is one of the largest evangelical movements in New York and is based in Brooklyn. Their two magazines *Awake!* and *The Watchtower* are published in at least 80 languages and boast a circulation of more than ten million copies. They are distributed door to door or in the street.

JUDAISM
More than a million Orthodox Jews from Eastern Europe emigrated to America between 1880 and 1910. Many of them settled in New York. They started daily newspapers, theater companies, socialist political groups and unions. After World War II, American Jews gave their support to the creation of a Jewish state in Palestine and lobbied the government for economic and military aid to Israel.

NATIVIST PROTESTANTS
Protestantism was the city's main religion until the mid-19th century. But by 1864, following the immigration of Irish and German Catholics, half of the population was Catholic. This cartoon by Thomas Nast (above), which depicts some parents protecting their children from the invading Catholic bishops, conveys Protestant distrust of Catholics, whom they criticized for their proposed changes to the educational system such as discontinuing Bible-readings and attempting to obtain state subsidies for their own schools.

> "It was clean, but not brisk, nothing like the urgency of New York, rude often, premised on a notion that time was flying."
>
> Janet Hobhouse

LUBAVITCHER COMMUNITY
The Lubavitcher Chassidic Movement, based in Brooklyn, is a mystical branch of Judaism. Its members, who are all men and can be recognized by their black suits, beards and sidecurls, include some eminent Talmud experts.

ISLAM
This religion became widespread in New York only in the second half of the 20th century. The Islamic Center of New York, opened in 1991, sits on the corner of 96th St and 3rd Ave. Its axis forms an angle of 29 degrees with the street, so that the building is facing Mecca.

BUDDHISM
The impressive statue of Shinran-Shonin, who founded the Buddhist sect Jodo Shinshu, watches over the New York temple, built in 1938 on Riverside Drive. This statue, originally erected in Hiroshima, 1½ miles from the center of the explosion, was brought to New York in 1955 as a reminder

of the horrors of atomic warfare and a symbol of hope for lasting peace in the world.

BLACK CHRISTIAN COMMUNITIES
At the end of the 18th century, in response to discrimination and racial segregation, a group of Black New Yorkers formed their own denomination, the African Methodist Episcopal Zion Church. Today most of the Black churches in New York, including the famous Abyssinian Baptist Church ▲ *359*, can be found in Harlem. The largest Black denominations are the Baptists, the Methodists and the Pentecostalists.

Since the 18th century, Manhattan has hosted countless political, civic, religious and military events both annual and, in some cases, one-time events. The first well-known festival took place in 1788; it celebrated the ratification of the American Constitution with a huge parade and a banquet for five thousand guests.

FEAST OF SAN GENNARO
In September, Mulberry Street, in Little Italy ▲ 196, hosts the parade for the patron saint of Naples.

DISTINGUISHED GUESTS
These have included the French hero of the American Revolution the Marquis de Lafayette, who was received in 1824 with a profusion of speeches and parades. A lavish ball was also held in his honor.

THE CIVIL WAR
The armed forces have often been involved in noteworthy festivals in the city's history. In 1865 thousands of soldiers marched through Manhattan to celebrate the end of the Civil War.

TICKER TAPE PARADES
At the end of the 19th century, in the Financial District ▲ 158, official guests used to be bombarded with ticker tape thrown from the office buildings. Despite the fact that the practice of holding these parades has declined somewhat, due to the traffic and prohibitive cleaning costs, it nevertheless continues to this day (*left and right*), only now with shredded computer paper. The victories of New York's baseball team, the Yankees, are traditionally celebrated by a ticker tape parade.

PUERTO RICAN DAY PARADE
New York City's largest street party of the year, the Puerto Rican Day Parade has been held every June since 1958. More than 1,000,000 people line Fifth Avenue and fill Central Park to celebrate the city's largest immigrant community.

ST. PATRICK'S DAY PARADE

The St. Patrick's Day Parade takes place unfailingly every year on March 17th. This cultural event was organized for the first time in the 1760's by Irish soldiers stationed in New York. Since 1838, the parade has been sponsored by the Ancient Order of Hibernians, an Irish Catholic brotherhood. This major festival, which has become extremely popular, symbolizes the solidarity of the Irish community.

MACY'S THANKSGIVING DAY PARADE

This parade, which has taken place since the 1920's, has numerous floats, giant balloons of cartoon characters and brass bands (*left*). It is sponsored by Macy's ▲ 249, the city's largest department store.

GAY AND LESBIAN PRIDE MARCH

This annual march commemorates the first major protest in favor of gay rights, the Stonewall Inn Riots ▲ 212, which broke out in Greenwich Village on June 30, 1969. As many as 500,000 people have attended this event over the past few years.

CHINESE NEW YEAR
Firecrackers are one of the attractions of this lavish celebration that takes place in late winter in Chinatown ▲ 190. For thirty-six hours, traditional dragon figures weave their way through the quarter (*above*).

GREENWICH VILLAGE HALLOWEEN PARADE
Several thousand people don elaborate costumes for this immensely popular Halloween celebration (*left and right*).

● THE WRITTEN PRESS

THE "PENNY PRESS"
The first mass-circulation newspapers
emerged in the early 1830's and early 1840's
with the founding of the *New York Sun*, the
New York Herald and the *New York Tribune*.

The New

Copyright 1911 by

and as Second-Class Matter,
office at New York, N. Y.

NEW YORK MO

For almost 300 years New York's vibrant and occasionally unruly press has played a central role in the life of the nation. One of the earliest battles over press freedom was fought, and won, by a New York printer, and the city has long been the home of many of the most influential newspapers and magazines. The New York press's robust contribution to the uniquely American cultural milieu, as well as to the nation's continuing impulse for political and social reform, endows it with a rich and varied history.

THE ZENGER TRIAL

Charged by New York's colonial governor with spreading "Scandalous, Virulent, False and Seditious Reflections upon the Government" in his *New York Weekly Journal*, colonial printer John Peter Zenger's acquittal in 1735 helped to establish a central tenet of the freedom of the press: the right to publish criticism of government officials.

"YELLOW JOURNALISM"

In the 1890's, intense competition for readers between William Randolph Hearst's *New York Journal* and Joseph Pulitzer's *New York World* led to unparalleled levels of journalistic sensationalism and chauvinism. The featured sex, sin and violence came to be termed "yellow journalism", a name derived from the Yellow Kid, a popular character in Richard F. Outcault's *Sunday World* comic strip "Hogan's Alley", about life in tenements.

THE TABLOID NEWSPAPERS

The *New York Post* and the *New York Daily News*, direct descendants of the Penny Press, did not merely deal with the most sordid aspects of life in the city; they also tackled political issues of national concern.

ork Times.

Y ork Tibe‌t Company:

, DECEMBER 8, 1941.

THE NEW YORK TIMES

Founded in 1851, *The New York Times* has been the most influential national newspaper since World War II. It has a circulation of around one million during the week and this doubles on Sundays. In 1967 the international edition of *The New York Times* merged with those of the *New York Herald Tribune* and *The Washington Post* to become the *International Herald Tribune*.

THE "MUCKRAKERS"

In the early years of the 20th century, *McClure's* and other crusading magazines exposed many of society's ills. They were called "muckrakers" by Theodore Roosevelt (after the Man with the Muckrake in *Pilgrim's Progress*). Ida Tarbells' *History of Standard Oil*, Lincoln Steffen's *The Shame of the Cities*, and Ray Stannard Baker's reports on working conditions shaped much of the Progressive agenda of the period and fostered much-needed urban and industrial reforms.

THE NEW YORKER

Since the 1920's this urbane, intellectual, weekly magazine has focused on society, politics and culture in the city. Its contributors have included such well-known writers as Dorothy Parker, John McPhee and Seymour Hersh, and artists and photographers such as Saul Steinberg, Richard Avedon and Brigitte Lacombe.

MAGAZINES

The United States' most famous magazines, which are read throughout the country and abroad, include *Vogue, Time, Newsweek, Rolling Stone, Esquire, Vanity Fair*, and *People*.

In 1907 Lee De Forest patented the audion, an amplifier that was the precursor of the cathode ray tube. This invention heralded the advent of the crystal set, which was sold during the 1920's in Manhattan by mail order and in kit form. A decade later, people in New York witnessed the beginnings of television. Today, Manhattan is home to three major national private networks (ABC, CBS and NBC) and receives more than 250 other stations and cable channels.

LEE DE FOREST'S AUDION
Lee De Forest used this device to broadcast the voice of the famous tenor Enrico Caruso from the stage of the old Metropolitan Opera House. This feat of technology amazed the world. De Forest started the first amateur radio station at his home in the Bronx.

DAVID SARNOFF
Sarnoff saw the potential of radio as big business. As early as 1916 he stated that this "music box" would rapidly become useful around the home. In 1921 he became general manager and later president of RCA, parent of NBC (the National Broadcasting Company).

FELIX THE CAT
Following the invention of the electronic movie camera by Vladimir Zworykin and of the cathode ray tube, RCA (the Radio Corporation of America) decided, in 1923, to use the famous comic strip hero Felix the Cat for their first experiments in animation.

GEORGE BURNS AND GRACIE ALLEN
For seventeen years this pair of vaudeville actors were a great success in a popular comedy broadcast on the NBC radio network. In 1950 the program was transferred to television.

WALTER CRONKITE
A newscaster of the evening news at CBS (the Columbia Broadcasting System) from 1962 to 1981, Cronkite ended all of his programs with his own distinctive catchphrase, "And that's the way it was."

"SESAME STREET"
Since 1969, this program and its star, Big Bird, have taught innumerable children how to read and count.

IMPORTANT DEBATES
In 1960 John F. Kennedy and Richard M. Nixon, both presidential candidates, took part in the first series of televised election debates. After the last one, which took place in New York, Kennedy was elected president. Since then, television has become a key platform for political confrontations.

SPORTS PROMOTION THROUGH THE MEDIA
In the 1960's and 1970's, ABC sportscaster Howard Cosell broadcast games live and interviewed sports personalities in their locker rooms. He brought sports into everyone's home, sharing his boisterous enthusiasm with his viewers,

HOME BOX OFFICE AND MUSIC TELEVISION
Renowned for such first-rate series as *The Sopranos* and *Sex and the City*, HBO was the first pay cable network and the first to employ satellite broadcasting. MTV has become one of the most powerful broadcasting media for pop culture throughout the world.

BARBARA WALTERS
In 1964 Barbara Walters made her debut as an interviewer on the *Today Show* for NBC; she was then co-anchor of the ABC evening news broadcast before finally becoming a star with her own television specials. Her success helped to promote women in the profession.

"THE WAR OF THE WORLDS"
"Poisonous black smoke, death rays, an army wiped out, people dropping like flies. Monstrous Martians landing all over the country . . ." In 1938 a tidal wave of panic swept New York when Orson Welles broadcast, on CBS, his hyper-realistic description of a Martian invasion, inspired by H. G. Wells's famous novel *The War of the Worlds*.

● THE MUSICAL

The musical – the form of theater that best evokes Broadway – derives from operetta, which was introduced to New York by European composers in the early 20th century. These light operas caused some lovers of vaudeville and burlesque sketches to develop a taste for more refined entertainment.

GEORGE AND IRA GERSHWIN
The two brothers, Ira the lyricist and George the composer (top), born into a humble Jewish family, created some of Broadway's greatest hits. In 1930 their *Girl Crazy* made a name for Ethel Merman and Ginger Rogers.

"SHOW BOAT"
Show Boat (1927), based on the novel by Edna Ferber with music and lyrics by Jerome Kern and Oscar Hammerstein II, is an outstanding example of the Broadway musical that was revived in 1994, 67 years after its debut. "Old Man River" and "Only Make Believe" are just two of the songs that have made this love story, set in the deep South, an enduring American classic.

"OKLAHOMA!"
This innovative musical by Rodgers and Hammerstein, with choreography by Agnes de Mille, used neither showgirls nor chorus lines. Opening in 1943 it ran for 2,248 performances. In 2001 Cameron Mackintosh and the Royal National Theater staged a wildly successful new production with choreography by Susan Stroman.

"KISS ME KATE"
Cole Porter composed some of Broadway's greatest songs, including "Kiss Me Kate", "Anything Goes", "Night and Day" and "Can Can".

58

> "New York was a Yukon–Salem where you could get spiritual riches, save yourself, and flee, one way or another, a kind of poverty and death."
>
> Janet Hobhouse

BOX-OFFICE HITS
For a long time Michael Bennett's *A Chorus Line*, a musical about the world of show business, was the longest-running show on Broadway. It was overtaken by *Cats* which topped the bill for more than seventeen years and ran for over 7,000 performances. *Les Misérables*, adapted from Victor Hugo's novel, and more recently *The Lion King*, inspired by the Walt Disney cartoon and staged at the New Amsterdam Theater ▲ 258, are also among Broadway's greatest hits.

PRICES
In 1927, the cost of a ticket for *Show Boat* was $4.50. Today you can pay as much as $100 to see a hit Broadway musical.

BOB FOSSE
Fosse was one of just a few Broadway choreographers who also made movies. In addition to his resounding stage success of *Dancin'*, he directed the movies *Cabaret*, *Lenny* and the autobiographical *All That Jazz*.

LAVISH PRODUCTIONS
Sophisticated machinery, lighting, sets and eye-catching costumes are now integral parts of the musical. In *Les Misérables*, a barricade is built (center); in *Cats*, a spaceship appeared; in *Phantom of the Opera*, a huge chandelier came crashing down; in *Miss Saigon*, a helicopter landed and took off.

59

COTTON CLUB PARADE

Although jazz was born in New Orleans, it came of age in New York. During the 1920's, Harlem was the capital of the African-American world, a mecca for the Black intelligentsia. In the prevailing climate of creative activity – both intellectual and financial – many new clubs sprang up, providing more opportunities for jazz musicians. They flocked to Harlem, and new styles of jazz were created by the many bands formed in this period.

DUKE ELLINGTON

Duke Ellington was one of the great jazz composers of the 20th century. As a star attraction at the Cotton Club, between 1927 and 1931, he developed "jungle music", an exotic style of jazz to accompany the sinuous dancing of chorus girls.

COTTON CLUB

The Cotton Club opened in Harlem in 1922. Despite the fact that all the bands and acts performing there were Black, Blacks were barred from the audience, because its gangster owners wanted the club to be a gathering place for the city's white *glitterati*.

BIG BANDS

The popularity of the big bands, which were aimed primarily at dance audiences, hit an all-time high between the two world wars. Above, the Fletcher Henderson band in 1925, with Coleman Hawkins on tenor saxophone (bottom, second left) and Louis Armstrong on cornet (top, third left).

Duke
Ellington
22 USA

SMALL BANDS: BEBOP

This provocative style with its insistent, fiendish beat and piercing dissonances, was well suited to small bands. It was very popular during the 1940's with young jazz "intellectuals", including saxophonist Charlie Parker, trumpeter Dizzy Gillespie, and pianist Thelonius Monk. Their younger colleague, trumpeter Miles Davis, created "cool", an introverted style in marked contrast to the aggressive exuberance of bebop. From left to right, Tommy Potter, Charlie Parker, Dizzy Gillespie and John Coltrane at Birdland in 1951.

> "Freedom and Jazz go hand in hand."

Thelonius Monk

CAB CALLOWAY
The dancer-singer-conductor, who with his swinging jazz orchestra used to perform in Harlem, was nicknamed the "Hi-De-Ho Man" because of his strange way of mixing slang and yodeling in performance. In the 1930's, he wrote the *Hipster's Dictionary*, a work that revealed the secrets of his new mode of expression.

APOLLO THEATRE ▲ 358
Ella Fitzgerald and Sarah Vaughan made their debut performing in the Apollo Theatre's "amateur nights". Today this legendary theater is taking advantage of the Harlem revival and presents some first-rate shows and music. There's also a very popular TV program, *Showtime at the Apollo*, broadcast live from the theater.

ELLA FITZGERALD
Fitzgerald took first prize at the Apollo in 1934. Four years later she had her first hit with *A Tisket a Tasket, I Lost my Yellow Basket*.

JAZZ AT LINCOLN CENTER The new Jazz at Lincoln Center facilities, a 100,000-square-foot performance, education, and broadcast space designed by Rafael Viñoly, is no longer based at Lincoln Center. It is now located in the new Time Warner Building on Columbus Circle, but it is still run by Wynton Marsalis, of the famed New Orleans musical family.

In the 20th century New York has been a fertile breeding ground for daring essays in choreography. Ballet has explored new dimensions and the city has witnessed the birth of many companies. Three great pioneers of modern dance, Isadora Duncan, Ruth St. Denis and Martha Graham, began their careers in New York. Martha Graham, the only one to remain here, stimulated and influenced this art, both in the works she created and through her teaching methods.

MARTHA GRAHAM
Her powerful, abrupt, angular style was resolutely innovative. After her debut as a soloist in 1926 she stated, "My dance is urban, not pastoral".

THE NEW YORK CITY BALLET

In 1934, in response to a request by Lincoln Kirstein, George Balanchine (1904–83) founded the School of American Ballet. Their highly creative collaboration eventually resulted in the founding of The New York City Ballet Company in 1948.

PAUL TAYLOR
This former swimmer formed his own company which first performed in 1957. His bold, flowing choreography is often informed by a sense of humor.

MERCE CUNNINGHAM

Cunningham founded his troupe in 1953 and soon became famous for his avant-garde creations. For some forty years he collaborated with the composer John Cage, as well as contemporary American artists Jasper Johns, Robert Rauschenberg and Andy Warhol. The company's work profoundly influenced young choreographers such as Trisha Brown, Douglas Dunn and Randy Warshaw.

"THE NUTCRACKER"

In 1954, George Balanchine created a new version of this great classical ballet. Since then, *The Nutcracker* has become an American tradition. During the Christmas season, the New York City Ballet gives as many as forty-five performances.

"GISELLE"

The multi-ethnic Dance Theater of Harlem set the action of this classical ballet in New Orleans, while preserving the original choreography. The company was founded in 1969 in the crypt of a Harlem church by Arthur Mitchell, the first Black dancer to perform with the New York City Ballet.

37 ARTS

This International Dance Center (450 W. 37th St.) houses the Mikhail Baryshnikov Foundation.

"REVELATIONS"

This is the best-known creation by the Alvin Ailey American Dance Theater, a mainly Black company formed in 1958. The exciting work produced by this troupe draws its inspiration from Black American tradition, Alvin Ailey's own roots, and traditional gospel music.

THE NEW GENERATION

Since the 1960's, Twyla Tharp, Meredith Monk (right) and, more recently, the greatly talented Mark Morris, to name only three, have helped to revitalize modern dance and the New York dance scene, one of the most fertile in the world.

New York has always been closely associated with the world of sports. On June 19, 1845, the first baseball game was played just across the Hudson River in Hoboken. New York also boasts two of the country's most famous stadiums: Yankee and Shea.

ALEXANDER JOY CARTWRIGHT (1820–92)

Although Abner Doubleday was long regarded as the father of baseball, credit was subsequently given to Cartwright; he adapted the rules of cricket, designed a new field and organized the first game in America.

BABE RUTH (1895–1948)

Babe Ruth, considered to be the greatest of all baseball players, moved from the Baltimore Orioles, where he started in 1914, to the Boston Red Sox to the Yankees. With the Yankees, in 192[] he set a new record of 6[] home runs for one seaso[] He hit 714 home runs in major league play, a reco[] that held until 1974. He also led the Yankees to seven pennants (1921–3, 1926–8, 1932).

At any moment, a great moment.

MADISON SQUARE GARDEN

Built then rebuilt four times between 1879 and 1968, the most famous sports complex in New York has virtually never been closed. Among the many celebrities

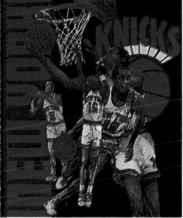

JOE NAMATH

His amazing skill as a quarterback at the University of Alabama earned him a three-year no-cut contract of over $400,000 from the New York Jets before he had ever played as a professional. Years before carrying off the Super Bowl in 1969, this high-spirited, charismatic player was the subject of gossip in the New York tabloids as well as being the idol of football fans.

NEW YORK YACHT CLUB

The New York Yacht Club, one of the oldest sailing clubs in the world, is situated in the heart of Manhattan ● 93, ▲ 251. This venerable institution manned the *America*, the first holder of the cup of that name. This trophy, which is competed for every three years, left the premises of the New York Yacht Club only in 1983, after 132 years of American invincibility.

JOHN McENROE

Raised in Queens, trained on Long Island, and now living in Manhattan, John McEnroe is more closely associated with New York than any other tennis player. Before retiring, McEnroe, who won the U.S. Open four times between 1979 and 1984, helped to make the two weeks at Flushing Meadows a highlight of international tennis.

NEW YORK MARATHON

The New York Marathon, which usually takes place at the end of October, was first organized in 1970, when the vogue for jogging was at its peak. In the space of only a few years, this race has acquired an international reputation, due not only to its setting, but to the caliber of its participants and its generous prizes.

who have appeared in the Garden are Sarah Bernhardt, Marilyn Monroe, player Jimmy Connors and Muhammad Ali. The Garden's home teams are the Knicks ▲ 249 (above) and the Rangers (left).

TIFFANY LAMPS

These lamps, with brightly colored shades made of iridescent glass, set in lead like stained glass windows, are among the most eye-catching creations of Louis Comfort Tiffany, son of the jeweler Charles Lewis Tiffany, founder of the famous Tiffany & Co.

At the end of the 18th century, New York's master craftsmen – mainly European-born – satisfied their customers' desire for the latest fashions by copying and adapting the styles of the Old World. In the last few years of the 19th century, they adopted a showy, luxurious style of interior design which corresponded to the city's extraordinary growth. The single-story mansion on Fifth Avenue belonging to multi-millionaire William H. Vanderbilt was a perfect example of these excesses: its decoration cost $1,800,000 in 1882.

640 FIFTH AVENUE

Above: a detail of the Vanderbilt house ▲ *284*. The dining room was decorated in the so-called "esthetic" style, which was then all the rage. Parisian interior designer Pierre Victor Galland created the *trompe l'œil* ceiling in this room, combining an unusually rich blend of Chinese, Japanese and Turkish influences. The house was crammed with works of art which, for the most part, reflected the tastes of the time. Once a week, Vanderbilt opened his art gallery to the public, showing off his collection of 19th-century European painting. The house was demolished in 1946.

GOTHIC REVIVAL STYLE

Many different styles emerged in the 19th century, each more eclectic than the last. This piece by A. J. Davis reveals the considerable influence of architecture ● *86* on furniture design. The chair's pointed arches suggest the ogive windows of medieval cathedrals.

THE CLASSICAL PERIOD

A neo-classical style, which emphasized harmony and symmetry, prevailed between the end of the American Revolution and the beginning of the 19th century. The carved eagle on the back of this dining room chair symbolizes the new American republic.

"SKYSCRAPER" BOOKCASE

The rising set-back design of this work by Paul Frankl reflects the silhouette of 1920's skyscraper architecture in New York ● *97*.

CHIPPENDALE-STYLE CARD TABLE

This table has three features typical of furniture made in New York: the fifth leg, which permits the extension of the table-leaf, the ornamental design of the legs and the gadrooning just below the table top.

ROCOCO REVIVAL STYLE

This style is distinguished by its luxuriant floral ornamentation. A typical example is the dining room table, by John Henry Belter, which is encrusted with a tangle of branches, leaves and bunches of grapes.

Founded in New York in 1921, *Lindy's* restaurant is famous for its cheesecake.

The two recipes (Jewish and Italian) for the American cheesecake originated in New York in the early years of the 20th century. What is now called New York cheesecake by out-of-towners is closer to the Jewish recipe. It is heavier than the Italian recipe, whose main ingredient is *ricotta* cheese, and has a smooth texture which comes from the cream and cream cheese used.

2. Melt the butter then mix in a bowl with the graham crackers. Place the mixture in a mold lined with waxed paper.

3. Press down with a glass to obtain a ½-inch thick base. Place in the refrigerator for about 45 minutes.

6. Gradually add the cream cheese to the mixture.

7. Then pour in the heavy cream and add the vanilla and the orange zest.

11. Leave to rest for an hour and a half, then unmold and decorate with the strawberries.

12. To make the syrup cook the strawberries, the sugar and the water over a low heat.

INGREDIENTS

Topping: 1 cup sugar, 3 tbsp/4½ tbsp cornstarch, 3½ cups cream cheese, 2 eggs, ½ cup heavy cream, 1 sachet of vanilla, orange zest, 18 oz strawberries.
Syrup: ¼ lb strawberries, ¼ cup sugar, 1½ tbsp water.
½-inch mold.

Base: 4 tbsp butter, 9 oz graham crackers.

1. To make the base, first crush the graham crackers.

4. Cream the sugar and the cornstarch.

5. Add the eggs.

8. Mix the ingredients well.

9. Pour the topping into the mold.

10. Cook in a hot oven (400°–450°F) for 45 minutes.

13. Strain the mixture and use to glaze the cheesecake.

BAGELS

These ring-shaped rolls, often served with smoked salmon and cream cheese, are a Jewish specialty.

You can buy large, chewy pretzels, hot and salted, from sidewalk vendors (above, a pretzel vendor in the 1940's).

A placemat depicting the presidents of the U.S.; a coffee cup illustrating a New York deli's ideals of service; in a more exotic vein, the spices sold on 9th Ave. at International Food.

The traditional doggy bag in which customers at some restaurants take home their leftovers. They are given to customers at the Carnegie Delicatessen, a typical New York establishment specializing in Jewish food from Central Europe, famous for its gargantuan servings of pastrami.

WALDORF SALAD

The ingredients of this dish, created in the 1930's at the Waldorf-Astoria Hotel, include apples, walnuts and celery.

Certain pubs – New York institutions such as McSorley's Old Ale House, Pete's Tavern and the Peculiar Pub – serve locally brewed beer.

Jigsaw puzzles and ties are among New York's souvenirs.

Architecture

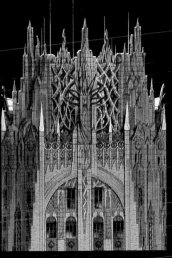

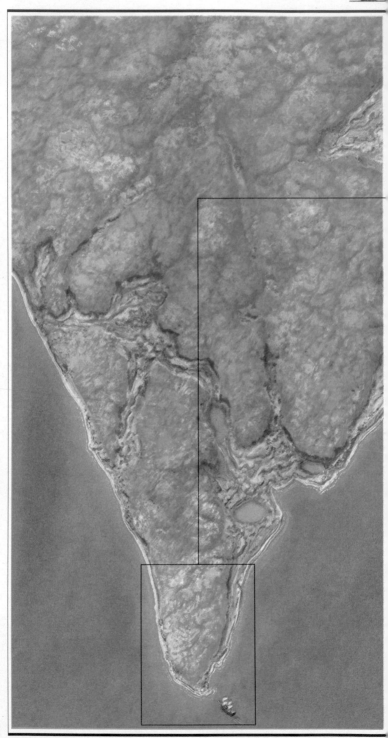

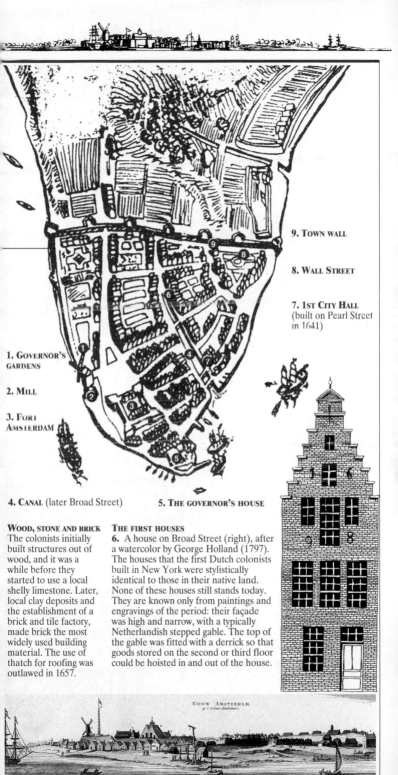

9. TOWN WALL

8. WALL STREET

7. 1ST CITY HALL
(built on Pearl Street
in 1641)

1. GOVERNOR'S
GARDENS

2. MILL

3. FORT
AMSTERDAM

4. CANAL (later Broad Street)   5. THE GOVERNOR'S HOUSE

WOOD, STONE AND BRICK
The colonists initially
built structures out of
wood, and it was a
while before they
started to use a local
shelly limestone. Later,
local clay deposits and
the establishment of a
brick and tile factory,
made brick the most
widely used building
material. The use of
thatch for roofing was
outlawed in 1657.

THE FIRST HOUSES
6. A house on Broad Street (right), after
a watercolor by George Holland (1797).
The houses that the first Dutch colonists
built in New York were stylistically
identical to those in their native land.
None of these houses still stands today.
They are known only from paintings and
engravings of the period: their façade
was high and narrow, with a typically
Netherlandish stepped gable. The top of
the gable was fitted with a derrick so that
goods stored on the second or third floor
could be hoisted in and out of the house.

1. DRAINAGE DITCHES
Ditches were dug to drain and dry marshy areas. Earth and rubble from neighboring hills were then used as landfill for the ditches.

2. GREENWICH STREET

3. ST. PAUL'S CHAPEL
The oldest building in Manhattan (1764–66) ▲ *176*.

4. BROAD WAY STREET

5. LITTLE QUEEN STREET, LATER CEDAR STREET

6. TRINITY CHURCH ▲ *154*
The original church was built in 1696, destroyed in 1776.

7. 2ND CITY HALL ▲ *182*
Built in 1701, destroyed in 1812.

8. FORT GEORGE ▲ *142*

9. NEW BATTERY

**THE COUNTRY HOUSES OF WEALTHY MERCHANTS
AND SHIPOWNERS**
The only such house still standing today is
the typically splendid Morris-Jumel Mansion
(above) ● *82*, in W. 160th St. The former
Stuyvesant manor house (**18**) ▲ *224* once
stood at what is now 2nd Ave. and E. 10th St,
on a farm of 120 acres.

**17. BOWERY
LANE**

15. COLLECT POND
Manhattan originally
had a generous supply
of clean drinking
water in the form of a
small lake. However,
it soon became
polluted by the rapidly
expanding population
and such commercial
activities as tanning.
It silted up and
disappeared in about
1817. It was on the
site of today's Foley
Square ▲ *182*.

**16. THE FIRST
ROW HOUSES** ● *83, 85*

**COLONIAL NEW YORK
AND FEDERAL NEW YORK**
The Declaration of Independence was quickly
followed by the strengthening of military
defenses around the bay and on the island.
A new battery was built. The end of the war,
however, made these installations redundant
and from 1789 they were dismantled to make
way for a new phase of urban construction,
including the further extension of Broad Way
toward the natural water supply. During this
period, certain streets and other places in the
town were given a different name: King Street
became Pine Street; Little Queen Street
became Cedar Street; Queen Street became
Pearl Street; and King College became
Columbia College.

**14. QUEEN STREET,
LATER PEARL STREET**

**13. KING STREET,
LATER PINE STREET**

THE ISLAND WAS DOTTED WITH FARMSTEADS

12. WALL STREET

11. BROAD STREET

10. PEARL STREET

1. UNION SQUARE
(1831) ▲ *222*
Originally a residential area, by the end of the 19th century the square had become one of the city's playgrounds, with numerous theaters and shops.

2. WASHINGTON SQUARE
(1824) ▲ *198*

3. BROADWAY

4. 8 THOMAS STREET, in neo-Gothic style ● *87*

5. CARY BUILDING, in Italianate style (1856) ▲ *209*

6. CASTLE CLINTON
▲ *143*

17. 13TH STREET CHURCH,
in the Greek Revival style ▲ *219*

16. ASTOR PLACE ▲ *226*

15. COLONNADE ROW ▲ *227*

CAST-IRON APARTMENT BLOCKS ● *94*
14. Haughwout Store, 1857 ▲ *204*.
Fear of fires, the desire for
economical building methods and
technical advances led to a completely
new architectural style, the precursor
of modern architecture.

13. CANAL STREET

12. THE 3RD AND PRESENT CITY HALL
(1812) ▲ *168*

11. Construction of **BROOKLYN
BRIDGE** (1867–83) ▲ *186*

9. CROTON FOUNTAIN
up until 1842, then the
CENTRAL POST OFFICE
(destroyed in 1913) ▲ *170*

**8. FEDERAL HALL
NATIONAL MEMORIAL**
(1834–42) ▲ *162*

**7. THIRD MERCHANT'S
EXCHANGE** (1842)

FIRES ● *38*
10. Warehouses on John Street ● *85*.
Frequent fires were one of the causes
of constant rebuilding in the city.
These warehouses on John Street
were built after the fire of 1835 in
the Greek Revival style that was
fashionable at the time.

1. WASHINGTON ARCH, WASHINGTON SQUARE (1892) ▲ 198

2. WOOLWORTH BUILDING (1909–13) ▲ 180

3. NY TELEPHONE CO. BUILDING (1923–6) ▲ 140

4. EQUITABLE BUILDING (1912–15) ▲ 153

5. LIBERTY TOWER ▲ 159

6. SINGER BUILDING ▲ 152 (demolished in 1970)

7. 90 WEST STREET (1905–7) ▲ 140

8. CUNARD BUILDING (1921) ▲ 155

9. STANDARD OIL BUILDING (1922) ▲ 156

10. THE US CUSTOM HOUSE (1907) ▲ 157

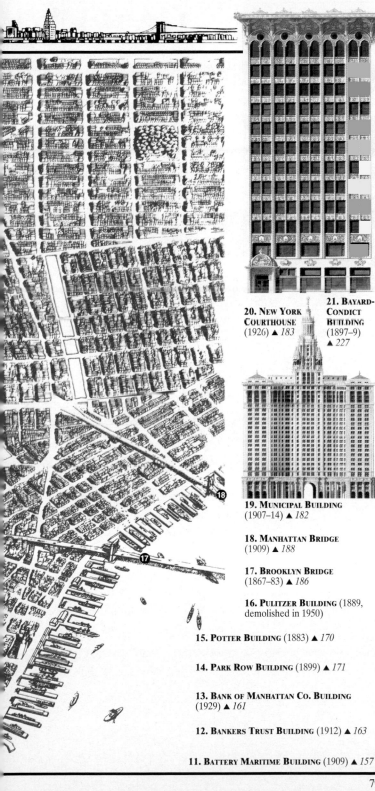

20. NEW YORK COURTHOUSE (1926) ▲ *183*

21. BAYARD-CONDICT BUILDING (1897–9) ▲ *227*

19. MUNICIPAL BUILDING (1907–14) ▲ *182*

18. MANHATTAN BRIDGE (1909) ▲ *188*

17. BROOKLYN BRIDGE (1867–83) ▲ *186*

16. PULITZER BUILDING (1889, demolished in 1950)

15. POTTER BUILDING (1883) ▲ *170*

14. PARK ROW BUILDING (1899) ▲ *171*

13. BANK OF MANHATTAN CO. BUILDING (1929) ▲ *161*

12. BANKERS TRUST BUILDING (1912) ▲ *163*

11. BATTERY MARITIME BUILDING (1909) ▲ *157*

BARCLAY/VESEY ST.

CHURCH ST.

NEW YORK
MERCANTILE
EXCHANGE AND
COMMODITIES
EXCHANGE

NORTH COVE

WASHINGTON ST.

GREENWICH ST.

TRINITY PLACE

WEST ST.

SOUTH COVE

HUDSON RIVER

BATTERY

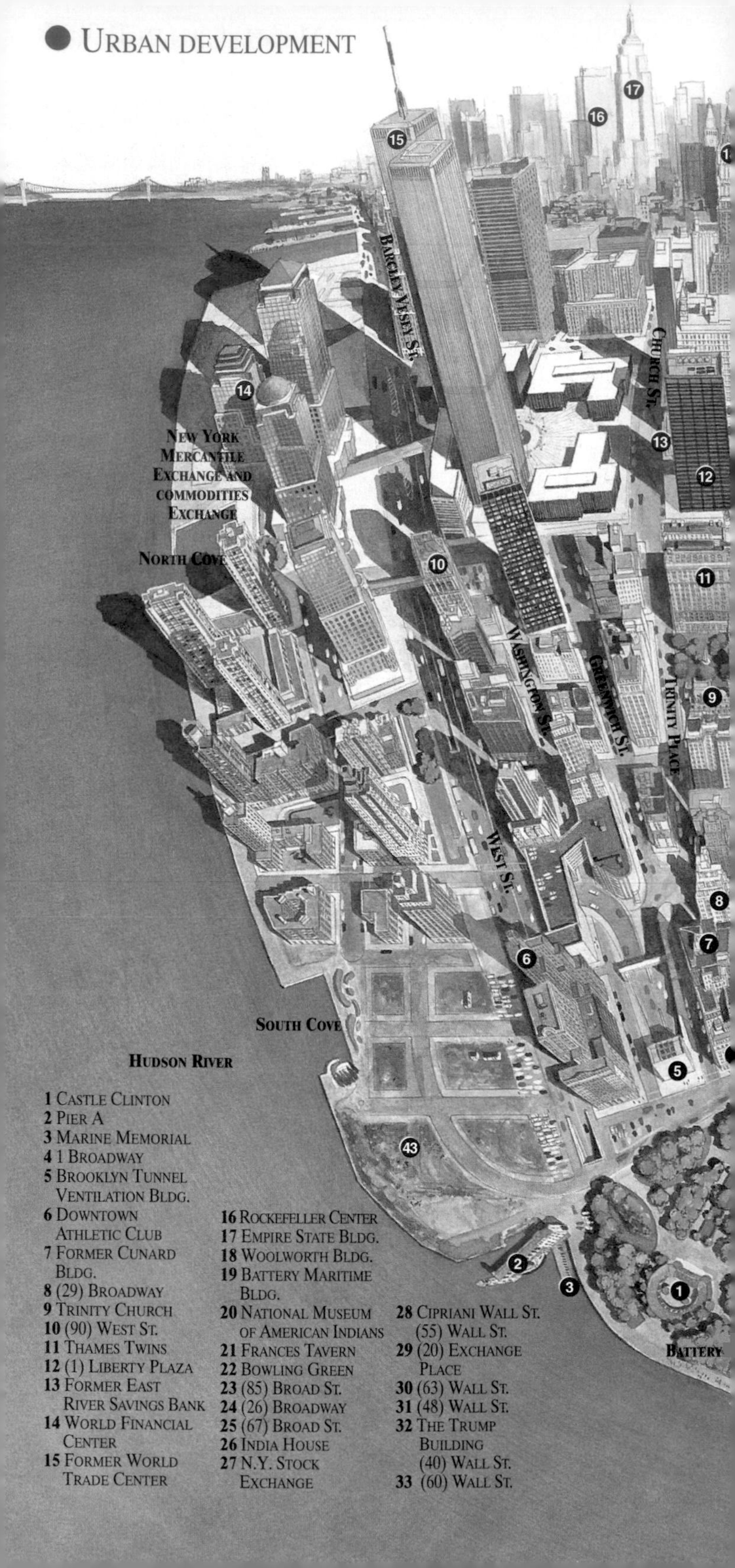

1 CASTLE CLINTON
2 PIER A
3 MARINE MEMORIAL
4 1 BROADWAY
5 BROOKLYN TUNNEL
   VENTILATION BLDG.
6 DOWNTOWN
   ATHLETIC CLUB
7 FORMER CUNARD
   BLDG.
8 (29) BROADWAY
9 TRINITY CHURCH
10 (90) WEST ST.
11 THAMES TWINS
12 (1) LIBERTY PLAZA
13 FORMER EAST
   RIVER SAVINGS BANK
14 WORLD FINANCIAL
   CENTER
15 FORMER WORLD
   TRADE CENTER

16 ROCKEFELLER CENTER
17 EMPIRE STATE BLDG.
18 WOOLWORTH BLDG.
19 BATTERY MARITIME
   BLDG.
20 NATIONAL MUSEUM
   OF AMERICAN INDIANS
21 FRANCES TAVERN
22 BOWLING GREEN
23 (85) BROAD ST.
24 (26) BROADWAY
25 (67) BROAD ST.
26 INDIA HOUSE
27 N.Y. STOCK
   EXCHANGE

28 CIPRIANI WALL ST.
   (55) WALL ST.
29 (20) EXCHANGE
   PLACE
30 (63) WALL ST.
31 (48) WALL ST.
32 THE TRUMP
   BUILDING
   (40) WALL ST.
33 (60) WALL ST.

MANHATTAN IN 1990

MANHATTAN BRIDGE

BROOKLYN BRIDGE

EAST RIVER

WATER ST.

HELIPORT

STATE ST.

36 FEDERAL
RESERVE BANK
37 (70) PINE ST.
38 CHASE
MANHATTAN BANK
39 LIBERTY TOWER
40 FEDERAL HALL
41 DELMONICO'S
42 MUNICIPAL BLDG.
43 MUSEUM OF JEWISH

34 SOUTH STREET
SEAPORT
35 EQUITABLE BLDG.   HERITAGE

Colonial style and Federal style

Vestiges of colonial New York, whether Dutch or English, are few and far between, although several remaining old Colonial houses in Manhattan hint at the look of the city in the late 18th century. Much more common are the early 19th-century houses built in the Georgian style dubbed "Federal" which developed in the early years of Independence.

DYCKMAN HOUSE, 1783 (204th St. and Broadway) ▲ *361*
Dyckman House is the only surviving example of the type of farmhouse built in Manhattan up until the mid-19th century by settlers of Dutch origin. Its double-sloped gambrel, or mansard, roof is typical of Dutch colonial houses.

Splayed stone lintels above windows, with or without keystone, are typical features of the Georgian style.

MORRIS-JUMEL MANSION, 1765 (W. 160th St. and Jumel Terrace) ▲ 361
This is the only Georgian country house remaining in New York from the English colonial period. The grand Corinthian portico and corner quoins are reminiscent of the English Palladian style, which was widely adopted by wealthy Americans in the mid-18th century. The carved balustrade on the crest of the roof is a more typically American feature.

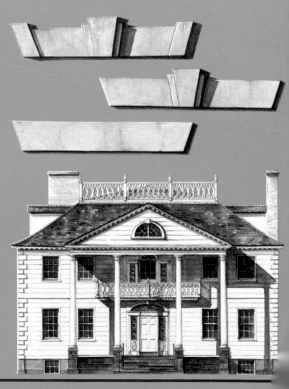

THE ROOF
Some Federal-style houses have pitched roofs pierced with dormer windows.

THE ENTRANCE
The most striking feature of Federal-style houses is the main entrance. The doorway of 59 Morton Street, with its engaged colonettes, is crowned with a fanlight and flanked by sidelights.

Typical Federal-style lintels.

EDWARD MOONEY HOUSE, 1785–9 (18 Bowery).
The Edward Mooney House is an example of transitional architecture. Its façade, overlooking the Bowery, displays Georgian elements, while the gable end (on Pell Street), with its top-story quarter round windows, anticipates the Federal style.

ROMAN CATHOLIC ORPHAN ASYLUM, 1826–06 (32 Prince St.)
This former Catholic orphanage, a typical structure from the Federal period, now houses a convent and a school. Its features – so-called Flemish bond brickwork, dormer sash windows and fanlight – are reminiscent of domestic architecture.

The 1830's were prosperous years for New York. They witnessed the flowering of the Greek Revival style, which was widely applied to large civic, religious and commercial buildings, as well as houses. Although it was a development of late 18th-century European neo-classicism, the Greek Revival style also represented a tribute from an idealistic America to ancient Greek democracy.

The cast-iron railings of 10 Washington Square are a combination of Grecian geometric and floral motifs and classical scrolls.

COLONNADE ROW, 1833, Seth Greer (428–34 Lafayette St.) ▲ 227
Four houses remain out of the nine that originally made up LaGrange Terrace (the name was derived from the French country home of the Marquis de Lafayette). The Greek architectural features of this residential structure – from the restrained decoration to the vast Corinthian-order portico – were modified to suit domestic typology.

VILLAGE COMMUNITY CHURCH, 1847, Samuel Thomson (143 West 13th St.) ▲ 219
In the 19th century many New York parishes commissioned new buildings modeled on the classical Greek temple. A typical example is this old church in Greenwich Village. Such buildings were constructed out of brick, granite, polished marble or limestone; softer materials, such as sandstone or wood, were used for the columns. These austere exteriors often conceal richly decorated interiors.

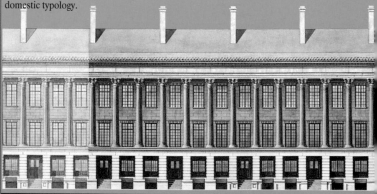

An attic story is a characteristic feature of Greek Revival houses, like this one in Cushman Row, with its regular small square windows surrounded by laurel wreaths.

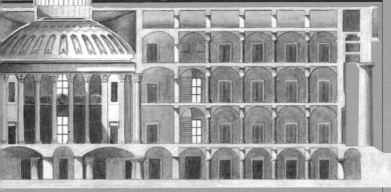

FEDERAL HALL, 1834–42, Town & Davis (28 Wall St.) ▲ 162

The most imposing examples of Greek Revival style in Manhattan are public buildings, and among these the most eye-catching is the former Federal Customs House. The restraint of its marble Doric exterior, modeled on the Parthenon, belies the sumptuous interior, which boasts a domed, coffered ceiling resting on marble Corinthian columns and adorned with elegant classical ironwork.

WAREHOUSES

After the fire of December 1835, many warehouses were built in the same basic design: granite ground floor, brick upper stories and a façade sometimes totally made of granite, as here, at 170–6 John Street.

PORCHES

Porches were set back within the façade so as not to encroach on the narrow New York streets. The main entrance, typically framed in solid granite, was illuminated by side lights and a fanlight.

CUSHMAN ROW, 1840 (406–418 W. 20th St.) ▲ 220

This is a group of identical row houses. The two most characteristic features of this style of house are the cornices and the attic story, concealing a flat roof.

The bays and the cornice are the only form of decoration. Here, wealth goes hand in hand with austerity.

The arches of Grace Church, ▲ 224, on Broadway, are adorned with figurative reliefs.

The Gothic Revival style appeared in New York in the 1830's. Although it was applied primarily to religious structures, elements found their way into civic architecture. The early form of Gothic Revival, with its rural medieval architecture, gave way, in the 1860's, to a more complex style, High Victorian Gothic, and later, at the end of the century, to Neo-Gothic, whose idiom was closer to that of 14th-century Gothic; St Thomas's, on Fifth Avenue, is an outstanding example.

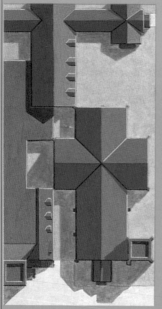

When building the Church of the Holy Communion, Upjohn made every effort to reproduce the appearance of English rural churches down to the smallest detail, even to the point of choosing uneven blocks of stone, in different shades, to give the church the weathered look of old stone.

The Church of the Holy Communion is typical of American parishes in combining the place of worship with a building devoted to social activities.

CHURCH OF THE HOLY COMMUNION, 1846, Richard Upjohn (6th Ave at 20th St.) ▲ 220
In 1846, Upjohn, the architect of Trinity Church ▲ 154, designed the first asymmetrical Gothic Revival church in America, similar to those built in the English countryside. This church became the model for many others in the United States.

The Gothic Revival grillwork of
Grace Church on Broadway.

High Victorian Gothic, inspired by Italian and
French Gothic architecture, showed the
influence of John Ruskin's theories. It became
very fashionable in New York in the 1860's.

For a short time
during the 1840's the
property developers
of rowhouses applied
Gothic elements to
their buildings, as can
be seen on the doors
of 135 E. 12th Street
▲ 85.

**THOMAS STREET INN, 1875, J. Morgan Slade
(8 Thomas St.)** ▲ 209
This is an example of High Victorian Gothic
as applied to a commercial building.
The use of brick and stone and
the polychrome decoration are
distinctive features of this style.

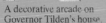

A decorative arcade on
Governor Tilden's house.

**DECORATIVE
IRONWORK**
One of the most
striking features of
neo-Gothic style is
the use of cast iron
for screens and
balconies, which
often had pointed
quatrefoil and trefoil
motifs.

**MEDIEVAL
INSPIRATION**
Some granite façades
had medieval features
such as lancet arch
doorways and ogee
arches.

**NATIONAL ARTS CLUB,
formerly GOVERNOR
TILDEN'S HOUSE,
1884, Calvert Vaux
(15 Gramercy Park
South)** ▲ 230
Here the architects
combined sculpture
and polychrome
decoration in the
purest Ruskinian
tradition. Note the
stringcourses under
the windows and the
curved arcading,
suggestive of
northern Italian
Gothic architecture.

● ITALIANATE AND SECOND EMPIRE STYLES

The doorway of the Salmagundi Club (47 5th Avenue), crowned with a semicircular fanlight, has double doors. The lavishly carved architrave is topped with a pediment.

As early as 1845, but primarily in the 1850's and 1860's, two new styles took Manhattan by storm – one inspired by the Italian Renaissance and the other by Second Empire French architecture. The two styles could be combined so that "Florentine" façades were crowned with mansard roofs. It was during these years of heady economic and urban growth that architects began to make use of new materials such as cast iron.

THE ITALIANATE CORNICE
The Italianate façade is articulated by deeply recessed windows with ledges. The building is crowned by a projecting cornice supported by corbels, often made of galvanized iron.

CARY BUILDING, 1857, King and Kellum (105–107 Chambers St.) ▲ 209
Italianate-style commercial buildings were often constructed of cast-iron elements, bolted onto conventional brick or wooden structures. The façades of these cast-iron buildings were painted to resemble stone – which was too expensive – as on the Haughwout Building ● 94, ▲ 204, or here, on the Cary Building.

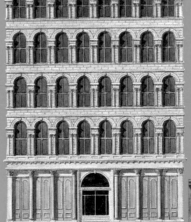

ANALOGY
Features common to both Italianate and Second Empire styles are strong horizontal divisions, grouped columns, deeply recessed window arches and projecting cornices, as seen on the Cary Building (left) and Gilsey House (above, right).

BROWNSTONES
Thousands of Italianate-style rowhouses were constructed between 1845 and 1870, a period of great economic growth. They were built of brownstone, a type of rich brown sandstone quarried in Connecticut and New Jersey. This material became so popular that New Yorkers still call these houses "brownstones". This (right) is the Langston Hughes House, at 20 E. 127th Street, in Harlem.

Italianate-style rowhouses were simple three-story structures (right) resting on a rugged rusticated basement. They have segmental arch bay windows (left) with very large windowpanes.

The ironwork on the roof of 881 Broadway is reminiscent of that on Napoleon III's addition to the Louvre.

GILSEY HOUSE, 1871
(1200 Broadway) ▲ *234*
Several New York buildings, such as the Gilsey House, with its cast-iron façade, built by Stephen Decatur Hatch, were directly inspired by Haussmann's neo-Baroque style. The double-slope, so-called mansard roof, a key feature of this style, marks the first significant influence of French architecture in New York.

The Gilsey House's façade (below) overlooking Broadway, and a detail (left) of the pyramidal pavilion roof at the corner. Geometric and scattered polychrome patterns are created by the slates.

Another example of slate patterns at 19 Gramercy Park ▲ *230.*

70 PERRY ST., 1867
The popular mansard roof had begun to replace flat roofs in the 1830's. Adding a mansard roof to an Italianate façade gave the owner an additional story to rent out.

QUEEN ANNE STYLE AND ROMANESQUE REVIVAL

A stylistic change took place in the years following the depression of the 1870's. The Italianate style was replaced by two picturesque modes: Queen Anne and Romanesque Revival. The first combined Medieval, Renaissance, classical and even Japanese features to create a sometimes eccentric architecture. The second, a pragmatic, weighty style introduced by H. H. Richardson, combined Romanesque and Byzantine influences.

Brick was commonly used in the Queen Anne style for its formal and decorative potential, in combination with other materials. This varied effect is seen to good advantage in the Potter Building, Park Row ▲ *170*.

The Japanese-style glazing bars of the Century Building ▲ *223* and the floral-motif ironwork of the Chelsea Hotel ▲ *220* – are typical of the Queen Anne style.

The sunflower became the archetypal motif of Queen Anne decoration.

Most Queen Anne structures in New York are polychromatic, with brick façades enhanced with stone and terracotta trimmings.

QUEEN ANNE-STYLE ROW HOUSES, 1894, W. Holman Smith (35–45 W. 94th St.)
These houses still have their eccentric gables, a galvanized metal cornice, punctuated alternately by small triangular and scrolled pediments, decorated with pinecones. The regularity of the façades is interrupted by picturesque bow windows.

Stone, terracotta and brick used together in a Romanesque Revival lintel.

GILBERT KIAMIE HOUSE formerly the Grolier Club, 1895 (29 E. 32nd St.)

Romanesque Revival façades are typically articulated by bold semicircular bays, divided by thick mullions and transoms, occasionally embellished with leaded glass panes. The bonding is richly varied, incorporating rubble stone, terracotta and reliefs featuring carved plant forms, strapwork and grotesque motifs.

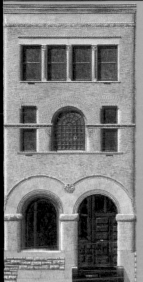

WALLACE BUILDING, 1893–4, Oscar Wirz (56–8 Pine St.).

This is one of the few examples of Romanesque Revival being applied to skyscraper architecture. Note the intricate Byzantine detailing of the semicircular bays (opposite).

On the Wallace Building Romanesque Revival decoration has been adapted to suit the proportions of the skyscraper.

The juxtaposition of rustication and dressed stone is typical of Romanesque Revival (seen here at 112 E. 17th St.). The contrast is accentuated by the use of bas-relief elements.

The grilles of the DeVinne Press Building employ a motif similar to those used on Rouen Cathedral in France.

DEVINNE PRESS BUILDING, 1885–6, Babb, Cook and Willard (393–9 Lafayette St.) ▲ 227

In the prosperous 1880's, many Romanesque Revival factories and warehouses, including this printing press, were built in New York. Tall round-arched bays such as these came to influence commercial architecture at the end of the century.

● "Beaux Arts" style

Between 1846 and 1914, more than four hundred
American architects studied in Paris at the École
des Beaux-Arts. In fact, the United States had no
architectural school until 1867. The prestige enjoyed by Paris-
trained architects prompted their younger colleagues to follow
in their footsteps, and nearly half of these graduates practised
in New York. "Beaux Arts"-style buildings are now coming
back into favor among certain Postmodern architects.

**NEW YORK PUBLIC LIBRARY, 1911, Carrère & Hastings (5th Ave., between 40th and
42nd sts.)** ▲ *252.* The key feature of this monumental building is the clearly organized and
balanced plan (left), a characteristic of Beaux Arts training
found in major public commissions. The wide corridors,
punctuated by columns, are conducive to circulation and make
every department of the New York Public Library easily
accessible. The triple arcade, accentuated by columns and
surmounted by groups of carved figures (above), gives the
main entrance the monumentality of a triumphal arch.

**HENRY VILLARD HOUSES, 1884, McKim, Mead and White
(451–5 Madison Ave., between 50th and 51st sts.)** ▲ *284.* This group
of six private residences, arranged around a central courtyard, is a
replica of a traditional Italian palazzo. The south wing was intended for
Henry Villard, one of America's wealthiest railway magnates, who
commissioned the project. The houses now form part of a hotel.

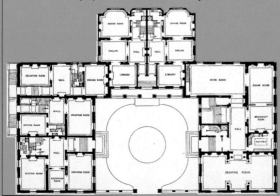

The main source of
inspiration for the
Henry Villard Houses
was the Palazzo della
Cancelleria in Rome,
whose decoration was
simplified and limited
to the window frames,
the balconies and
the quoins.

THE PIERPONT MORGAN LIBRARY, 1906, McKim, Mead & White (33 E. 36th St.) ▲ *241*
"I want a gem": these were the words of the financier J. Pierpont Morgan, an ardent admirer of Italian Renaissance architecture, when he commissioned a private library-cum-museum from McKim. The three rooms are linked by a vestibule extended by an apse. The allegorical paintings on the walls are adapted from Raphaël's frescos in the Vatican.

The decoration of the cornice on the Racquet and Tennis Club of New York ▲ *286* sets up a subtle balance between picturesque and monumental elements.

NEW YORK YACHT CLUB, 1900, Warren and Wetmore (37 W. 44th St.) ▲ *251*
The architects of this sailing club imaginatively designed three classical bays decorated with galleon sterns, which could have come straight out of *Peter Pan*; they overhang 44th Street, bringing dolphins, seaweed and shells in their wake.

LOW MEMORIAL LIBRARY, 1897, McKim, Mead & White (Columbia University) ▲ *352*
Between 1894 and 1903 Charles McKim designed the general plan for the Columbia campus, located between West 116th and 120th streets. The overall scheme, dense and homogeneous, is one of the most characteristic examples of the "City Beautiful" movement, the urban design equivalent of the "Beaux Arts" style. The focal point of the composition is this library, with its awe-inspiring peristyle and dome. However, the proportions remain on a human scale and the steps, which serve as a podium, have become a popular student gathering place.

The birth of the skyscraper, in the 1860's, was a response to the spatial constraints imposed by the tight urban fabric of Lower Manhattan. It was made possible by the design of light steel frames, the invention of the electric passenger elevator and the fact that the rocky terrain lent itself to the laying of foundations. But there was another reason: the desire to go higher than the competition. Although the techniques were new, the forms and the decoration remained eclectic.

In 1913 the Woolworth Building, dubbed the "eighth wonder of the world", was New York's tallest building at 792 feet ▲ *180*.

HAUGHWOUT BUILDING, 1857, J. P. Gaynor (488 Broadway, at Broome St.) ▲ *204*. This forebear of the skyscraper was built by Daniel D. Badger, to plans by Gaynor, with prefabricated cast-iron elements which made it possible to incorporate large areas of glass. The Haughwout Building was originally a department store selling glass, china, clocks and watches.

Decorative elements were cast in factories and then bolted onto the structure.

CAST-IRON ASSEMBLY
Standardized cast-iron parts were assembled and bolted on at the construction site. This job did not require skilled workmen and the process was cheaper than stone construction. But the cast iron was not initially strong enough to be used for buildings with a large number of stories; in addition, its low resistance to fire represented a very real danger for the building's occupants. Behind the metal façade, the load-bearing structures continued to be made of wood or conventional masonry: it was not until the invention of the Bessemer process (1856) and the popularization of high-resistance steel, that a homogeneous frame was developed ▲ *203*.

BAYARD BUILDING, formerly CONDICT BUILDING, 1898, Louis Sullivan and Lyndon P. Smith (65 Bleecker St.) ▲ *209*
This is the only building in New York designed by the master of the Chicago School. A projecting cornice stabilizes the rhythm of the decorative pilasters, alternately thick and thin, and achieves an innovative balance between horizontal and vertical elements.

Detail from the terracotta decoration of the Bayard Building. Here Sullivan was exploiting the interlaced geometrical motifs which were a hallmark of his style.

In 1857, in the Haughwout Store, Elisha Otis installed the first passenger elevator fitted with a safety device.

ANSONIA HOTEL, 1904, Paul E. M. Duboy and Michael Graves (2109 Broadway) ▲ *347*. The French-born architect endeavored to give this apartment building a Parisian look. This was no easy task, as it entailed maintaining a harmonious sense of proportion in a huge apartment building with disparate façades, combining a whole spectrum of materials, whose height was three times that of its Parisian counterparts.

THE ECLECTICISM OF THE FIRST SKYSCRAPERS

Diagram showing the assembly of a terracotta facing.

At the turn of the 20th century the technology necessary for erecting tall buildings came of age; the number of stories multiplied and skyscrapers shot up all over Manhattan. But these skyscrapers still needed to find their own aesthetic, instead of wavering between neo-Classicism and neo-Gothic.

MUNICIPAL BUILDING, 1914, McKim, Mead & White (1 Centre St.) ▲ *182*
Designed by prominent champions of classicism, this skyscraper evokes a classical column in its tripartite composition, distinct base, shaft and capital. The Stalinist-era skyscrapers of Moscow, which also sport Corinthian pilasters and engaged columns, were inspired by this style.

FLATIRON BUILDING, formerly FULLER BUILDING, 1902, Daniel H. Burnham & Co. (175 5th Ave.) ▲ *233*
Equipped with a system to prevent the spread of fire, this was the first self-sufficient skyscraper. It had an electric generator providing all its electricity and heating.

The plans drawn up in 1922 by the Viennese architect Adolf Loos for the headquarters of the *Chicago Tribune* (left) were a literal reference to the tripartite division of the skyscraper and suggest a giant Doric column.

THE TOPS
The tops of 14–16 Wall Street ▲ *163*, Woolworth ▲ *180* and Metropolitan Life Insurance Company ▲ *234* buildings were inspired respectively by classical mausoleums, Gothic steeples and the campanile in Saint Mark's square in Venice. This was not for ideological reasons but rather to give each building a distinctive identity on the Manhattan skyline.

ZONING RESOLUTION
In 1916 a set of building regulations was passed to prevent the "canyon" effect ■ *16*, Skyscrapers could be built with a height relative to the width of the street. Successive setbacks were then employed to make them narrower and allow light into the street. When the building size had been reduced to a quarter of the site at street level, the tower could continue to rise ad infinitum.

EQUITABLE BUILDING, 1912–15 (120 Broadway)
▲ *153*. Designed before the zoning law, the Equitable Building (left) should, according to its criteria, have been built in the shape of a pyramid (right).

During the property boom of the 1920's, New York architects drew their inspiration from European movements – Viennese Secession, German Expressionism, French Art Deco – and even transcended them. The Chrysler Building ▲ *266* is one of the most striking examples of this trend. The geometric, streamlined aesthetic of Art Deco was ideally suited to the tapering shape of the new skyscrapers.

FRIEZES IN ABUNDANCE
An abundance of decorative friezes appeared during the Art Deco period. Here, a detail of one at 2 Park Ave. built by Ely Jacques Kahn.

THE FIRST ART DECO SKYSCRAPER
The main entrance of the Barclay-Vesey Building, 1923–6 ▲ *140* (140 West St.) is decorated with bells, the logo of the Bell Telephone Company.

Former RCA VICTOR BUILDING, 1930–1, Cross & Cross (570 Lexington Ave. at 51st St.) ▲ *286*
The summit of this spire is stunning in its originality and exuberance. The lacy ornamental stonework, brickwork and glazed ceramic veneer, gilded in places, suggest Flamboyant Gothic; yet, apart from the stylized pinnacles, none of these varied motifs had any precedents; the chevrons and bolts of lightning symbolize the Hertzian waves broadcast by the Radio Corporation of America, the original owner of this tower.

DYNAMIC COMPOSITIONS
The radiator grills in the Chanin Building, 1929 (122 E. 42nd St.) ▲ *272.* These grills, the work of the sculptor René Chambellan, combine rays and chevrons, spirals and ripples.

THE SKYLINE

In 1929 the Multiple Dwelling Act authorized the construction of very tall apartment houses and hotels. Central Park West was subsequently endowed with a number of soaring residences, some with twin towers. On the East Side, the towers of the Waldorf-Astoria Hotel (1930–1, Schultze & Weaver) joined the Chrysler and General Electric buildings on the Midtown skyline.

FORMER AMERICAN STANDARD BUILDING (40 W. 40th St.)

▲ *254*. This has one of the earliest pyramidal silhouettes. The black brick facing employed by Raymond Hood, a former pupil at the École des Beaux-Arts, was an innovative step. It enabled him to minimize the contrast between the building's solid masses and the windows.

FILM CENTER BUILDING, 1928–9, Buchman & Kahn (630 9th Ave.) ▲ 256

The lobby of this building, designed by one of the masters of the Modern Jazz style, is a prime example of this style's typical features. Certain motifs, like those of the mosaics, were directly inspired by Mayan art.

The Gothic pinnacles on the setbacks of the American Standard Building are enhanced with gold.

TWO NEW DECORATIVE ELEMENTS

The horizontal bands of blue-green glazed terracotta and the giant stylized letters, which form part of the decoration of the entrance and the top of the McGraw-Hill Building, were introduced by architect Raymond Hood.

FORMER McGRAW-HILL BUILDING, 1930–1, Hood, Godley & Fouilhoux (330 W. 42nd St.) ▲ 256.

This skyscraper, whose use of horizontal lines and rounded corners at the top creates a dynamic effect, doubled as headquarters and printing works for a large publishing company. An early example of streamlining, this building displays a functionalism akin to that of the International Style.

The term "international style" was first used, in 1932, by the architect Philip Johnson and the art historian Henry-Russell Hitchcock to describe the exhibition of modern European architecture held at MOMA in the same year. However, New York architects were not ready to embrace European modernism and the city did not become a testing ground for modern architecture until around 1950.

W. LESCAZE HOUSE, 1934 (211 E. 48th St.) ▲ 262
This townhouse was the architect's home and place of work and one of the first International Style buildings in New York. It contrasts sharply with the neighboring brownstone residences. Ribbon windows and glass block panes let the light filter in while maintaining privacy.

MOMA ▲ 290, reconstruction of the original façade, 1939, Philip Goodwin and Edward Durell Stone (11 W. 53rd St.) The original building to house the Museum of Modern Art formed a marked contrast with the adjacent rowhouses.

THE INITIAL COMPOSITION The emphasis is on horizontal and vertical lines. The functions are divided as follows: a welcoming, glazed ground floor, two levels of windowless exhibition rooms, two office stories and a roof terrace. The geometric severity of the building is tempered by the curve of the canopy and the round openings in the roof.

LEVER HOUSE, 1952, Skidmore, Owing & Merrill (390 Park Ave.) ▲ 286. The generation of "minimalist" skyscrapers, with their pared-down lines, came of age with this building. Using on a quarter of the available area, its main vertical structure is set a right angles to Park Avenue. Under threat in 1983, it is now liste as a landmark and has recently undergone a major restoration.

A NEW APPROACH TO PUBLIC OPEN SPACES. Because Lever House rests on stilts, a pedestrian area opens up at street level. Trees grow up through the opening in the roof terrace (left). The airy effect breaks the uniformity of the avenue.

Narrow decorative bronze I-beams punctuate the windows of the Seagram Building and accentuate the vertical thrust of the metal frame.

SEAGRAM BUILDING, 1958, Ludwig Mies van der Rohe in collaboration with Philip Johnson (375 Park Ave.) ▲ 286
The German-born architect was already an established name in Chicago when he received the commisssion for this building. A 38-story-high rectangle composed of three major bays, it is proportioned according to classical canons. The building is set back from Park Avenue, creating space for a deep plaza from which this minimalist skyscraper can be admired. Its austere lines were realized in rich materials and the Seagram Building topped all records for cost per square meter.

DECORATIVE BRONZE
The vertical structure is accentuated by decorative bronze I-beams; the corner posts are also clad in bronze.

The top is sliced off at a 45° angle, making Citicorp easy to distinguish on the Manhattan skyline.

CITICORP CENTER, 1978, Hugh Stubbins & Assoc. (Lexington Ave., between 53rd and 54th Sts.) ▲ 286
This 46-story tower, sheathed in aluminum panels, sits on four pillars and a central column. A sunken plaza occupies the area which has been liberated at ground level.

FORD FOUNDATION, 1967, Kevin Roche, John Dinkeloo & Assocs. (321 E. 42nd St.) ▲ 264. The technical and stylistic innovation of this building is its brick and glass façade. It was built using girders made of exposed steel (Cor-ten) which is resistant to atmospheric corrosion.

A BETTER BALANCE BETWEEN PUBLIC AND PRIVATE SPACES
At the end of the 1960's, architects endeavored to improve the relationship between public and private spaces. The Ford Foundation is one successful example: two office wings open onto an immense enclosed atrium-garden which can be seen from the street.

Detail of the polished steel elevator
door-plaques inside the Sony Building.

In the 1980's and 1990's the prosperity
enjoyed by big business gave the
skyscraper a new lease on life.
In New York, one of the hotbeds of
Postmodernism since the 1970's,
architects and real estate developers
viewed the revival of past forms as
an antidote to the International Style,
and a means of restoring to larger
corporate buildings
a symbolic dimension.

**SONY BUILDING formerly AT&T
BUILDING, 1979–83, Philip
Johnson and John Burgee
(550 Madison Ave.)**
The era of the Postmodern
skyscraper dawned with this
building. To make his "small"
37-story building more
monumental, Johnson revived
tripartite composition. His
Chippendale-style pediment
aroused great controversy.

**THE RISE OF
POSTMODERNISM**
With the AT&T headquarters
(now the Sony Building),
which appeared on the
covers of *Time* and *The
New Yorker*, Johnson's
firm launched a new
fashion; and Johnson –
once an exponent of
the International Style
– maintained his
position as an arbiter
of taste in New York.
The place of honor in
the main lobby was
held by a statue,
the *Spirit of
Communication*,
brought from the
previous headquarters.

**WASHINGTON COURT, 1986, James Stewart Polskek & Partners ▲ *212*
(6th Ave., between Waverly Place and Washington Square)**
Postmodernism has also had its effect on residential architecture: these rowhouses,
with their harmonious façades, reflect the spirit of Greenwich Village.

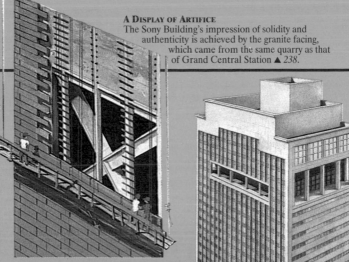

A DISPLAY OF ARTIFICE
The Sony Building's impression of solidity and
authenticity is achieved by the granite facing,
which came from the same quarry as that
of Grand Central Station ▲ 238.

**PHILIP MORRIS INC. BUILDING, 1982,
Ulrich Franzen & Assocs.
(42nd St. at Park Ave.)**
Franzen employed a pluralist architectural
language, midway between the International
Style and classicism. This building has two
different tripartite façades which work well
with the busy thoroughfares they overlook.

**WORLD FINANCIAL CENTER, 1981–8,
Cesar Pelli (Battery Park City)**
▲ 141. This complex is the focal
point of the district of Battery Park
City. Its four towers, ranging from
33 to 50 stories, are built around a
plaza and winter garden. Architect
Cesar Pelli has used the
mirror effects of his
glass towers to
emphasize their tiered
façades and
designed their
tops in Art
Deco style.

103

Because of the recession, some projects designed in the 1980's never saw the light of day. Neither the skyscrapers scheduled to be built on Columbus Circle nor Donald Trump's 150-story dream tower were realized. However, on the West Side, the redevelopment of the banks of the Hudson reveals a new approach to urban design.

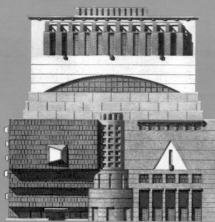

WHITNEY MUSEUM, 1966, Marcel Breuer & Assocs. (Madison Ave. at 75th St.) ▲ *326*

This building, built by a former professor at the Weimar Bauhaus to house a collection of modern American art, quickly became too cramped. The plans for enlarging it, designed in 1986 by Michael Graves, rekindled the quarrel of the Moderns and the Postmoderns. Three plans were scuttled, but by 2004, the museum again made a commitment to expand based on a plan by Italian architect Renzo Piano, who has also designed new headquarters for the *New York Times*.

Plans for a tower by Pederson and Fox at 383 Madison Avenue were abandoned.

WHITEHALL FERRY TERMINAL

In 1992 the Postmodernist architect Robert Venturi was commissioned to build a new maritime terminal on the tip of Manhattan. He reproduced the proportions of the façade from the neighboring Battery Maritime Terminal and topped the building with a startling clock over 98 feet in diameter, which called to mind the slogan "Time is Money". This approach follows the tradition of large American neo-Classical railroad stations.

104

New York
as seen by
painters

"What a sight these towers of Manhattan are, glittering with millions of golden specks, soaring endlessly, as if they were going to touch the sky!"

Langston Hughes

Wherein lies New York's quintessential nature? Georgia O'Keeffe (1887–1986) who painted *Radiator Building* (2; detail in 3) in 1927, felt that the skyscraper was the enduring symbol of the city. O'Keeffe painted what she saw from her own windows. She professed to be as interested in the spaces between the buildings, the "canyons", as in their architecture. Robert Henri (1865–1929) held that the real city was not to be found at the tops of the temples to Mammon but at the very bottom; in 1902, he painted *New York in Winter* (1).

| 1 | 2 |
| | 3 |

"A love of art is not enough to perceive the strength, meaning and spark of beauty in a gang of urchins from the East Side."

Robert Henri

M Prendergast (1859–1924) and Robert Henri ● *107*, members of "The Eight", specialized in painting scenes of American city life. Prendergast's fondness for the city is clearly visible in the 1901 paintings *East River* (2) and *Central Park* (1). In his watercolor *Grand Central Terminal* (3), 1987, Richard Haas captures this early skyscraper in a wintry twilight. A more mundane portrait of a skyscraper is *Chrysler Building under Construction* (1931) by Earl Horter.

| 1 | 3 |
| 2 | 4 |

> "I regarded this modern city as a sort of hell. The subway, hidden in the bowels of the earth, seemed to symbolize an environment that confounds the senses and destroys life."
>
> George Tooker

Edward Hopper (1882–1967; below), the most outstanding of Robert Henri's pupils, visited Paris where he began his career by painting in an impressionist style. He returned to New York in 1910, to devote himself to

more familiar American subjects. The works for which he became famous depicted lonely figures in such urban settings as cinemas, service stations, and hotel rooms. Hopper stated that his favorite subject was "sunlight striking the wall of a house". *Roofs of Washington Square*, 1926 (1), is the view from the roof of his studio. This canvas, a dazzling composition of light and airy distances, seems to offer an escape from the artificial lighting of the New York subway system, depicted in George Tooker's painting *Subway* (2; detail in 3). In this oppressively claustrophobic canvas, completed in 1950, the characters are lost in the alienating maze of technology. Hopper and Tooker both evoked a stark and lonely American landscape.

1	
2	3

111

These two paintings, *View of Manhattan West from Philip Morris at Park Avenue and 41st Street* (1982), by Richard Haas, with its jumble of buildings and erratic spaces, and – even more so – Joseph Stella's *Brooklyn Bridge, Variation on an Old Theme* (1939), with its Gothic arches, rigid steel cables and heavy traffic, enshrine the city in its own mythology.

New York
as seen by writers

NEW YORKERS

TALENT

Does the character of a city come principally from its buildings or its people? According to Timothy Dwight (1752–1817), writing in 1811, the city acts as a magnet for people of talent and is thus shaped by them.

❝In every large city there will always be found a considerable number of persons who possess superior talents and information; and who, if not natives, are drawn to it by the peculiar encouragement which it holds out to their exertions. The field of effort is here more splendid, and the talents are more needed, honored, and rewarded than in smaller towns. New York has its share of persons sustaining this character: men really possessing superior minds and deserving high esteem. Together with these, there is not a small number, here as elsewhere, who arrogate this character to themselves, and some of whom occasionally acquire and lose it: men accounted great through the favorable influence of some accident, the attachment of some religious or political party during a fortunate breeze of popularity, or the lucky prevalence of some incidental sympathy, or the ardent pursuit of some favorite public object in which they have happened to act with success. These meteors, though some of them shine for a period with considerable luster, soon pass over the horizon, and are seen no more.

The citizens at large are distinguished as to their intelligence in the manner alluded to above. To this place they have come with the advantages and disadvantages of education found in their several native countries. Some of them are well informed, read, converse, and investigate. Others scarcely do either, and not a small number are unable to read at all. Most of these are, however, Europeans.❞

TIMOTHY DWIGHT, *TRAVELS IN NEW ENGLAND AND NEW YORK*,
HARVARD UNIVERSITY PRESS, 1969

GILDED YOUTH

F. Scott Fitzgerald (1896–1940) glamorized the 1920's as a decade belonging to "gilded youth". In this autobiographical piece, he feels like an observer of the city rather than a participant because his future wife, Zelda, is in Alabama.

❝New York had all the iridescence of the beginning of the world. The returning troops marched up Fifth Avenue and the girls were instinctively drawn East and North toward them – this was the greatest nation and there was gala in the air. As I hovered ghost-like in the Plaza Red Room of a Saturday afternoon, or went to lush and liquid garden parties in the East Sixties or tippled with Princetonians in the Biltmore Bar I was haunted always by my other life – my drab room in the Bronx, my square foot of the subway, my fixation upon the day's letter from Alabama – would it come and what would it say? – my shabby suits, my poverty, and love. While my friends were launching decently into life I had muscled my inadequate

bark into midstream. The gilded youth circling around young Constance Bennett in the Club de Vingt, the classmates in the Yale-Princeton Club whooping up our first after-the-war reunion, the atmosphere of the millionaires' houses that I sometimes frequented – these things were empty for me, though I recognized them as impressive scenery and regretted that I was committed to other romance.**99**

F. SCOTT FITZGERALD, *THE CRACK UP*, © FITZGERALD ESTATE, 1932

STRANGERS AND NEIGHBORS

Edmund B. White (1899–1985), an American journalist, was very conscious of the city's previous illustrious inhabitants.

66On any person who desires such queer prizes, New York will bestow the gift of loneliness and the gift of privacy. It is this largess that accounts for the presence within the city's walls of a considerable section of the population; for the residents of Manhattan are to a large extent strangers who have pulled up stakes somewhere and come to town, seeking sanctuary or fulfillment or some greater or lesser grail. The capacity to make such dubious gifts is a mysterious quality of New York. It can destroy an individual, or it can fulfill him, depending a good deal on luck. No one should come to New York to live unless he is willing to be lucky.

New York is the concentrate of art and commerce and sport and religion and entertainment and finance, bringing to a single compact arena the gladiator, the evangelist, the promoter, the actor, the trader and the merchant. It carries on its lapel the unexpungeable odor of the long past, so that no matter where you sit in New York you feel the vibrations of great times and tall deeds, of queer people and events and undertakings. . . . I am twenty-two blocks from where Rudolph Valentino lay in state, eight blocks from where Nathan Hale was executed, five blocks from the publisher's office where Ernest Hemingway hit Max Eastman on the nose, four miles from where Walt Whitman sat sweating out editorials for the Brooklyn Eagle, thirty-four blocks from the street Willa Cather lived in when she came to New York to write books about Nebraska, one block from where Marceline used to clown on the boards of the Hippodrome . . . and for that matter I am probably occupying the very room that any number of exalted and somewise memorable characters sat in, some of them on hot, breathless afternoons, lonely and private and full of their own sense of emanations from without **99**

E. B. WHITE, *HERE IS NEW YORK*, HARPER BROS., 1949

LABORERS

First-generation immigrants add color and diversity to the masses thronging the streets of the city. Charles Dickens (1812–70) described some Irish laborers.

66 . . . let us see what kind of men . . . are . . . those two labourers in holiday clothes, of whom one carries in his hand a crumpled scrap of paper from which he tries to spell out a hard name, while the other looks about for it on all the doors and windows.

Irishmen both! You might know them, if they were masked, by their long-tailed blue coats and bright buttons, and their drab trousers, which they wear like men well used to working dresses, who are easy in no others. It would be hard to keep your model republics going, without the countrymen and countrywomen of those two labourers. For who else would dig, and delve, and drudge, and do domestic work, and make canals and roads, and execute great lines of Internal Improvement! Irishmen both, and sorely puzzled too, to find out what they seek. Let us go down, and help them for the love of home, and that spirit of liberty which admits of honest service to honest men, and honest work for honest bread, no matter what it be.

That's well! We have got at the right address at last, though it is written in strange characters truly, and might have been scrawled with the blunt handle of the spade the writer better knows the use of, than a pen. Their way lies yonder, but what business takes them there? They carry savings: to hoard up? No. They are brothers, those men. One crossed the sea alone, and working very hard for one half year, and living harder, saved funds enough to bring the other out. That done, they worked together side by side, contentedly sharing hard labour and hard living for another term, and then their sisters came, and then another brother, and lastly, their old mother. And what now? Why, the poor old crone is restless in a strange land, and yearns to lay her bones, she says, among her people in the old graveyard at home: and so they go to pay her passage back: and God help her and them, and every simple heart, and all who turn to the Jerusalem of their younger days, and have an altar-fire upon the cold hearth of their fathers.**

CHARLES DICKENS, *AMERICAN NOTES*,
LONDON, 1842

RAGING TORRENTS

Theodore Dreiser (1871–1945), the American novelist, writes here of the sheer masses of people going about their business in the city.

**Take your place on Williamsburg Bridge some morning, for instance, at say three or four o'clock, and watch the long, the quite unbroken line of Jews trundling pushcarts eastward to the great Wall-about Market over the bridge. A procession out of Assyria or Egypt or Chaldea, you might suppose, Biblical in quality; or, better yet, a huge chorus in some operatic dawn scene laid in Paris or Petrograd or here. A vast, silent mass it is, marching to the music of necessity . . . And they are New York, too – Bucharest and Lemberg and Odessa come to the Bowery, and adding rich, dark, colorful threads to the rug or tapestry which is New York.

Since these are but a portion, think of those other masses that come from the surrounding territory, north, south, east and west. The ferries – have you ever observed them in the morning? Or the bridges, railway terminals, and every elevated and subway exit?

Already at six and six-thirty in the morning they have begun to trickle small streams of human beings Manhattan or cityward, and by seven and seven-fifteen these streams have become sizable affairs. By seven-thirty and eight they have changed into heavy, turbulent rivers, and by eight-fifteen and eight-thirty and nine they are raging torrents, no less. They overflow all the streets and avenues and every available means of conveyance. They are pouring into all available doorways, shops, factories, office-buildings – those huge affairs towering so significantly above them. Here they stay all day long, causing those great hives and their adjacent streets to flush with a softness of color not indigenous to them, and then at night, between five and six, they are going again, pouring forth over the bridges and through the subways and across the ferries and out on the trains, until the last drop of them appears to have been exuded, and they are pocketed in some outlying side-street or village or metropolitan hall-room – and the great, turbulent night of the city is on once more.**

THEODORE DREISER,
THE COLOR OF A GREAT CITY,
THE DREISER TRUST, 1923 © 1923 BY
BONI & LIVERIGHT, INC.

A TRANSIENT POPULATION

Don DeLillo (b. 1936) picks some individuals out of the crowd – not celebrities but anonymous characters or people on the streets.

❝Harbors reveal a city's power, its lust for money and filth, but strangely through the haze what I distinguished first was the lone mellow promise of an island, tender retreat from straight lines, an answering sea-mound. This was the mist's illusion and the harbor's pound of flesh. Skippy tugged at licorice with her teeth, the black strands expanding between hand and jaw. She had a shaded face and she was ageless, a wanderer in cities, one of those children found after every war, picking in the rubble for scraps of food the gaunt dogs have missed. Such minds are unreclaimable but at the same time hardly dangerous and governments acknowledge this fact by providing millions of acres of postwar rubble. On our way to find a bus stop we saw the subway crowds drop into openings in the earth, on their way up the length of Manhattan or under rivers to the bourns and orchards, there to be educated in false innocence, in the rites of isolation. Perhaps the only ore of truth their lives possessed was buried in this central rock. Beyond its limits was their one escape, a  dreamless sleep, no need to fear the dare to be exceptional. Dozens of pigeons swarmed around a woman tossing bread crumbs. She was in a wheelchair held at rest by a young boy, both on fire with birds, the pigeons skidding on the air, tracing the upward curve of the old woman's arm. I watched her eyes climb with the birds, all her losses made a blessing in a hand's worth of bread. Pigeons and meningitis. Chocolate and mouse droppings. Licorice and roach hairs. Vermin on the bus we took uptown. I wondered how long I'd choose to dwell in these middle ages of plague and usury, living among traceless men and women, those whose only peace was in shouting ever more loudly. Nothing tempted them more than voicelessness. But they shouted. Transient population of thunderers and hags. They dragged through wet streets speaking in languages older than the stones of cities buried in sand. Beds and bedbugs. Men and lice. Gonococcus curling in the lap of love. We rode past an urban redevelopment project. Machine-tooth shovels clawed past half-finished buildings stuck in mud, tiny balconies stapled on. All spawned by realtor-kings who live in the sewers. Skippy coughed blood onto the back of her hand. The bus panted over cobblestones and I studied words drawn in fading paint on the sides of buildings. Brake and front end service. Wheel alignment. Chain and belt. Pulleys, motors, gears. Sheet-metal machinery. Leather remnants. Die cutting and precision measuring. Cuttings and job lots. Business machines. Threads, woolens, laces. Libros en español. We left by the back door and Skippy went back to whatever she was doing (or dealing) in that hotel. Rain blew across the old streets. The toothless man was still at his cart, a visitation from sunken regions, not caring who listened or passed, his cries no less cadenced than the natural rain. YOU'RE BUYING I'M SELLING YAPPLES YAPPLES YAPPLES.**❞**

DON DELILLO, *GREAT JONES STREET*,
RANDOM HOUSE INC., NEW YORK, 1989

"TALL BUILDINGS"

AMERICAN BEAUTY

In "The American Scene", Henry James (1843–1916) wrote of his impressions of a visit in 1906 after an absence of almost twenty years.

❝Memory and the actual impression keep investing New York with the tone, predominantly, of summer dawns and winter frosts, of sea-foam, of bleached sails and stretched awnings, of blanched hulls, of scoured decks, of new ropes, of polished brasses, of streamers clear in the blue air; and it is by this harmony, doubtless, that the projection of the individual character of the place, of the candour of its avidity and the freshness of its audacity, is most conveyed. The "tall buildings," which have so promptly usurped a glory that affects you as rather surprised, as yet, at itself, the multitudinous sky-scrapers standing up to the view, from the water, like extravagant pins in a cushion already overplanted, and stuck in as in the dark, anywhere and anyhow, have at least the felicity of carrying out the fairness of tone, of taking the sun and the shade in the manner of towers of marble. They are not all of marble, I believe, by any means, even if some may be, but they are impudently new and still more impudently "novel" – this in common with so many other terrible things in America – and they are triumphant payers of dividends; all of which uncontested and unabashed pride, with flash of innumerable windows and flicker of subordinate gilt attributions, is like the flare, up and down their long, narrow faces, of the lamps of some general permanent "celebration".

You see the pin-cushion in profile, so to speak, on passing between Jersey City and Twenty-third Street, but you get it broadside on, this loose nosegay of architectural flowers, if you skirt the Battery, well out, and embrace the whole plantation. Then the "American beauty," the rose of interminable stem, becomes the token of the cluster at large – – to the degree that, positively, this is all that is wanted for emphasis of your final impression. Such growths, you feel, have confessedly arisen but to be "picked," in time, with a shears; nipped short off, by waiting fate, as soon as "science," applied to gain, has put upon the table, from far up its sleeve, some more winning card. Crowned not only with no history, but with no credible possibility of time for history, and consecrated by no uses save the commercial at any cost, they are simply the most piercing notes in that concert of the expensively provisional into which your supreme sense of New York resolves itself. They never begin to speak to you, in the manner of the builded majesties of the world as we have heretofore known such – towers or temples or fortresses or palaces – with the authority of things of permanence or even of things of long duration. One story is good only till another is told, and sky-scrapers are the last word of economic ingenuity only till another word be written. **99**

HENRY JAMES, *THE AMERICAN SCENE*,
INDIANA UNIVERSITY PRESS, BLOOMINGTON
AND LONDON, 1968

RAPID RUINS

G.K. Chesterton (1874–1936), the English journalist, novelist and short-story writer, was impressed by the industry of the city's builders.

66There is one point, almost to be called a paradox, to be noted about New York; and that is that in one sense it is really new. The term very seldom has any relevance to the reality. . . . But there is a sense in which New York is always new; in the sense that it is always being renewed. A stranger might well say that the chief industry of the citizens consists of destroying their city; but he soon realises that they always start it all over again

> "A haven as cosy as toast, cool as an icebox
> and safe as skyscrapers."
>
> Dylan Thomas

with undiminished energy and hope. At first I had a fancy that they never quite finished putting up a big building without feeling that it was time to pull it down again; and that somebody began to dig up the first foundations while somebody else was putting on the last tiles. This fills the whole of this brilliant and bewildering place with a quite unique and unparalleled air of rapid ruin. Ruins spring up so suddenly like mushrooms, which with us are the growth of age like mosses, that one half expects to see ivy climbing quickly up the broken walls as in the nightmare of the Time Machine, or in some incredibly accelerated cinema. There is no sight in any country that raises my own spirits so much as a scaffolding. It is a tragedy that they always take the scaffolding away, and leave us nothing but a mere building. If they would only take the building away and leave us a beautiful scaffolding, it would in most cases be a gain to the loveliness of earth. If I could analyse what it is that lifts the heart about the lightness and clarity of such a white and wooden skeleton, I could explain what it is that is really charming about New York; in spite of its suffering from the curse of cosmopolitanism and even the provincial superstition of progress. It is partly that all this destruction and reconstruction is an unexhausted artistic energy; but it is partly also that it is an artistic energy that does not take itself too seriously. It is first because he is a stage carpenter. Indeed there is about the whole scene the spirit of scene-shifting. It therefore touches whatever nerve in us has since childhood thrilled at all theatrical things. **"**

G. K. CHESTERTON, *WHAT I SAW IN AMERICA,*
HODDER AND STOUGHTON, LONDON, 1922

A DELIGHTFUL WALK
George Templeton Strong (1820–75) wrote in his diary for June 11, 1859, about the development of Central Park in the midst of the city.

"Improved the day by leaving Wall Street early and set off with George Anthon and Johnny to explore the Central Park, which will be a feature of the city within five years and a lovely place in A.D. 1900, when its trees will have acquired dignity and appreciable diameters. Perhaps the city itself will perish before then, by growing too big to live under faulty institutions corruptly administered. Reached the park a little before four, just as the red flag was hoisted – the signal for the blasts of the day. They were all around us for some twenty minutes, now booming far off to the north, now quite near, now distant again, like a desultory "affair" between advanced posts of two great armies. We entered the park at Seventy-first Street, on its east side, and made for "The Ramble," a patch just below the upper reservoir. Its footpaths and plantations are finished, more or less, and it is the first section of the ground that has been polished off and made presentable. It promises very well. So does all the lower park, though now in most ragged condition: long lines of incomplete macadamization, "lakes" without water, mounds of compost, piles of blasted

119

stone, acres of what may be greensward hereafter but is now mere brown earth; groves of slender young transplanted maples and locusts, undecided between life and death, with here and there an arboricultural experiment that has failed utterly and is a mere broomstick with ramifications. Celts, caravans of dirt carts, derricks, steam engines, are the elements out of which our future Pleasaunce is rapidly developing. The work seems pushed with vigor and system, and as far as it has gone, looks thorough and substantial. A small army of Hibernians is distributed over the ground. Narrowness is its chief drawback. One sees quite across this *Rus in Urbe* at many points. This will be less felt as the trees grow. The tract seems to have been judiciously laid out. Roads and paths twist about in curves of artistic tortuosity. A broad avenue, exceptionally straight (at the lower end of the park) with a quadruple row of elms, will look Versailles-y by A.D. 1950. On the Fifth Avenue side, the hideous State Arsenal building stares at students of the picturesque, an eyesore that no landscape gardening can alleviate. Let us hope it will soon be destroyed by an accidental fire. From the summit of the rock mount in which "The Ramble" culminates, and from the little wooden framework of an observatory or signal flag tower thereon erected, the upper reservoir (lying on the north) is an agreeable object, notwithstanding the formalism of its straight lines. Johnny was delighted with his walk . . .**

THE DIARY OF GEORGE TEMPLETON STRONG,
THE MACMILLAN PUBLISHING COMPANY, NEW YORK, 1952

BROADWAY

The Russian futurist poet Vladimir Mayakovsky (1893–1930) was often out of favor with government regimes in his homeland but after his suicide, he was acclaimed by Stalin as "the best and most talented poet of our Soviet epoch".

**Tarmac like glass.
                    A clang with each step.
Trees,
        and blades of grass,
                        with crew-cuts.
Avenues
        run
                from North to South,
and streets
            from East to West.
Between –
        who could have stretched them that far! –
buildings
        a good mile high.
Some houses seem to touch
                        the stars,
while others
            reach for the sky.
Most Yanks are too idle
                    to go out walking.
They ride express
            elevators
                        throughout.

> "If Paris is the setting for a romance, New York is the perfect city in which to get over one, to get over anything. Here the lost *douceur de vivre* is forgotten and the intoxication of living takes over."

> Cyril Connolly

At seven hundred hours
                    the human tide rolls in.
And at seventeen hundred
                           rolls out.
Machines
         rattle
                clatter
                        chink
pedestrians
            go deaf and dumb,
while past them more
                     dumb people sprint
only stopping
              to spit out their chewing gum.
Yelling at a friend:
                    'Make money!'
A mother suckles her child:
                            'Don't holler!'
And the kid,
            with its nostrils runny
looks less like it sucks a breast than
                                        a dollar
and like everyone else,
                        in a hurry.
The workday done,
                  now all around
you're battered by
                   electric hurricanes.
You take the subway,
                     vanish underground,
or climb
         on the elevated
                         train.
You can ride as high
                     as a chimney stack
or dart
        between the feet of a house.
On Brooklyn Bridge, a tram
                           snakes its back
or under the Hudson,
                     sneaks like a mouse."

VLADIMIR MAYAKOVSKY, *BROADWAY*

THE VILLAGE

The development of Greenwich Village is described by Edmund Wilson (1895–1972) in his novel "I Thought of Daisy".

"Among those tangled irregular streets to the west of Washington Square, I caught occasionally, from the taxi, a glimpse, almost eighteenth-century, of a lampless, black-windowed street-end where the street-urchins, shrieking in the silence, were stacking up bonfires in the snow – those lost corners of the old provincial city, where the traffic of the upper metropolis no longer gnashed iron teeth, no longer oppressed the pavements with its grindings and its groans – where those soft moans and hoots of the shipping washed the island from the western shore. There they had come, those heroes of my youth, the artists and the prophets

of the Village, from the American factories and farms, from the farthest towns and prairies – there they had found it possible to leave behind them the constraints and self-consciousness of their homes, the shame of not making money – there they had lived with their own imaginations and followed their own thought. I did not know that, with the coming of a second race, of which Ray Coleman, without my divining it, had already appeared as one of the forerunners – a mere miscellaneous hiving of New Yorkers like those in any other part of town, with no leisure and no beliefs – I did not know that I was soon to see the whole quarter fall a victim to the landlords and the real-estate speculators, who would raise the rents and wreck the old houses – till the sooty peeling fronts of the south side of Washington Square, to whose mysterious studios, when I had first come to live in the Village, I had so much longed some day to be admitted, should be replaced by fresh arty pinks – till the very guardian façades of the north side should be gutted of their ancient grandeurs and crammed tight with economized cells – till the very configuration of the streets should be wiped out, during a few summer months when I had been out of New York on vacation, by the obliteration of whole blocks, whole familiar neighborhoods – and till finally the beauty of the Square, the pattern of the park and the arch, the proportions of everything, should be spoiled by the first peaks of a mountain-range of modern apartment-houses (with electric refrigerators, uniformed elevator boys and, on the street-level, those smartly furnished restaurants in which Hugo was soon to be horrified at finding copies of *Town and Country*), dominating and crushing the Village, so that at last it seemed to survive as a base for those gigantic featureless mounds, swollen, clumsy, blunt, bleaching dismally with sandy yellow walls that sunlight which once, in the autumn, on the old fronts of the northern side, still the masters of their open plaza – when the shadows of the leafless trees seemed to drift across them like clouds – had warmed their roses to red.**99**

EDMUND WILSON, *I THOUGHT OF DAISY*,
W. H. ALLEN, LONDON, 1920

FERRYBOAT RIDE

The novel "Manhattan Transfer" by John dos Passos (1896–1970) is a collection of hundreds of fictional and atmospheric episodes that take place in New York. The following extract describes a trip on the Ellis Island Ferry.

66It was blowing cold in his face and he was sitting on the front of a ferryboat when he came to. His teeth were chattering, he was shivering . . . .

Across the zinc water the tall walls, the birchlike cluster of downtown buildings shimmered up the rosy morning like a sound of horns through a chocolatebrown haze. As the boat drew near the buildings densened to a granite mountain split with knifecut canyons. The ferry passed close to a tubby steamer that rode at anchor listing towards Stan so that he could see all the decks. An Ellis Island tug was alongside. A stale smell came from the decks packed with upturned faces like a load of melons. Three gulls wheeled complaining. A gull soared in a spiral, white wings caught the sun, the gull skimmed motionless in whitegold light. The rim of the sun had risen above the plumcolored band of clouds behind East New York. A million windows flashed with light. A rasp and a humming came from the city. . . .

In the whitening light tinfoil gulls wheeled above broken boxes, spoiled cabbageheads, orangerinds heaving slowly between the splintered plank walls, the green spumed under the round bow as the ferry skidding on the tide, gulped the broken water, crashed, slid, settled slowly into the slip. Handwinches whirled with jingle of chains, gates folded upward. Stan stepped across the crack, staggered up the manuresmelling wooden tunnel of the ferryhouse out into the sunny glass and benches of the Battery. He sat down on a bench, clasped his hands round his knees to keep them from shaking so. His mind went on jingling like a mechanical piano.

There was Babylon and Nineveh, they were built of brick. Athens was goldmarble columns. Rome was held up on broad arches of rubble. In Constantinople the minarets flame like great candles round the Golden Horn. . . . O there's one more river to cross. Steel, glass, tile, concrete will be the materials of the skyscrapers. Crammed on the narrow island the millionwindowed buildings will jut, glittering pyramid on pyramid, white cloudsheads piled above a thunder storm . . . Kerist I wish I was a skyscraper.**99**

JOHN DOS PASSOS, *MANHATTAN TRANSFER*,
HARPER AND BROTHERS, NEW YORK AND LONDON, 1925

RAMSHACKLE STREETS

Joseph Heller, the novelist, was born in New York in 1923. His novel "Good As Gold" satirizes the politics of the city and this particular extract describes a drive along the southern rim of Brooklyn.

66Following the smooth parkway as it curved with the shoreline to the east, he soon saw in the distance on his right the gaunt structure of the defunct Parachute Jump standing on the narrow spit of land across Gravesend Bay and recalled, with some pride in his upbringing, how that Parachute Jump, the hit of the World's Fair in New York in 1939 or '40, was moved to the Steeplechase boardwalk afterward but had never proved adequately perilous for success to an indigenous population trained on the Cyclone and the Thunderbolt and on the Mile Sky Chaser in Luna Park. Now it looked forlorn: no one owned it and no one would take it away. Like those haunted, half-completed luxury apartment houses in Manhattan whose builders had run out of money and whose banks would not supply more, gaping with dismal failure and aging already into blackest decrepitude before they ever shone spanking new. A moment later came the skeletal outline of the giant Wonder Wheel, idled for the year by the chilly season, the only Ferris wheel left in Coney Island now that Steeplechase, the Funny Place, was bankrupt and gone. Hard times had descended there as in other places. Where Luna Park had last whirred in bright lights on summer evenings over thirty years earlier there now rose a complex of

high, honeycombed brick dwellings that looked drabber than ordinary against the lackluster sky. On the overpass spanning Ocean Parkway Gold turned his head for a speeding glimpse of Abraham Lincoln High School and bemoaned for the thousandth time the vile chance that had located him in classes there the same time as Belle and gulled him into a mismanaged destiny of three dependent children and a wife so steadfast. If a man marries young, he reasoned aristocratically in the self-conscious mode of a Lord Chesterfield or a Benjamin Franklin, as Gold himself had been minded to do, it will likely be to someone near him in age; and just about the time he learns really to enjoy living with a young girl and soars into his prime, she will be getting old. He would pass that precious homiletic intelligence on to both sons, if he remembered. If only Belle were fickle, mercenary, deceitful. Even her health was good.

He turned off the parkway past Brighton at the exit leading toward Sheepshead Bay and Manhattan Beach. The slender crescent on the southern rim of Brooklyn through which he'd driven was just about the only section of the area with which he was familiar. Almost all of the rest was foreign to him and forbidding. His thoughts went back to a ramshackle street he'd passed minutes before on which stood the same moldering antique police station to which he'd been brought as a small child the day Sid had abandoned him and gone off with his friends. What a heartless thing to have done. Gold must have been numb as he waited in the precinct house. If they asked him his address he might not have known it. The nearest telephone to his house then was in a candy store at the trolley stop on the corner of Railroad Avenue. Just a few years later he was earning two-cent tips for summoning girls from the flats for calls from boys phoning for dates. Brooklyn was a big fucking borough.**99**

JOSEPH HELLER, *GOOD AS GOLD*, JONATHAN CAPE, LONDON, 1979

BAYMEN

Joseph Mitchell (b. 1908) reminds us that New York is situated on the ocean and many make their living from fishing.

66The fish and shell fish in the harbor and in the ocean just outside provide all or part of a living for about fifteen hundred men who call themselves baymen. They work out of bays and inlets and inlets within inlets along the coasts of Staten Island, Brooklyn, and Queens. Some baymen clam on the public beds. Some baymen set eelpots. Some baymen set pound nets, or fish traps. Pound nets are strung from labyrinths of stakes in shoal areas out of the way of the harbor traffic. Last year, during the shad, summer herring, and mossbunker migrations, forty-one of them were set off the Staten Island coast, between Midland Beach and Great Kills, in an old oyster-bedding area. Some baymen go out in draggers, or small trawlers, of which there are two fleets in the harbor. . . . The majority of the men are Italian-Americans, a few of whom in their youth fished out of the Sicilian ports of Palermo and Castellammare del Golfo. Some of them tack saints' pictures and miraculous medals and scapular medals and little evil-eye amulets on the walls of their pilothouses. The amulets are in the shape of hunchbacks, goat horns, fists with two fingers upraised, and opened scissors; they come from stores on Mulberry Street and are made of plastic. The harbor draggers range from thirty to fifty feet and carry two to five men. According to the weather and the season, they drag their baglike nets in the Lower Bay or in a fishing ground called the Mud Hole, which lies south of Scotland and Ambrose lightships and is about fifteen miles long and five to ten miles wide. The Mud Hole is the upper part of the Old Hudson River Canyon, which was the bed of the river twenty thousand years ago, when the river flowed a hundred and twenty-five miles past what is now Sandy Hook before it reached the ocean. The draggers catch lower-depth and bottom feeders, chiefly whiting, butterfish, ling, cod, porgy, fluke, and flounder. They go out around 4 A.M. and return around 4 P. M., and their catches are picked up by trucks and taken to Fulton Market.**

JOSEPH MITCHELL, *UP IN THE OLD HOTEL,* PANTHEON BOOKS, NEW YORK, 1992

LIFE IN THE CITY

WALKING ON MIRRORS

Wallace Stevens (1879–1955), the American poet, made the following entries in his journal in the year 1900, during a visit to New York.

**Took dinner in a little restaurant – poached eggs, coffee and three crusts of bread – a week ago my belly was swagging with strawberries. Bought a couple of newspapers from a little fellow with blue eyes who was selling *Journals* and *Worlds* & who had to ransack the neighborhood for the ones I wanted. As I came back to my room the steps of the street for squares were covered with boarders etc. leaning on railings and picking their teeth. The end of the street was ablaze with a cloud of dust lit by the sun. All around me were tall office buildings closed up for the night. The curtains were drawn and the faces of the buildings looked hard and cruel and lifeless. This street of mine is a wonderful thing. Just now the voices of children manage to come through my window from out it, over the roofs and through the walls.

All New York, as I have seen it, is for sale – and I think the parts I have seen are the parts that make New York what it is. It is dominated by necessity. Everything has its price – from Vice to Virtue. I do not like it and unless I get some position that is unusually attractive I shall not stay. What is there to keep me, for example, in a place where all Beauty is on exhibition, all Power a tool of Selfishness, and all Generosity a source of Vanity? New York is a field of tireless and antagonistic interests – undoubtedly fascinating but horribly unreal. Everybody is looking at everybody else – a foolish crowd walking on mirrors. I am rather glad to be here for the short time that I intend to stay – it makes me appreciate the opposite of it all. Thank Heaven the winds are not generated in Yorkville, or the clouds manufactured in Harlem. What a price they would bring!

The carpet on the floor of my room is gray set off with pink roses. In the bathroom is a rug with the figure of a peacock woven in it – blue and scarlet, and black, and green, and gold. And on the paper on my wall are designs of fleur-de-lis and forget-me-not. Flowers and birds enough of rags and paper – but no more. In this Eden, made spicey with the smoke of my pipe which hangs heavy in the ceiling in this Paradise ringing with the bells of streetcars and the bustle of fellow boarders heard through the thin partitions, in this Elysium of Elysiums I now shall lay me down.**

**June 17, Sunday.

Last night I sat in an open square near the Washington Arch. A man passed me with his coat tightly buttoned, his hands in his trousers pockets, his head bent and his hat well pulled-down. His clothes were in rags. As he started to cross Fifth Avenue a 'bus drove by and he stopped to let it pass. On the top of the 'bus was a group of girls in neat Spring jackets and bonnets covered with cherries and roses.

This morning the church bells are ringing.

New York is the most egotistical place in the world. **"**

FROM HOLLY STEVENS, *SOUVENIRS AND PROPHECIES*, ALFRED A. KNOPF INC., NEW YORK, 1977

THE JANITOR
The Russian politician Lev Trotsky (1879–1940) was expelled from his homeland in 1924. He and his family wandered from country to country for a while before settling in Mexico. The following extract from his autobiography describes a spell in New York.

"We rented an apartment in a workers' district, and furnished it on the instalment plan. That apartment, at eighteen dollars a month, was equipped with all sorts of conveniences that we Europeans were quite unused to: electric lights, gas cooking-range, bath, telephone, automatic service-elevator, and even a chute for the garbage. These things completely won the boys over to New York. For a time the telephone was their main interest; we had not had this mysterious instrument either in Vienna or Paris.

The janitor of the house was a negro. My wife paid him three months' rent in advance, but he gave her no receipt because the landlord had taken the receipt-book away the day before, to verify the accounts. When we moved into the house two days later, we discovered that the negro had absconded with the rent of several of the tenants. Besides the money, we had intrusted to him the storage of some of our belongings. The whole incident upset us; it was such a bad beginning. But we found our property after all, and when we opened the wooden box that contained our crockery, we were surprised to find our money hidden away in it, carefully wrapped up in paper. The janitor had taken the money of the tenants who had already received their receipts; he did not mind robbing the landlord, but he was considerate enough not to rob the tenants. A delicate fellow indeed. My wife and I were deeply touched by his consideration and we always think of him gratefully. This little incident took on a

symptomatic significance for me – it seemed as if a corner of the veil that concealed the "black" problem in the United States had lifted. **"**

LEV TROTSKY, *MY LIFE*, CHARLES SCRIBNER'S SONS, NEW YORK, 1930

BEAUTIFUL GIRLS
Ogden Nash (1902–71) was famous for his light verse, of which the following is a good example.

"In New York beautiful girls can become more beautiful
by going to Elizabeth Arden,

> **"A hundred times I have thought, New York is a catastrophe,**
> **and fifty times: it is a beautiful catastrophe."**
>
> Le Corbusier

And getting stuff to put on their faces and waiting for
                          it to harden,
And poor girls with nothing to their names but a letter
                    or two can get rich and joyous
From a brief trip to their loyous.
So I can say with impunity
That New York is a land of opportunity.
It also has many fine theatres and hotels,
And a lot of taxis, buses, subways and els,
Best of all, if you don't show up at the office or at a
                          tea nobody will bother their head,
They will just think you are dead.
That's why I really think New York is exquisite.
And someday I'm going to pay it a visit. **"**

OGDEN NASH, *A BRIEF GUIDE TO NEW YORK*,
FROM *"VERSES FROM 1929 ON"*, 1940

THE HARLEM RENAISSANCE

Langston Hughes (1902–67) was one of the most impor-
tant figures of the Harlem Renaissance. Discovered by
the poet Vachel Lindsay, he wrote poetry, plays,
and novels whose language resonated with
dialect and jazz rhythms. In "The Big Sea"
(1940), his autobiography, Hughes
recounts a fascinating life in Paris
and Harlem when "the
Negro was in vogue".

"White people began to come to
Harlem in droves. For several years they
packed the expensive Cotton Club on Lenox
Avenue. But I was never there, because the Cotton Club
was a Jim Crow club for gangsters and monied whites. They were
not cordial to Negro patronage, unless you were a celebrity like
Bojangles. So Harlem Negroes did not like the Cotton Club and never
appreciated its Jim Crow policy in the very heart of their dark community. Nor did
ordinary Negroes like the growing influx of whites toward Harlem after sundown,
flooding the little cabarets and bars where formerly only colored people laughed
and sang, and where now the strangers were given the best ringside tables to sit and
stare at the Negro customers – like amusing animals in a zoo.
The Negroes said: 'We can't go downtown and sit and stare at you in your clubs.
You won't even let us in your clubs.' But they didn't say it out loud – for Negroes
are practically never rude to white people. So thousands of whites came to Harlem
night after night, thinking the Negroes loved to have them there, and firmly
believing that all Harlemites left their houses at sundown to sing and dance in
cabarets, because most of the whites saw nothing but the cabarets, not the houses.
Some of the owners of Harlem clubs, delighted at the flood of white patronage,
made the grievous error of barring their own race, after the manner of the famous
Cotton Club. But most of these quickly lost business and folded up, because they
failed to realize that a large part of the Harlem attraction for downtown New
Yorkers lay in simply watching the colored customers amuse themselves. And the
smaller clubs, of course, had no big floor shows or a name band like the Cotton
Club, where Duke Ellington usually held forth, so, without black patronage, they
were not amusing at all. **"**

LANGSTON HUGHES, *THE BIG SEA*, 1940

A COLLAPSING CITY

The following piece by John Updike (1932–), the American novelist, short-story writer
and poet, comes from an essay entitled "Is New York City Inhabitable?"

❝New York is of course many cities, and an exile does not return to the one he left. I left, in April of 1957, a floor-through apartment on West Thirteenth Street, and return, when I do, to midtown hotels and the Upper East Side apartments of obliging friends. The Village, with its bookstores and framer's shops, its bricked-in literary memories and lingering bohemian redolence, is off the track of a professional visit – an elevator-propelled whirl in and out of high-rise offices and prix-fixe restaurants. Nevertheless, I feel confident in saying that the disadvantages of New York life which led me to leave have intensified rather than abated, and that the city which Le Corbusier described as a magnificent disaster is less and less magnificent. Always, as one arrives, there is the old acceleration of the pulse – the mountainous gray skyline glimpsed from the Triboro Bridge, the cheerful games of basketball and handball being played on the recreational asphalt beside the FDR Drive, the startling, steamy, rain-splotched intimacy of the side streets where one's taxi slows to a crawl, the careless flung beauty of the pedestrians clumped at the street corners. So many faces, costumes, packages, errands! So many preoccupations, hopes, passions, lives in progress! So much human stuff, clustering and streaming with a languid colorful impatience like the pheromone-coded mass maneuvers of bees! But soon the faces and their individual expressions merge and vanish under a dulling insistent pressure, the thrum and push of congestion. As ever more office buildings are heaped upon the East Fifties – the hugest of them, the slant-topped white Citicorp building, clearly about to fall off its stilts onto your head – and an ever-greater number of impromptu merchants spread their dubiously legal wares on the sidewalks, even pedestrian traffic jams. One is tripped, hassled, detoured. Buskers and beggars cram every available niche. The sidewalks and subway platforms, generously designed in the last century, have been overwhelmed on both the minor and major entrepreneurial scales. The Manhattan grid, that fine old machine for living, now sticks and grinds at every intersection and the discreet brownstones of the side streets look down upon a clogged nightmare of perpetual reconstruction and insolent double parking. Even a sunny day feels like a tornado of confusion one is hurrying to get out of, into the sanctum of the hotel room, the office, the friendly apartment. New York is a city with virtually no habitable public space – only private spaces expensively maintained within the general disaster. While popular journalism focuses on the possible collapse of Los Angeles and San Francisco into chasms opened by earthquakes, here on the East Coast, on its oblong of solid granite, the country's greatest city is sinking into the chasm of itself.❞

JOHN UPDIKE, *ODD JOBS*, ALFRED A. KNOPF INC.,
NEW YORK, 1991

Itineraries in New York

▲ Central Park

▲ The Sherry Netherlands Hotel

Hotel Pierre

The former American Standard Building ▼

▲ 3 Park Ave.

The Waldorf-Astoria Hotel ▼

Lower Manhattan

The Twin Towers
The site was originally occupied by twelve dilapidated blocks called "Radio Row", a paradise for radio and photography

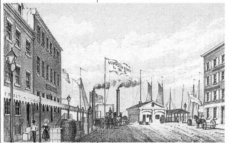

enthusiasts. The Twin Towers required foundations 69 feet deep; the 1.2 million cubic yards of earth excavated served as landfill for the future Battery Park City. It was also necessary to destroy a number of piers and warehouses along the Hudson (below, former cargo loading stations along the Hudson on the site of the World Trade Center). After they opened in 1973, the Twin Towers became one of the most compelling emblems of the city. Not only did the terrorist attacks of 9/11 claim thousands of lives, they also destroyed the most familiar landmark on the world's most famous skyline.

Lower Manhattan, the southern tip of the island, includes the site of the World Trade Center, Battery Park City and the Financial District, around Wall Street. Its early settlers – first the Dutch then the English – laid out narrow, winding streets here. Traces of this initial occupation are evident in the oldest of the streets; in their names, which date back to the 17th century, as well as their configuration – borrowed from that of Amsterdam. And, as was the case in the parent city, some of these streets, notably Broad Street, were originally canals ● *32*. Others, built later, reflect the well-known Dutch practice of reclaiming land from the sea by drainage; in fact, over the centuries, Manhattan has expanded well beyond its original boundaries. At the time of the Dutch settlements, the shape of the shoreline differed greatly from its present one. It ran alongside Water St to the east, along Greenwich St to the west and along State St to the south. The acres of land that were gradually gained – due to a buildup of abandoned ships, detritus, earth from excavation work for the construction of buildings and subway lines – are now some of the most expensive in the world. Among the few remaining traces of the English colonial period is the cemetery of Trinity Church, where some of the most famous names in American colonial history are buried. Just opposite, on the other side of Broadway, is Wall Street, the heart of the Financial District, which bankers and stockbrokers call simply "The Street". A harbor city, New York has grown through trade and shipping. Offshore in the distance stand the Statue of Liberty ▲ *144* and Ellis Island ▲ *148*, witnesses to the arrival of immigrants in their thousands. Over the years, architects have ceaselessly rebuilt the city in this area, superimposing many different chapters in its history. On September 11, 2001 one of these chapters came to an end as terrorist attacks destroyed the World Trade Center and other nearby buildings. Reeling physically and economically from these attacks, the area had to undertake a process of reconstruction, regeneration and recovery after an episode that traumatized the city and the country as a whole.

Around Ground Zero

In the thirty years since its construction, the World Trade Center, which was destroyed in the attacks of September 11, 2001, had become New York's key business and financial complex. Begun in 1962 and opened in 1973, it housed the offices of numerous public institutions and 500 companies. where more than 50,000 people worked. It also became a major tourist attraction. Each month, the World Trade Center received more than 200,000 visitors, who came to admire the breathtaking views of the city from its rooftop observation deck on the 110th floor or the

restaurant, Windows on the World, on the 107th floor.
Since its destruction, the site designed by Japanese
architect Minoru Yamasaki has been named "Ground
Zero". On December 18, 2002, seven teams of
prominent architects from around the world submitted
designs for the site. David Childs of Skidmore, Owings
& Merrill and Daniel Libeskind have been working
on the master plan for The Freedom Tower, the single
office building that will replace the twin towers, which at
1776 feet has been reconfigured to make it more secure.
Santiago Calatrava has designed the subway station, but
negotiations between the city, the state, and the
transportation authorities have been fraught and have
caused delays in redeveloping Ground Zero. The site
will contain a memorial, and as this may be in the original
footprint of the twin towers, extending deep into the ground,
some of the infrastructure of the buildings and transportation
would have to be moved. The Drawing Center, the popular
exhibition space for drawings which also had celebrated and
well-attended author readings, had planned to move from
Soho to be part of the Ground Zero complex but it became
a source of huge controversy and therefore will move
elsewhere. In general, the area has revived very quickly: the
celebrated designer discount shop, Century 21, is back; the
Winter Garden – the ten-story atrium which houses 16 palm
trees and a variety of restaurants and stores – reopened in
September 2002 after a $50 million restoration by its original
architect Cesar Pelli and his son, Raphael; an adjoining public

The Twin Towers
(above) overlooked
the World Trade
Center and the
Financial District.
The shopping
concourse in the
basement of the
complex had already
been targeted by a
bomb attack in 1993,
which claimed six
lives and left scores
of people wounded.

Because 90 West St was designed to be seen from a distance, its crown is dramatically illuminated at night.

Interior of the New York Telephone Building.

THE SPHERE
Pending the reconstruction of the World Trade Center site and the erection of a monument to the memory of the victims of 9/11 ● *46*, a sculpture by Fritz Koenig, The Sphere, which was located in the financial complex and found badly damaged after the attacks, has become a temporary memorial in Battery Park. People come here to sit quietly, reflect and remember.

West St., looking toward Liberty St., in 1900.

park has been redone; and nearby, new apartment buildings have been completed.

BARCLAY–VESEY/NEW YORK TELEPHONE CO. BUILDING ★. 140 WEST ST., BETWEEN BARCLAY AND VESEY STS. (1923–6, arch. Ralph Walker, McKenzie, Voorhees & Gmelin, 33 stories) ● *98*. When this Art Deco building, located north of the World Trade Center site, was completed, it was considered so striking an expression of the new industrial age that its designers were awarded the Architectural League of New York's gold medal of honor for 1927. The lobby, which runs the length of the building and which can be entered via Washington Street, is well worth a visit. The lobby floor is covered with bronze plates, which depict the workers laying the New York telephone system and the ceiling frescoes retrace the history of communication. To see the whole building at its best, you need only walk back to West Street then head toward the Hudson.

90 WEST STREET ★ (1905, arch. Cass Gilbert, 23 stories, 324 feet). This building was one of the first New York skyscrapers constructed using a fire-resistant frame. The lavish decoration of the neo-Gothic façade becomes increasingly more intricate as the building rises, culminating in an extravaganza of stalactites dripping from a cornice supported by consoles.

BATTERY PARK CITY

A DISTRICT RECLAIMED FROM WATER. Battery Park City covers an area of 112 acres to the west of WEST STREET, between BATTERY PARK to the south and CHAMBERS STREET to the north. This brand new complex comprising offices, apartment buildings, hotels, schools, museums and parks was built on top of landfill ■ *18*, supplied partly by excavation work when the foundations of the World Trade Center were laid. Although this development program was begun in 1979, it

dates back to a project conceived in the 1960s by the then governor of New York, Nelson A. Rockefeller, who wanted to rejuvenate this deserted part of Lower Manhattan as well as the banks of the Hudson. Its major attraction is the ESPLANADE ★, a riverside pedestrian walkway that affords a magnificent view of the bay and runs the entire length of the district. There are two parks, Robert F. Wagner Jr. in the south and Nelson A. Rockefeller Park in the north, as well as a picturesque small marina, SOUTH COVE, with a PLATFORM that is an abstract replica of the crown of the Statue of Liberty directly opposite. The Ground Zero redevelopment project should make it possible to reconnect Battery Park City, a new district inhabited mainly by young couples and isolated by the fast-moving West Side Highway, to New York's historic center, which is more family-orientated.

WORLD FINANCIAL CENTER. (1981–8, arch. Cesar Pelli). Both heart and centerpiece of Battery Park City is the World Financial Center. It consists of four TOWERS of polished granite and glass, topped with geometric shapes identifying the owners. These are, from the north-west tower: Merrill Lynch (step pyramid, dome); American Express (pyramid); Dow Jones-Oppenheimer (mastaba). The building uses a profusion of materials, with floors of multicolored marble, shining black columns and glossy, luxurious lobbies. WINTER GARDEN, the pavilion at the entrance to the World Financial Center, is a vast greenhouse planted with giant palms and is the central point of the complex. Badly damaged when the north tower of the World Trade Center collapsed ● 46, the Winter Garden has now been entirely reconstructed. The former walkway linking it to the World Trade Center, which was also destroyed, has not been rebuilt though there is a temporary covered walkway. A fifth building, the work of the famous architects Skidmore, Owings & Merrill, erected in 1997, completes the ensemble on the shores of the Hudson. This last building houses the New York Mercantile Exchange and Commodities Exchange (NYMEX-COMEX), two commodities markets founded in 1872 and 1933 respecively. It has a small museum,

THE HOBOKEN FERRY (NEW JERSEY)
You can board the ferry – nicknamed the "Penguin Boat" due to the number of people it regulary carries between the financial district and Hoboken – at the northenmost point of North Cove. The crossing gives one an opportunity to enjoy a fabulous view of Manhattan. Hoboken is the birth place of Frank Sinatra. In 1954, film maker Elia Kazan directed *On the Waterfront* here with Marlon Brando (below). New York Harbor provided a realistic backdrop for a story of union corruption and for the private drama of a weak man who, in his search for happiness, is plagued by his conscience.

On The Waterfront

View of New York Harbor in 1878.

and it is possible to observe the trading halls from the two Visitors Galleries. The towers of the World Financial Center surround NORTH COVE MARINA, forming what one critic has enthusiastically described as a "Saint Mark's Square on the Hudson". The guardrail along the marina's esplanade is engraved with quotations from WALT WHITMAN and THOMAS O'HARA, former inhabitants of Lower Manhattan, celebrating the history and beauty of this site.

DOWNTOWN ATHLETIC CLUB. 19 WEST ST. (1930, arch. Starrett & Van Vleck, 38 stories). With a height of 535 feet, this building was one of the tallest in Manhattan for its time. Every year the club awards the HEISMAN TROPHY for the best college football player in the nation. To visit the TROPHY HALL, lined with the portraits of prizewinners since 1935, take the elevator; press the button marked "H". This building, like many in the Financial District, is slated to be converted in luxury apartments

MUSEUM OF JEWISH HERITAGE, A LIVING MEMORIAL TO THE HOLOCAUST. 18 FIRST PLACE (1997). This museum, which opened in September 1997, traces the history of the Jews in the 20th century, from before World War II through the Holocaust and up to the present day. Along with the photographs and archival material are documentaries made by the Shoah foundation set up by Steven Spielberg.

BATTERY PARK

The southern tip of Manhattan, once of strategic importance, was until the early 1800's the site of batteries of artillery. Today the public gardens of Battery Park are arranged around Castle Clinton, the old fort where tickets for Ellis Island and the Statue of Liberty ▲ *144* are sold.

A "NEW" FORT. In 1635, on the site of what is now the US Custom House, the Dutch built FORT AMSTERDAM later re-named FORT GEORGE by the British. In addition, the British built another fort on a man-made island 295 feet offshore. Between 1807 and 1811, in anticipation of war with Britain, a new fort, designed by JOHN McCOMB was erected on the island. This fortification, called West Battery, formed a pair with East Battery on Governor's Island at the entrance to the East River. In 1815 West Battery was demilitarized and renamed CASTLE CLINTON, in honor of the mayor of New York, De Witt Clinton, who later instigated the construction of the

Erie Canal ● 27. Foreign dignitaries were officially welcomed at Castle Clinton; among them was Lafayette in 1824. Earlier that year the fortress had been renamed CASTLE GARDEN and later became a concert hall seating 6,000 people, where New Yorkers could attend the opera for 50 cents. In 1855, Castle Garden was transformed into the MAIN IMMIGRANT LANDING DEPOT, where immigrants could obtain information, medical care, currency and job offers. By the time the center was transferred to Ellis Island ▲148, in 1892, eight million people had already passed through its doors. The land between Castle Clinton's island and Manhattan was gradually filled in, and in 1896 the fort was turned into the AQUARIUM, which attracted millions of visitors. The aquarium was closed in 1941 to permit the construction of the BROOKLYN-BATTERY TUNNEL, and then moved to Coney Island. The fort was saved from demolition by ELEANOR ROOSEVELT, restored and listed as a National Historic Monument in 1946

PIER A ★. S.W. CORNER OF WEST ST. AND BATTERY PLACE (1886, eng. George Sears Green, Jr.). This is the oldest pier in Manhattan. A clock tower was added in 1919, in homage to the victims of World War One. Its bells used to signal the watches that were kept on board ship. Until 1959 the pier was used as a headquarters for the harbor police and the maritime fire department.

A PLUCKED NIGHTINGALE
On September 11, 1850, Jenny Lind, the "Swedish Nightingale", made her American debut at Castle Garden, promoted by P. T. Barnum. The latter caused a controversy in the New York press by praising the diva in public while panning her singing performance in print using various pseudonyms. This ruse pushed the ticket price up to $25 for her first night. Several years later, the soprano was just a memory.

A FORT-AQUARIUM
The aquarium had numerous species on display to the public. It also served as a breeding farm for fish which were later released into the state's rivers.

Tip of Lower Manhattan (below) with Battery Park.

In 1886, the people of France presented the United States with a huge statue, "Liberty Enlightening the World". The idea was conceived by Edouard-René Laboulaye, champion of liberalism, as a symbol of Franco-American friendship. In discussion with the statue's sculptor, Bartholdi, Laboulaye declared: "This will not be the revolutionary Liberty wearing a red bonnet and carrying a pike but the American Liberty, who brandishes not an incendiary torch, but one that lights the way." Erected in New York Harbor, the statue, a World Heritage Site since 1994, has become a symbol of both freedom and the United States.

A TRIP THROUGH THE BODY OF A GIANT
The Statue of Liberty's colossal heel is the first sight to greet the visitor's eye. Once inside the base, you can visit a museum (renovated in 1986), that relates the statue's history. An elevator will take you to the top of the pedestal, then a metal spiral staircase leads to the crown with a view out over the harbor. Entrance to the torch is now prohibited for reasons of safety. The cartoon (right) from *The World*, May 16, 1885, shows Uncle Sam congratulating Miss Liberty.

BARTHOLDI: A SCULPTOR'S APPRENTICESHIP
Frédéric Auguste Bartholdi was born on April 2, 1834, in Colmar, Alsace, France. Family connections introduced the sculptor to a network of influential republican contacts.

Legend has it that the sculptor used his mother as a model for the statue's face (her portrait, center, by Ary Scheffer), while his wife-to-be posed for the body.

JULY IV MDCCLXXVI

THE SYMBOL OF AMERICA ✪

Allow about 3 hours, including time spent waiting for the ferry to leave. The short crossing between Circle Line Pier and Liberty Island only take a few minutes and affords lovely views of Manhattan rising above the water. The tedious climb to the top of the crown is best avoided in favor of the small museum at the base of the monument which documents the history of the statue's construction. If you have a few more hours to spare, visit the American Museum of Immigration on Ellis Island ▲ *148*, which is reached by taking the same ferry from the statue.

EIFFEL TO THE RESCUE OF LIBERTY
At a height of 145 feet, the statue was vulnerable to high winds. The engineer Gustave Eiffel was hired to solve this

problem. The ¹⁄₁₀-inch-thick copper gown is riveted onto a flexible steel frame, which allows the statue a measure of give.

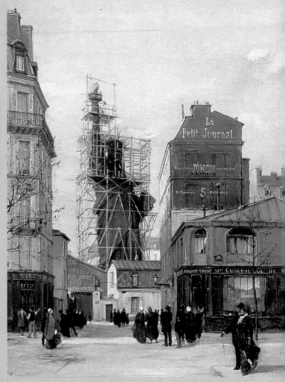

"LIBERTY" EXHIBITED IN PARIS
At the Paris Universal Exposition of 1878, visitors could climb inside a life-size model of the statue's head. For a time it towered above the roofs of Paris; for 50 centimes, one could climb as far as the crown and the torch. Although the Parisians, led by Victor Hugo, did not want to allow "their" statue of Liberty to leave Paris, it was nevertheless dismantled, packed in 214 crates, and shipped to America on the frigate *Isère*.

RICHARD MORRIS HUNT, ARCHITECT OF THE PEDESTAL
Hunt designed a high pedestal, a Doric base topped with a neo-classical loggia made of reinforced concrete and granite, to accentuate the size of the statue. The first stone was laid – following Masonic rites – in spring 1884.

The statue, which has been administered by the National Park Service since 1937, was given a facelift for her centennial in 1986. A Franco-American team was given the task of correcting the right arm and the head, which were slightly askew due to an error made when the statue was originally assembled. With a

new torch, its flame gilded in gold leaf, and her freshly cleaned gown, Miss Liberty was ready to take up her duties again for another century. Many people forget her French origins – so thoroughly has she come to symbolize the United States.

DEDICATION

On October 28, 1886, the statue, her face veiled by the Tricolor, was dedicated (above). Apart from her symbolic role at the entrance to New York, she has become a universally recognized figure, the subject of all sorts of products, from jam to pasta (top); she has "posed" for painters (Andy Warhol made multiple portraits of her) and appeared in films, such as Hitchcock's *Saboteur* (1942) and Schaffner's *Planet of the Apes* (1968).

Arrival of immigrants at Ellis Island in about 1900.

Immigrants arriving in New York harbor during the era of the great sailing ships (opposite). Painting by Samuel Waugh.

"Rumour had it . . . that some of us would be refused entry into the United States and would be sent back to Europe. The very thought brought me out in a cold sweat . . . Later, having mastered these anxieties, I was gripped by the fear that I would catch the mumps, smallpox, or some other disease . . . I didn't sleep a wink. I shook all night, listening to all those passengers snoring and dreaming aloud in a dozen different languages."
Louis Adamic, describing his crossing in 1913

ISLE OF TEARS, ISLE OF HOPE

The history of the United States is to a certain extent a story of immigration, and this story has had some grim moments. By the end of the 19th century, immigrants were being attacked, even murdered, due to a rising tide of xenophobia in American society. Public opinion, which had turned against Central and Southern European nationals, forced the Federal Government to assume responsibility for immigration, which had hitherto been left to the discretion of individual states. Institutions were restructured, committees were established, and strict immigration quotas were imposed. In 1892 the United States Immigration Station was established on Ellis Island. For millions of immigrants this was the waiting room for the Promised Land.

HOW TO GET TO ELLIS ISLAND. From Manhattan, take the same ferry as for the Statue of Liberty (Battery Park, southwest point of Manhattan). The crossing takes twenty minute, after which you will alight at the impressive redbrick landing stage, topped by a glass canopy, which leads to the Main Building.

MUSEUM OF IMMIGRATION. Within the building's precincts,

facing the sea, a wall of honor has been erected. It is some 98 feet long and is covered with a sheet of engraved copper bearing the names of 200,000 immigrants. A museum was opened following restoration in 1990. The BAGGAGE ROOM on the ground floor, with its collection of trunks, suitcases, baskets and assorted belongings, all of which accompanied the immigrants on their journey, has been reconstructed on the ground floor, where various signboards indicate the route to follow. If you are in a hurry, you can take the elevator directly to the second story; but visitors with plenty of time may wish to begin their visit with an overview of the history of American immigration, which is provided in the main hall on the ground floor. This exhibition takes the form of individual

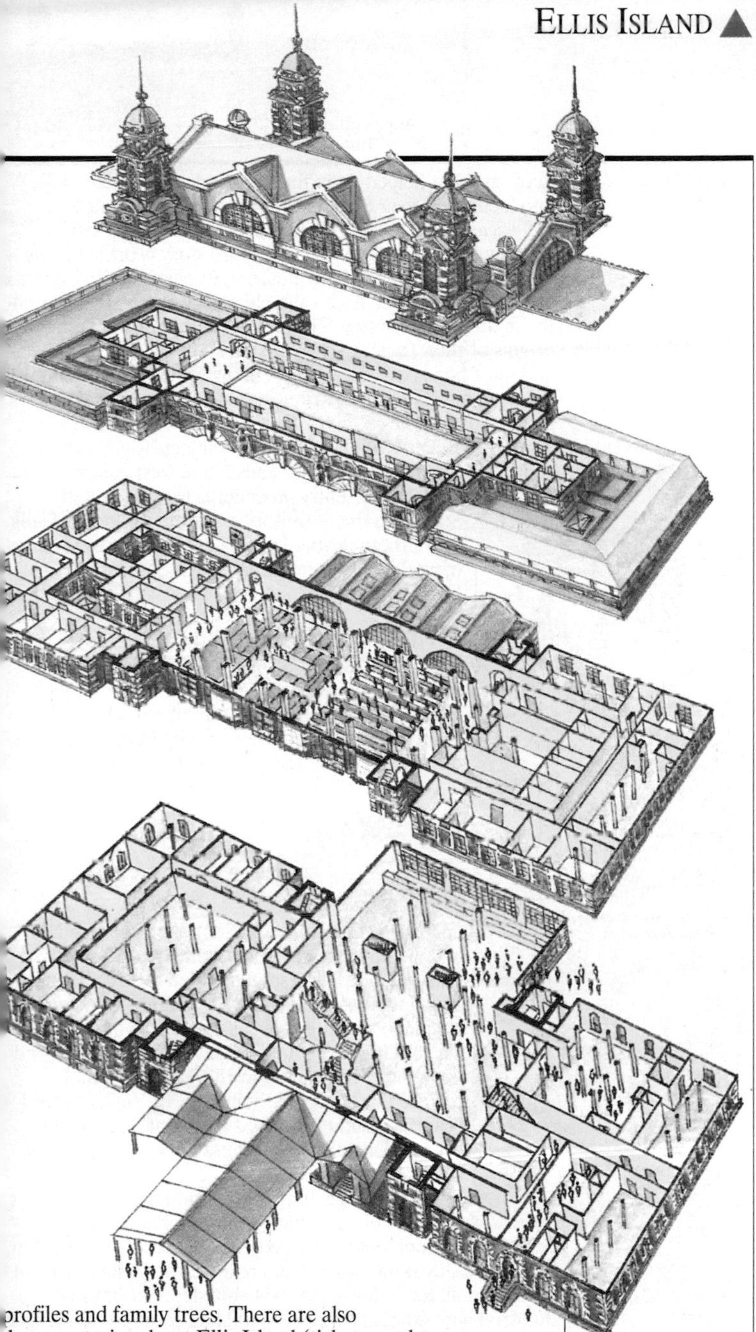

profiles and family trees. There are also
documentaries about Ellis Island (tickets can be
obtained in the entrance hall). On the second story, two
semicircular galleries, west and east of the large Registry Hall,
or Great Hall, document the lengthy process immigrants had
to endure before being admitted to the United States
(medical examinations, literacy tests) and list the marriages
contracted in Manhattan in cases where the name of one of
the spouses was registered on Ellis Island. This room also
contains testimonies supplied by immigrants and their
children. These statements bear witness to the new arrivals'
gradual integration into American society with the support of

IMMIGRATION CENTER
Between 1892 and
1954 nearly seventeen
million people passed
through this
building's vast waiting
rooms, dormitories,
offices and medical
examination rooms.

Main entrance to
Ellis Island.

THE MEDICAL EXAMINATION

All the immigrants to the United States (below in the 19th century and in 1914) had to undergo a medical examination. Those suffering from contagious diseases such as trachoma (inflammation of the eyes), were rejected. Between 6 and 11 percent were deported for health reasons.

networks that helped them find jobs and acquire new skills and facilitated their children's rapid assimilation into American life. There is a second movie theater for visitors wanting further information. The third story is probably the most fascinating part of the museum; its east gallery displays a collection of objects, both valuable and everyday, that shared the immigrants' odyssey. They illustrate the wide-ranging origins of their owners – a Scottish teapot, an Austrian pipe – and their hopes and dreams – wedding shoes, religious books, a sewing machine, a typewriter, flatirons, tools for a new life in a new land. The room of "Forgotten Voices", which is just as moving, focuses on the abandoned objects found before Ellis Island was restored. This leads to the west gallery where display cases detail the entry procedures for the United States, via the dormitories. Another doorway leads into a room devoted to small temporary exhibitions of works by contemporary artists depicting Ellis Island.

A HISTORICAL SITE, THE HISTORY OF A SITE

THE COST OF ASYLUM. Immigration laws were successively tightened to prohibit entry into the United States by anyone suffering from contagious diseases, by polygamists, prostitutes, the indigent,

anarchists, the Chinese (1882), the Japanese (1907) and the illiterate (1917). Despite being a narrow strip of land (it was soon doubled in size) Ellis Island was the ideal site for weeding out, detaining and deporting possible candidates for immigration. The original structure, which was far too small and was destroyed by a fire in 1897, was ultimately replaced by thirty-five buildings. In 1907, a record year, the Island processed a total of one million people. The majority of these hopeful candidates, who had often reached their destination after a grueling voyage, had only to endure another five or six hours of examination and interviews before reaching freedom, but approximately 20 percent were held in dormitories to await money from relatives or further medical examination. Each dormitory probably slept about three hundred immigrants and the hospital had room for as many as five hundred patients. About half of the detained were ultimately deported.

Some 3,500 people died on Ellis Island, and 350 were born there.

AT THE GATES OF OBLIVION. The 1924 laws regarding immigration quotas were the start of Ellis Island's slow decline. In 1933, for the first time, immigrants returning to their homeland outnumbered those who were just arriving. In 1937 the center

"A stranger who greeted us,
a hard man, asked:
'And how's your health?'
He examined us. His eyes
Like a dog's
scrutinized us . . .
One thing is certain,
If he could have plumbed
the depths of our hearts
He would have seen–
the wound."
Avrom Reisen

SORTING IMMIGRATION CANDIDATES
This room (left) is where the immigrants were divided into categories based on criteria laid down in American legislation. This process often lasted for five hours and 400–500 hundred people were dealt with every day.

"New York is an ugly city, a dirty city. Its climate is a scandal, its politics are used to frighten children, its traffic is madness, its competition is murderous. But there is one thing about it – once you have lived in New York and it has become your home, no place else is good enough!"
John Steinbeck
The Making of New York

dealt with only 160 deportees and thirty prisoners. During World War II Ellis Island became a detention center for "enemies of the United States". The occasional Jewish refugee rubbed shoulders with Nazis and Communists from all over America. Finally, as Ellis Island was no longer

Ellis Island at the turn of the 20th century.

cost-effective, given the meager service it provided, it was permanently closed in 1954.

THE RESTORATION OF ELLIS ISLAND. Neglect brought decay: the decorated buildings, the historic objects in storage there, the surrounding land were all left to the mercy of vandals, looters and the elements. Nature reclaimed the rooms that once had thronged with countless immigrants; all that remained were walls rotted by damp, gaping roofs, crumbling ceilings and parquet floors. In 1965 President Johnson's administration took action, making Ellis Island a National Monument, affiliated with the Statue of Liberty. The sea wall was strengthened and rebuilt in places. From 1976, when it was opened to the public, fifty thousand people have visited this site every year. In 1982, a campaign alerted public opinion to the dilapidated condition of the monument. Donations flooded in from all over the nation to save this part of its cherished heritage. The site was closed in 1983 for restoration. A detailed inventory was drawn up of everything worth salvaging: the registry hall ceiling, which had been constructed and covered with terracotta tiling in 1918, using Catalan technique, was restored; the walls were repaired, saving some of the messages that had been carved into the plaster at the beginning of the 20th century – moving testimonies of the immigrants' hopes and fears. The restoration of Ellis Island was one of the most expensive projects of its kind undertaken in the history of the United States ($156 million). However, the museum, opened on September 10, 1990, receives two million visitors every year.

AN ERUDITE IMMIGRANT
Albert Einstein on his arrival in New York on October 27, 1933.

MOVING MEMORIES
For one hundred million Americans these buildings are evocative of the memories of parents, grandparents and other family members. Ellis Island was the point of entry to the New World for some twelve million immigrants, at the beginning of the 20th century.

151

HYPER-REALISM
In fine weather, bankers and stockbrokers sit on the steps of Liberty Plaza, their ties flicked over their shoulders, eating sandwiches bought in one of the Broadway delis. One of them,

seated on a bench, is checking the contents of his briefcase, sifting through documents from the Merrill Lynch brokerage firm. This is actually a startlingly lifelike statue, entitled *Double Check* (J. Seward Johnson Jr., 1982); the documents are perfectly legible. Another interesting sight is the clock set in the sidewalk at 174 Broadway. This belongs to a nearby jewelry store, William Barthman Jewelers.

LANDMARKS PRESERVATION LAW
The Singer Building (right), destroyed in 1970, is one of New York's most sorely missed masterpieces. Since then, the New York Landmarks Preservation Commission has consolidated its power of veto and widened its sphere of influence: it also has the right to preserve building interiors that are open to the public. There are more than 1,500 designated landmarks in New York today.

This itinerary runs from the former World Trade Center down Broadway, the most famous thoroughfare in Manhattan, which crosses the island from north to south. It was originally an old Indian trail that curved around forests and hills. During the building of Fort Amsterdam the Dutch widened it south of what is now Bowling Green and named it "Breede Wegh" (Broadway). "Lower Broadway" is now so densely lined with buildings that you cannot see their tops from street level: the disorderly layout of old New York and the heavy traffic hem you in. Many of the buildings have spacious lobbies covering an entire block.

AROUND LIBERTY PLAZA

CENTURY 21, FORMER RIVER SAVINGS BANK BUILDING. 26 CORTLANDT ST., BETWEEN CHURCH, DEY AND CORTLANDT STS. (1934, arch. Walker & Gillette, 5 stories). This former bank is an Art Deco gem ● 98. The breathtaking scale of the red, black and brown marble former banking hall, with its barrel-vaulted ceiling and its floor patterned with optical geometrical motifs, makes the building well worth a visit. It is now the home of Century 21, the discount store famous for selling designer labels at unbeatable knockdown prices.

1 LIBERTY PLAZA/165 BROADWAY. (1974, arch. Skidmore, Owings & Merrill, 53 stories). The construction of this glass box ● 100, which occupies the block bounded by Broadway, Church, Cortlandt and Liberty streets, was to blame for the demolition of the Singer Building – doomed because its usable floor space was five times smaller. A Beaux Arts masterpiece, designed by ERNEST FLAGG, the Singer Building was,

The circular brass seal of the East River Savings Bank, flanked by two eagles, used to adorn the parapet overhanging the side entrances.

The Sky Lobby (left) of the Equitable Building.

in many respects, a forerunner of the modern skyscraper. The tallest building ever built at the time of its completion (1908), then the tallest building ever to be pulled down (1970), it could withstand wind pressure of 350 tons. It also anticipated the Zoning Resolution of 1916 ● 97 since its slender, elegant tower formed a setback in relation to the larger mass below, thereby allowing sunlight to reach the street. At the time of its demolition, the New York City Landmarks Commission, only five years old, was not sure enough of its powers to halt the plans of the new landlord, US Steel.

HONG KONG CHINA BANK. 140 BROADWAY, BETWEEN LIBERTY AND CEDAR STS. (1967, arch. Skidmore, Owings & Merrill). This flat-roofed monolith, a typical example of the International Style ● 100, is devoid of all decoration. Instead, the building has a single, striking work of art: the red cube sculpture (below) by Isamu Noguchi (1973).

EQUITABLE BUILDING ● 97 ★. 120 BROADWAY (1915, arch. Ernest R. Graham of Graham, Anderson, Probst & White). Stone eagles and lions adorn the lower part of the façade of this neo-Renaissance building which covers a surface area thirty times larger than that of the original building of the same name. Its construction raised a general outcry, as New Yorkers were concerned that Lower Manhattan should not be entirely smothered by such "monsters". The Equitable Building is, however, a designated landmark and boasts one of New York's most impressive lobbies, with its vaulted, coffered ceiling adorned with gilded ceiling rosettes, its floor of pink marble, quarried in Tennessee, and its sandy-colored marble walls. It has four entrances, one for each of the adjacent streets. The lower part of the building occupies a whole block, while its body, with its five thousand windows, is H–shaped. The "Sky Lobby", former headquarters of the exclusive Banker's Club on the 38th floor, can be visited by appointment. From here, you can enjoy a panoramic view over the neighboring roofs.

The Equitable Building in 1914.

The Trinity Building, as seen by a reveler, takes on a strange appearance. . .

THAMES TWINS/TRINITY AND REALTY BUILDINGS ★. 111–115 BROADWAY (1905 and 1907, arch. Francis H. Kimball). These twin buildings, linked by a walkway that straddles Thames Street, are one of New York's architectural gems and make for a pleasant surprise deep in the heart of the bustling Financial District. The façades call to mind the Gothic lines of Trinity Church, and the interiors are treated in a similar style, with stained-glass windows and gilded elevator doors, grotesques and gilded ornaments.

AROUND TRINITY CHURCH

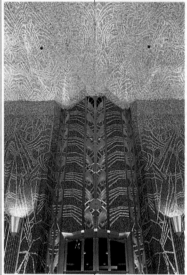

FORMER IRVING TRUST BUILDING
The ground-floor banking hall of this building glows with red and gold mosaics.

AN ENGLISH CHURCH
Trinity Church (right, as rebuilt in 1846) was the first Manhattan parish established by the Church of England. When it was built, in the 1690's, all residents, whatever their religion, had to pay a tax for its construction.

BANK OF NEW YORK, FORMERLY IRVING TRUST BUILDING ★. 1 WALL ST., S.E. CORNER OF BROADWAY (1932, arch. Voorhees, Gmelin & Walker, 50 stories). The Greek practice of fluting columns to enhance the illusion of height and delicacy was adapted for the walls of this building. The plain limestone cladding and the abstract Art Deco motif of the façade enhance the building's monolithic appearance. Although built during the Great Depression, the building exudes a feeling of confidence. The name of the former owners of the building is derived from the American author, Washington Irving, who used to live at 3 Wall Street. To view the building as a whole, walk back to Rector Street.

TRINITY CHURCH ★. BROADWAY AT WALL ST. (1846, arch. Richard Upjohn). Trinity Parish, founded by a charter granted by William III in 1697, was given extensive pasture lands in Manhattan, which eventually made it the richest church in America. This is the third building of the same name to be built on this site; the first church, built in 1698, was destroyed by a fire in 1776 and the second was demolished in 1839 due to a defective roof frame. Completed in 1846, the present Gothic Revival church is clad in brownstone and boasts a bell tower whose slender spire soars to 280 feet. Until the end of the 19th century Trinity Church was the tallest building in New York; it used to serve as a landmark for ships. The stained glass window over the choir is one of the earliest made in the United States. The three bronze porch doors, designed by Richard Morris Hunt and constructed by Karl Bitter, Charles Niehaus, and J. Massey Rhind illustrate Adam and Eve's expulsion from Paradise. The hundred-year-old oak trees in the church burial ground shelter the graves of Alexander Hamilton, the first Secretary of the Treasury, Robert Fulton, inventor of the steam warship ▲ 174, Captain

James Lawrence, a hero of the War of 1812, William
Bradford, the founder of the first newspaper ● *54* in New
York, and ALBERT GALLATIN, statesman and a founder of New
York University ▲ *200*. The oldest tombstone dates from
1681. An ossuary contains the ashes of two thousand
prisoners who died during the American Revolution. After
the attacks of September 11, 2001 ● *46*, the churchyard
railings served as a makeshift monument – covered in signs,
flags, clothing and photographs – to the memory of the
victims and the bravery of the firefighters.

29 BROADWAY. (1931, arch. Sloan & Robertson, 31 stories).
The lobby, with its wealth of jade marble, engraved glass
doors and radiator grills, is a perfect example of Art Deco
style. Cross the street to appreciate the design of the building.

AROUND BOWLING GREEN

FORMER CUNARD BUILDING. 25 BROADWAY (1921, arch.
Benjamin Wistar Morris; Carrère and Hastings, 22 stories).
Cunard's first ship, *Britannia*, berthed in New York on
July 4, 1840. By the 1920's, after its merger with the White
Star Line, Cunard had become the leading passenger
steamship company. Their former headquarters used to
house the NEW YORK CITY POLICE MUSEUM (on the top
floor), which traces the history of
the New York police from its
beginnings up to the present day
and is now on Oldslip St. The
sumptuous main entrance, set in a neo-Renaissance
façade, leads into an immense lobby, illuminated by
antique chandeliers, with a vaulted ceiling and walls
lined with polychromatic terracotta.

**AN AMERICAN
CHURCH**
After the fire of 1776
the original Trinity
Church (above)
remained in ruins
throughout the
American Revolution.
A second church was
built after the war.
Like other Anglican
Churches in the
United States, it
became part
of the new,
independent
Episcopal Church.

**LOBBY OF THE
FORMER CUNARD
BUILDING**
The octagonal main
hall, 65 feet high, is
surmounted by three
domes. The interior
walls of the building
are decorated with
charts showing
Cunard's lines and
illustrated by flags
from former French
and English colonial
empires (by the
artist Ezra Winters).
The pendentives
supporting the main
dome are decorated
with paintings of the
ships of four famous
sailors: Christopher
Columbus, Leif
Eriksson, John Cabot
and Sir Francis
Drake.

Government House in 1797, on the site of the future US Custom House.

1 BROADWAY. This was the first office building to be built (in 1884), along the longest and most famous street in New York. It was originally called the Washington Building. In 1922 it was refurbished to house the headquarters of the United States Line, one of the many shipping companies based on Steamship Row. The reservation and ticket sales office (now converted into a bank) was on the ground floor. Note the compass dial set in the floor and the words "First-Class tickets" which still appear outside.

FORMER STANDARD OIL BUILDING. 26 BROADWAY (1922, arch. Carrère & Hastings and Shreve, Lamb & Blake, 31 stories). The neo-Renaissance façade of the former Standard Oil

Building (left) cunningly curves here in a fan shape to follow the contour of Broadway. The names of the founders of the oil company, including John D. Rockefeller, grace the lobby which is lined with pilasters and columns. Note the STANDARD OIL CLOCK, on which the "S" indicates the minutes and the "O" the hours. As you approach Bowling Green, you can see the top of the building's pyramidal tower, whose main axis is aligned east-west, at an oblique angle to the main part of the building. This building now houses THE MUSEUM OF AMERICAN FINANCIAL HISTORY.

BOWLING GREEN. (rest. 1978, landscape architect, Paul Friedberg). Created in 1733, Bowling Green is the oldest park in the city. It occupies the site of a former Dutch parade ground, which had originally been adjacent to a cattle market. The new park consisted of a green where gentlemen could bowl (hence its name) for an annual fee of one peppercorn, paid to the municipal government. It was here that PETER MINUIT bought Manhattan from the Indians ● 30. At the center of the green, in 1766, New Yorkers raised a gilded statue of George III to show their gratitude at the repeal of the Stamp Act, which had placed a tax on all written documents. Although the 18th-century railings that surrounded the park are still there, the statue was melted down for making bullets during the American Revolution. In 1842 a fountain was built in the park. It was supplied with fresh water from the Croton Reservoir, which gave New Yorkers, for the first time, access to clean water, instead of the well water that caused so many epidemics ● 34 in the city.

"BOWLING GREEN BULL". This enormous bronze bull (Arturo di Modica, 1989), stands at the entrance to the Financial District ▲ 158, at the northernmost end of Bowling Green. The bull and the bear represent the two trends of the stock market: rising and declining.

"The bull strives to crush the bear, which is waiting for the best time to throttle it."
André Kostolamy,
Si la Bourse m'était contée

NATIONAL MUSEUM OF THE AMERICAN INDIAN, FORMER US CUSTOM HOUSE ★. 1 BOWLING GREEN (1907, arch. Cass Gilbert, 6 stories) ● 92.

This museum, which forms part of the Smithsonian Institute in Washington, was founded in 1916; its collections cover ten thousand years of American Indian civilization. Originally based in Harlem ▲ 358, it moved to the former US Custom House in 1994. This Beaux Arts-style building was built in 1907 to receive customs duties. At that time, there was no income tax so customs duties were the Federal Government's primary source of income. Most of this revenue was provided by New York and as a result the US Custom House accounted for most of the money that kept the American economy afloat. The double-height marble HALL leads into a sumptuous oval rotunda

illuminated by an elliptical picture window and crowned by a dome decorated by eight frescoes (1937, Reginald Marsh). These frescoes depict the first explorers arriving in New York as well as Greta Garbo disembarking from a transatlantic liner which has just entered the harbor. In 1973, the Customs House moved to the former World Trade Center.

TOWARD THE SEA

CHURCH OF OUR LADY OF THE ROSARY. 7–8 STATE ST. (1793–1806, arch. John McComb, rest. 1965, Shanley & Sturges). This church can be found in a house with a Georgian-style east wing (1793) and a Federal-style west wing (1806) ● 82. It belonged to shipowner James Watson who would spend long hours watching the harbor activity from his house; its columns were made from ships' masts.

BATTERY MARITIME BUILDING. 11 SOUTH ST. (1909, arch. Walker & Gillette). Until 1938 the MUNICIPAL FERRY PIERS served as landing stages for the various BROOKLYN ferryboat lines. They are now used by the GOVERNOR'S ISLAND ferry. The inland side of this building, which gives access to the piers, has a colonnade and arches facing the water.

ALLEGORICAL ORNAMENTS

The steps of the main entrance to the US Custom House are adorned with statues by Daniel Chester French, symbolizing four continents. The building's front-facing windows bear the heads of the eight "races" of mankind (Caucasian, Hindu, Latin, Celtic, Mongolian, Eskimo, Slavic and African); above the cornice are twelve statues representing the great commercial centers in Western history.

SAINT ELIZABETH ANN SETON

In 1809 Elizabeth Seton (1774–1821), who lived at 7–8 State St., founded the Sisters of Charity, the first American order of nuns. A member of the New York aristocracy, she was ostracized for her conversion to Catholicism. She was canonized in 1975, becoming the first female American saint ● 50. There is a statue of her in the Shrine of St. Elizabeth Ann Seton.

THE FINANCIAL DISTRICT
The Financial District, which dates back to 1792 with the creation of the first Stock Exchange, was once dominated by the spire of Trinity Church ▲ 154. With the advent of the skyscraper, the area's appearence changed radically.

"ONCE UPON A TIME IN AMERICA"
A scene (below) for the movie, *Once Upon a Time in America*, made in 1984 by Sergio Leone and filmed in the Federal Reserve

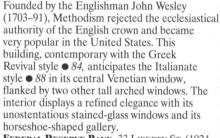

Bank. In this movie the director explores another face of the "American dream": the birth of great cities and the stranglehold of mob rule.

AROUND THE FEDERAL RESERVE BANK

JOHN STREET METHODIST CHURCH. 44 JOHN ST. (1841, arch. William Hurry). This church (the third on this site) was the home of the first Methodist congregation in America. Founded by the Englishman John Wesley (1703–91), Methodism rejected the ecclesiastical authority of the English crown and became very popular in the United States. This building, contemporary with the Greek Revival style ● *84,* anticipates the Italianate style ● *88* in its central Venetian window, flanked by two other tall arched windows. The interior displays a refined elegance with its unostentatious stained-glass windows and its horseshoe-shaped gallery.

FEDERAL RESERVE BANK. 33 LIBERTY ST. (1924, arch. York & Sawyer). The Federal Reserve Bank was founded in 1913 by President Woodrow Wilson to centralize the American banking system. The New York Reserve Bank, a key part of the Federal Reserve System, is where monetary policy is implemented for the Federal Reserve, influencing interest rates and economic activity throughout the nation.

The gold reserves from eighty countries and some foreign banks and international organizations, over one quarter of the world's stock, are stored 80 feet below ground in this massive rectangular fortress built of limestone and sandstone. Its impregnable appearance is modeled on Florentine Renaissance palaces. The strong rooms can be visited by appointment, and it used to be possible to watch old banknotes being destroyed. LOUISE NEVELSON PLAZA, farther east, at the intersection of Maiden Lane and Liberty and William streets, affords the best view of the crenelated turret that tops this building. This pedestrian area contains an abstract sculpture, *Shadows and Flags*, created by Louise Nevelson in 1977.

CENTRAL BANK OF CHINA, FORMER NEW YORK CHAMBER OF COMMERCE. 65 LIBERTY ST. (1901, arch. James B. Baker). This architectural gem is one of the finest Beaux Arts-style ● *92* buildings in New York and a product of the "City Beautiful" movement. The three pedestals on the façade once bore statues, which did not survive the ravages of pollution.

CHASE MANHATTAN BANK. 1 CHASE MANHATTAN PLAZA (1960, arch. Skidmore, Owings & Merrill). This building marked a watershed in the postwar

development of Lower Manhattan, being the first International Style ● *100* office building to be constructed in this part of the city. It was an expression of the confidence that David Rockefeller, the bank's president, had in the future of Downtown at a time when businesses were moving Uptown. The tower's plain rectangular shape contrasts markedly with the slender spires surrounding it. The Chase Manhattan Bank boasts a superb art collection and its huge plaza contains work by Isamu Noguchi – a sunken Japanese garden with an arrangement of seven rocks – as well as a sculpture by Dubuffet (above), *Group of Four Trees*, created in 1972. The plaza affords a spectacular view of the neighboring buildings, especially 70 Pine Street.

AMERICAN INTERNATIONAL BUILDING ★. 70 PINE ST. (1932, arch. Clinton and Russell; Holton and George). This Art Deco ● *98* skyscraper, which originally housed the CITIES SERVICE COMPANY, responsible for the

LIBERTY TOWER Situated at 55 Liberty St., this neo-Gothic tower decorated with finials and gargoyles once housed the Standard Oil Company ▲ *156*. The

frescos in its lobby depict the building in 1909, as well as the Singer Building ▲ *152*, which stood on the site of the present Liberty Plaza.

159

The French franc, which was hard currency at the time, is carved on the pediment (above) of the main door of 20 Exchange Place.

60 WALL STREET Built in 1988, the Morgan Bank's new building, is a heavy Postmodern tower, contrasting sharply with its more graceful neighbors. However, the lower part of the building is composed of a colonnade, echoing the one at 55 Wall St., just opposite. It houses a

vast atrium (above), open to the public in accordance with city-planning regulations.

The deeply recessed main entrance to Citibank behind its colonnade.

city's substructural work, was designed to create an impression of power and wealth. The Chase Manhattan Plaza affords a good view of its Gothic tower, which is one of the Financial District's three most prestigious tops, along with 40 WALL STREET and 20 EXCHANGE PLACE. A limestone model of the building is carved onto the central column of the entrance. The triangles on the main doors are the Federal Reserve's emblem. Behind Egyptian-style doors in the lobby are two elevators: one for odd and one for even floors.

WALL STREET

The financial world's most famous street once marked the northernmost boundary of New Amsterdam. In 1653 the Dutch erected a wooden palisade as a form of protection, first against the Native Americans, then against the English ● *32*. From 1792, when the first stock exchange was organized in this neighborhood ▲ *164*, Wall Street began to establish its reputation as a financial center.

72–74 WALL STREET. (1926, arch. Benjamin Wistar Morris). The ships and anchors that adorn the ashlar façade are a reminder of this building's previous occupant. The lobby of no. 72, with its decorative brass grilles, paneled doors and gilded ceiling, is a masterpiece. The central door, opposite the elegant bank of elevators, is crowned with a brass bas-relief depicting a lighthouse.

63 WALL STREET. (1929, arch. Delano and Aldrich). The building rises in a series of setbacks to a top decorated with ornamental gargoyles, a better view of which can be obtained farther back up Wall Street. Note the coins adorning the façade and take a look at the corner lobby.

22 WILLIAM STREET, BETWEEN BEAVER ST. AND EXCHANGE ST. ★. (1931, arch. Cross & Cross). Built for the CITY BANK FARMERS' TRUST COMPANY, this office tower fills a trapezoid-shaped block and has a façade with bevelled quoins. Take a look at the bronze doors decorated with trains, boats, planes and airships, typical Art Deco ● *98* motifs. On the cornice of the lower part of the building, huge helmeted centurions seem to watch the passersby. There is a better view of the lofty, slender tower farther west from William Street. The lobby offers a profusion of marble, mosaics, paintings and tin. Note the central dome, vaulted ceilings, elevator doors, floor and glass telephone booths.

CIPRIANI-WALL STREET, FORMER CITIBANK. 55 WALL ST. (1836–42, arch. Isaiah Rogers; 1907, arch. McKim, Mead & White). This neo-classical building, with its two-story colonnades, was built on the site of the first Merchants' Exchange, which had been destroyed by fire in 1835. The lower part of the building, which dates from 1836, served as the US Custom House from 1863 ▲ *157* until 1899. After that tenant departed, "55 Wall Street" was enlarged to house Citibank (then called the First National City Bank). A Corinthian-order colonnade was added to the Ionic one by the architects McKim, Mead & White. The huge lobby, which measures 198 by 132 feet in height, is once again a reception hall. The rest of the building has been converted into a luxury hotel.

> "This is a district overflowing with gold, a true miracle, and you can even hear the miracle through the doors with its sound of dollars being counted . . . "

Louis-Ferdinand Céline

BANK OF NEW YORK BUILDING. 48 WALL ST. (1927, arch. Benjamin Wistar Morris III). Cross the street to appreciate the setbacks of this skyscraper which draws its inspiration from the Italian Renaissance and whose topmost aedicula is crowned with an eagle. The Bank of New York, the first bank in the newly independent state, was founded in 1784 by Alexander Hamilton ▲ *154, 352, 360*, Washington's former aide-de-camp and first Secretary of the Treasury. Alexander Hamilton died after being shot in a duel on July 11, 1804 by Aaron Burr, a rival in politics as well as in business.

THE TRUMP BUILDING ★. 40 WALL ST. (1929, arch. H. Craig Severance and Yasuo Matsui, 69 stories). The name of this building's current owner, DONALD TRUMP, ▲ *296*, who renovated and modernized the building, is displayed in large gilt letters at the top of the tower (below). Constructed for the Bank of Manhattan Company, the skyscraper (left) bears a certain resemblance to the Empire State Building ▲ *242* (like the latter, it was even hit by a plane in the 1940's). It was the tallest building in the world for just a few days before being overtaken by the Chrysler Building ▲ *266*. The top, a Gothic Revival green pyramid, similar that of the Woolworth Building ▲ *180*, can easily be recognized on the Lower Manhattan skyline – the northeast corner of Broad and Beaver streets provides a good vantage point. The Bank of Manhattan Company, originally the Manhattan Water Company, was founded by Aaron Burr in 1799 to supply drinking water. In 1842, when the Croton Aqueduct was opened, the company, which had also engaged in banking activities, dropped its water supply function and took the name of the Bank of Manhattan.

30 WALL STREET. (1919, arch. York and Sawyer). This building was built on the site of the United States Assay Office which was designed by Martin E. Thompson and completed in 1823; it was demolished in 1915. Its façade is displayed in the American Wing of the Metropolitan Museum of Art.

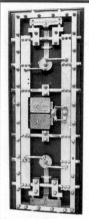

Former subtreasury vaults.

In 1883, a statue of George Washington by John Quincy Adams Ward was placed outside the entrance to Federal Hall, at the approximate spot where he took his oath of office and where (right) President Benjamin Harrison made a speech.

26 WALL STREET
Built in 1842, the U.S. Custom House displays a Doric austerity in contrast to the Stock Exchange (1903), whose façade, with its profusion of figures and Corinthian opulence, recalls Caesar's Rome.

FEDERAL HALL NATIONAL MEMORIAL ★. 26 WALL ST. (1834–42, arch. Town & Davis) ▲ *85*. In 1701, the second New York CITY HALL was built on this site ▲ *168*. Remodeled in 1788 by Pierre-Charles L'Enfant (architect and city-planner for Washington, D. C.), the building, now renamed Federal Hall, served briefly as the headquarters of the American government until the capital was moved to Philadelphia in 1790. This building, later demolished, housed the first meeting, in March 1789, of the new Congress, and was the site of George Washington's inauguration as the first president of the United States, on April 30 of that year. The present Greek Revival building was built in 1842 to house the first U.S. Custom House ▲ *157*, then, between 1862 and 1920, it became the headquarters of a U.S. subtreasury. Exhibits in the museum are focused on American history.

MORGAN GUARANTY TRUST COMPANY. 23 WALL ST. AT S. E. CORNER OF BROAD ST. (1913, arch. Trowbridge & Livingston). In 1907, financier and businessman J. Pierpont Morgan managed to stem the tide of panic then threatening Wall Street by locking the leading city bankers in his 5th Avenue home and forcing them to come up with a plan to rebuild people's confidence. While the "prisoners" were working, Morgan played solitaire – which indicates his status

> 'All the major financial markets have grown up in the heart of a capital city. The American stock exchange is an exception: it was created in a port, on the outskirts of a city which is not even the capital.'
>
> M. Turin

among them. His bank at 23 Wall Street was the last building to be built at this key intersection, around which were grouped the US subtreasury (now the FEDERAL HALL NATIONAL MEMORIAL), to the north: the NEW YORK STOCK EXCHANGE, to the west; and, opposite, BANKERS TRUST, a rival occupying, in 1912, the tallest building in the world. By building this low, four-story structure, Morgan intended to create the impression that "Less is more". The bank had no identifying sign – the Morgan establishment did not need one! The Morgan family's highly reactionary stance brought them many enemies: a bomb exploded outside the building on September 16, 1920, killing thirty-three people and wounding hundreds of others. Those responsible were never found.

"WALL STREET"
The pediment over the entrace to the New York Stock Exchange depicts a group of sculpted figures entitled *Integrity Protecting the Works of Man* (John Quincy Adams Ward). In the center, the winged figure of Integrity looms over Science, Industry and Invention; on the right, Agriculture; and on the left, the Mining Industry.

BROAD STREET AND NEW YORK STOCK EXCHANGE

BROAD STREET. This street, which runs from Wall Street down to the tip of Manhattan, was originally a canal dug by the Dutch in 1660. In 1676, it was filled in ● 76. Although "Wall Street" is considered the world over to be synonymous with the US stock market, the New York Stock Exchange, the center of for most of the district's financial activity, is actually on Broad Street.

NEW YORK STOCK EXCHANGE ★.
8 BROAD ST. (1903, arch. George B. Post), The largest stock exchange in the . world first opened on May 17, 1792 under a sycamore tree, near the intersection of Wall and William streets. Here

twenty-four American brokers met to impose some sort of order on a chaotic market and signed the "Buttonwood Agreement". The tree was felled in 1865 by a storm, but a commemorative plaque was laid in front of 8 Broad Street. On March 8, 1817, the market adopted a constitution and a name, the New York Stock and Exchange Board, and moved into 40 Wall Street. In 1863, the Board shortened its name to the New York Stock Exchange and moved into larger premises at 10–12 Broad Street. Thirty-five years later, in 1903, it settled in its present home at 8 Broad Street. The history of the New York Stock Exchange is filled with eccentric figures. One of the most famous was Hetty Green, nicknamed the "Witch of Wall Street", who, in the 1880's, transformed her inheritance into a fortune worth more than $100 million. She achieved this without ever showing her face on the floor of the Exchange . The classical façade of the New York Stock Exchange conceals a vast and highly sophisticated trading floor, one of the few remaining floors where brokers buy and sell millions of stocks and shares every day. The sound is deafening, punctuated by the clacking of the electronic wallboards.

The pyramid that tops the building at 14–16 Wall Street ● 97 is one of the most distinctive sights on the Manhattan skyline.

A hard currency – the dollar – a buoyant economy and a well-established banking system have made the New York Stock Exchange the leading money market in the world. Since its founding in 1792 it has survived many crises, including the crash of 1929. Instrumental in generating many of the technical innovations and new financial products used in trading halls since the beginning of the 20th century, Wall Street has created a new generation of stockbrokers.

"BLACK FRIDAY" AT THE NEW YORK STOCK EXCHANGE
On September 24, 1929, Jay Gould's attempt to corner the market having collapsed, the price of gold dropped nearly 20 percent. A panic in the securities market followed.

"CURB EXCHANGE"
Early in the 20th century small-scale stockholders carried out transactions at cash desks in stockbrokers' offices located along Broad St., and even in the street itself (below, in 1918).

ON TICKER TAPE
In order to send the rates on the Stock Exchange's Big Board to stockbrokers all over the country, Wall Street began, in 1867, to use teletype.

BATTLE OF THE "BEARS" AND THE "BULLS"
This animal metaphor, now used in all the money markets of the world, originated in America. "Bears" sell stocks and shares because they believe the market is falling; "bulls" buy them because they are gambling on a rising market. The behavior of the two groups generate Stock Market prices ▲ 156.

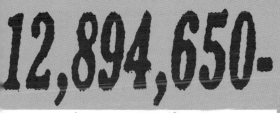

12,894,650 -

After the attacks of September 11, 2001, the New York Stock Exchange closed for four days running, an unprecedented move. During the four subsequent trading sessions, the Dow Jones dropped 14.25 percent before gradually rising again. However, although a crash was avoided after the terrorist attacks, a series of financial scandals, like the Enron and WorldCom affairs, caused a much more drastic fall in stock exchange indexes and seriously undermined investors' confidence in the system itself.

The New York Times.

"All the News That's Fit to Print."		THE WEATHER

| GRUNDY SAYS LOBBY IS NEEDED TO UPHOLD PARTY TARIFF VOWS | HUMBERT ESCAPES ANTI-FASCISTS SHOT AT BRUSSELS TOMB | WORST STOCK CRASH STEMMED BY BANKS; 12,894,650-SHARE DAY SWAMPS MARKET; LEADERS CONFER, FIND CONDITIONS SOUND |

PANIC ON WALL STREET

"Worst Stock Crash Stemmed By Banks" ran the headline in *The New York Times* on Friday October 25, 1929. The day before, the share prices of the big names in American industry had plummeted and 12,894,650 stocks and shares had changed hands. America was about to plunge into the Great Depression. In 1934, to prevent a catastrophe of this scale from recurring, Congress instituted the Securities and Exchange Commission, which established strict regulations to prevent violent market fluctuations.

In the 1980's, there was a staggering increase in the number of illegal schemes: hostile takeover bids – the targeted company would be shut and stripped of its assets – and junk bonds. Unscrupulous financial geniuses such as Michael Milken (right) built up huge fortunes in this way. In 1990 he was imprisoned for fraud.

VIETNAM WAR VETERANS' MEMORIAL

The writing on the memorial (above) to soldiers who fought in the Vietnam War (Vietnam Veterans' Plaza, S.E. Water St.), include extracts from letters, military dispatches and newspaper clippings.

The sign in front of the Fraunces Tavern.

INDIA HOUSE

This building, at 1 Hanover Square, housed the Hanover Bank, the N.Y. Cotton Exchange and the W. R. Grace & Co., in quick succession. India House is a classic example of an Italianate-style ● 88 brownstone residence. It is now occupied by a businessmen's club and restaurant and contains a collection of art and naval objects.

FORMER INTERNATIONAL TELEPHONE BUILDING. 67 BROAD ST. (1928, arch. Buchman & Kahn). The best view of the spectacular verticality of this 35-story Gothic Revival ● 86 building is from the corner of Beaver Street and Broadway. The allegorical frescoes of the lobby, which take communication as their theme, depict mythological figures. The alcove of what used to be the main entrance, on the corner of William Street, is embellished with a mosaic (right).

MARITIME EXCHANGE BUILDING. 80 BROAD ST. (1930, arch. Sloan & Robertson). The entrance of this Art Deco ● 97 building, topped with four silver sea horses, leads into the lobby, whose ceiling is covered with paintings of ships, illustrating the history of ship-building. The building has Tiffany-style ● 66 stained glass windows, depicting cars, trains, boats and planes.

85 BROAD STREET. (1983, arch. Skidmore, Owings & Merrill). A brass plaque bearing a map of Lower Manhattan c.1660 is placed below the archway leading into this building. The lobby follows the curve of the intersection with Stone Street. When the foundations were being laid, objects from the Dutch era were found; these are now exhibited in Pearl Street.

FRAUNCES TAVERN BLOCK HISTORIC DISTRICT

The Fraunces Tavern Block, located between Broad, Pearl and Water streets and Coenties Slip, occupies land salvaged from the sea by the Dutch in 1689.

FRAUNCES TAVERN. 54 PEARL ST. This house is an architectural conjecture of one built in 1719 for a wealthy merchant, Étienne (or Stephen) de Lancey. It was bought in 1762 by Samuel Fraunces who opened a restaurant in it called Queen's Head Tavern. After Independence, he changed its royalist name to his own. The tavern was frequented by members of the New York élite. George Washington was one of the establishment's patrons, and it was here, in 1783, that he gave a farewell dinner for his officers. In 1785, his business on the wane, Fraunces sold the tavern and became Washington's steward. The building, in Georgian style, was bought in 1904 by the Sons of the Revolution and restored in 1907 by William Mersereau. It houses a museum on early New York history and American decorative arts.

HANOVER SQUARE. This square was originally called Printing House Square in homage to William Bradford ● 54, who founded the first American printing works here in 1693. It was renamed "Hanover" by the English, in honor of the reigning dynasty. Many streets in the district followed suit, taking the names of members of the royal family. After Independence, only Hanover Square retained its name. A statue of Abraham De Peyster, Mayor of New York between 1691 and 1693, stands in this square.

DELMONICO'S. 56 BEAVER ST. (1891, arch. James Brown Lord). This restaurant was founded in 1827 by two Italian immigrants, the Delmonico brothers. It has a white marble portico, with columns that are said to come from Pompeii. The interior contains photos, engravings and tapestries of old New York.

166

Around City Hall

Civic Center, New York City.

CITY HALL
TOWARD SOUTH STREET SEAPORT

1 CITY HALL
2 CITY HALL PARK
3 PRINTING HOUSE SQUARE
4 PACE UNIVERSITY
5 POTTER BLDG.

The area now occupied by the Civic Center, the nation's second largest administrative complex after that of Washington D.C., employing 50,000 people, was a tranquil patch of countryside covered with fields and marsh lands. To the south stands City Hall, the offices of the mayor of New York since 1812, and Park Row, once the center of the theater district and also known as "Newspaper Row" because of the many newspapers based here. Farther southeast lies South Street Seaport, a remnant of the city's commercial, maritime past. To the west towers the Woolworth Building, while to the northeast administrative buildings and courthouses for the city and the State of New York are grouped around Foley Square.

CITY HALL
In paying homage to the Georgian and Louis XVI styles, the architects who designed City Hall (above, in 1826) were deliberately rejecting the monumental form of neo-classicism favored for the new capital, Washington. On top of City Hall's clock tower (below) stands a statue of Justice.

AROUND CITY HALL

CITY HALL ★. Between PARK ROW and BROADWAY (1803–12, arch. Joseph François Mangin and John McComb, Jr) This was New York's third City Hall. The first, built in 1641 during the Dutch occupation, was situated at about 71 Pearl Street, opposite the site where the Fraunces Tavern block ▲ *166* now stands. The second, built in 1701 on the corner of Broad and Wall streets, was demolished in 1812. On the same site, the U.S. CUSTOM HOUSE, now the FEDERAL HALL NATIONAL MEMORIAL ▲ *162* was constructed. City Hall served as the seat of Manhattan's administrative offices until the creation of "Greater New York" in 1898, which brought together the five boroughs – the Bronx, Queens, Brooklyn, Staten Island and Manhattan – following which the MUNICIPAL BUILDING ▲ *182* was built. It still houses the Mayor's office and is used for official ceremonies. The courtrooms and the office (open to the public) used by "Hizzoner" (the traditional New York nickname for the mayor) are reached by the building's main staircase.

Center, the cupola of City Hall.

CITY HALL PARK. The apple trees of this former public grazing ground (1686) were once used as gallows by the British. JACOB LEISLER, a Dutch merchant who was proclaimed "leader of Free New York" during the city's rebellion against excessive taxation by JAMES II, was hanged here for treason in 1691. The statue of another legendary convict – although executed elsewhere – also stands in the park ▲ *262*: NATHAN HALE, a hero of the American Revolution, was summarily hanged by the British for spying. His last words were, "I only regret that I have but one life to lose for my country." The

& PLACE TOWER
7 PARK ROW BLDG.
8 TITANIC MEMORIAL LIGHTHOUSE
9 PECK SLIP
10 FORMER AT&T BLDG.
11 ST PAUL'S CHAPEL
12 N.Y. COUNTY LAWYERS ASS.
13 FORMER N.Y. EVENING POST B.
14 FEDERAL OFFICE BLDG.
15 ST PETER'S CHURCH
16 WOOLWORTH BLDG.
17 FOLEY SQUARE
18 MUNICIPAL BLDG.
19 US COURTHOUSE
20 N.Y. COUNTY COURTHOUSE
21 N.Y.C. CRIMINAL COURT BLDG
22 THOMAS PAINE PARK
23 N.Y.C. DEPARTMENT OF HEALTH

24 ENGINE COMPANY N° 31
25 JAVITS FEDERAL OFFICE BLDG
26 CITY OF NEW YORK OFFICE BLDG
27 "TWEED COURTHOUSE"
28 SURROGATE'S COURT
29 COLUMBUS PARK

SOUTH ST. SEAPORT

FULTON FISH MARKET

BROOKLYN BRIDGE ✪

⏳ **Six hours**
◆ **A** A2-A3 **B** D2-D3

...ole on the green commemorates the "Liberty Poles" raised by New Yorkers in 1767 to mark the first anniversary of the repeal of the STAMP ACT ● *27*. This was also where a huge crowd gathered on July 9, 1776 to hear a reading of the Declaration of Independence, a document written mainly by Thomas Jefferson (1743–1826) and adopted by the Continental Congress in Philadelphia, on July 4, 1776.

THE CROTON FOUNTAIN
In 1842 a fountain was built on the site of the ornamental pond in City Hall Park (above) to celebrate the city's first supply of piped drinking water from the Croton Reservoir. The fountain was demolished in 1875.

FORMER POST OFFICE
This post office (opposite), which replaced the Croton Fountain, stood in front of City Hall. It was torn down in 1939 when the General Post Office was built on 8th Ave. ▲ 249.

NEWSPAPER ROW
In 1895 around fifteen daily newspapers were located near Park Row (below), including the *Times, World, Tribune, Sun, Post, Journal* and *Staats Zeitung*. Children used to sell

BENJAMIN FRANKLIN. PRINTING HOUSE SQUARE (1872, Ernst Plassman). In this square, east of City Hall, stands a statue of BENJAMIN FRANKLIN, printer, writer, scientist, statesman and signatory of the Declaration of Independence. From 1729 Franklin was editor of the *Pennsylvania Gazette*. Between 1732 and 1757 he published *Poor Richard's Almanack*.

PARK ROW, FORMERLY "NEWSPAPER ROW"

This area was the center of journalism during the second half of the 19th century. The proximity of City Hall and of the theater district around Theater Alley, was ideal for the newspapers, which took advantage of the inexhaustible supply of scandal afforded by these establishments. Although some of the buildings are still standing, the newspapers and the theaters have moved uptown to the vicinity of Times Square.

PACE UNIVERSITY, FORMERLY THE NEW YORK TIMES BUILDING. 41 PARK ROW (1889, arch. George B. Post). This building, occupied by Pace University since 1952, has such sturdy foundations (to accommodate the printing presses) that it was able to bear the extra weight when the height of the building was raised in 1905. The *New York Times* moved in 1903 to offices on what became Times Square ▲ 255.

POTTER BUILDING. 38 PARK ROW (1883, arch. Nathan Starkweather). This replaced the NEW YORK WORLD BUILDING, which had been destroyed by a fire though it was said to be fireproof due to its terracotta construction. The ornamental treatment of the façade was a first for an office building. The *Daily News*, the *New York Press* and the *Daily Observer*

the morning and evening editions on the street with the familiar shout "Extra! Read all about it!". The office buildings had cavernous basements which housed heavy printing presses.

subsequently occupied this building in turn.

THE FORMER AMERICAN TRACT SOCIETY BUILDING.
150 NASSAU ST. (1896, arch. R. H. Robertson). The COLONNADE on top is all that remains of a penthouse suite built on top of the sloping copper roof. It was demolished when the height of the TIMES BUILDING was raised, thereby blocking its view. Visit the semicircular lobby, with its original marble moldings and coffered ceiling. This building has some of the last manually operated elevators in New York.

The muse who now rules the press."
Anthony Trollope

ARK ROW BUILDING. 15 PARK ROW (1899, rch. R. H. Robertson). This building was the allest skyscraper in the world when it was opened, and s twin-domed crown used to dominate the skyline. The alconies thrusting away from the façade at intervals seem to e magically secured by magnets, and four stone goddesses atch over the entrance. Make sure to see the reception area nd the lobby, with its semicircular elevators. The lobby still as its original decoration: solid brass ramps, delicate marble im and a coffered ceiling.

OWARD THE SOUTH STREET SEAPORT

ITANIC MEMORIAL LIGHTHOUSE. FULTON ST., between PEARL nd WATER STS. This monument, erected in memory of those ho went down with the *Titanic*, once sat on top of the eamen's Church Institute Building (on State Street). The *itanic* Memorial Lighthouse was moved to this site in 1976 nd marks the entrance to South Street Seaport. Its clock is ighly original: every day, at noon exactly, a black ball slides own from the top of a post.

ECK SLIP ★. PECK SLIP at FRONT ST. n the 18th century this eighborhood boasted any Federal-style ouses belonging to e élite. In 1973 the on Edison company emolished several locks to build a sub-tation, despite the ngry protests of esidents. Its wall s decorated with trompe l'oeil ainting by Richard laas, which depicts he demolished site, he arches of the outh Street Viaduct nd the Brooklyn Bridge ▲ 186.

DRAFT RIOTS, JULY 11–13, 1863
During the Civil War (1861–5) New York was hit by three days of violent rioting. The Draft Riots erupted in protest against the first draft list from Abraham Lincoln's Act of Conscription. The rioters converged on City Hall, also attacking certain newspapers, especially the *New York Tribune*, which "dared" to print the comment that "a negro is worth as much as an Irishman".

JOURNALISM AND LITERATURE
The press, which had been free from the beginning, tended to favor journalistic methods that appealed to a mass market. The Civil War (1861–5) confirmed this trend and, during the 19th century, many writers who published their work in the newspapers gave rise to a type of journalism that appropriated the techniques of literature.

Park Row Building in construction (left) and in 1917 (below).

Since 1967
the South Street Seaport
Historic District, which
covers eleven blocks in Lower
Manhattan and extends along three piers on the
East River, has managed to preserve some of the
last buildings to house shipowners' and merchants'
offices during the golden age of the clipper ships.
Schermerhorn Row, built in 1811 (opposite), was
preserved in this way. The old Fulton Ferry
Hotel, which faces the river,
dates back to the 1860's.
South of the block, the
A. A. Low warehouse
(1850) still stands.

Lettie G. Howard

Pioneer

Peking

Wavertree

A fleet of historic ships evokes the hustle
and bustle of this neighborhood during the
19th century, when the long booms virtually
touched the façades of the buildings – and
when oysters (left) were cheap.

PIER 15, PIER 16

Along pier 15 (above right) lies the *Wavertree*, built in England in 1885. In the center is the *Peking* (made in Germany in 1911); to the left of Pier 16 is the *Ambrose* (1907), a bright red lightship serving at the entrance to the Ambrose Channel, excavated in 1899, which enabled New York Harbor to accommodate the giant transatlantic liners of the 20th century.

Behind the poop of the *Peking* are the *Pioneer*, the *Andrew Fletcher*, which offers excursions around the harbor in the summer, and the *Lettie G. Howard*, a fishing schooner of 1893 (moored between the prows of the two square-rigged schooners).

FULTON FERRY HOTEL

This establishment's varied clientele included captains of trading vessels, farmers with produce to sell at the local markets, traders and businessmen.

A. LOW WAREHOUSE

The warehouse, designed by A. A. Low in 1875, a clipper owner and merchant involved in the China trade, houses an exhibit of maritime artifacts.

SOUTH STREET SEAPORT MUSEUM
★ BOAT BUILDING SHOP ★

173

During the 19th century New York was the scene of several of the greatest technological advances in shipbuilding which had been made possible by the industrial revolution. It was in New York in 1807 that Robert Fulton built the first profit-making steamboat; in 1814 he designed and launched the first steam battleship.

SHIPBUILDING IN NEW YORK
During the era of steel shipbuilding, New York's shipyards, in Brooklyn (above, in 1883) launched several of the country's great warships, including the *Maine* (above, left), whose sinking in Havana harbor in 1898 was one of the main causes of the Spanish-American War.

THE "MONITOR"
Built in 1862 by the Swedish engineer John Ericsson, the *Monitor* was the first battleship in the world to have its cannons housed in an armor-plated turret. Here it is shown in battle with the Confederacy's own ironclad, the *Virginia*.

The New York shipyards, which are located in Brooklyn, Staten Island and on the Jersey shore, still do a lively business repairing and refitting all types of ships including the ocean liners, small tugs and barges that use the harbor.

WELCOME
South Street Seaport Museum
INFORMATION

Seafaring paraphernalia in local shop window (left) and fish signboard (right).

FULTON FISH MARKET
This original market (for produce) opened in 1821; eventually benefiting from the busy harbor activity, it became the city's wholesale fish market.

THE FISH MARKET
The flat-roofed Fulton Fish Market is located right on the East River front. The fish are no longer delivered by fishing boats; they arrive at night in refrigerated trucks from all over the country. Fish is on sale from midnight until 9am.

NEW YORK CENTRAL NO. 31
The pilothouse on exhibit on Pier 13 at the South Street Seaport Museum was taken from a steam tug boat built in 1923.

Oysters and clams are two of New York's natural resources and for a long time were a local tradition in the city. Here and there you can still find "oyster bars" ▲ 238, where you can savor the famous Manhattan clam chowder.

South Street Seaport's two oldest restaurants are on Schermerhorn Row; Sloppy Louie's (early 1900's) is opposite on South St., and Sweet's Restaurant (mid-19th century) is in the old Fulton Ferry Hotel.

SOUTH STREET SEAPORT MUSEUM AND HISTORIC DISTRICT
The historic district covers eleven blocks between Pier 17 and Water, John and Beekman streets. The museum holds temporary and permanent exhibitions in various buildings as well on the old ships. Below, the A. A. Low warehouse, at 171 John Street.

An exhibition of model ships (above) in the Fish Market.

The huge cathedral of commerce that is Woolworth Building along with Saint Paul's Chapel, which in 1776 marked the city's northernmost boundary, are both situated to the west of the Civic Center. Another local landmark is the former AT&T Building.

FORMER AT&T BUILDING ★. 195 BROADWAY (1915–22, arch. William Welles Bosworth). This building conveys a feeling of strength. The huge Doric columns, 40 feet high, with their purity of line, are echoed by those in the lobby (below, left). One element strikes a false note with the classical Greek decoration: the vertical joins of the columns reveal that the stone is merely a cladding. Against the lobby's west wall a monument to the glory of communication trumpets the vocation of the building's previous occupant, AT&T: "Service to the Nation in peace and war". The lobby also boasts a statue of *Adonis*. Another sculpture, by E. B. LONGMAN, was erected on the roof of the building. This statue, called *Spirit of Communication*, or more affectionately *Golden Boy*, was moved in 1984 to the lobby of the new AT&T building at 550 Madison Avenue ▲ *289.* When Sony bought the building in 1993, the statue left Manhattan for its new home in New Jersey.

ST. PAUL'S CHAPEL ★

St. Paul's Chapel, at the intersection of Broadway and Fulton streets, is a part of Trinity parish. Having miraculously escaped unscathed from the many fires that

TELECOMMUNICATIONS
For just over a century, AT&T provided virtually all the telephone services in the United States. In 1981, the company had more than one million employees, an annual turnover of 60 billion dollars and more than three million shareholders. An AT&T investment was the archetypal gilt-edged investment; in other words, it was completely risk-free. In 1982, the company lost its monopoly and was forced to part with its Bell subsidiaries. Since then, AT&T has restructured several times in response to the continuing deregulation of the US telecom industry.

> "A black moonless night; Jimmy Herf is walking alone up South Street. Behind the wharfhouses ships raise shadowy skeletons against the night."
>
> John Dos Passos

evastated most of Lower Manhattan ● *38*, his building is the only monument in the neighborhood predating the American Revolution. Completed in 1766, it is the oldest church in New York. The building, designed by Thomas McBean, was constructed of regular-sized blocks of Manhattan schist. It resembles St. Martin's-in-the-Fields, in London, whose architect, James Gibbs, taught McBean. Entry to St. Paul's used to be through the churchyard on Church Street. Above the present-day entrance, on Broadway, there is a NICHE containing a statue of St. Paul armed with a sword. Just below, in the middle of the porch, there is the tomb and monument of Brigadier General Richard Montgomery, who died in 1775 during the American Revolution at the battle of Quebec. The interior, painted in pastel colors, is graced by a barrel vaulted ceiling and an exquisite organ loft. The church service following George Washington's inauguration as President, on April 30, 1789, was held here. His PEW, as well as that of New York State's first governor, De Witt Clinton, can still be seen. The church and churchyard had to be cleaned and restored following the collapse of the nearby Twin Towers in 2001. For eight months, teams of firefighters and volunteers clearing the site would come to this peaceful spot to take a well-earned break. Free concerts are given in the chapel twice a week at noon.

WEST OF BROADWAY

NEW YORK COUNTY LAWYERS' ASSOCIATION.
14 VESEY ST. (1930, arch. Cass Gilbert). This austere neo-Georgian building ● *82*, constructed of Vermont marble and limestone, was designed by the

GEORGE WASHINGTON IN ST. PAUL'S CHAPEL. Above George Washington's pew hangs the first oil painting of the Great Seal of the United States, designed in 1789, shortly after the election of the first president. George Washington's regimental flag is displayed at the rear of the nave.

Saint Paul's Chapel (center), a painting (1940) by Saul Berman.

THE CHURCHYARD OF ST. PAUL'S CHAPEL This churchyard is an astonishing oasis of peace with its trees and squirrels, and employees from the Financial District and tourists come here to unwind. Most of the

tombstones date back to the 18th century. The churchyard has a timeless atmosphere that presents a striking contrast with the surrounding neighborhood.

Façade of the Federal Office Building.

architect of the WOOLWORTH BUILDING ▲ *180*, the CUSTOM HOUSE ▲ *157* and the U.S. COURTHOUSE. It is the headquarters of the New York County Lawyers' Association and has been dubbed "the house of law". The retrospective style of this building, designed for a conservative body concerned with projecting a traditional image, made it conspicuous at a time when architecture in the United States was going through a more bold, forward-looking phase. Its large auditorium (which is open to the public on request) is modeled on the main hall of Philadelphia's Independence Hall.

FORMER GARRISON BUILDING. 20 VESEY ST. (1906, arch. Robert D. Kohn, sculptor Gutzon Borglum). At one time, this building housed the *New York Evening Post*. In 1801 Alexander Hamilton, who is buried not far from here in Trinity churchyard, founded the newspaper which is now published as the *New York Post*, but was then a mouthpiece for conservative Federalist opinions. Later, another famous writer, William Cullen Bryant, who edited the *Post* from 1829 to 1878, gradually moved it toward a more working-class ethic. The building's façade is structured by limestone piers which rise in unbroken lines to the fine curb roof. The side walls were left plain, as future plans included other buildings on either side. Cross to the opposite side of the street to admire the ornamental Art Nouveau sculptures on top of the building, allegorical figures representing the "Four Periods of Publicity". They are the joint work of Estelle Rumbald Kohn (the architect's wife) and Gutzon Borglum. The latter also created the famous NATIONAL MEMORIAL in South Dakota where the gigantic heads of Presidents WASHINGTON, JEFFERSON, LINCOLN and ROOSEVELT are carved into the side of Mount Rushmore.

FEDERAL OFFICE BUILDING & U.S. POST OFFICE. 90 CHURCH ST. (1935, arch. Cross & Cross, Pennington Lewis & Mills Inc., Lewis A. Simon). There is no doubt that this building, complete with majestic eagles and occupying the entire block, is the property of the federal government, even if the main entrance, rather than being a triumphal focus of attention, is minimized by the sides of the building. The architects of this building combined architectural forms with alternating vertical and horizontal lines: the stocky twin towers rise from a setback which sits above a sturdy neo-classical temple, an attempt to marry the characteristic verticality of New York with the horizontality of Washington. Enter the building on Church Street to discover one of the finest post office interiors in the city, with its intricately worked grilles and monumental black Doric columns echoing the ones on the façade. Be sure to make a detour to see the stunning Art Deco stained glass windows and the inlaid work of the floor and ceiling – from which light is diffused through square panels, creating the effect of coffering. The building also boasts a magnificent lobby.

ST. PETER'S CHURCH. 16 BARCLAY ST. (1838, arch. John R. Haggerty and Thomas Thomas). This church was built on the site of an earlier St. Peter's Church, erected in 1785, the year after a ban on Roman Catholicism in New York was lifted. This was the parish church of the first Black American saint, Pierre Toussaint, whose ashes now lie in a crypt in St. Patrick's Cathedral on 5th Avenue ▲ *283*.

The eagle that adorns the entrances and façades of many New York buildings became the emblem of the United States on June 20, 1782. After six years of deliberation, Congress adopted the bald eagle, an American species with a dark body and white head and tail, as the central figure of the republic's Great Seal. A symbol of power and independence, suitable for the new nation's self-image, the eagle quickly became a very popular motif. From the American Revolution to the Civil War, scarcely any kind of everyday object escaped eventually being decorated with an eagle. Initially it was portrayed with a long neck and rather frog-like feet, following the style of English heraldry, but around the beginning of the 19th century, it began to reflect the influence of neo-classicism, inspired by ancient Greece and Rome. In the 20th century it has undergone another transformation, its characteristics being severely stylized (left) in the Art Deco style.

A RECORD TO BEAT
With its 60 stories and a height of 792 feet, this was the world's tallest building – 92 feet taller than the Metropolitan Life Tower. It was relegated to third place by the Chrysler Building ▲ *266* and 40 Wall St. in 1929.

In 1909 Frank Woolworth, the "king" of two hundred five-and-ten-cent stores, embarked on the creation of a headquarters for the company which had made him a household name. He bought a plot of land on Broadway. Cass Gilbert, the epitome of the eclectic architect, urged his client to build the tallest building in the world. The foundations of this "cathedral of commerce" were laid in August 1911 and work proceeded at the rate of one and a half stories a week. Woolworth paid for his skyscraper in cash: $15.5 million.

SIGNED IN STONE
The sort of humor sometimes found in cathedral carvings can be seen in the building's sculptures: one of the consoles (left) depicts Frank Woolworth counting the nickels and dimes that made his fortune.

THE "EIGHTH WONDER OF THE WORLD"
The official opening of the building took place in April 1913 with a gala for 800 people, during which President Woodrow Wilson turned on the building's lights from the White House.

A COPPER PINNACLE ON TOP OF A "TERRACOTTA" CATHEDRAL

Influenced by his travels in Europe, Woolworth insisted that his architect employ a Gothic style ● 86, reminiscent of French cathedrals and of London's Houses of Parliament.

Labor

THE LOBBY

The lobby, with entrances on Broadway, Barclay St. and Park Place, is a vast shopping arcade in the shape of a Latin cross. The walls are sheathed in marble and the vaulted ceilings in mosaics of Byzantine inspiration (above), which extol the virtues of labor and commerce. The Woolworth Building was one of the first buildings to provide direct access to the subway.

At the beginning of the 19th century, a new wave of immigrants in search of cheap housing settled on the intersection of Baxter, Park and Worth streets. This small triangular park, which was the setting for all kinds of entertainment, soon came to be called "Paradise Park". During the 1820's, the neighborhood began to deteriorate, becoming the haunt of gangsters and prostitutes. In 1845 the Five Points Mission (above) was set up.

Most of the buildings of the Civic Center can be found to the north of the City Hall. They represent a host of architectural styles, their construction having spanned more than a century. Some of them were built in neo-classical styles inspired by Greco-Roman democratic tradition, frequently favored in the United States for government buildings. Architects and their clients, however, who were keen to build higher, often used the model of neo-classical temples as bases on which to erect loftier structures. As the 20th century progressed, New York, whose architecture had been influenced previously by London, then Paris, began to create its own distinctive style.

FOLEY SQUARE

This square occupies the site of what was once COLLECT POND ● *74*, which had disappeared by 1811. Before Independence, a gallows stood on the island in the center. In 1854 the FIVE POINTS MISSION was founded in this section of New York to help the poor in the nearby slums of Five Points ● *191*, who were being decimated by cholera. Thomas Foley (1852–1923), whose name was given to the square in 1926, had run a bar in the neighborhood before going into politics: he became alderman and sheriff of the County of New York and played a key role in getting Al Smith elected governor. Foley used to say that he enjoyed being involved in political intrigue for its own sake. He attributed his success to the fact that he always told the truth, adding: "People don't like it, but they come back six months later."

MUNICIPAL BUILDING ★. 1 CENTRE ST. AT 4 CHAMBERS ST. (1914, arch. McKim, Mead & White) ● *96*. When the Bronx, Queens, Brooklyn and Staten Island were linked to Manhattan in 1898 to create Greater New York, it was decided that new administrative offices were needed. This building, which looks like a square-shouldered giant guarding City Hall, made such an impression on Stalin that the University of Moscow was later modeled on it. The architects, who were searching for a style of administrative architecture that best symbolized America and the 20th century, were influenced by the *City Beautiful*

The Municipal Building (right).

movement which sprang up after the 1893 World's Columbian Exposition in Chicago and which focused on the creation of grand public buildings in elegantly landscaped parks. Their building consists of a fourteen-story u-shaped block crowned with a "Renaissance palace" rising from a monumental base with a neo-classical colonnade. The building is topped with three tiered drums, the bottom of which is flanked by four pinnacle turrets symbolizing the four boroughs joined to Manhattan. On the top stands a statue, *Civic Fame*, by Adolph A. Weinman. The building straddles Chambers Street with a central arch, through which vehicles crossing the Brooklyn Bridge ▲ *186* could formerly pass; thus the building became known as the "Gate of the City". A pedestrian walkway, over the bridge, starts here and is well worth following, as it affords an extraordinary view over Manhattan and leads to Brooklyn Heights ▲ *366*.

U.S. COURTHOUSE ★. 40 CENTRE ST. AT S. E. CORNER OF PEARL ST. (1936, arch. Cass Gilbert and Cass Gilbert, Jr) This was the last of Cass Gilbert's New York buildings. Here neo-classicism seems to be played out: a marble platform supports a CLASSICAL TEMPLE, pierced by a modern twenty four story tower with a gilded top. During the week, one can attend hearings in the various courtrooms. The basement houses a SHOOTING GALLERY for F.B.I. agents.

NEW YORK COUNTY COURTHOUSE. 60 CENTRE ST. (1926, arch. Guy Lowell). The New York County Courthouse is an imposing Corinthian temple approached by a monumental staircase. At the center this hexagon-shaped building is a domed circular area, which is linked to each of the six wings by corridors. Thirty years later, this layout was adapted by the architects of the Pentagon. The central area is decorated with fine murals and a polychrome marble floor inlaid with brass medallions representing the signs of the zodiac. Outside, statues entitled *Law, Truth and Equity* stand on the pediment of the main entrance.

NEW YORK CITY CRIMINAL COURT BUILDING, 100 CENTRE ST. BETWEEN WORTH AND LEONARD STS. (1939, arch. Harvey Wiley Corbett and Charles B. Meyers). This building once housed the men's prison. It was the third generation of municipal prisons: the esplanade opposite stands on the site of the two previous buildings. The first, dating from 1838, was built in the Egyptian Revival style, which gave the building its nickname of "The Tombs", a nickname also applied to its two successors. One of the most famous anecdotes relating to the original prison concerns John Colt. This man, sentenced to be hanged in 1842, was allowed to marry and enjoy an hour-long honeymoon. At the end of the allotted hour he was found dead, stabbed through the heart with a knife. A second, French Renaissance-style prison was built on the ruins of the first which was demolished in

"In New York, everyone is afraid of the burly Irish cop: he only has to blow on his whistle to commandeer vehicles or to obtain help from everyone. Like ambulances and fire engines, the police have right of way on the road and priority use of the telegraph system and the telephone. This peace force whose job is to send people to Sing-Sing", as described by Paul Morand in *New York*, was divided into specialist squads concentrating on areas such as robbery or bootlegging.

"THE TOMBS"
In *Ragtime*, a novel based on real characters which takes place in New York at the turn of the century, the writer E. L. Doctorow tells the story of a multi millionaire in a cell in "The Tombs". Above, the first, Egyptian-style prison.

183

Bas-reliefs from the Paine St. façade of the N.Y.C. Department of Health.

THE FIREHOUSES
When horses were first used to pull fire engines, they were kept in stables on the ground floor of firehouses (above, Engine Company no. 31). The men, who slept on the second floor, above, protested violently, so it was decided to move the stables to the back of the building. However, the firemen soon changed their mind about this because by the time they had harnessed up the horses to the vehicles, the fire had, in many cases, destroyed everything. Many horses who had spent their early working lives with the fire department found it very hard to retire to a more tranquil life as carriage horses: whenever they heard a fire engine's siren, they would gallop off, putting their new owner in grave danger.

1893. This in turn was destroyed in 1947. The third prison was moved to Rikers Island in 1974. The present Art Deco building houses the courts, a popular attraction for New Yorkers who can attend trials held here.

DEPARTMENTS OF HEALTH, HOSPITAL AND SANITATION.
125 WORTH ST. (1935, arch. Charles B. Meyers). This Art Deco ● *98* temple was built to celebrate the victory of medicine over cholera, smallpox and tuberculosis. Previously, the department had occupied run down premises, inadequate for the task of trying to control the health and hygiene of the city's 6 million inhabitants. Note the bas-reliefs depicting the medical sciences (above) and the splendid torchères (below, right) that grace the south and east entrances.

ENGINE COMPANY NO. 31. 87 LAFAYETTE ST. AT N. E. CORNER OF WHITE ST. (1895, arch. Napoleon Le Brun & Sons). The architect, who specialized in building firehouses, designed this building like a Loire Valley chateau, a style then very popular for the houses of the rich. Firemen used to live full-time in the firehouse. This building, which is no longer used for its original purpose, is now a designated landmark.

JACOB K. JAVITS FEDERAL BUILDING AND CUSTOMS COURTHOUSE.
26 FEDERAL PLAZA (1967, arch. Alfred Easton Poor, Kahn & Jacobs, Eggers & Higgins). This Inter-national Style ● *100* building is clad in a facing whose motifs are designed to disguise its massive frame. Every day long lines of hopeful citizenship candidates stretch back from the checkpoint.

CITY OF NEW YORK OFFICE BUILDING, FORMER EMIGRANT INDUSTRIAL SAVINGS BANK.
51 CHAMBERS ST. (1912, arch. Raymond F. Almirall). This precursor of the Municipal Building is a mixture of styles: its Renaissance Revival twin towers with Art Deco tops stand on a neo-classical base. It was once the headquarters of the Emigrant Savings Bank, founded in 1851 by the Irish to help their fellow countrymen who were living in the slums of Five Points ▲ *191*. In time it became one of the most powerful banks in the country. Enter

through the west door to admire the gilded elevator cages.

"Tweed Courthouse", Old New York County Courthouse. 52 Chambers St. (1858–78, arch. John Kellum, Leopold Eidlitz). The former New York County courthouse stands as a monument to the heights of corruption reached by William Marcy, Tammany Hall's "Boss" Tweed ● 40. Until his arrest in 1871, Boss Tweed pocketed huge amounts of city funds. A total of $14 million was eventually spent on the construction of this building, which was completed twenty years later and whose original cost had been estimated at $250,000. The municipal government then paid for an order – which was never delivered – of enough carpeting to cover City Hall Park three times over. The campaign led by George Jones, editor of *The New York Times*, and Thomas Nast, the cartoonist, finally led to Tweed's downfall. He was tried and sentenced, and died behind bars in 1878. The building, which was completed without the dome or marble facing originally planned, has a Central Rotunda (below).

Detail from the façade of the Emigrant Savings Bank.

Tweed Courthouse
The scandal surrounding the construction of the old New York Courthouse (below left) clearly demonstrates the type of methods that "Boss" Tweed stooped to as early as 1852 when he was an alderman. He would inflate costs on orders issued by the municipal government and pocket the difference. No one ever knew just how much Tweed and his ring embezzled.

Hall of Records, Surrogate's Court ★. 31 Chambers St. at n. w. corner of Centre St. (1899–1911, arch. John R. Thomas, Horgan & Slattery). This impressive building, which serves both as surrogate's court and as home for the New York city archives, was originally intended to serve as the Municipal Building, but in the event it was deemed too small for this purpose. Work on the building was stopped, only to be restarted to build the Hall of Records. The architect used the popular Beaux Arts style ● 92 to reproduce the affluence of the Paris Opera House.

Under the Hall of Records
This building occupies, in part, the site of an old cemetery for Blacks; recently discovered, it was designated a landmark. Several hundred bodies have been exhumed, some of them still wearing 18th-century British uniforms; the British offered freedom to slaves who fought on their side in the American Revolution.

The neo-Baroque rotunda (left) of the Hall of Records and Surrogate's Court, designed by John R. Thomas.

185

▲ Brooklyn Bridge

Ferryboats replaced by a bridge
In the mid-19th century, 50 million people a
year crossed the East River on the slow,
overcrowded ferryboats.

Manhattan, cut off from the mainland by a wide estuary and a
great river, the Hudson, needed bridges if it was to grow; but it
took many years before engineers
were able to construct bridges of
the required length. The oldest is
the Brooklyn Bridge, completed
in 1883.

Granite from Hallowell, Maine
The granite used on this bridge was the
same as the one used in the Tombs prison
and for the reservoir in Central Park.

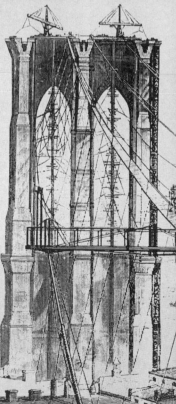

A STEEL AND GRANITE MONSTER
This was the longest, highest bridge of
the 19th century, with its two granite
towers and its steel cables and its metal
roadway with a span of 1,595 feet,
towering 148 feet above the water.

A DIZZY TRIP OVER THE EAST RIVER ✪
Crossing the bridge,
120 feet above
the East River, on
the pedestrian
footbridge that
overhangs the road
is an unforgettable
experience.
The view of the
skyscrapers from
the footbridge is
stunning. To avoid
making the trip
both there and
back on foot, and to
enjoy the best view,
take the subway, line
A or C, go down to
High Street at
Brooklyn and return
on the footbridge in
the direction of
Manhattan. Allow
1 to 2 hours.

GIANT CABLES
In 1867 the State of
New York authorized
the construction
of the suspension
bridge in line with
plans drawn up
by John
Roebling
(1806–69),
who arrived
from
Germany
in 1831.

k 14 years to build and
$16 million, exceeding
all expectations.

A FAMILY OF ENGINEERS
Due to an accident at
work, Roebling developed
tetanus and died in 1869. His son
Washington took over but was disabled

The Manhattan
skyline seen
from Brooklyn,
before
September 11,
2001.

by "caisson disease"; Washington's
wife, Emily, then became a
liaison between Washington
and the crew.

The New Harlem Bridge over the Harlem River (here in 1868) linked Harlem and the Bronx.

STATISTICS OF SOME NEW YORK BRIDGES
(1) Brooklyn: span 1,595 feet
(2) Manhattan: span 1,470 feet
(3) Williamsburg: span 1,600 feet
(4) Queensboro: max. span 1,182 feet
(5) Verrazano: span 4,260 feet
(6) George Washington: span 3,500 feet

THE BRIDGES OF MANHATTAN

For twenty years the Brooklyn Bridge remained the only link (apart from ferries) between Manhattan and Long Island, which – along with its beauty and virtuoso engineering – accounted for its popularity. Then, in the first decade of the 20th century, to satisfy the demands of a growing city, three other bridges were built over the East River.

ACROSS THE EAST RIVER. These were the Williamsburg Bridge in 1903, followed by the Queensboro bridge (commonly called the 59th Street Bridge) in 1909, and the Manhattan Bridge, in

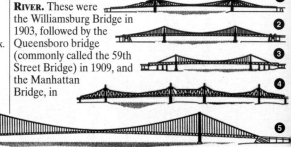

1912. At the same time, the railroad and subway companies began to dig tunnels under the East River. In the 1930's, despite the Depression, a fifth bridge was built: the Triborough Bridge, a three-pronged bridge connecting the Bronx and Queens to Manhattan.

ACROSS THE HUDSON. The George Washington Bridge, designed by Othmar Ammann and completed in 1931, remains the city's only bridge over the Hudson River. It is a suspension bridge, linking Manhattan, at 178th Street, to Fort Lee in New Jersey. Its span is over 3,500 feet – twice as long as that of the Brooklyn Bridge. This was the first major project to be completed by the Port of New York Authority, an interstate body created in 1921 to coordinate transportation in the metropolitan region. Although originally conceived as a railroad bridge, it was finally designed for motor traffic; a lower level was added in 1962.

WILLIAMSBURG BRIDGE
The Brooklyn Bridge (1883), then the Williamsburg Bridge (1903, shown right) made it much easier for wealthy New Yorkers, who in the early years of the 20th century had elected Brooklyn as the place to live, to travel to their offices in Manhattan every day.

ACROSS THE NARROWS. At one time the longest suspension bridge in the world, the Verrazano-Narrows Bridge (1964) spans the strait dividing Brooklyn from Staten Island at the mouth of the Upper Bay. This bridge, also designed by Ammann, has a span of 4,260 feet and a total length of 13,700 feet. In addition to its practical value in easing traffic congestion in Manhattan by providing a direct route from New Jersey to Long Island and its airports, the bridge serves as a spectacular gateway to the city.

Lower East Side

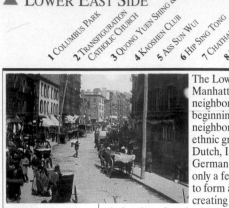

"THE BIG ONION"
During the 1870's, the Lower East Side was called "The Big Onion". Although at the time this was a pejorative term, it has now acquired a new significance. In a sense, this neighborhood does resemble an onion: every time a layer is peeled away, there is another underneath, each representing a part of the neighborhood or another ethnic group.

The Lower East Side is one of Manhattan's liveliest, most historical neighborhoods. From the city's very beginnings this has been an immigrant neighborhood. An astonishing variety of ethnic groups have chosen to live here: Dutch, Irish, Jewish, Italian, Chinese, German and Latin American, to mention only a few. Each of these groups has tried to form a self-sufficient community, creating its own social organizations as a bulwark against the demands of city life. These mutual aid institutions have played a vital role in finding work and accommodation for new immigrants and introducing them to the ways of the "New World". Religious and ethnic subgroups were formed within each community, so that there were organizations not simply for Jews, but for Russian Jews, Romanian Jews and Hungarian Jews, for example. Similarly Italian immigrants settled on the Lower East Side not as Italians but as Neapolitans, Sicilians and Milanese. This continual influx of immigrants also imported its share of marvelous national recipes – some of the best and cheapest restaurants in New York can be found on the Lower East Side.

CHINATOWN ✪

COLUMBUS PARK. BAYARD AND MULBERRY (1892) was originally a patch of cultivated land belonging to the Bayard family, at the corner of Bayard Street and Mulberry Street. In the 19th century, the curved part of Mulberry Street was known as Mulberry Bend. This street led to Five Points, deep in the heart of the Sixth District, called by many

CHINATOWN, AN ASIAN JOURNEY ✪
This neighborhood is a labyrinth of vibrant streets teeming with life. Allow at least 4 hours to explore the area, starting with Doyers, Mott and Pell streets in Old Chinatown, where the street signs are still written in Chinese characters. The small Museum of Chinese in the Americas and the sprawling Pearl River bazaar on Canal Street are both musts. And, obviously, you should not leave Chinatown without a meal in one of the many restaurants that serve superb food.

Four hours

◆ B C3-D3-D4

MUSEUM OF CHINESE IN THE AMERICAS
The Chinatown history museum occupies one floor of the public school on the corner of Bayard and Mulberry sts. It contains a collection of documents and personal letters written by the local inhabitants.

people the "Bloody old Sixth". This was the worst slum area in the history of New York. Until the mid-19th century, it was predominantly Irish; then Italians flocked here in search of cheap accommodation, cramming themselves into tiny apartments and living on top of each other, sometimes twelve or more to a room. In 1892 the slums of Five Points were demolished and replaced by Columbus Park. Almost as soon as it was built the park became a favorite site for open-air concerts and patriotic ceremonies. On Columbus Day and other public holidays, local musicians would gather in the park to play Italian melodies; street peddlers sold refreshments and the festive mood was heightened by fireworks displays.

CHURCH OF THE TRANSFIGURATION. 25 MOTT ST. This Georgian-style church, built in 1801 by the community of the First Episcopal Church of Zion, has seen some extraordinary changes. In 1853, the Catholic Church bought the building for its thriving Italian and Irish communities. Then, in the 1950's, an increasing number of Chinese joined the parish, which is now almost exclusively Chinese. Under the times of services posted at the entrance to the church, there is a notice explaining that Mass is celebrated in Mandarin, Cantonese and English.

QUONG YEUN SHING & CO. 32 MOTT ST. This store is opposite the Church of the Transfiguration. It was founded in 1877 by the Lee family and is the oldest store in Chinatown. This establishment started life as a grocery store, which doubled variously as a post office, a social center, a message service and a bank. It still has its original interior and façade and is a remnant of old Chinatown.

KAOSHEN CLUB. 12 MOTT ST. The headquarters of a secret political organization used to be based in this building (Kaoshen means "high mountain"). In 1895, Doctor Sun Yat-sen (founder and first president of the Republic of China) set

GREETINGS FROM

up the New York branch of the secret revolutionary party Hsing Chung Hui in this building. This party brought about the demise of the Ch'ing imperial dynasty and established a republican government in China.

SUN WEI ASSOCIATION. 24 PELL ST. The exterior of this building offers an interesting example of Chinese symbolism. It is topped with an intricately carved wood pagoda, decorated with two carved fish representing financial profit. The association's colors are red, gold and green. Red symbolizes luck, gold symbolizes wealth and green symbolize success in business.

HIP SING TONG. 16 PELL ST. This was one of the fraternal Chinese organizations, whose name, "tong", originally meant "hall" or "meeting place". Membership of these societies is shrouded in mystery and their money-making "activities" are

THE STREETS OF CHINATOWN
In the 19th century Doyers St. and Pell St. (above, in 1927) were dotted with Irish bars. A Chinese restaurant, Pell's Dinty (at 25 Pell St.) retains the name of the previous establishment. The Chinatown post office now occupies the site where one of the most popular bars of the time, Callahan's, used to stand. These bars used to employ scantily dressed waitresses and singers to draw in customers. Al Jolson and Irving Berlin were two very popular performers who used to work in Callahan's.

requently the subject of controversy. The tongs were secret raternal societies created in China several hundred years ago and known then as "Triads". They were established in New York at the end of the 1870's to protect their members' nterests. Over the years some tongs became involved in criminal activities including drug trafficking, embezzlement, prostitution, gambling and usury. However, today most tongs remain social organizations, helping new immigrants to find accommodation and employment

CHATHAM SQUARE. CORNER PARK ROW, BOWERY and EAST BROADWAY. This part of the city, which has been a prosperous center for trade since 1800, owes its name to the first Earl of Chatham, William Pitt the Elder. Lord & Taylor and Brooks Brothers opened their first clothing stores here. The arch in the center of the square was erected in 1962 as a memorial to Benjamin Ralph Kim Lau, a resident of Chinatown who died during World War Two, and to all the other Chinese soldiers who served under the American flag during the war. It is also sometimes called Kim Lau Square.

FIRST SHEARITH ISRAEL GRAVEYARD. 55 ST. JAMES PLACE. Half a block from Chatham Square, the first graveyard of the Spanish and Portuguese synagogue Shearith Israel, runs the length of St. James Place. This site, designated a "National Historic Landmark" and a "New York City Landmark" dates back to 1682. It is the oldest Jewish cemetery in the United States and one of the oldest cemeteries in New York.

ST. JAMES CHURCH. 132 JAMES ST. (1837). Although the parish was created in 1827 by Irish immigrants, St. James Church, now designated a "New York City Landmark", was not built until 1837. As can be seen from the plaque to the right of the entrance, its first pastor was Father Felix Valera (1788–1853), who was born in Cuba. To the left of the entrance, another plaque commemorates the formation, in 1836, of the Ancient Order of Hibernians, Hibernia being the Latin name for Ireland. The A.O.H. helped Irish immigrants to find work and gave them legal and occasional financial aid, as required.

MARINERS' TEMPLE. 12 OLIVER ST. (1842, arch. Minard Lafever). This Ionic-order, Greek Revival church was built by a Baptist congregation to serve the spiritual

DOYERS STREET
At the end of the 18th century this street served as a cart lane for a distiller, Anthony H. Doyer. A hundred years later, the bend half way down Doyers St. was nicknamed "Bloody Angle" during a "tong war" which raged in Chinatown at the time. The Hip Sing and the On Leong used to battle here for control of local criminal activities.

NATOWN, NEW YORK

needs of mariners, a purpose commemorated by the huge ship bell to the right of the porch. A similar function was served by the SEA AND LAND CHURCH (61 Henry Street), renamed the First Chinese Presbyterian in 1866. Today the Mariners' Temple belongs to a Black Baptist Congregation and boasts an excellent gospel choir.

BROAD AVENUES
At the end of the 19th
century, the Bowery
(right), which in the
17th century led to
Dutch farmland, was
populated by the
homeless, and
the neighborhood
also had a high
concentration of bars
dealing in all kinds of
illegal activities. In
1884, 27 percent of
arrests in New York
were made in the
Bowery. That year,
the neighborhood
numbered 82 bars, an
average of six per
block.

**THE EDUCATIONAL
ALLIANCE**
The Educational
Alliance, on the
southeast corner of
East Broadway and
Jefferson St., was
founded in 1891 by
German Jews from
Uptown to help
Eastern European
immigrants adjust to
the American way of
life. It offered lessons
in English, civics and
health education.

THE JEWISH NEIGHBORHOOD

ELDRIDGE STREET SYNAGOGUE. 12–16 ELDRIDGE ST. (1886,
arch. Herter Brothers). This Moorish-style building was built
by Russian-Polish Jews. It is open to the public; guided tours
take place on Sunday, Tuesday and Thursday. The façade has
a rose window similar to those found on some churches, but
the interior is a classic Orthodox synagogue, with women's
galleries and an ark for holding the Torah scrolls.
FORMER JARMULOWSKY BANK. Southwest corner of CANAL
and ORCHARD STS. (1912). This eleven-story building was built
by Sender Jarmulowsky, who arrived in America in 1856 from
Poland and opened his bank in 1873. His customers were
mainly Jewish immigrants who were sending money back to
the Old World to help their families to cross the Atlantic. By
1913 the bank was doing well, a state of affairs that continued
until the outbreak of World War One, when a large number
of the bank's customers withdrew their money.
Because they did not trust paper money, they
demanded gold and silver coins. There was
such a rush on the counters that the federal
controller shut the Jarmulowsky bank on
August 4, 1914.
LOWER EAST SIDE TENEMENT MUSEUM.
90 ORCHARD ST. This museum is housed
within a former tenement building, whose
many rooms were once filled to bursting with
immigrant families. The building, which dates
from 1863, is now listed as a landmark.
Several of the apartments have been
decorated to reflect the different periods
in its history and to give an idea of the
immigrants' living conditions.
GARDEN CAFETERIA. Corner of EAST
BROADWAY and RUTGERS ST. The Wing
Shoon Restaurant stands on the site
once occupied by the Garden
Cafeteria, a famous rendezvous
of the local intelligentsia. Some
of the most eminent socialists,
communists and anarchists used to meet
here for a cup of tea. Among them were

> "Not to have seen those hucksters and their carts, and their merchandise, and their extraordinary zest for bargaining is to have missed a sight that once seen declines to be forgotten."

Harper's Weekly

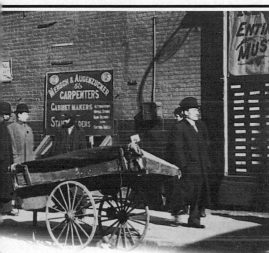

the Russian anarchists Emma Goldman, Alexander Berkman, Leon Trotsky, and Nikolay Bukharin. Isaac Bashevis Singer is said to have written many of his books at the Garden Cafeteria.

FORWARD BUILDING. 175 EAST BROADWAY (1912, arch. George A. Boehm). The former Forward Building stands southeast of Nathan Straus Square. The Jewish community still regards this apartment building, with its huge clock and the Yiddish word "Forverts" carved into the stone at the top, as a symbol of the power of socialism and the workers. Until 1975 it was the headquarters of the Jewish *Daily Forward*, once one of the major socialist Yiddish publications in the world. The building now houses a church and a Bible-making works, the New York Ling Liang Church. On the west façade of the building a Mandarin slogan that translates, "Through Christ you will find salvation" highlights the changes that have taken place in the neighborhood's ethnic make-up.

GUSS'S PICKLES Essex St. is the heart of the old Jewish business district. The famous Guss's Pickles can be found at no. 35. On Sundays New Yorkers come to buy his famous gherkins at 25 cents apiece, a good deal more than the 5 cents they once used to cost.

SEWARD PARK. Corner of EAST BROADWAY and ESSEX ST. This park, which dates from 1901, was designed to provide an open space in New York's most densely populated neighborhood. One of the memorable moments in the history of

Seward Park occurred during the Cloakmakers' Strike in 1910. About sixty thousand striking workers from many different trades thronged the corner of East Broadway and Essex, opposite the Forward Building. This was also where immigrant workers used to congregate with their signs in Yiddish, Italian and English, calling for better pay and work conditions.

BETH HAMEDRASH HAGODOL SYNAGOGUE. 60 NORFOLK ST. This is the synagogue of the oldest Orthodox Ashkenazic community in the United States. It was founded in 1852 and used to be situated on Allen Street. The Ashkenazic community bought the building, originally the Norfolk Baptist Church, in 1885. The synagogue, open to the public during daily prayers, has retained the fine Gothic interior of the original Baptist church.

AT THE MARKET Around 1910 hundreds of thousands of Jews lived in this neighborhood, many working as street vendors. Hester St. was the busiest, liveliest part of the Lower East Side, especially on Thursday evenings, when women came to buy provisions for the Sabbath.

Washday on Monday, c. 1900, in the tenements of Little Italy.

ITALIAN & AMERICAN RECORDS
MACARONI MACHINES ☆
RAVIOLI · MAKERS ITALIAN FLAGS
SPAGHETTI BOWLS ★
ITALIAN & ENGLISH COOK BOOKS

SICILIANS, MILANESE, NEAPOLITANS
The Italian stretch of Mulberry St. (also known as Via San Gennaro) is still lined with shops selling fresh pasta, freshly baked bread and cheese made on the premises (above, at the turn of the 20th century). The Caffè Roma is on this street. In the 1930's it was a haunt of Italian actors. Migliaccio, a popular performer of Neapolitan folk songs who appeared in theaters in the Bowery under the name of Farfariello (meaning "little butterfly"), lived nearby. His act consisted of making good-humored fun of the people living in the neighborhood.

LITTLE ITALY

BANCA STABILE. 189 GRAND ST. Corner of S.W. MULBERRY and GRAND STS. (1885). This building used to house an Italian bank, a family business founded in 1865 to help immigrant Italians. The Stabile offered various other services in addition to banking, including translation and steamship reservations. This can be seen from the gilt lettering above one of the counters, where tickets for transatlantic crossings could be bought. Note the tin ceilings, the terrazzo floor, the huge vault and the original brass grilles.

240 CENTRE STREET. (1909, arch. Hoppin, Koen & Huntington) This huge stone building in French-Baroque style was originally built for the New York police headquarters. At the time, this neighborhood was a hive of criminal activity. The headquarters were deliberately situated near the city's main prison, called "The Tombs" ▲ 183, itself not far from the insalubrious "Five Points" area ▲ 191. The building was converted into condominiums in the late 1980's.

MOST HOLY CRUCIFIX CHURCH. 378 BROOME ST. This Neapolitan Catholic church was consecrated in 1926. At that time, so the story goes, a group of Neapolitans had established a community in the neighborhood. When they wrote home, they told their families that they worshipped together, so their wives decided to dispatch a priest to New York from the village of their birth. The only land they could build on within a radius of three blocks was this plot, between Mott and Mulberry streets. The church was built extremely swiftly, so that when he arrived the priest would find a parish in which he could preach and hold services.

OLD SAINT PATRICK'S CATHEDRAL. CORNER OF MOTT AND PRINCE STS. (1809–15, arch. Joseph Mangin). This building was New York's first Catholic cathedral; constructed before the present St. Patrick's, which is Uptown on 5th Ave. A fire in 1868 destroyed much of the old cathedral, but it was rebuilt only as a parish church. The new cathedral at 50th St. and 5th Ave. was completed in 1879.

Around
Washington Square

▲ WASHINGTON SQUARE TO SOHO-TRIBECA

1 WASHINGTON SQUARE · 2 N.Y. UNIVERSITY · 3 ASCH BLDG · 4 E. HOLMES BOBST LIBRARY · 5 JUDSON MEMORIAL CHURCH · 6 MILLS HOUSE Nº 1 · 7 MACDOUGAL SULLIVAN GARDENS · 8 FORMER LITTLE SINGER BLDG · 9 FORMER HAUGHWOUT STORE · 10 FORMER ROOSEVELT BLDG · 11 100 6TH AVE.

⚔ Seven hours

◆ **B** B1-B2-C1-C2-D1-D2

A FORMER MILITARY PARADE GROUND
Washington Square sits on former marshland which was drained and converted into a military parade ground in 1826 (above, in 1851). When it was not an arena for military parades, it was used as a park where various entertainments were

staged. This park, which was dearly loved by New Yorkers, gave the neighborhood a new lease on life. When the park was redesigned in 1971, the central island, which sports a fountain and was once used by buses for turning around, was closed to traffic by the municipal government.

WASHINGTON SQUARE ★

This square has been the artistic and intellectual hub of Greenwich Village since the turn of the century. Until the end of the 18th century, it was simply a vast tract of marshland with a stream, the MINETTA BROOK ▲ 202, running through it. It was then converted into a potter's field, for the interment of victims of the great cholera and yellow fever epidemics. In the early 1800's it also served as the site of public hangings – events commemorated by the great elm that stands at the northwest corner of the park, which was used as a gallows. During his trip to New York in 1824, Lafayette was invited to watch the hanging of twenty highwaymen there. In 1826, when the streets were being laid and the surrounding lands were developed for sale as building lots, the municipal government drained the swamp and built the WASHINGTON MILITARY PARADE GROUNDS, which were inaugurated on July 4, 1828. The area around Washington Square soon became popular with wealthy New Yorkers, who built imposing residences around the park. Henry James, who was born in 1843 at 27 Washington Place, not far from the Square, immortalized this neighborhood in his novel *Washington Square*. The WASHINGTON ARCH, which has stood at the north of the park since 1895, perfectly encapsulates the main cultural trend of the time, which has

Washington Square (right) in the early 1900's.

12 FORMER N.Y. MERCANTILE EXCHANGE
13 HOUSE OF RELIEF, NEW YORK HOSPITAL
14 SCHEPP BLDG
15 DUANE PARK
16 WESTERN UNION BLDG
17 HIGH PRESSURE SERVICE HEADQUARTERS
18 CARY BLDG
19 CONDICT STORE
20 AT&T BLDG
21 THE CLOCKTOWER
22 JAMES BOGARDUS WAREHOUSE
23 DAVID BROWN STORE

been described as the "American Renaissance". The statues that grace its piers were added later; these are "Washington in War", by Hermon A. MacNeil (1916) and "Washington in Peace", by A. Stirling Calder (1918). The second half of the 19th century brought a fresh influx of European immigrants into Greenwich Village, a neighborhood lying west and south of Washington Square, which became a French and Italian enclave. At that time most of the houses were converted into apartments or replaced by tenements. Many artists chose to live in this part of the city, lured by its beauty and sense of history, while the gentry, who lived north of the square, gradually moved Uptown, deserting the district.

WASHINGTON ARCH
To commemorate the centenary of George Washington's inauguration ● *27*, on April 30, 1889, the architect Stanford White was commissioned to create a temporary wooden triumphal arch. It stood at the north of the park at the bottom of 5th Ave. and was garlanded with strings of lights. The arch was such a resounding success that the city arts council asked White to build another, this time in marble, modeled on those in Rome and Paris.

From the beginning of the 20th century this neighborhood was largely bohemian in atmosphere, attracting those who wanted to mix with avant-garde artists. The writers Eugene O'Neill, Edna St. Vincent Millay and Theodore Dreiser followed in the footsteps of their famous forebears, Edgar Allan Poe, Herman Melville, Mark Twain and Henry James. Painters, including the members of the Ashcan school ▲ *217*, set up their studios in some of the old houses. You have only to look upward when crossing certain streets to see the large skylights that crown these buildings. The former speakeasies, theaters, cafés and jazz clubs are still haunted by the memory of the celebrities who used to frequent them.

National Academy
of Design, opened
in 1826 ▲ *320*. Nine
years later he became
a lecturer in art at
N.Y.U., where he also
set up a laboratory
in its Main Building
for his scientific
experiments.
He patented his
telegraph system
in 1837.

**JUDSON MEMORIAL
CHURCH**
This church, which
is dominated by a
Romanesque-style
campanile, is
decorated with Italian
Renaissance motifs
adorned with
terracotta
moldings.

SOUTH VILLAGE

NEW YORK UNIVERSITY, MAIN BUILDING. 100 WASHINGTON
SQUARE EAST (1894–5, arch. Alfred Zucker). New York
University (N.Y.U.), founded in 1831 by ALBERT GALLATIN,
a member of Thomas Jefferson's cabinet, is the largest private
university in the United States. The MAIN BUILDING, at the
center of a campus which is spread throughout the Village,
occupies the site of the first university building, completed
in 1833. This building created a furor, as the administrators,
eager to cut costs, had employed convicts from Sing Sing
prison – a cost-free work force – on the building. Local
construction workers staged a union demonstration, one of
the first of its kind organized in New
York. When it degenerated into violence,
the "Stone Cutter's Guild Riot", as it
became known, had to be quelled by the

National Guard. This building is also famous for
occupants such as SAMUEL F. B. MORSE, the
inventor of the telegraph, and SAMUEL COLT,
the designer of the famous revolver. All that
remains of this building, destroyed in 1894,
is a turret on Washington Square East.
**THE BROWN BUILDING, FORMERLY THE
ASCH BUILDING.** 29 WASHINGTON PLACE.
In 1911 this manufacturing loft, later
converted into lecture halls for N.Y.U.,
was devastated by a fire that claimed 146
victims, all of them young women employed by the TRIANGLE
SHIRTWAIST CO., one of the "sweatshops" in the clothing
industry ● *38*. At the request of the *International Ladies'
Garment Workers' Union*, founded in 1900, a plaque was fixed
to the building to commemorate this tragedy.
ELMER HOLMES BOBST LIBRARY. 70 WASHINGTON
SQUARE SOUTH (1972, arch. Philip Johnson and
Richard Foster). This library, built for New York
University, owes its nickname of "Redskin" to its red
sandstone façade. The interior boasts a fine atrium
and a checkerboard floor of gray, white and black
marble based on one in the church of San
Giorgio Maggiore in Venice.
JUDSON MEMORIAL CHURCH. 55 WASHINGTON
SQUARE SOUTH (1888–93, arch. McKim, Mead &
White) ● *90*. This church was built in homage to
Adinoram Judson, the first American Baptist
missionary in Burma, and financed partly by
JOHN D. ROCKEFELLER ▲ *276*, who devoted some
of his fortune to the city's Baptist congregations.

Program cover for an Off-Broadway show in Greenwich Village.

HE "LATIN QUARTER". In the 1850's, "Frenchtown" was the nickname given to the area south of Washington Square inhabited by a community of French immigrants. However, most of the French families moved out of the neighborhood by 1875 because the many brothels and sleazy dance halls had cheapened the area. Toward the end of the 19th century, a new wave of Italian immigrants settled in the neighborhood. They opened cafés and restaurants next door to the French stores that were still in business and the sector was named the "Latin Quarter".

The neighborhood, which was very popular with intellectuals at the beginning of the 20th century, became a magnet for jazz musicians and, later, in the 1950's, for "beat generation poets". In the 1960's Bob Dylan and other folk singers transformed it into a center for folk music. It is still the place to go if you want to catch up-and-coming stars or linger over an espresso on a Sunday afternoon. Bleecker Street is lined with numerous picturesque bars: the Bitter End, the Peculiar Club, Kenny's Castaways and the Back Fence. On MacDougal

So this is Gay Paree... Come on along with me — we're stepping out to see the LATIN QUARTER

STREET you will find the Caffè Dante, the Caffè Reggio, opened in 1927, the Café Borgia and Le Figaro Café.

PROVINCETOWN PLAYHOUSE. 133 MACDOUGAL ST. The Provincetown Players, an improvisational theater company, made their debut in New York at no. 139 MacDougal Street before moving into this former stable (below). They were responsible for launching the young playwright Eugene O'Neill, by giving the first performance of his play *Bound East for Cardiff*, in 1916. The writer later received the Pulitzer Prize and became one of America's most celebrated playwrights. The company disbanded in 1930 but the theater was rebuilt around 1940 and is now part of New York University.

201

At the end of the 1850's the engineers James Bogardus and Daniel Badger produced the first sales catalogue of cast-iron architectural decorative pieces ● 84. The catalogue contained details of ready-made models, with understated ornamentation in the latest styles. It was

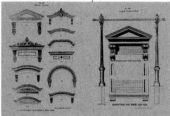

possible to buy a façade by the foot.

The clothes market on Spring St. (opposite).

RICHMOND HILL HOUSE
In 1831, the manor house on the Richmond Hill estate was converted into a theater (below in 1832). In 1849 it was destroyed to build offices and workshops to meet the needs of a neighborhood going through a period of intense commercial growth.

MINETTA STREET.
This street follows the erstwhile course of Minetta Brook, filled in around 1820, and was home to a large population of Blacks in the 18th century, hence its former nickname of "Little Africa". In the mid-19th century, the neighborhood deteriorated, becoming squalid and dangerous because of the brawls that regularly broke out there, especially at the time of the Draft Riots ● 28, ▲ 171, 212. The following decades saw the street gradually fill up with Italian, French and then German immigrants ● 44. Nearby, at 113 MacDougal Street, is the MINETTA TAVERN, a real "drinkers' museum", its walls covered with caricatures of Village personalities.

THE ATRIUM, FORMERLY MILLS HOUSE
No. 1. 160 BLEECKER ST. (1896, arch. Ernest Flagg). At the end of the 19th century, many tenements were built south of Washington Square. The architect Ernest Flagg, who was interested in this type of housing, designed this Renaissance-style building. It was made up of 1,500 units, arranged around a grassy courtyard. These rooms were mostl for newly arrived immigrants who could spend the night there for the modest sum of 20 cents. Subsequently, the courtyard was paved over, then covered, and the building became a shabby hotel, the Greenwich, before being converted into a private residence complete with ATRIUM in 1976.

MACDOUGAL-SULLIVAN GARDENS ★.
Designated a "Historic District", this neighborhood consists of twenty-four Greek Revival ● 84 houses built back-to-back on two streets. Its layout served as a model for similar housing plans in New York in the 1920's. By 1923 the houses were badly run-down. They were bought and renovated by property developer, William Sloane Coffin. He removed the entrance steps, standardized the façades, using a style influenced by colonial architecture, and gave each house its own garden opening onto a central walk.

CHARLTON-KING-VANDAM HISTORIC DISTRICT.
Between 6TH AVE. and VARICK ST. This historic enclave, which abuts on an industrial area, is a fine example of New York residential town planning in the last century. It boasts the longest unbroken row of Federal-style ● 82 townhouses in the city, dating from the 1820's, and a number of Greek Revival houses built between 1830 and 1850, the most eye-catching examples of which are nos. 37 and 39 Charlton Street and no. 203 Spring Street. This district occupies the former site of Richmond Hill, an estate of some 25 acres, whose Georgian manor house served as George

Joe Gould, a resident of MacDougal St. (above, in the 1950's) and of Minetta Tavern claimed to be writing an "oral history of the world" in order to earn money at meal times from the restaurant clientele. After his death in 1957 no manuscript was found, only a series of disconnected conversations.

Washington's headquarters in 1776 ● 27. The lands were subsequently bought by Aaron Burr ▲ 161, 228, who laid out the present network of roads in 1797 in order to divide up the estate into building lots. He unfortunately had to sell the estate to JOHN JACOB ASTOR ▲ 226, 313, who completed the task of parceling it out.

SoHo Cast-Iron Historic District ★

Around 1850, the area now called SoHo (a contraction of "South of Houston Street") was the major industrial and commercial center of New York. This historic district contains the highest concentration of cast-iron structures ● 94 in the United States, presenting an amazingly homogeneous urban landscape. These palaces of commerce were built for grocers, textile merchants and furniture store owners who, above all, needed vast interior spaces and attractive shop fronts. Initially, architects tried to give the cast iron the appearance of stone, by covering it with paint mixed with sand (the HAUGHWOUT BUILDING, of 1857 ▲ 204 is a typical example). Then, in the light of its success, they began to exploit the properties of cast iron, creating new motifs, including the slender colonnettes called "Sperm candles". This craze for the new material brought about a volte-face, and stone began to imitate the appearance of cast iron, as at 502 Broadway (A foolproof way of telling the difference is to use a magnet.) By the beginning of the 1960's, SoHo had lost its commercial importance, and many former warehouses and industrial premises stood empty – not unlike London's Covent Garden during the same period. Consequently, artists looking for large, bright, reasonably priced studios began to move in, and the area acquired a somewhat Bohemian atmosphere. A special artists' statute, responding to tenants' requirements, authorized the conversion of these buildings into studios and apartments. Little by little, the area began to attract a new, alternative kind of commerce – cutting-edge galleries, furniture stores and innovative young fashion designers, some of whom, like Palma, Jane Wilson-Marquis and Legacy, have been continuously in business since the late 1970's. Nowadays, SoHo is a vibrant, stylish neighborhood with

CAST IRON
The bolting process can be seen in the old and new façade of this factory in TriBeCa.

203

The red-brick building (right) that used to house the Guggenheim Museum of SoHo before it was converted into a store.

modern art galleries, some delightful restaurants and a number of luxury stores that have made this area the equal of Madison Avenue, south of Manhattan. Prada's flagship store, housed in the former annex of the Guggenheim Museum at 575 Broadway, is a sign of the renewed commercial interest in this neighborhood. This store, originally a warehouse with brick façades and cast-iron window frames (1881–2, arch. Thomas Stent, opposite), is worth a visit for the futuristic look of the building as much as the clothes. The vast space designed by Dutch architect Rem Koolhaas boasts many innovative features. The SoHo of the 1980's – full of galleries and artists' studios – has now been "malled".

RICHARD MORRIS HUNT
Richard Morris Hunt was the first American architect trained at the École des Beaux Arts and a founder of the American Institute of Architects. He represented a whole generation of architects inspired by the Old World. His work includes the Roosevelt Building (below) as well as mansions for the élite.

FORMER LITTLE SINGER BUILDING ★. 561–563 BROADWAY (1904, arch. Ernest Flagg). This L-shaped Art Nouveau building was designed for the famous sewing machine manufacturer. When Flagg designed a larger Singer Tower ▲ *152* in 1908, he called this one the "Little Singer". Flagg's aesthetic sense, developed at the École des Beaux Arts in Paris, can be seen in the building's prefabricated metal frame and interlaced floral motifs.

HAUGHWOUT BUILDING. 488–492 BROADWAY AT BROOME ST. (1856–7, arch. John P. Gaynor) ● *94*. When Eder V. Haughwout, a specialist in tableware, commissioned this building, he had one of the very first cast-iron masterpieces, complete with open-cage elevator, installed by ELISHA OTIS.
ROOSEVELT BUILDING. 478–482 BROADWAY (1873–4, arch. Richard M. Hunt). This building shows how much could be achieved with cast iron. Three wide bays with colonnettes give the structure a sense of grace and lightness. When it was first built the building boasted superb brightly colored ornamental motifs. The ground floor and the basement, like several of the other buildings in the neighborhood, are occupied by stores – in this case, a fabric store (left).
GREENE STREET ★. This street has the most remarkable assortment of cast-iron buildings, and its cobblestone paving, recently repaired, is an unusual sight in New York. Between nos. 8 and 34, a collection of cast-iron façades sets up a subtle, regular rhythm of alternating solid and hollow forms, light and shadow, as a counterpoint to the fire escapes.

Built between 1872 and 1896, these buildings are the work of Warner, Wright, Duckworth and Snook.

N.Y. CITY FIRE MUSEUM. 278 SPRING ST. (1904, arch. Edward P. Casey). This small, fascinating and little-known museum is housed in a neo-classical fire station built at the start of the 20th century. It retraces the history of fire fighting in the city, and boasts a superb collection of exhibits, including wooden firemarks dating from the 17th century and old fire engines, as well as children's drawings and paintings, sent to the firefighters after September 11, 2001 ● 46.

THE EAR INN, FORMERLY THE JAMES BROWN RESIDENCE. 326 SPRING ST. (1817) This Federal-style house originally stood on the edge of the Hudson River. As port traffic became heavier over the years, the river was filled in as far as West Street, so that more docks could be constructed. The house was then converted into a distillery, and after that, during the time of Prohibition, into a brothel with a speakeasy upstairs. It is now a slightly timeworn, but nonetheless lively, bar.

"DAYLIGHT FACTORIES"
The façade of this Art Deco industrial building (1928) is decorated with bas-reliefs depicting laborers and craftsmen. This is a typical example of what was called a "daylight factory", several of which were built during the 1930's near the Holland Tunnel.

HOLLAND TUNNEL
The mouth of the tunnel, which was built in 1927 to link Manhattan with New Jersey, is adjacent to the site of a former railroad depot. Until 1850, this was a stylish residential area around St. John's Park. In 1869 Cornelius Vanderbilt bought the park and built the depot there. The freight trains had to run alongside the Hudson on West St. to reach St. John's Park. The depot was demolished in 1936, two years after a new terminal had been constructed a few blocks south.

"THE CLOCKTOWER"
The former headquarters of the New York Life Insurance Company ▲ 209 boasts one of the last mechanical clocks in New York. It is worth a visit to admire the machinery.

TRIBECA WEST HISTORIC DISTRICT

TriBeCa – a recent coinage derived from "TRIangle BElow CAnal" – is bounded by CANAL STREET to the north, BROADWAY to the east and the HUDSON RIVER to the west. It falls into two distinct areas; the eastern part, which has Italianate palaces of commerce with marble façades, and the western part, with Romanesque Revival warehouses and factories ● 90, as well as two influential skyscrapers of the 1920's – the Western Union Building and the New York Telephone Company Building.

THE HISTORY OF THE NEIGHBORHOOD. During the English colonial period, the land belonged to Anthony Lispenard and the parish of Trinity Church ▲ 154, which had been given this grant of land by Queen Anne in 1705. When the lands were later mapped for development and sold off, the streets were given the names of these landowners – Lispenard and his children Leonard, Thomas and Anthony (today Worth Street) – or of key figures in the parish such as Chambers, Murray, Duane, Reade and Watts. Between

850 and 1920 the western part of what is now TriBeCa was
he trading center for wholesale fruit and vegetables and dairy
roducts and supplied Washington Market, which covered
art of the site once occupied by the World Trade Center.

INDUSTRIAL ARCHITECTURE. The sector's trading activities
ere given a boost by the new piers and warehouses and by
he extension of rail facilities thanks to the NEW YORK
CENTRAL & HUDSON RIVER RAILROAD
FREIGHT DEPOT, built in 1869 for
Cornelius Vanderbilt ▲ 260. This
huge freight depot stood on the
te of ST. JOHN'S PARK (a
esidential public square with
andscaped garden) and was
emolished in 1936 when the
HOLLAND TUNNEL, linking
Manhattan and New Jersey, was
uilt. TriBeCa is mainly a
eighborhood for warehouses
85, whose utilitarian function
s still apparent from their
oading ramps, metal canopies
nd security gates. The district
oasts a whole range of styles,
rom the starkest lines,
epresented by the minimalism
f the WAREHOUSE AT 135
HUDSON STREET (1886–7, arch.
Kimball & Ihnen, right), to the
most elaborate, such as the
FLEMING SMITH WAREHOUSE
1891–2, arch. Stephen Decatur
Hatch) in Flemish style, at nos.
51–453 Washington Street. There are still some wholesale
tores around the small triangle of DUANE PARK but the rest
f TriBeCa has become a residential area. Buildings are being
estored and businesses are constantly springing up.
FORMER NEW YORK MERCANTILE EXCHANGE. 6 HARRISON ST.
1886, arch. Thomas R. Jackson). In 1872 the dairy farmers
ounded the BUTTER AND CHEESE EXCHANGE on Greenwich
treet. Some ten years later, this Queen Anne-style building
vas built, and business carried out in the huge hall paved with
olychromatic flags. After the Mercantile Exchange moved
o the former World Trade Center in 1977, this building was
onverted into apartments; one of New York's finest
estaurants, Chanterelle, now occupies the ground floor.
HARRISON STREET ROW. 25–41 HARRISON ST. (1796–1828).
Most of the houses in this residential neighborhood were
lemolished during the second half of the 19th century to
llow Washington Market to expand and to make way for the
levelopment of the docks. In 1975 it was decided to save the
ew remaining houses that now form this row. Two of them
nos. 31 and 33) stood here originally, while the others came
rom adjacent Washington Street. At the end of the street,

**WASHINGTON
MARKET**
After the Civil
War and the
development of
steamship traffic, the
narrow straits of the
East River were
abandoned for the
wider stretches of
the Hudson. Docks
gradually sprang up
all along the bank,
and as a result, the
part of southwest
Manhattan now
called TriBeCa
underwent a period
of intense commercial
growth. Products
were unloaded and
taken to Washington
Market (above, in
1888).

The Hudson River alongside West St. in 1921.

Manhattan COMMUNITY COLLEGE's walkway over Harrison Street affords a view of what is now Ground Zero ▲ *138*.

ORIGINALLY HOUSE OF RELIEF, NEW YORK HOSPITAL. 67 HUDSON ST. (1893, arch. Cady, Berg & See). This square Renaissance-Revival structure was an annex of New York Hospital, the oldest medical institution in the city, its charter granted by George III in 1771. The old ambulance garage can be reached by a covered walkway that bestrides Staple Street.

165 DUANE STREET. (1881, arch. Stephen D. Hatch). This imposing, ten-story Romanesque Revival ● *90* factory used to house the headquarters of Leonard Schepp's company, which imported fine foods and spices. Schepp was responsible for introducing exotic products such as shredded coconut to the United States. The building is now residential.

DUANE PARK. This triangular park, dating from 1795 and once bordered by dairy product wholesalers, is now surrounded by furniture and design stores, a sign that the neighborhood is changing. Notice the small building whose original cast-iron ▲ *203* structure can be seen in front of the new façade.

The Franklin St. elevated railroad, opened in 1870 (here, in 1878), linked southwest Manhattan to Broadway.

WESTERN UNION BUILDING. 60 HUDSON ST. (1928–30, arch. Voorhees, Gmelin & Walker). This sheer mountain of brick occupies a whole block. Once the headquarters of the Western Union telegraph company, the building is notable for its bold masses interrupted by recesses and for the complexity of its brick motifs. It shows how strongly American architecture was influenced by Dutch and German Expressionism. The lobby's dramatically illuminated orange brick walls set off a basket arch ceiling faced with "Guastavino" glazed tiles, named after their manufacturer.

HIGH PRESSURE SERVICE HEADQUARTERS OF THE N.Y. CITY FIRE DEPARTMENT. 226 WEST BROADWAY (c. 1905, arch. August D. Shepard, Jr). The most striking characteristic of this municipal building, with its neo-classical façade covered in cream glazed terracotta, is the use of utilitarian symbols – fire hydrants, valves and hosepipes – as ornaments.

2 WHITE STREET HOUSE. (1808–9). This old wooden house with brick façade, sloping roof and dormer windows is one of the last vestiges of the period when TriBeCa was a residential neighborhood. It was built before wooden structures were banned as a fire hazard and probably always housed a shop on the ground floor.

El Teddy's Mexican restaurant, 219 West Broadway.

FORMER CARY BUILDING

This building, at 105–107 Chambers St. (left), built in 1857 by the architects King & Kellum ● 88, is a perfect example of a "first generation" cast-iron building, with its two Italianate façades (which imitate stone). It was built for the grocery store Cary, Howard & Sanger and remains a monument to the commercial prosperity around City Hall in the mid-19th century.

AT&T (AMERICAN TELEPHONE & TELEGRAPH COMPANY).

32 6TH AVE. (1930–2, arch. Ralph Walker). This beautiful Art Deco building originally housed the technical offices for transatlantic communications. In 1984, after the new headquarters building at 550 Madison Avenue was sold to Sony, the company moved its main offices into the 6th Avenue building. The linear quality of the façades and their ornamentation, the vast tiled map of the world on the wall of the lobby, as well as the mosaic allegories on the ceiling, endow the building with an industrial aesthetic in keeping with its function.

"THE CLOCKTOWER" ★. 346 BROADWAY (1894–9, arch.

Stephen D. Hatch and McKim, Mead & White). This neo-Renaissance building ▲ 206, built for the New York Life Insurance Company, now serves as offices for the City of New York. A visit to the CLOCKTOWER GALLERY is a must. This gallery forms part of the PSI Contemporary Art Center, a museum in Queens and affiliated with MoMA ▲ 290 since 1999. You can enjoy a superb view of the Woolworth Building ▲ 180, and Foley Square ▲ 182 from its terrace.

JAMES BOGARDUS WAREHOUSE. 85 LEONARD ST. (1861).

This cast-iron building was built to house the grocery store KITCHEN, MONTROSS & WILCOX. It is one of the few remaining structures designed by the architect James Bogardus, who did pioneering work with this material.

DAVID BROWN STORE. 8 THOMAS ST. (1875–6, arch. J. Morgan

Slade). This building, commissioned by a soap and eau de toilette manufacturer, is an exceptional example of High Victorian Gothic as applied to a commercial building ● 86.

This building, at 55 White St., built by John Kellum & Son in 1861, sports a cast-iron version of the stone "Sperm candle" façade built by the same architect for 502 Broadway.

⏱ Five hours
◆ **B** B1-B2-C1

1 JEFFERSON MARKET COURTHOUSE LIBRARY
2 WASHINGTON COURT
3 NORTHERN DISPENSARY
4 CHRISTOPHER PARK
5 SHERIDAN SQUARE
6 GREENWICH HOUSE
7 175–179 W. 4TH ST.

GREENWICH VILLAGE ✪

GANSEVOORT MEAT MARKET

A LIVELY VILLAGE IN THE HEART OF MANHATTAN ✪
Allow a day for exploring Greenwich Village, founded at the end of the 17th century in what was then open countryside. Washington Square and the streets to the south of the square are the hub of the village, but its most picturesque and peaceful areas are situated to the west of 7th Avenue, near Bedford, Grove and Commerce streets. End your visit with a leisurely stroll down to the beautiful riverside park that runs along the Hudson between Christopher and Bank streets.

JEFFERSON MARKET
View of Jefferson Market with its Fire Tower, in 1830.

GREENWICH VILLAGE ✪

A "VILLAGE" WITHIN A CITY. With its low buildings and crooked streets, this neighborhood has, visually, something of the character of a small provincial town, deliberately rejecting the grid system typical of most of Manhattan. Nevertheless, its heterogeneous population is in perfect accord with New York's cosmopolitan character. Earlier inhabitants of Manhattan, the CANARSIE INDIANS, called this swampy, wooded area *Sapohanikan*. They set up a trading post – dealing in goods between Hoboken and Manhattan – on the shore, near what is now Gansevoort Street. Tobacco farming was very important during the Dutch period (1613–64) and Governor Wouter Van Twiller appropriated 222 acres of "Northwyck" (as the Dutch called this area) for a private plantation. In 1696, Van Twiller's *Bossen Bouwerie* "wooded farm", was renamed Greenwich Village by the English. Over the next century or so, houses in various styles – Georgian, Federal and Greek Revival ● *82, 84* – were built bordering the huge estates. The area became a thriving, prosperous village, whose activity was centered around the shipping industry. In the 1820's, as a result of an influx of New Yorkers from lower Manhattan, fleeing the cholera and yellow fever epidemics, Greenwich Village experienced rapid urbanization. In 1829 the male population of Newgate Prison, in the heart of the Village, was transferred to Ossining, along the Hudson River. Today Greenwich Village is a multifarious neighborhood offering an overview of three centuries of architecture.
"BOHEMIA". In the early 20th century, various social reformers interested in art joined the "Bohemians" living in the Village. These included the anarchist Emma Goldman and the "vagabond poet", Harry Kemp, who, around 1910, used to publish his writings in *The Masses*, a daily newspaper edited by Max Eastman, and in

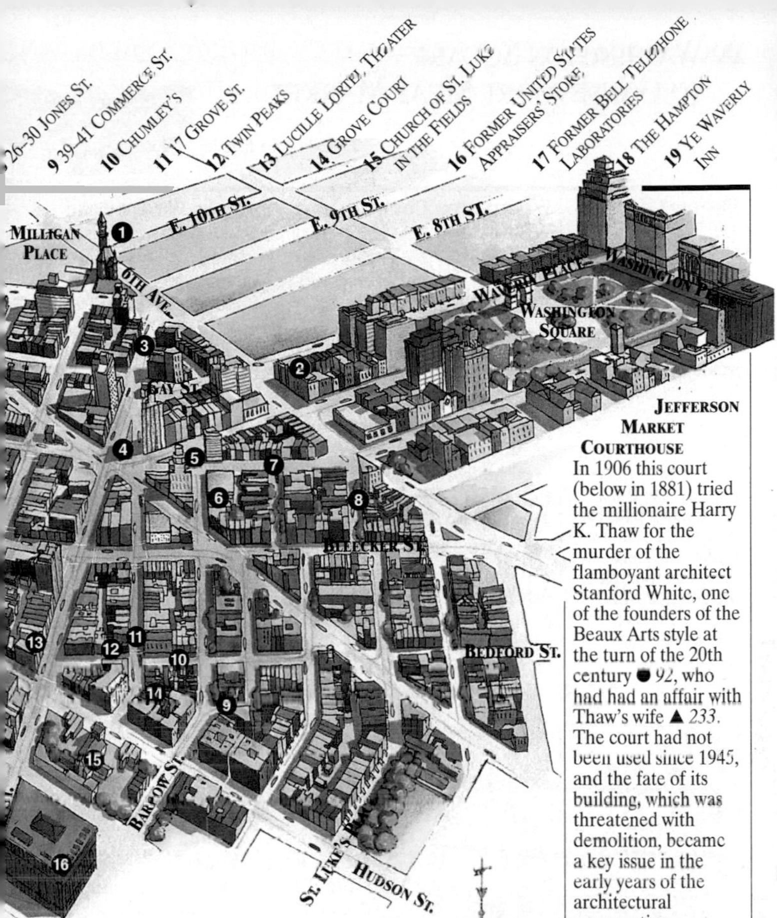

MILLIGAN PLACE

E. 10TH ST.

E. 9TH ST.

E. 8TH ST.

6TH AVE.

GAY ST.

WAVERLY PLACE

WASHINGTON PL.

WASHINGTON SQUARE

BLEECKER ST.

BEDFORD ST.

BARROW ST.

HUDSON ST.

ST. LUKE'S PLACE

JEFFERSON MARKET COURTHOUSE

In 1906 this court (below in 1881) tried the millionaire Harry K. Thaw for the murder of the flamboyant architect Stanford White, one of the founders of the Beaux Arts style at the turn of the 20th century ● 92, who had had an affair with Thaw's wife ▲ 233. The court had not been used since 1945, and the fate of its building, which was threatened with demolition, became a key issue in the early years of the architectural preservation movement. The local residents financed the restoration of the tower and hounded the municipal government until it granted the requisite funds for the building's conversion into a branch of the New York Public Library. It was restored by Giorgio Cavaglieri in 1967.

Seven Arts, a magazine that published such writers as D. H. Lawrence and the Marxist journalist John Reed. Although the golden age of the Village came to an end at the beginning of the 1930's when many of the "bohemians" settled down or left the neighborhood, the influence of this period can still be felt.

JEFFERSON MARKET COURTHOUSE LIBRARY ★. 425 6TH AVE., at 10TH ST. (1874–7, arch. Withers & Vaux). This Victorian-Gothic building combines intricately carved, brightly colored materials with naturalistic ornaments. Built on the site of the old Jefferson Market ● 86, the courthouse was converted into a public library in 1967.

Detail of the façade
of Bigelow's Pharmacy

BREVOORT HOUSE
The hotel which has now been torn down made the news when its Basque owner, Raymond Orteig, promised a reward of $25,000 to a pilot who would fly non-stop from New York to Paris. Charles Lindbergh, who landed his monoplane *Spirit of Saint Louis* in Paris in May 1927, was the first pilot to achieve this. On his return, Lindbergh was carried in triumph to the hotel, on 5th Avenue (below), where Orteig gave him the prize.

WASHINGTON COURT. 6TH AVE., between WAVERLY and WASHINGTON PLACES (1986, arch. James Stewart Polshek & Partners) ● *102*. This group of Postmodern-style apartments blends in well with the profile of the Village.

BIGELOW CO. PHARMACY. 414 6TH AVE., at 9TH ST. (1902, arch. John E. Nitchie). This pharmacy, founded in 1838, is a fine example of early 20th-century commercial architecture, with its three striking Beaux Arts-style double bays. The interior, recently restored, still boasts its apothecary jars and all the prescriptions made up since the pharmacy opened, including one they had prepared for Mark Twain, who lived nearby.

PATCHIN PLACE (W. 10TH ST.) **AND MILLIGAN PLACE** (6TH AVE.) (1848–52). These two cul-de-sacs, enclosed by iron gates, are lined with redbrick houses which once served as accommodation for staff at the nearby Brevoort House. Among the most famous residents of Patchin Place are the poet e. e. cummings and John Reed, the left-wing journalist who covered the Russian Revolution and wrote *Ten Days that Shook the World* (1919). Reed was indicted for sedition in the Red Scare of 1919–20.

GAY STREET. This narrow lane, which epitomizes the neighborhood's charm, served as a mews in colonial times. The stables were later replaced by a harmonious group of late Federal-style houses (1827–31) and later by some Greek Revival houses (1844–60). Note the graceful columns flanking the doors, the brick masonry and the wide dormer windows of nos. 12 and 14 (1827–8).

NORTHERN DISPENSARY. 165 WAVERLY PLACE (1831). The Northern Dispensary was established by a group of citizens to care for the poor and is one of New York's oldest public hospitals. The triangular Greek Revival building was completed in 1831 and an extra story was added in 1854. The writer Edgar Allan Poe, one of the Northern Dispensary's benefactors, was treated at the hospital for a head cold in 1837.

"GAY LIBERATION"
In 1992, in Christopher Park, two statues by George Segal – two couples, one male, one female – were erected in honor of the gay rights movement. Since the 1969 riot, a "Gay Pride March" has been organized every year. It starts at the Stonewall Inn, where there is now a commemorative plaque.

CHRISTOPHER PARK AND SHERIDAN SQUARE. These two squares stand side by side. The larger of the two is Christopher Park, in which a statue of the Union general Philip Sheridan, by Joseph Pollia, was erected in 1936. Sheridan Square is a small garden at the southeast end of Christopher Park. At the height of the Civil War, Christopher Park was the site of the Draft Riots of July 1863 ▲ *171*: poverty-stricken Irishmen, who feared that if they had to go to war their jobs would be taken by Blacks, went on the rampage. Despite the forceful intervention of the National Guard, eighteen Blacks were lynched by the Irish. A century later, Christopher Park was also the site of the Stonewall Inn Riot; on the night of June 28, 1969, the police raided the Stonewall Inn, a gay bar at 51 Christopher Street. The raid ended in a riot, which marked the start of the Gay Rights Movement ● *53*.

ROBERT FRYER presents

Rosalind Russell
THE NEW MUSICAL COMEDY
Wonderful Town

175–179 W. 4TH STREET (1833–4). These houses feature the original door frames as well as Flemish bonding, overhanging roofs pierced by dormers at nos. 177 and 179 and the dimensions characteristic of the Federal style.

26–30 JONES STREET (c. 1830). The distinctive features of these three Greek Revival houses are their dentiled cornices, their wrought-iron stoop railings (nos. 28 and 30), their lantern-embellished doors (nos. 26 and 28) and their small-paned windows.

GREENWICH HOUSE. 29 BARROW ST. (1917, arch. Delano & Aldrich). This neo-Georgian structure, built to serve as a social center for immigrants, is still used for socio-cultural activities.

AROUND ST. LUKE'S IN THE FIELD

With its array of well-preserved brick- and brownstone-Italianate houses built 1852–3 (nos. 5–16), St. Luke's Place is one of the most attractive streets in Greenwich Village.
39 AND 41 COMMERCE STREET (1831–2). Contrary to popular legend, these two houses, nicknamed the "Twin Sisters", were not built by a naval officer for his two daughters, but by a milkman, Peter Huyler. They have a somewhat old-fashioned air, with their leafy courtyard and their mansard roofs, which were added after 1870, and give the Greek Revival architecture a top-heavy appearance.

"My Sister Eileen"

CHUMLEY'S. 86 BEDFORD ST. (1831). During Prohibition, this innocuous-looking building housed one of the best-known speakeasies in New York. Its clientele included Edna St. Vincent Millay, Upton Sinclair, John Dos Passos and Theodore Dreiser. The owner disguised the façade with a garage front in order to put the police off the scent and his

Ruth McKenney, who lived at 14 Gay St. in the 1920's, published a group of stories in *The New Yorker* set against the bohemian backdrop of the Village. It described the ups and downs of life there with her younger sister, an actress finding it difficult to break into the big time. The stories were used as material for a Broadway hit musical called *Wonderful Town*.

ST. LUKE'S PLACE
In 1922 the writer Theodore Dreiser moved into 16 St. Luke's Place and began work on his novel *An American Tragedy*. The gas lamps that stand in front of No. 6 mark the residence of Mayor James J. Walker, who was notorious in the 1920's for his dissolute lifestyle. The playground on the other side of the road is a former graveyard in which Edgar Allan Poe once liked to stroll.

213

customers used to enter discreetly through the old stables at the back, at 58 Barrow Street. Two traditions that persist to this day are the absence of an inn sign and a display of the dust jackets from books by regulars. Take a look at 95 BEDFORD STREET, where another old stable, built in 1894, was converted into apartments in 1927. The building still has its wide original doors.

17 GROVE STREET (1822). This frame house is one of the few vestiges of the period before laws were passed banning this type of structure in Manhattan for reasons of safety. The beautiful Greek Revival entrance is original, whereas the cornice and decorative wooden panels date from 1870, when another story was added.

TWIN PEAKS. 102 BEDFORD ST. (c. 1830). This "neo-Alpine

style" half-timbered building was created by the artist Clifford Reed Daily. He converted this residence in 1925, aiming for a startling effect in defiance of the homogeneous Federal style of the other houses on this peaceful street. He even managed to persuade Otto Kahn, his wealthy patron, to finance the project.

LUCILLE LORTEL THEATER. 121 CHRISTOPHER ST. In the 1950's the former Hudson Cinema was converted into a theater specializing in experimental

Grove St. at the corner of Bedford St. (above).

productions ▲ *258*. It is named after one of its famous directors.
GROVE COURT ★. THROUGH THE GATE BETWEEN 10–12 GROVE ST. (1853–4). This address marks the entrance to six small houses, built by Samuel Cocks, a local grocer, to rent to workers. The courtyard once bore the name "Mixed Ale Alley", probably because of the inhabitants' propensity to drink. The houses were restored around 1920 and given their current name.

CHURCH OF ST. LUKE IN THE FIELDS. 485 HUDSON ST. (1822, arch. James N. Wells). Built by local residents with funds supplied by Trinity Parish ▲ *154, 361*, this was originally a village church adjoining several farms along the riverbank. Some parishioners used to come to church by boat – easier than traveling by road at that time. The brick exterior, whose simplicity verges on the severe, gives the church a distinctively rural look even today. The row of Federal-style houses bordering the old churchyard – especially the numbers 473 to 477 and 487 to 491 Hudson Street – creates an attractive setting for the church and its garden. The writer Bret Harte spent his boyhood at no. 487.

FORMER UNITED STATES APPRAISERS' STORES. 666–668 GREENWICH ST. (1892–9, arch. Willoughby J. Edbrooke). This massive Romanesque Revival structure, with its sturdy brick arcading, was used as a bonded warehouse when port activity was at its peak. The building was later used to house archives before being converted, in 1988, into apartments. Only the name of the MELVILLE BAR, on the corner of Barrow and Washington streets, evokes the ghost of the writer Herman Melville, who once worked as a customs inspector.

214

WEST VILLAGE

FORMER BELL TELEPHONE LABORATORIES. 463 WEST ST. and 155 BANK ST. (1880–1900, arch. Cyrus W. Eidlitz). The first transcontinental telephone call was made from here on January 25, 1915, when Alexander Graham Bell spoke to Thomas Watson in San Francisco; the first experimental radio set, the 2XS, was invented here, as was the sound projector, in 1925, which paved the way for the talkies. It was also here, on April 7, 1927, that journalists attended the first television broadcast, during which the Secretary of Commerce and future President, Herbert Hoover, made a speech from the Capitol, Washington, D.C. ● *54*. The building now forms part of a complex of lofts and studios for artists.

THE HAMPTON. 80–82 PERRY ST. (1887, arch. Thom & Wilson). The distinctive features of this apartment building, which blends in well with its surroundings, are its Moorish arches, its intricate brick decoration and its brownstone reliefs.

PIERRE DEUX. 369 BLEECKER ST. (1867). This attractive home decoration store, founded by two antique dealers both answering to the name of Pierre, occupies a complex designed to be divided into apartments, with commercial space on the ground floor. It was one of the first apartment buildings in New York.

301–319 W. 4TH STREET (1836–7). Out of these ten Greek Revival houses, nos. 311 and 313 still have their original proportions, while the others have been heightened with Italianate cornices ● *88*. The original wrought-iron railings still adorn the front steps.

YE WAVERLY INN. 16 BANK ST. (1844–5). This inn is part of a group of buildings that combine elements of late Greek Revival style with typical Gothic Revival decoration, such as the motifs on the carved lintels. The inn has low beamed ceilings and wooden alcoves.

GANSEVOORT MEAT MARKET. This covered wholesale meat market can be found east of 9th Avenue, between Gansevoort and 14th streets. Visit the market at dawn, when the auctioneering begins, or in the evening to eat at Florent, a 24-hour restaurant which is popular with the city's night owls.

⏲ **Four hours**

◆ **B** A1-A2-B1-B2

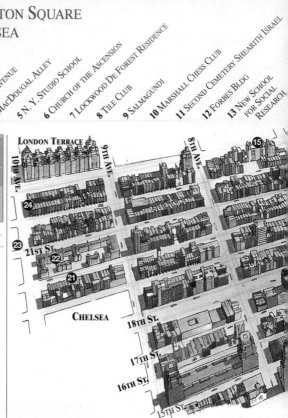

FROM WASHINGTON SQUARE TO 14TH STREET

CONSTRAINTS ON PROPERTY DEVELOPERS
Rows of identical townhouses were built in response to the conditions laid down by landowners in their tenants' leases. How the land was used, the size of the residences (in case of construction), materials, even their decoration, were all strictly regulated. These constraints meant that homeowners often had to build their stables at some distance from their dwellings.

THE ROW. 1–13 WASHINGTON SQUARE NORTH (1832–3). Some elegant residences were built around the square after the parade ground was constructed. This group is the most important row of early 19th-century houses in the city, and in their time they served as a model for adapting the Greek Revival style to private residences in New York. They are handsome redbrick houses, with porches, stairs and balustrades of white marble and railings embellished with acanthus finials and other classical motifs.
No. 3 was occupied, among others, by certain members of the Eight ● *109* and, later, by the painter Edward Hopper. The houses at nos. 19–26 (1828–39) are in the same style but offer greater diversity, with their balconies and French doors, their varying shades of brick and their rich decoration.
WASHINGTON MEWS ★. BETWEEN UNIVERSITY PLACE AND 5TH AVE. This charming cobblestone alley behind The

Row is lined on the north side by its former stables, now converted into houses. The south side was built in 1939.
ONE 5TH AVENUE. (1929, arch. Helmle, Corbett & Harrison; Sugarman & Berger).

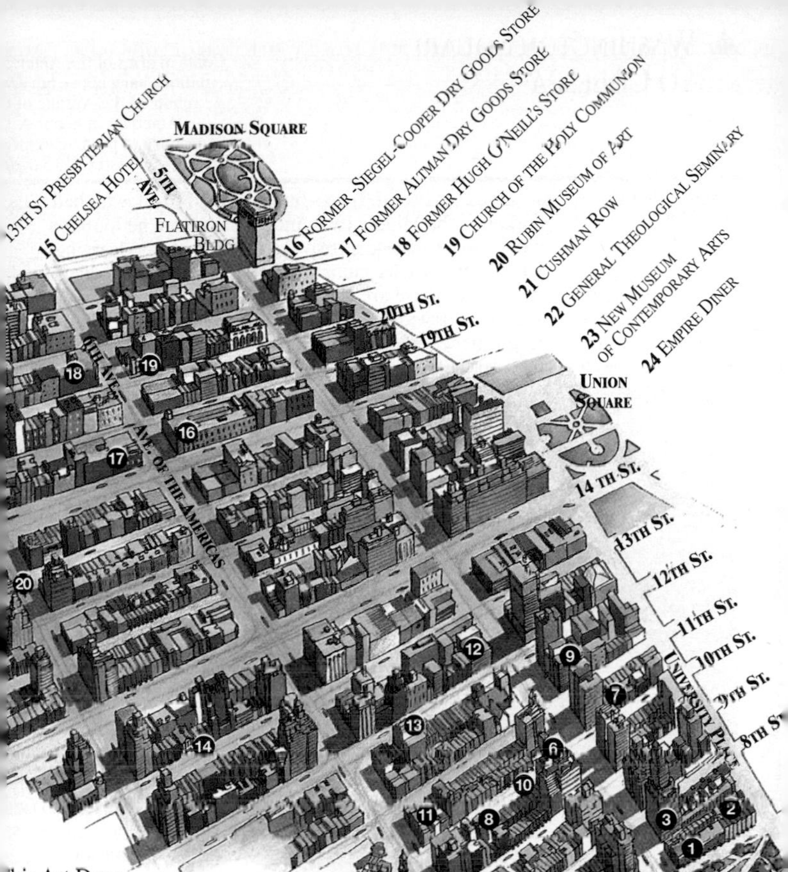

MADISON SQUARE
5TH AVE
FLATIRON BLDG
UNION SQUARE
20TH ST.
19TH ST.
14TH ST.
13TH ST.
12TH ST.
11TH ST.
10TH ST.
9TH ST.
8TH ST.
UNIVERSITY PLACE
WASHINGTON SQUARE NORTH

This Art Deco monument looms above a landscape of smaller houses. Having been rather insensitively restored, it has lost the subtle original shading of its brick cladding.

MacDougal Alley. MacDougal St., between 8th St. and Washington Square North (1833–8). The former stables of this cul-de-sac were renovated at the turn of the century and rented out cheaply, attracting artists who converted them into studios.

New York Studio School. 8 W. 8th St. (1838, altered in 1931 and 1936 by Auguste L. Noel). In 1907 the sculptor Gertrude Vanderbilt Whitney opened the Studio Club in MacDougal Alley. She championed American avant-garde and collected neglected works by her friends in the Eight. In 1931, she converted these three houses on 8th Street into a private gallery and residence. In 1936 they became the first home of the WHITNEY MUSEUM OF AMERICAN ART ▲ 326. An Art Deco stucco was added at a later date.

Lockwood DeForest Residence. 7 E. 10th St. (1887, arch. Van Campen Taylor). This house boasts an extravaganza

"Ashcan school"
Gertrude Vanderbilt Whitney, granddaughter of Cornelius Vanderbilt and wife of the financier Harry Payne Whitney, was the patron of the group of the Eight. These artists were also known as the "Ashcan school", because they flew in the face of academic tradition and concentrated on realistically portraying city life's grittiness as well as its beauty. The Whitney Collection moved Uptown in 1954 and the 8th Street museum became the New York Studio School of Drawing, Painting, and Sculpture.

217

Coats of arms of the Americ
nations hang above 6th Av
renamed the Avenue of t
Americas in honor of t
founding of the Organizati
of American States, 1948 *(righ*

CHURCH OF THE ASCENSION
This Episcopal church, on 5th Ave. at 10th St., was built in 1841 by Richard Upjohn. The interior was remodeled in 1885–9.

MARCEL DUCHAMP
(1887–1968). When he settled in New York in 1915, Duchamp (below right) abandoned painting to concentrate on his "ready-mades", everyday objects that he presented as works of art. Around 1935 the artist turned from the world of art to the art of chess. His anti-art stance had a great impact on all the major artistic trends of the day.

of carved teakwood. It was built for De Forest, who had worked in the Middle East and India, where he founded studios to encourage a revival in the art of woodcarving.
THE CLUBS. Artists' clubs once abounded in the Village, and those that survive are open to the public. They were formed when friends with the same taste in art and conversation began to meet regularly. Among them are the TILE CLUB (58 West 10th St) founded in 1877, and the SALMAGUNDI CLUB ● *88*, formed in 1870 and located at 47 5th Avenue since 1917. This club owes its name to the journal run by Washington Irving, *Salmagundi*, an essentially mysterious name possibly from the French for a kind of "mixed salad". Women painters, who were barred from these clubs, founded the PEN & BRUSH (16 East 10th Street) in 1893; its beautifully appointed Victorian rooms are regularly used for exhibitions, concerts and receptions. The MARSHALL CHESS CLUB, at 23 West 10th St, was founded in 1915 by Frank J. Marshall, United States champion between 1909 and 1936. Businessmen such as Edward Cornell and Gilbert Colgate rubbed shoulders here with the likes of Sinclair Lewis and Marcel Duchamp. Bobby Fischer, world chess champion in 1972, played his first competitive matches here. It is not unusual to see people playing it in Washington and Abingdon squares.
18 WEST 11TH ST. (1845). This house was originally part of a group of rowhouses, but in March 1970 the façade was blasted away by a bomb being made by the daughter of the owner of the house and her cohorts, a terrorist organization called the *Weathermen*. For years, the maimed house showed its gaping holes to passersby until a controversial modern design with a projecting rough brick façade was built.

SECOND SHEARITH ISRAEL CEMETERY. 72–76 W. 11TH ST. (1805–25). This tiny enclave is all that remains of the second graveyard of the oldest American Jewish community, most of whose tombs have been moved to another graveyard on 21st Street.
FORBES BUILDING ★. 60–62 5TH AVE. N. W. CORNER 12TH ST. (1925, Carrère & Hastings and Shreve & Lamb). This neo-

classical building was the headquarters of the MACMILLAN publishing house (which published *Gone with the Wind* in 1936); it later became the offices of *Forbes* magazine.

NEW SCHOOL FOR SOCIAL RESEARCH. 66 W. 12TH ST. (1930, arch. Joseph Urban). This innovative institution, founded in 1919 by two lecturers from Columbia University, moved, in 1930, into this Bauhaus-inspired building ● 98. Three years later the New School developed a curriculum for scholars and academics fleeing Nazi Germany; it became a veritable "university in exile" for the social sciences.

VILLAGE COMMUNITY CHURCH. 143 W. 13TH ST. (1847, attrib. Samuel Thompson) ● 84. This former Presbyterian church, inspired by the Theseum in Athens, is one of the finest examples of Greek Revival style. It was converted into apartments in 1982.

CHELSEA

This neighborhood, which lies between 14th and 34th streets from 6th Avenue to the Hudson River, is named after Captain Thomas Clarke, a retired English naval officer who, in 1750, bought a large plot of land along the river here for a country estate. He named it Chelsea in honor of the Chelsea Royal Hospital in London. His randson, the scholar Clement Clarke Moore (author of "A Visit from St. Nicholas"), parceled out the estate with the aim of creating a middle-class neighborhood. Although Chelsea was never to become the residential haven that Clarke had imagined, this

Below, galleries on West 24th St, in the heart of the new art neighborhood.

219

Siegel Building.

area and the neighboring blocks did attract wealthy families. However, by the end of the 19th century, Chelsea had lost some of its residential character due to the arrival of the department stores that drove away the wealthy residents. Warehouses and piers sprang up in the west of the neighborhood, attracting poor immigrants in search of work, and tenements were built to house them. Chelsea is now a fashionable neighborhood: luxury boutiques abound and various galleries of contemporary art have moved from SoHo to some of the old warehouses near the Hudson, between 16th and 26th streets, and 9th and 11th avenues.

FORMER SIEGEL-COOPER DRY GOODS STORE ★. 616–632 6TH AVE., between 18TH and 19TH STS. (1895–7, arch. DeLemos & Cordes). On September 12, 1896, 150,000 spectators jostled at the inauguration of this department store (above), which the advertising campaign boasted was "a city in itself". The man behind the idea, Henry Siegel, revolutionized commerce by using every form of advertising available and by handing out samples to customers.

FORMER B. ALTMAN DRY GOODS STORE. 621 6TH AVE., between 18TH and 19TH STS. (1877, arch. D. & J. Jardine). The oldest cast-iron department store on 6th Avenue and famous for its sophisticated clothing, its silks, velvets and satins. In 1913, ALTMAN gave his collection of Italian Renaissance and Baroque paintings to the Metropolitan Museum of Art.

FORMER HUGH O'NEILL'S STORE. 655–671 6TH AVE. between 20TH AND 21ST STS. (1875, arch. Mortimer C. Merritt, additions 1890–5). Hugh O'Neill's low prices were aimed at the working classes rather than a wealthy clientele. In 1902, at O'Neill's death, no one wanted to take over from the "Fightin' Irishman of 6th Avenue". The establishment closed in 1915. The cast-iron building was later made into offices and the two cupolas that used to crown the building's corners disappeared.

CHURCH OF THE HOLY COMMUNION ★. 49 W. 20TH ST. (1846, arch. Richard Upjohn) ● 86. This was the first asymmetrical Gothic Revival church in the United States. Despite its conversion into a nightclub, Limelight, the interior has not changed. There is an excellent view of the Empire State Building from the corner of 6th Avenue and 23rd Street.

CUSHMAN ROW. 406–418 W. 20TH ST. (1839) ● 84. Greek Revival rowhouses, built by Don Alonzo Cushman.

GENERAL THEOLOGICAL SEMINARY ★. (mainly 1883–1902, arch. Charles C. Haight). Clement Clarke Moore gave the land in 1818 for the seminary. An exhibition on the history of Chelsea is now housed in the building.

RUBIN MUSEUM OF ART. 150 W 17TH ST. (7th Ave.). This museum, devoted to the art of the Himalayas and surrounding regions, is housed in the former Barney's Building.

NEW MUSEUM OF CONTEMPORARY ART. 556 W 22ND ST. Founded in 1977 by Marcia Tucker, this museum aims to promote living artists, neglected by other museums of contemporary art, in particular exponents of conceptual art.

CHELSEA PIERS. 23RD ST. AND HUDSON RIVER. This complex has facilities for golf, bowling, rock climbing, tennis, soccer, as well as restaurants and banquet rooms.

"The most famous apartment house [located at 222 W. 23rd St.] inaugurated in 1884, still exists. The Chelsea Hotel, whose semi-Victorian, semi-Gothic architecture still stirs passersby. These early buildings were striking because of their extremely flexible approach to composition."

Anka Muhlstein,
Manhattan

THE DINERS
Long before the arrival of fast food chains, the American "diner" – originally shaped like a railroad dining car – served inexpensive food at all hours of the day and night. The Empire Diner (below), founded in 1943, is located at 210 10th Ave.

Around Union Square

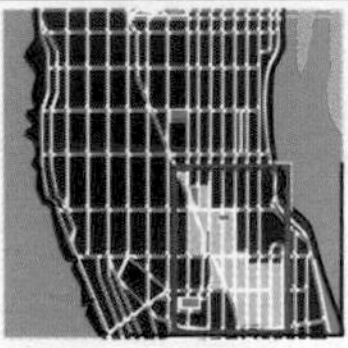

⏱ Five hours

◆ **B** B2-B3-C2-C3

On April 10, 1927, *The New York Times* led with the story of Sacco and Vanzetti's

The New York Times.
"All the News That's Fit to Print."

SACCO AND VANZETTI GUILTY, SAYS FULLER, AND MUST DIE;
BAY STATE GOVERNOR UPHOLDS JURY, CALLS TRIAL FAIR;
HIS BOARD UNANIMOUS, EXECUTION OF PAIR SET FOR AUG. 10

death sentence. The execution was deferred until August 23. A strike was called and on the 22nd some 5,000 workers converged on Union Square, where they kept vigil until the time of the execution.

Located at the intersection of BROADWAY and 4th Avenue (which in colonial times led to Albany and Boston), Union Square was laid out in 1831 and opened in 1839. In the 1840's this was a wealthy residential area; after the Civil War, it became New York's theater district, with the presence of the ACADEMY OF MUSIC on 14th Street (the site now occupied by the Con Edison building), and several other theaters. In the 1880's, with the development of the Ladies' Mile, commercial establishments moved to the neighborhood and a few early skyscrapers were erected to the west of Union Square. After 1910, as commercial and artistic establishments moved uptown, it became a favorite site for labor-union gatherings and political demonstrations, particularly between the wars. These have included such historic gatherings as the demonstration on August 22, 1927 against the execution of Sacco and Vanzetti, and the protest march of 35,000 unemployed workers in March 1930, during the Great Depression. A fruit and vegetable market now occupies Union Square four days a week.

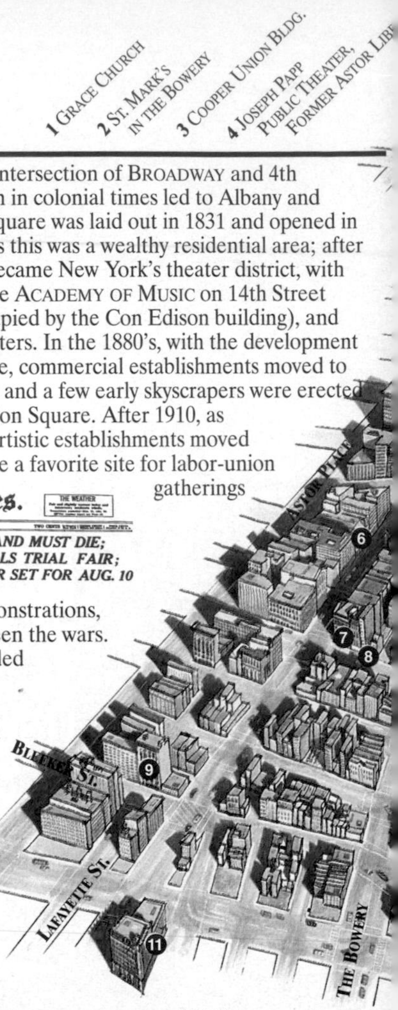

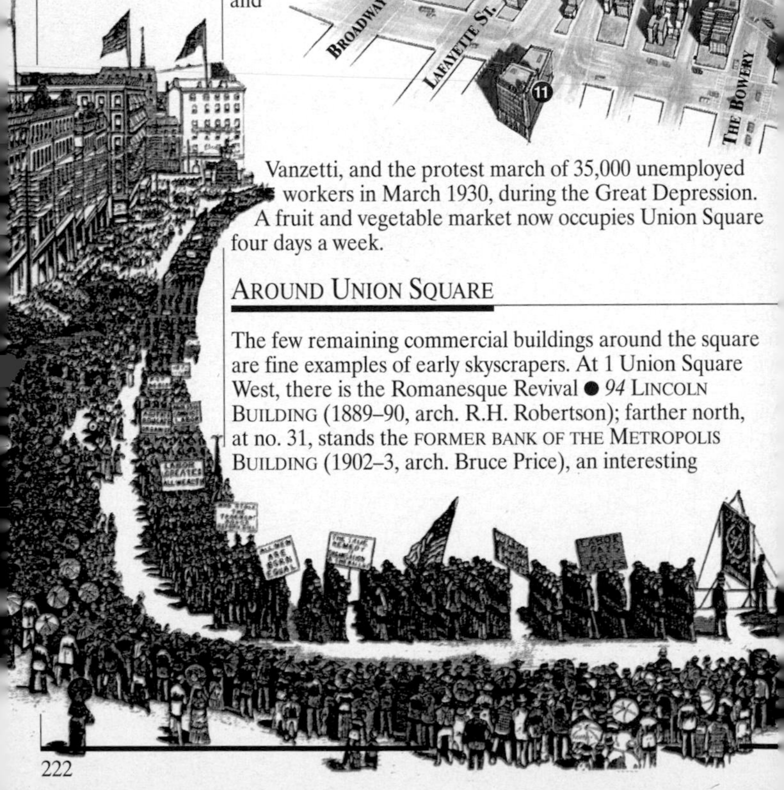

AROUND UNION SQUARE

The few remaining commercial buildings around the square are fine examples of early skyscrapers. At 1 Union Square West, there is the Romanesque Revival ● *94* LINCOLN BUILDING (1889–90, arch. R.H. Robertson); farther north, at no. 31, stands the FORMER BANK OF THE METROPOLIS BUILDING (1902–3, arch. Bruce Price), an interesting

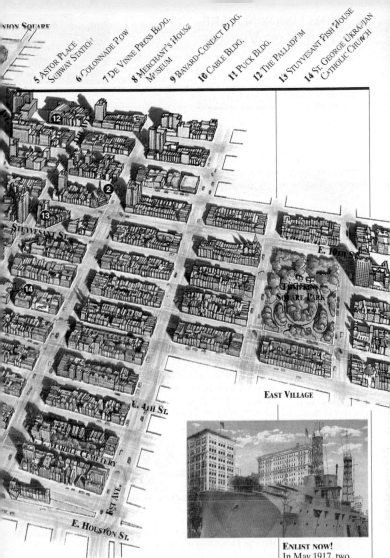

UNION SQUARE

5 ASTOR PLACE SUBWAY STATION 6 COLONNADE ROW 7 DE VINNE PRESS BLDG. 8 MERCHANT'S HOUSE MUSEUM 9 BAYARD-CONDICT BLDG. 10 CABLE BLDG. 11 PUCK BLDG. 12 THE PALLADIUM 13 STUYVESANT FISH HOUSE 14 ST. GEORGE UKRAINIAN CATHOLIC CHURCH

EAST VILLAGE

ENLIST NOW!
In May 1917, two months after the US entered World War One, John Mitchell, Mayor of New York, had a model of a warship *The Recruit* constructed in Union Square. In this building naval officers recruited marines to fight in the war.

example of neo-Renaissance tripartite architecture as applied to the skyscraper; and, close by, at no. 33, the Moorish-style DECKER BUILDING ★ (1892–3, arch. John Edelman), which for a time housed the Decker Piano Company. The finest building on Union Square is arguably the CENTURY (1880–1, arch. William Schickel) ★, at 33 East 17th Street, in Queen Anne style ● *90*, with its abundance of highly fanciful ornaments. It was once the headquarters of the Century Publishing Company, which in the late 1800's, published various magazines including the *Century* and, for children, *St. Nicholas*. On the east side of the square, at no. 20, stands the former UNION SQUARE SAVINGS BANK.

This severely neo-classical granite building (1924, arch. Henry Bacon) was designed by the architect of the Lincoln Memorial in Washington, D.C.

A demonstration in Union Square (opposite) in the 1880's.

Cooper Square
(opposite) at the turn
of the century.

The entrance of
legendary punk-rock
venue CBGB (below
right), on the Bowery.

**PETER STUYVESANT
(1592–1672)**
This stern, moralistic
man, always dressed
in black, was the last
governor of New
Amsterdam (1647–
64). He established
a 200-acre *bouwerie*
(farm) on Indian
territory, between
Broadway and the
East River and what
are now 3rd and 23rd
streets, from which
the present-day
Bowery takes its
name. The Federal-
style house at
21 Stuyvesant St. was

given by his
great-grandson to his
daughter as a wedding
present in 1804. Since
1861 the site has been
occupied by a group
of Italianate brick
and brownstone
houses, known as the
Renwick Triangle.

EAST VILLAGE

Formerly part of the Lower East Side ▲ *189*, the East Village
lies east of the Bowery and north of Houston Street. At the
end of the 19th century, many immigrants – mainly Germans
at first – moved into the neighborhood, where they settled in
the local tenements, especially around
Tompkins Square. A couple of wealthy
German benefactors, Oswald and Anna
Ottendorfer, founded the GERMAN
POLIKLINIK (Dispensary) and the FREIE
BIBLIOTHEK UND LESEHALLE on 2nd
Avenue to help the poorest inhabitants.
THE NEW BOHEMIA. After World War II a
new generation of artists moved into this
neighborhood, where rents were lower
than in Greenwich Village ▲ *210*. They
created a new Bohemia and gave the area
its present name. The 1950's saw the arrival of the founders of
the beat generation: the writers Allen Ginsberg, Jack
Kerouac, William Burroughs and poet Gregory Corso; also
the writer Norman Mailer, the artist Andy Warhol, the jazz
musicians Thelonius Monk, Charles Mingus and Ornette
Coleman who created the underground movement.
GRACE CHURCH. 800–804 BROADWAY AT E. 10TH ST. (1845–6,
arch. James Renwick, Jr) ● *86*. This Gothic Revival church
with its delicate octagonal spire, was built where Broadway

veers to the west, a location that makes it visible, even today,
many miles to the south. The interior boasts a fine mosaic
floor and some magnificent stained glass windows, such as
the "Te Deum" in the choir (1879).

ST. MARK'S HISTORIC DISTRICT

The neighborhood to the northeast of
Stuyvesant Street belonged to Peter
Stuyvesant's bouwerie, in the 17th century,
and the street that now bears his name was
once a private alley between Bowery Road
and his mansion. His great-grandson,
Petrus, divided up the estate for
development at the end of the 18th century.
The church of St. Mark's-in-the-Bowery,
the Stuyvesant-Fish House and the
Nicholas William Stuyvesant House date
from this period. Today, St. Mark's Place,
which runs between 3rd Avenue and
Tompkins Square, is a lively street lined
with bars and restaurants.
ST. MARK'S-IN-THE-BOWERY ★ 2ND AVE.
AT E. 10TH ST. (1799). The land on which
the private chapel of Stuyvesant's

bouwerie is believed to have stood was sold to the Episcopal Church in the late 18th century for a token dollar. The small Georgian-style church built in 1799 was enhanced by a Greek Revival steeple in 1828 and an Italianate cast-iron porch in 1854.

LAFAYETTE STREET HISTORIC DISTRICT

In its heyday, the second quarter of the 19th century, this area, lying east of Broadway and running the length of Lafayette and Bond streets, was an elegant residential neighborhood, rivaling Washington Square as Manhattan's smartest address. Two of the most influential businessmen of the 19th century, Peter Cooper and John Jacob Astor, contributed to its growth by building the Cooper Union and the Astor Library. After the Civil War, as the city continued to spread northward, this neighborhood became a commercial district.

COOPER UNION BUILDING. COOPER SQUARE (1859, arch. Frederick A. Peterson). This Italianate brownstone building ● *88*, was built to house the college founded by Peter Cooper in 1859. It incorporated various structural innovations such as an iron-frame elevator. The top-floor studios added in the 1890's, were lit by glass roofs and contained an exhibition of decorative arts which became

COOPER UNION
This school of art and engineering was founded in 1859 by Peter Cooper (1791–1883), an industrialist, inventor and philanthropist who wanted to provide free education in the arts and sciences for working-class people. Cooper designed the first American steam locomotive, called "Tom Thumb", produced the first

steel train rails and started his own telegraph company.

The first Wanamaker's department store (below), at 4th Avenue and East 9th Street (1862, arch. Daniel Hudson Burnham).

ASTOR PLACE RIOT
When the curtain of the Astor Place Opera House rose on the English actor William Macready in the title role of *Macbeth* on May 10, 1849, the audience, giving vent to anti-British feelings, booed and hissed. Meanwhile, a crowd numbering ten to twenty thousand gathered in the square and threw stones at the theater's entrance. The 7th Regiment of the Tompkins Market Armory quelled the riot by firing into the crowd, killing thirty-one people and wounding one hundred fifty others. The former Mercantile Library at 13 Astor Place now stands on the site of the opera house.

Astor Place Subway Station (right).

the nucleus of the future Cooper-Hewitt Museum ▲ *320* and which were used by the students as models. The building's Great Hall became a forum for lectures by such celebrities as Mark Twain, Andrew Carnegie, Fiorello La Guardia and Orson Welles. Above all, the hall is famous as the scene of Abraham Lincoln's first speech on slavery, "Right Makes Might", in 1860, which was a decisive factor in his election as President.

JOSEPH PAPP PUBLIC THEATER, FORMER ASTOR LIBRARY.
425 LAFAYETTE ST. (south wing 1849–53, arch. Alexander Saeltzer; center wing 1856–9, arch. Griffith Thomas; north wing 1879–81, arch. Thomas Stent). JOHN JACOB ASTOR founded the first public library in New York. Constructed in three stages, the building reflects the German influence on commercial architecture in mid-19th-century New York. In 1965, the theatrical director and producer JOSEPH PAPP persuaded the city to buy the building which, one year later, became the home of the SHAKESPEARE FESTIVAL.

ASTOR PLACE SUBWAY STATION (1904, arch. Heins & La Farge). This is one of the few subway stations that still has its original decoration, including a plaque representing a beaver,

The logo of one of Theodore De Vinne's publications.

symbol of the Astor fortune, which originated in the fur trade. A black steel cube, entitled "Alamo" (1966), by Bernard T. Rosenthal, stands in the center of this square.

COLONNADE ROW. 428–34 LAFAYETTE ST. (1832–3, attributed to Seth Geer) ● *84*. These Greek Revival houses, with their marble façades, once ranked among the most magnificent residences in New York – home to such families as the Vanderbilts and the Astors. The series of Corinthian columns imposes a stylistic unity on the houses, which have suffered from lack of maintenance and infelicitous alteration. Only four of the nine original houses – formerly called LaGrange Terrace after Lafayette's estate in France – are still standing.

DE VINNE PRESS BUILDING. 393–9 LAFAYETTE ST. AT E. 4TH ST. (1885–6, arch. Babb, Cook & Willard) ● *91*. This was one of several printing press buildings on Lafayette Street. The printer Theodore De Vinne (1828–1914) published books and magazines such as the popular monthly, *The Century*.

MERCHANT'S HOUSE MUSEUM ★. 29 E. 4TH ST. (1831–2, attributed to Minard Lafever) ● *82*. This building (left), originally one of a group of six, was built by the property developer JOSEPH BREWSTER, and sold in 1835 to a wealthy hardware dealer, SEABURY TREDWELL. In 1936 it was converted into a museum evoking the life of a prosperous New York family in the 19th century.

BAYARD-CONDICT BUILDING ★. 65–69 BLEECKER ST. (1897–9, arch. Louis Sullivan and Lyndon P. Smith) ● *94*. This is the only work in New York by LOUIS SULLIVAN, one of the foremost architects of the Chicago school of architecture and Frank Lloyd Wright's revered "Master".

CABLE BUILDING. 621 BROADWAY (1894, arch. McKim, Mead & White). This building was once the headquarters and power station for Manhattan's streetcars. Its arcaded bays, classically inspired stone carvings and prominent cornice, with its acanthus-motif ridgepole, make it one of the finest commercial buildings by the firm of McKim, Mead & White.

PUCK BUILDING. 295–309 LAFAYETTE ST. (1885–6 and 1892–3, arch. Albert Wagner, John Wagner). The originality of this 19th-century Romanesque Revival building lies in its wide arched windows and highly elaborate brickwork. It was built to house the satirical magazine *Puck*. The building was constructed in three stages, the last of which was when Lafayette Street was widened in 1899.

A statue of Puck, a character from Shakespeare's *A Midsummer's Night's Dream*, with the words "What fools these mortals be", keeps watch over both entrances to the Puck Building. The statue at the former main entrance on Houston St. is the work of Caspar Buberl; the one on Lafayette St. is by Henry Baerer.

The cover of *Puck* Magazine of September 13, 1899 (above), attacking corruption.

Tammany Hall decorated for the national convention of July 4, 1868. During this period, the Democrats were based on 14th Street, next to the Academy of Music, on the site of the future Con Edison Building.

During the 1840's, the area between Union Square and Gramercy Park became New York's newest and most glamorous residential neighborhood. Large private mansions sprang up along parks and avenues, cheek by jowl with the humblest row houses in adjacent streets. In the following decades, while the area west of 4th Avenue (now Park Avenue South) developed commercially around the "LADIES' MILE" of shops and stores, the area to the east remained strictly residential. Around the turn of the 20th century, Gramercy Park became the chosen neighborhood of wealthy New Yorkers who preferred its artistic, bohemian style to the more staid luxury of Uptown.

AROUND IRVING PLACE

NEW YORK FILM ACADEMY, FORMER TAMMANY HALL. E. 17TH ST N. E. CORNER OF UNION SQUARE E. (1928, arch. Thompson, Holmes & Converse). The Tammany Society – whose name was derived from TAMMANEND, a Delaware chief famed for his wisdom – was initially a patriotic organization, founded in 1789 as a response to the aristocratic Federalist party. Ten years after it was formed, the society began to take an interest in politics. Eventually it became the powerful New York Democratic Party machine, notorious for its corruption – especially under "Boss" Tweed ● *40*. Between 1866 and 1871 the Tweed Ring, which controlled key posts in the city government, pocketed several million dollars ▲ *185* of city funds. In 1928 the Tammany Society which, even after the death of "Boss" Tweed, still had a stranglehold on local politics, commissioned this Colonial-style building, inspired by Federal Hall (on Wall Street). In 1943 the International Ladies Garment Workers Union bought the building and turned it into their union headquarters. It now houses the New York Film Academy.

BOSS TWEED
Caricature of "Boss" Tweed, the notorious leader of the ring of the same name, who embezzled a huge amount of money from the city between 1866 and 1871.

WASHINGTON IRVING HOUSE. S.W. CORNER OF IRVING PL. AND 17TH ST. This house was designed in 1845 and its cast-iron verandah, wrought-iron balconies and wooden hood molding set it apart from the other 19th-century townhouses on the street. Elsie de Wolfe, the first professional interior designer in the country, lived here with her companion, the playwright Elisabeth Marbury, from 1894 to 1911.

WASHINGTON IRVING HIGH SCHOOL. 40 IRVING PLACE (1908–13, arch. C. B. J. Snyder). This school, which was originally a women's college until 1986,

takes its name from the writer WASHINGTON IRVING, author of *A History of New York from the Beginning of the World to the End of the Dutch Dynasty* (1809), a satirical history of the city written under the name of Dietrich Knickerbocker. The neo-Gothic entrance hall is decorated with very fine murals by BARRY FAULKNER depicting scenes from Irving's work.

CON EDISON BUILDING. CORNER OF 14TH ST. AND IRVING PLACE (1915–29, arch. Henry Hardenbergh). This is the headquarters of the Consolidated Edison Company, which provides New York's gas and electricity. Its tower (1926–9, arch. Warren & Wetmore) which is brightly illuminated at night and called the "Tower of Light", was erected in memory of company employees who died in World War I. The building stands partially on the site of the Academy of Music, a huge concert hall, opened in 1854, which hosted performers such as Jenny Lind, Adelina Patti and Edwin Booth until it was superseded in 1883 by the old Metropolitan Opera House, on Broadway.

PETE'S TAVERN. 129 E. 18TH ST. This bar, opened in 1864, remained open even during Prohibition ● *40*. In its years as a speakeasy, customers entered through the door of the cold room in a florist's shop next door. The walls are lined with photographs and press clippings on the bar's history and the notables who used to drink here, including politicians from Tammany Hall and the short-story writer O. HENRY, who wrote "The Gift of the Magi" here.

THE "BLOCK BEAUTIFUL" The townhouses on 19th Street were remodeled in the 1920's and many were given stucco façades adorned with painted, glazed tiles, wrought iron and sculptures, such as these lawn jockeys (left). Their faces were originally black, but were later repainted, as they were considered racist stereotypes.

The Con Edison Building.

Samuel B. Ruggles
Born in 1800 in New Milford, Connecticut,

Samuel Ruggles attended Yale University, then studied law under his father, an influential lawyer twice elected to the Connecticut legislature. In 1820 he moved with his wife, Mary R. Rathbone, to New York, where he established his own practice.

Behind the railings of Gramercy Park stands the statue of Edwin Booth, a bronze commissioned by the Players Club from Edmond T. Quinn, who has portrayed

the actor in the role of Hamlet. It was erected in 1918.

Carved faces of Franklin, Milton, Goethe and Dante adorn the façade of the National Arts Club in true Italianate style, as was the fashion at the time of the building's restoration. The façade has been listed as a landmark since 1966. Woody Allen used this building for one of the scenes in his film *Manhattan Murder Mystery*.

Gramercy Park ★

The name "Gramercy" is an anglicization of the Dutch names *Krom Moerasje*, "crooked little swamp", which described a meandering brook that used to run through here. In the early 1830's, Samuel B. Ruggles, who owned the land and who advocated planning towns around green spaces, designed the park and sold sixty-six building lots around it, stipulating that their owners would maintain the park and have exclusive access to it. To this day, Gramercy Park remains the only private square in New York.

Early Houses. Of the houses and other buildings designed in Ruggles' time, a few remain along the west and south sides of the park – among them nos. 3 and 4 **Gramercy Park West** and the Friends' Meeting House, at 28 Gramercy Park South. Designed by King & Kellum for the Quakers between 1857 and 1859, this Italianate building was renovated in 1975 and sold to its current owners, the **Brotherhood Synagogue**. At 34 Gramercy Park East, the **Gramercy**, built in 1883 by the architect George da Cunha, was one of Manhattan's first cooperative apartment buildings. It is also a fine example of New York Queen Anne style ● *90*, with its use of contrasting materials: brick, terracotta, wrought iron and stone. The sumptuous lobby boasts a mosaic floor and stained glass ceiling. Close by, at 36 **Gramercy Park East**, stands the residence built between 1908 and 1910 by the architect James Riley Gordon. This building is almost entirely clad in terracotta with motifs of medieval inspiration.

The Players. 16 **Gramercy Park South** (1845; remodeled 1888–9, arch. Stanford White). In 1886, two years before founding The Players Club, the actor Edwin Booth wrote: "An actors club has been a dream of mine for many years. Having quite a number of theatrical books, pictures, etc., etc.,

I have dreamed of furnishing such an establishment with them someday. When I step aside and before I go, I hope to accomplish something of this kind." The only condition stipulated by Booth was that he should have an apartment at the club. The chosen premises, a townhouse in Gothic Revival style ● *86*, were remodeled by Stanford White (free of charge) who added the porch, the impressive iron railings and the cornice graced with theatrical masks. The Players soon became the haunt of actors and their friends, including Mark Twain, John Barrymore, Eugene O'Neill and Helen Hayes.

National Arts Club. 15 **Gramercy Park South** (1845) ● *87*. The two original townhouses here were combined and remodeled between 1881 and 1884 by Calvert Vaux for the lawyer **Samuel J. Tilden**, who had been governor of New York between 1874 and 1876. The elegant Victorian Gothic façade, with brick cladding in contrasting shades, is in typical

The stained glass roof (above) of the National Arts Club, executed by MacDonald.

Ruskinian style; note the carved medallions of birds and plants over the windows and the busts on the first floor. The panels to the right of the porch are engraved with plants, animals and insects indigenous to New York. Three rooms were knocked together to house Tilden's library. This became the property of the New York Public Library in 1886 after the politician's death. In 1906 the residence was bought by the National Arts Club. This club, founded in 1898, was one of the first in New York to welcome women as members. The residence was refurbished for its new owners, but the original decoration was preserved. A temporary exhibition hall provides a taste of the sumptuous interiors.

3 AND 4 GRAMERCY PARK WEST

These two residences boast the finest cast-iron porches in New York. The two lamps that stand in front of no. 4 are a reminder that the house was the home of James Harper, Mayor of New York between 1844 and 1845 (and one of the founders of the publishers J. & J. Harper), Following a tradition dating back to Dutch times, the entrance to the mayor's house was flanked by two lamps which were lit when he was at home.

▲ FROM UNION SQUARE TO MADISON SQUARE

1 TAMMANY HALL   2 49 IRVING PLACE   3 W. IRVING HIGH SCHOOL   4 CON EDISON BLDG.   5 PETE'S TAVERN   6 GRAMERCY PARK   7 THE PLAYERS AND NATIONAL ART CLI

Between the 1860's and 1910, "Ladies' Mile", the stretch of Broadway, 5th and 6th avenues (left) running from 8th to 23rd streets, was the most fashionable area in New York. The most elegant shops and department stores of the "Ladies' Mile" were clustered along Broadway between Union Square and Madison Square. There was a constant stream of fashionable ladies in pursuit of luxury goods. Most of the shops that were here have long since closed down or moved Uptown.

VESTIGES OF THE COMMERCIAL ERA

TEDDY BEAR
A Brooklyn manufacturer decided to make a plush bear after he learned that president Theodore Roosevelt (shown below as a child) had spared a small bear while hunting. The president agreed to let it be called Teddy's Bear, in memory of his generous gesture.

FORMER ARNOLD CONSTABLE & CO. 881–7 BROADWAY, S. W. CORNER OF 19TH ST. (1868–9, arch. Griffith Thomas). In 1825 Aaron Arnold, an English immigrant from the Isle of Wight, opened a little dry-goods store on Pine Street, in Lower Manhattan. Business thrived, and in 1853 his son-in-law, James Constable, became his partner. Subsequently, the store moved farther north several times, before opening on the "Ladies' Mile" in 1869. The new store was such a success that it had to be extended on 19th Street up to 5th Avenue. The extension is a cast-iron building with a mansard roof, the most striking in New York.

FORMER W. & J. SLOANE. 884 BROADWAY, S. E. CORNER OF 19TH ST. (1881–2, arch. W. Wheeler Smith). For more than a century, Sloane's has been a renowned dealer of luxury furniture and carpets (the store supplied furnishings for the coronation of Tsar Nicholas II). The superb cast-iron store front is still intact. Note also the plants carved around the columns inside.

FORMER GORHAM MANUFACTURING COMPANY. 889–91 BROADWAY, N. W. CORNER OF 19TH ST. (1883–4, arch. Edward Kendall). This impressive Queen Anne-style ● 90 building housed the main New York outlet of the GORHAM SILVER COMPANY.

FORMER LORD & TAYLOR DRY GOODS STORE. 901 BROADWAY, S. W. CORNER OF 20TH ST. (1867, arch. James H. Giles). This cast-iron building has a corner turret which was designed to attract customers. The store, founded around 1830 by two Englishmen, Samuel Lord and George W. Taylor, was originally a small shop in Lower

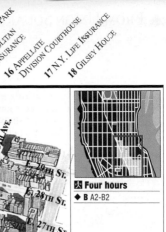

Four hours

◆ **B** A2-B2

The Broadway
Central Hotel c. 1900

LADIES' MILE
"Looking out from
Union Square, as this
oasis in the desert of
buildings is called, we
get an idea of how
interminable a
Broadway crowd is.
About a quarter of a
mile farther north,
Madison Square
relieves the confine-
ment of the street
with fountains, grass,
shrubs and trees, and
between the two such
a parade may be seen
on fine afternoons,
especially Saturdays,
as no other city in
America and few
other cities in the
world, can show. The
great retail houses of
the Stewarts, the
Tiffanys, the Arnold
Constables, and the
Lords and Taylors,
are concentrated
within these limits . . .
and women in their
most elegant attire
appear in quest of
new addition to their
already voluminous
apparel."

*Harper's New
Monthly Magazine,
1878*

Manhattan.
Later it became one
of the big names in
retailing, offering a wide range
of ready-to-wear clothing – as it
still does on 5th Avenue at 38th Street.

THEODORE ROOSEVELT'S BIRTHPLACE. 28 E. 20TH ST.
President Theodore Roosevelt was born here in 1858.
The present building is a reconstruction dating from 1923,
undertaken by his sisters, who engaged one of the first
women architects, Theodate Pope Ridde, for the work.
Inside, High Victorian Gothic rooms contain a MUSEUM
devoted to Roosevelt's achievements as explorer, naturalist
and politician.

FLATIRON BUILDING ★. BROADWAY AND 5TH AVE. AT 23RD ST.
(1902, arch. D. H. Burnham & Co.) ● 96. This slender

Madison Square Garden, New York City.

building, originally called the FULLER BUILDING after its developer, soon acquired its present name by virtue of its triangular shape – dictated by the awkward site. Its dramatic silhouette made it a familiar symbol of New York as well as a favorite subject for photographers and artists at the beginning of the 20th century ● *109*. This corner of 23rd Street and 5th Avenue was a popular haunt for "voyeurs", who took advantage of the air currents that swirled around the building, lifting women's skirts, to catch a glimpse of their ankles.

Madison Square

This square, which was named in memory of JAMES MADISON (1751–1836), president of the United States from 1809 to 1817, was established as a park on this site in 1811. The commemorative statues in the square include one of ADMIRAL DAVID FARRAGUT, who was a hero of the Mobile Bay naval battle, during the Civil War. This is the work of Augustus Saint-Gaudens (1880): the base, in the form of a bench, was designed by Stanford White.

MADISON SQUARE GARDEN NEW YORK.
THE WORLD FAMOUS METROPOLITAN HOME OF THESE COMBINED STUPENDOUS SHOWS.

It was on the roof of Madison Square Garden (above, 1910) on June 25, 1906, that architect Stanford White was killed by Harry Thaw, husband of Evelyn Nesbit, a former mistress.

FLATIRON BUILDING
This name was consequently given to other buildings on triangular sites, which occurred because of Broadway's irregular shape within the checker-board town plan.

METROPOLITAN LIFE TOWER ★. 1 MADISON AVE. (1893, 1909, arch. Napoleon LeBrun & Sons) ● *96*. The tower at the corner of 24th Street (modeled on Saint Mark's Campanile in Venice) is the company's symbol and was erected in order to make the building the tallest in the world (it was surpassed by the Woolworth Building ▲ *180* in 1913). In 1932 Met Life enlarged its premises with another building on the opposite side of the 24th Street, whose Italian marble lobby is particularly worth a visit. The existing building is a partial version of the project (above) which called for a tower nearly 100 stories high; it was left incomplete because of the Depression.

APPELLATE DIVISION COURTHOUSE ★. 27 MADISON AVE. (1900, arch. James Brown Lord) ● *92*. This small building, a Beaux Arts masterpiece, houses the Appellate Division of the New York State Supreme Court. The classical façade is adorned with sculptures depicting key figures from the history of law and various allegories evoking different aspects of Law and Justice. The lobby and the courtroom, which are richly decorated with murals and magnificent stained glass windows, are open to the public.

NEW YORK LIFE INSURANCE COMPANY. 51 MADISON AVE. (1928, arch. Cass Gilbert). This neo-Gothic skyscraper ● *86* stands on the site of the first two Madison Square Gardens.

GILSEY HOUSE. 1200 BROADWAY (1869–71, arch. Stephen D. Hatch) ● *89*. This building, with its enormous mansard roof, now an apartment building, was originally one of the city's most luxurious hotels.

Around Grand Central Terminal

"Five dollars. Grand Central. Three fifty. Penn Station. [He] got into the gleaming taxi. Horns were hooting everywhere . . ."
J. P. Donleavy

"Grand" is certainly the word for the large and imposing Grand Central Terminal, now restored to its former glory and considered one of the finest public buildings in the United States. It is the focal point of an area that embraces an interesting mixture of architectural styles and includes three more of New York's most distinguished landmarks: the Chrysler Building ▲ 266, the Empire State Building ▲ 242 and the New York Public Library ▲ 254. The United Nations headquarters ▲ 264, at the easternmost end of 42nd Street, as well as the many consulates and diplomatic residences, gives the eastern end of this area an international flavor. Just to the south of Grand Central Terminal lies Murray Hill, one of the most sought-after residential addresses in the city. To the west, along 5th Avenue, are some of the city's most elegant stores; farther west, Times Square

⏳ Five hours

◆ C C1-C2-C3-D1-D2-D3

GRAND CENTRAL DEPOT Grand Central Depot (below), the predecessor of the present terminal, was the first station opened in 1871 by the "Commodore".

and the Theater District. Times Square has been upgraded with brighter lights, more billboards, and new skyscrapers (Conde Nast and Reuters); Renzo Piano's skyscraper for *The New York Times* is slated for 2005.

GRAND CENTRAL TERMINAL

AUSPICIOUS BEGINNINGS. The original terminal (commonly called Grand Central Station) was built in 1871 by "Commodore" Cornelius Vanderbilt. The present building dates from the time of his grandson, William K. Vanderbilt, chairman of the New York Central Railroad, which included three major rail networks operating out of Manhattan. In 1903 a closed competition was launched for the reconstruction of the station. The winning firm, Reed & Stem, planned the layout of the station; later, Warren & Wetmore were asked to aid in the revision of the original design.

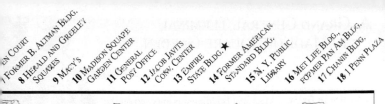

The new station was opened in 1913. It was a state-of-the-art design, with tracks running on two levels under Park Avenue.

The terminal was central to an ambitious town-planning project devised by William Wilgus, the chief engineer of the New York Central Corporation. This program included electrifying the network and laying down and organizing the underground tracks. Concerned with getting a good return on its investment, the railroad company rented out the building rights to the land above the tracks. Hotels, offices and luxury apartments were built along Park Avenue, which became one of the most prestigious addresses in Manhattan. The view down the avenue toward the station, crowned by the New York Central Building (now the Helmsley Building) was one of the most desirable. When, in 1963, the huge Pan Am (now

"I must admit, however, that I am starting to become reconciled with the Pan Am Building, which juts out of Grand Central Station like the shoulder piece of a bayonet sticking out of a fine animal that has been stabbed in the back."

Donald Westlake,
Strange Brothers

PEDIMENT OF GRAND CENTRAL TERMINAL
The central sculptural group on the station's pediment represents, Mercury (shown right), flanked by Hercules and Minerva. According to Warren, they embody, respectively "the glory of commerce", "moral energy" and "mental energy". The work was commissioned from Jules Coutan.

Grand Central Terminal underwent a complete renovation in the 1990's (below).

MetLife) Building was imposed on the station, thus spoiling this view, it raised a storm of public protest.

A CLASSICAL FAÇADE. The 42nd-Street façade, by the Beaux Arts-trained Whitney Warren, who was responsible for the station's exterior decoration, is a piece of architectural bravura. The architect saw the terminal as a triumphal gateway to the city and the façade, a stone facing on a metal frame, is remarkable for its use of a limited number of unusually large, boldly defined elements.

THE INTERIOR. The layout of Grand Central Terminal was revolutionary for its time. A system of ramps, which can be reached via the subway or from outside the station, helps prevent disorderly crowds, a common problem in other stations. The VAULTED CEILING of the vast MAIN CONCOURSE is decorated with the signs of the zodiac and the constellations: electric bulbs representing 2,500 stars, joined by a gilt border to form the "celestial figures". The ARRIVAL HALL, which is much smaller, formed part of the former Biltmore Hotel, now replaced by an office building. Originally, the MAIN CONCOURSE was exclusively used for long-distance trains while suburban trains ran from the hall on the lower level.

GRAND CENTRAL TRM
Sectional View from Biltmore Hotel Looking East Toward Le...
SHOWING PASSAGEWAYS TO HOTELS, OFFICE

1 - Hotel Commodore
2 - Biltmore Hotel
3 - Hotel Roosevelt
4 - New York Central Bldg. —230 Park Ave.
5 - Graybar Building
6 - Grand Central Terminal Office Building

Ⓐ - Cab Baggage Service
Ⓑ - Travel Information Bureau
Ⓒ - Newsreel Theatre
Ⓓ - Lower Level
Ⓔ - Stairways from Vanderbilt Ave. to Upper & Lower Levels
Ⓕ - Ticket Offices

EXPRESS TRAINS

SUBURBAN TRAINS

TO INCOMING TRAINS

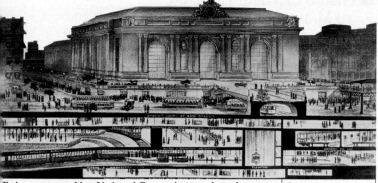

Trains to upstate New York and Connecticut are the only ones that run from this station.

THE "PALACE OF DEPARTURE". This is how French writer Paul Morand labelled the terminal, whose monumentality, comfort and cleanliness are a source of admiration for European visitors. Movie-makers have filmed some unforgettable farewell scenes and chases here. For example, Alfred Hitchcock used it for some sequences for *North by Northwest*, starring Cary Grant and Eva Marie Saint. Grand Central Terminal's passenger figures reached a peak, in 1947, of 65 million – more than 40 percent of the US population at that time. These days the terminal is always busy with commuters, college students and tourists. In recent years the terminal almost suffered the fate of Pennsylvania Station, which was demolished in 1963 to make way for the new Madison Square Garden ▲ *249*. In 1968, the Penn Central Corporation, the railroad's new owners, planned to demolish Grand Central's 42nd-Street façade and the waiting rooms to construct a 55-story tower. The terminal was saved by a high-profile campaign led by Jacqueline Kennedy Onassis and the architect Philip Johnson, and the station was listed on the National Register of Historic Places in 1983. The entire station was restored to its past splendor in the 1990's. It houses some 100 stores including a great gourmet food hall and restaurants such as Métrazur, Cipriani Dolci, Oyster Bar and Michael Jordan Steak House.

Cross section of Grand Central Terminal.

The renovated Main Concourse of Grand Central Terminal, completed in 1998.

"The evening she arrived at Grand Central Station was the turning point of her life. Disoriented, scared, she had crossed the huge concourse of the station, carrying her one and only suitcase; she had looked up and had stopped dead. She was probably one of the few people to have immediately realized that the heaven of the great vaulted ceiling had been painted back to front. The Eastern stars were in the West."
Marry Higgins Clark, *The Night of the Fox*

239

A PATRIOTIC WOMAN
According to a
Revolutionary War
legend, Mrs Murray
(whose family name
survives in Murray
Hill (right, during the
1860's) played a trick
on the British. By
inviting General
Howe and his officers
– who had just landed
with their troops –
to tea, she enabled
George Washington
and his men to retreat
to northwest
Manhattan.

MURRAY HILL

Façade, 149 E. 38th St.

POLISH CONSULATE
233 Madison Ave.
This mansion, built in
Second Empire style,
was formerly the
headquarters of the
National Democratic
Club. Its interior
(below) is as opulent
as its exterior.

This neighborhood, lying between 34th and 42nd streets and
between 5th and 3rd avenues, takes its name from Robert
Murray, who, during the British colonial period, owned a
country house in the center of this area. At the end of the
19th century, Murray Hill consisted of a collection of stables
and outbuildings belonging to the private mansions on
5th Avenue owned by "The Four Hundred". This referred to
the four hundred people from the most distinguished families
in New York, who were invited to Mrs Astor's annual ball
(her ballroom being able to accommodate that number).
When the mansions on 5th Avenue were demolished at the
beginning of the 20th century to make way for department
stores, a number of these outbuildings were refurbished. They
now rank among the most sought-after addresses in the city.
PHILIP MORRIS INC. BUILDING. 120 PARK AVE. (1982, arch.
Ulrich Franzen and Associates) ● *103*. The ground floor of
the New York headquarters of this well-known cigarette
manufacturer (open to the public) houses an enclosed garden,
a café and an annex of the Whitney Museum of Modern Art
▲ *326*, which mounts temporary exhibitions.
38TH STREET. With its varied styles of houses, the blocks of

38th Street between Park and 3rd avenues
epitomize the charm of the neighborhood.
At no. 108, a small Art Deco building, built
in 1930, proffers a "Cubist" façade, its
redbrick bonding enhanced with
polychromatic stringcourses made of
glazed terracotta. At the corner of
Lexington Avenue two PRIVATE MANSIONS
stand opposite each other: no. 136, in
Victorian style with little windowpanes
made of blown glass, and no. 125, a well-
preserved example of Old Charleston style.
Farther east, at no. 149, is a Flemish
Renaissance-style carriage house (above,
left) decorated with the heads of bulldogs
and horses. At no. 150–152, there is a
Federal-style residence from 1858
(remodeled in 1935), dating from the time
when Murray Hill was still a suburb of New
York. This was the home of a member of
the family of Martin Van Buren, the eighth
President of the United States (1837–41).

MORGAN, FATHER AND SON
John Pierpont Morgan, Sr (1837–1913) and his son, John Pierpont, Jr (1867–1943), built up the most influential financial trust in America before the 1929 crash. Their bank served the most important families in New York, such as the Astors, Vanderbilts and Guggenheims, and it saved the city from bankruptcy on three occasions. Until 1933 a letter of credit from the Morgan bank was regarded as an impeccable testimonial.
J. Pierpont Morgan, Sr (above) was not only the greatest financier of his time but also an unrivaled collector of rare books and manuscripts, for which he built his private library (left). It was opened to the public in 1924, in accordance with his wishes.

SNIFFEN COURT HISTORIC DISTRICT ★. 150–158 E. 36TH ST. (1850–60). Grouped around a small court, these ten Romanesque Revival brick houses once served as stables for some wealthy 5th Avenue residents. In the 1920's they were converted into homes, studios and offices.

UNION LEAGUE CLUB. S. W. CORNER OF PARK AVE. AND E. 37TH ST. (1931, arch. Morris and O'Connor). This imposing building in neo-Georgian style is the headquarters of a club founded in 1863 by some Republican former members of the Union Club. A conflict had arisen between them and some other members over the Club's admission of some Confederate sympathizers. To express their staunch support for the Northern cause and President Lincoln, these Republicans formed their own club, which they called the Union League.

PIERPONT MORGAN LIBRARY ● 93 ★. 29 AND 33 E. 36TH ST. AND 231 MADISON AVE. The Pierpont Morgan Library comprises three buildings. At 29 E. 36th Street, the grand and luxurious former library of J. P. Morgan, Sr ● 93 (designed by Benjamin W. Morris) contains his collection of works of art and antique manuscripts and books, including a Gutenberg Bible. The main entrance to the library is through the annex at 29 E. 36th Street, a museum that mounts temporary exhibitions. A pleasant covered garden leads to 231 Madison Avenue, a brownstone ● 88 that was once the home of J. P. Morgan, Jr. It was bought in 1990 by the museum to house a bookshop and a conference hall.

241

The plans for the Empire State Building, located on the corner of 5th Avenue between 33rd and 34th streets, were unveiled to the press on August 29, 1929. John J. Raskob, the prime mover behind this project and vice-president of General Motors, decided to go one better than his rival, Chrysler: the building was to reach a height of 1,250 feet, taller than the Chrysler Building by 202 feet, to become the highest building in the world until the construction of the World Trade Center and the Sears Roebuck Tower in Chicago in the early 1970's. The Empire State Building also set a new record for the speed of construction – more than four floors per week – and because of the Depression it cost less than the estimate ($41 million instead of 60).

Below, work begins on the Empire State Building.

"CATHEDRAL IN THE SKY" ✪
No visit to New York would be complete without the ascent to the top of the Empire State Building. Its two observation platforms on the 86th and 102nd floors afford breathtaking views of the city's densely packed buildings, streets and avenues. Go in the morning when it opens at 9.30am or at sunset to avoid long lines and to enjoy the best views. At nightfall, the sparkling lights of the city are a magical sight. The last elevator leaves the top at 11.30pm.

TEAMWORK
The construction of the Empire State Building was captured in a series of amazing pictures by photographer Lewis Hine (right and opposite).

The Waldorf-Astoria (left), demolished in 1929 and replaced by the Empire State Building.

AN ENORMOUS PROJECT
The photomontage on the right shows an early design for the Empire State Building superimposed onto the background of the city. This design was not, in the end, used.

"THE HAPPY WARRIOR"
Alfred E. Smith (right), a former governor of the State of New York and president of the corporation that managed the building, announced the project in 1929.

A FAILURE
When it was opened on May 1, 1931, the "Empty State Building" had rented out only 46 percent of its office space, despite an extensive publicity campaign.

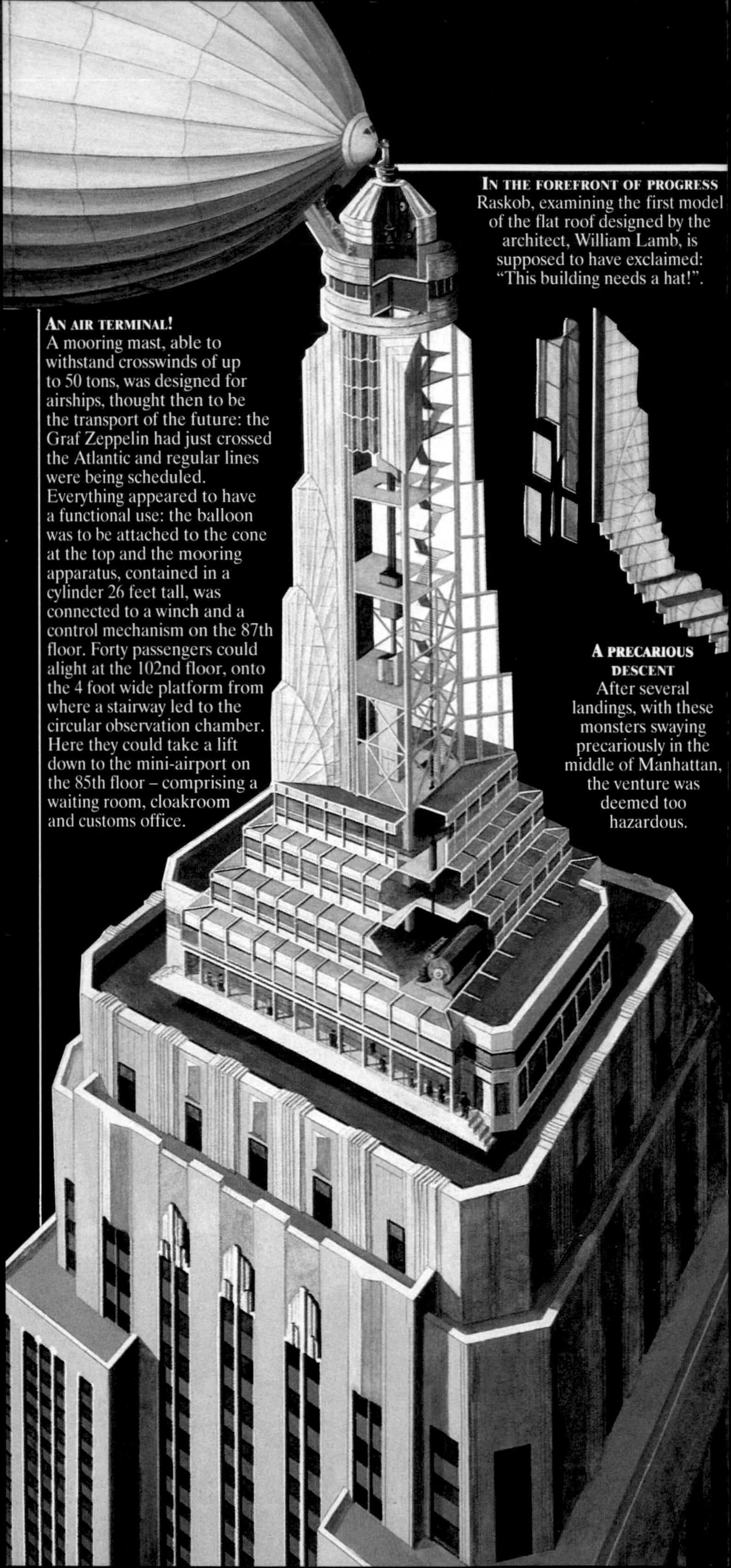

In the forefront of progress
Raskob, examining the first model of the flat roof designed by the architect, William Lamb, is supposed to have exclaimed: "This building needs a hat!".

An air terminal!
A mooring mast, able to withstand crosswinds of up to 50 tons, was designed for airships, thought then to be the transport of the future: the Graf Zeppelin had just crossed the Atlantic and regular lines were being scheduled. Everything appeared to have a functional use: the balloon was to be attached to the cone at the top and the mooring apparatus, contained in a cylinder 26 feet tall, was connected to a winch and a control mechanism on the 87th floor. Forty passengers could alight at the 102nd floor, onto the 4 foot wide platform from where a stairway led to the circular observation chamber. Here they could take a lift down to the mini-airport on the 85th floor – comprising a waiting room, cloakroom and customs office.

A precarious descent
After several landings, with these monsters swaying precariously in the middle of Manhattan, the venture was deemed too hazardous.

The top illuminated
to celebrate
St Patrick's Day,
Independence Day,
Easter Week,
Halloween, Memorial
Day, Christmas and
New Year, Gay Pride,

5,000 VISITORS PER DAY
The observatory on the 86th floor
is an invaluable source of income
for the Empire State Building.

MOST FAMOUS
FAMOUS BUILDING
SOUVENIR OF VISIT TO THE
MOST FAMOUS BUILDING IN THE WORLD
EMPIRE STATE OBSERVATORIES
3155175
EMPIRE S OBSERVAT
3155113

TWO SIGNS OF THE FUTURE
Utopian architects and science-
fiction authors dreamt of a union
of skyscrapers and air transport.

STARS
The terrace has
welcomed heads of
State and government
(Mussolini, Churchill,
Castro, Khrushchev),
royalty and a throng
of celebrities. On the
west side of the glass
observatory, there
are comfortable rattan
chairs where you can sit
and admire the sunset.

HIGH WAVES
The mooring mast,
having become
obsolete, was
topped with a
telecom-
munications
antenna, like the
Eiffel Tower in
Paris.

245

REAL CATASTROPHES
The Empire State Building has been the scene of many spectacular disasters, at least as dramatic as the one in the legendary film, *King Kong*.

THE BIG JUMP
Sixteen people have committed suicide by jumping off the top of the platform on the 86th floor. A railing was erected to stop suicide attempts, but has not managed to discourage the truly desperate. This figure is actually fairly low given that 70 million visitors have come up to admire the view; the Eiffel Tower has recorded 400 suicides.

FACT IS STRANGER THAN FICTION
On July 28, 1945, a B-25 bomber, piloted by William Smith, flew over Manhattan at more than 186 mph and at an altitude of 1148 feet, less than half the minimum authorized altitude. It is not known why he was weaving between the skyscrapers of Midtown but at 9.52am, having just missed the Helmsley Building, he crashed into the Empire State Building, devastating the north façade of the 79th floor. One of the engines went straight through the tower and crashed down on the other side of 33rd St. The outcome of this catastrophe was fourteen dead and twenty-six wounded. Luckily, as it was a Saturday, the offices were all virtually deserted.

MIRACLE ON 3

Gust of wind saves woman who leaped from 86th floor of Empire State Building

Left, lightning striking the spire.

A DETOUR TOWARD THE JACOB JAVITS CONVENTION CENTER
This exhibition center between 11th and 12th aves., 34th and 37th sts., was inaugurated in 1986 and has the facilities to accommodate nearly 86,000 visitors daily. Its architect, I. M. Pei, designed a glass structure that is opaque by day and reflects the skyline of Midtown but becomes transparent when illuminated at night.

AROUND THE EMPIRE STATE BUILDING

FORMER B. ALTMAN BUILDING ▲ *361*. 5TH AVE. BETWEEN 34TH AND 35TH STS. (1906, arch. Trowbridge & Livingston). Benjamin Altman was the first to open a department store in this previously residential neighborhood. He built it in the style of a grand Italianate palace to blend in with the surrounding mansions. The store closed in 1990, but the building now houses the New York Public Library's ▲ *252* Science and Industry collection (entrance on Madison Ave.).

HERALD AND GREELEY SQUARES. INTERSECTION OF 6TH AVE., BROADWAY AND 34TH ST. These two triangular squares face each other. Herald Square commemorates the New York Herald Building (founded in 1835 by James Gordon Bennett) whose headquarters, built in 1893, stood just north of here. The clock that used to crown the building, which was demolished in 1921, now stands over the square. Two bronze figures, nicknamed Stuff and Guff, chime the hours. The statue of Horace Greeley, founder of the *New York Tribune* (1841) and a crusading journalist, particularly in the cause of the abolition of slavery, seems to watch them from Greeley Square, just to the south. The statue was erected in 1890.

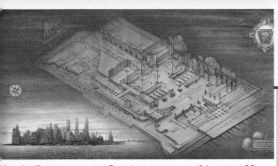

AN INSTITUTION
Every year Macy's organizes the Thanksgiving Day Parade ● *53*. Early in the morning, the parade leaves the Museum of Natural History, on Central Park West, and heads for the store.

Macy's logo, a red star, was once the emblem of Macy the whaler captain.

MACY'S. BROADWAY AND 7TH AVE., BETWEEN 34TH AND 35TH STS. (1901, arch. De Lemos & Cordes, additions 1924–31, arch. Robert D. Kohn). R. H. Macy, the former captain of a whaler, founded what was to become "the world's largest store" (as trumpeted by the huge billboard on the Broadway façade) in 1858. After occupying premises in the vicinity of 14th Street, Macy's moved to Broadway and 34th Street in 1902. Over the years the store was extended west to 7th Avenue. The 34th Street entrance still possesses its superb original decorations: four caryatids hold the emblems of commerce and abundance in their hands.

MADISON SQUARE GARDEN CENTER. BETWEEN 31ST AND 33RD STS., 7TH AND 8TH AVES. (1968, arch. Charles Luckman Assocs.). A masterpiece, Penn Station was destroyed in 1963 to make way for this vast leisure and office complex. The original Pennsylvania Station was one of the few "grand horizontals" left in an increasingly "vertical" New York. Built in 1910 and only four stories high, it covered 12 acres of land. Its architects, McKim, Mead & White, drew their inspiration directly from the great buildings of the Roman Empire. The general waiting room, which was modeled on the Baths of Caracalla, and the steel and glass roof over the train concourse, were particularly fine features. The demolition of the station gave rise to the first major public outcry in support of preserving landmarks. By contrast, the present Penn Station is unobtrusively hidden underground, below Madison Square Garden. This massive complex, which offers cultural and sporting events all year round, is the third with this name; the first was located at Madison Square and the second on 9th Avenue at 49th Street. All of them fell victim to fire.

GENERAL POST OFFICE OF NEW YORK
Between 8th and 9th aves., 31st and 33rd sts. Impressed by McKim, Mead & White's Penn Station, the government commissioned this firm to design the General Post Office, which was completed in 1913. Forty percent of its mail used to come via the station, which it faced across 8th Ave. It is, however, merely a pale reflection, aesthetically, of its former neighbor. The width of the façade bears a quotation, loosely adapted from Herodotus: "Neither snow nor rain nor heat nor gloom of night stays these couriers from the swift completion of their appointed rounds."

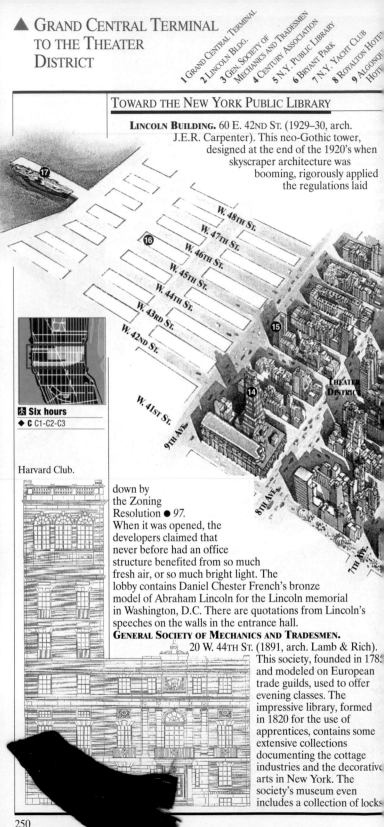

▲ GRAND CENTRAL TERMINAL TO THE THEATER DISTRICT

1 GRAND CENTRAL TERMINAL
2 LINCOLN BLDG.
3 GEN. SOCIETY OF MECHANICS AND TRADESMEN
4 CENTURY ASSOCIATION
5 N.Y. PUBLIC LIBRARY
6 BRYANT PARK
7 N.Y. YACHT CLUB
8 ALGONQUIN HOTE
9 ROYALTON HOTE

TOWARD THE NEW YORK PUBLIC LIBRARY

LINCOLN BUILDING. 60 E. 42ND ST. (1929–30, arch. J.E.R. Carpenter). This neo-Gothic tower, designed at the end of the 1920's when skyscraper architecture was booming, rigorously applied the regulations laid

🕐 Six hours

◆ C C1-C2-C3

Harvard Club.

down by the Zoning Resolution ● 97. When it was opened, the developers claimed that never before had an office structure benefited from so much fresh air, or so much bright light. The lobby contains Daniel Chester French's bronze model of Abraham Lincoln for the Lincoln memorial in Washington, D.C. There are quotations from Lincoln's speeches on the walls in the entrance hall.

GENERAL SOCIETY OF MECHANICS AND TRADESMEN. 20 W. 44TH ST. (1891, arch. Lamb & Rich). This society, founded in 178? and modeled on European trade guilds, used to offer evening classes. The impressive library, formed in 1820 for the use of apprentices, contains some extensive collections documenting the cottage industries and the decorative arts in New York. The society's museum even includes a collection of locks

THE CLUBS. This neighborhood is the home of some of the city's most venerable clubs. Leading universities such as Yale, Princeton and Harvard have established their clubs here, and admission is reserved exclusively for former students. The lobby of the Yale Club, at the corner of Vanderbilt Avenue and 44th Street, contains a commemorative plaque for one of the university's former students, Captain Nathan Hale, ▲ 171, a hero of the American Revolution.

CENTURY ASSOCIATION
7 W. 43rd St. This distinguished Italianate-style club, founded in 1891 to provide a forum for artists and intellectuals, takes its name from its original number of members – one hundred.

NEW YORK YACHT CLUB ★. 37 W. 44TH ST. ● 93
1901, arch. Warren & Wetmore). The façade of this building, with its carvings of waves, shells and seaweed, and its extraordinary windows suggesting the stern of an 18th-century ship ● 93, indicate this club's sphere of activity. Founded in 1844, the New York Yacht Club, the patriarch of American yacht clubs, successfully defended the America's Cup ● 65 for 132 years until 1983, when the Australians wrested it away.

THE AMERICA'S CUP
In 1851, when Queen Victoria asked who had come second in the race, she received the answer "But, Ma'am, there is no second place".

251

The lobby (right) of the Royalton Hotel.

ALGONQUIN HOTEL Dorothy Parker, George S. Kaufman, Robert Benchley, Edna Ferber, Ring Lardner, Harold Ross and James Thurber used to engage in sparkling conversation around the Round Table in the Oak Room of the Algonquin. It was here, in 1925, that Ross founded the witty, intellectual magazine, *The New Yorker* ● 54.

N.Y. PUBLIC LIBRARY The main façade, which is set back from 5th Avenue, is dominated by a triumphal arch crowned by allegorical figures by Paul Wayland Bartlett, representing, from left to right, History, Drama, Poetry, Religion, Romance and Philosophy. The statues above the fountains on the terrace are the work of Frederick MacMonnies, while the two white marble lions guarding the steps (dubbed Patience and Fortitude) are by Edward Clark Potter. In fine weather the terrace is an ideal spot from which to watch the world go by – perhaps while having a drink in one of its two cafés.

ROYALTON HOTEL. 44 W. 44TH ST. The ultra-modern lobby of this hotel, designed by Philippe Starck, is worth a visit. The writer William Saroyan used to stay here for long periods of time; this is where he was living when he was awarded the Pulitzer Prize for his play *The Time of Your Life* in 1940.

CITY CLUB HOTEL. 55 W. 44TH ST. This luxury hotel is housed in a building dating from 1904. Its interior was redesigned by Jeffrey Bilhubber. The restaurant here, run by chef Daniel Boulud, is well worth a visit.

ALGONQUIN HOTEL. 59 W. 44TH ST. (1902, arch. Goldwyn Starrett). In the 1920's, this hotel served as a meeting place for leading figures in theatrical and literary circles. The place to be seen in now is the Blue Bar in the lobby.

FRED F. FRENCH BUILDING ★. 551 5TH AVE. AT N. E. CORNER OF 45TH ST. (1927, arch. H. Douglas Ives and Sloan & Robertson). The faience mosaics decorating the upper setbacks of this building were sharply criticized when it was completed. Nowadays they are praised for their originality. The lobby is typical of those found in skyscrapers of this period.

NEW YORK PUBLIC LIBRARY

HISTORY. With its valuable collections and majestic, lavishly decorated architecture, the Main Branch of the New York Public Library ranks among the great libraries of the world.

ts research collection was founded on May 23, 1895, with a equest from Samuel J. Tilden which enabled the collections f the Astor and Lenox libraries to be consolidated. New ork's municipal government agreed to contribute a plot of nd on the condition that the library be open to the public in ne evenings and on Sundays and public holidays. The library ite, on 5th Avenue between 40th and 42nd streets, had ormerly been occupied by the Croton Reservoir, which was rected in 1842 to supply the city with drinking water. The ew library, designed by the Beaux Arts architects John M. arrère and Thomas Hastings, was opened in 1911. Built of hite marble, it sits grandly back from the street on a terrace, pproached by wide steps flanked by two haughty-looking one lions.

HE INTERIOR. On the first floor, the Gottesman Exhibition Hall mounts some extremely interesting temporary xhibitions. Since 1983 the murals by Richard Haas, depicting ne headquarters of New York's leading newspapers and ublishing houses, have graced the De Witt Wallace eriodical Room. This room owes its name to the founder of ne *Reader's Digest*, who recopied the rst texts he was to publish here. The nain Reading Room, on the top floor, which is divided by the delivery desk, uns the length of the building and can ccommodate seven hundred readers. here is a guided tour which includes all ne rooms.

HE COLLECTIONS. The library holds bout 36 million objects, including 11.3 nillion books. Its specialist departments nclude the Jewish, Slavic and Oriental ivisions; the History and Genealogy epartment, which boasts a collection of 00,000 views of New York; the Scientific epartment, in which Edwin Land, nventor of the Polaroid camera and hester Carlson, inventor of xerography, id research; and the Economics epartment, which houses 1.5 million ooks and 11,000 periodicals. The library also the proud owner of some rarities uch as a Gutenberg Bible and a globe ating from 1519, the first one to show merica.

In 1970 the small shops lining the Avenue of the Americas, or 6th Avenue (above) between 43rd and 44th streets, were knocked down and 1133 (below) was built, continuing the transformation of the avenue.

AMERICAN STANDARD BUILDING
The carved allegories on the façade of this building, first owned by the American Radiator Company, symbolize the transformation of matter into energy. This figure (right) embodies hydraulic energy.

1133 Avenue of the Americas.

FROM THE NEW YORK PUBLIC LIBRARY TO TIMES SQUARE

FORMER KNOX HAT BUILDING. 452 5TH AVE., S. W. CORNER 5TH AVE. AND 40TH ST. (1902, arch. John H. Duncan). This Beaux Arts-style building originally housed an enormous hat store owned by Colonel Edward M. Knox, known as the "hatter of presidents".

BRYANT PARK. The site of Bryant Park – and of the New York Public Library ▲ 252 – was a potter's field in 1823. In 1853 the Crystal Palace ● 39 (a replica of the one in London) was built on this site to host the first American world's fair; it was destroyed by fire five years later. The park was named after the poet and journalist William Cullen Bryant in 1894 and redesigned in its present form in 1934. During lunch hour people working in the neighborhood come to unwind in this green oasis, the only one in Midtown. It affords a splendid view of the surrounding buildings.

FORMER AMERICAN STANDARD BUILDING ★. 40 W. 40TH ST. (1924, arch. Hood & Fouilhoux). This was the first Art Deco building ● 99 constructed in New York by Hood, who subsequently designed the *Daily News* Building ▲ 272 and much of Rockefeller Center ▲ 274. Its characteristic features are the black brickwork with gold terracotta trimmings of the top and the bronze and black granite façade of the ground floor. It was built for the American Radiator Company, later American Standard.

BUSH TOWER. 132 W. 42ND ST. (arch. Helmle & Corbett). This slender skyscraper was regarded as a prototype for the next ten years. It was built in 1918 to house the headquarters of the Bush Terminal Company, a shipping firm.

FORMER KNICKERBOCKER HOTEL. 1466 BROADWAY, AT S. E. CORNER OF 42ND ST. (1902, arch. Marvin & Vavis). This hotel was built by Colonel John Jacob Astor IV. One of its famous residents, Enrico Caruso, lived here between 1908 and 1920. Mary Pickford, the silent movie star, also stayed here in 1916, the year she met actor Douglas Fairbanks, her future husband.

TIMES SQUARE

Times Square owes its name to *The New York Times*, which in 1904 moved into the Times Tower, at the south end of the square. (In 2005 they will have a new building, on the east side of 8th Avenue between 40th and 41st streets, designed by Renzo Piano). Since the beginning of the 20th century this intersection of Broadway and 7th Avenue has been the center of the performing arts in New York ▲ 258. Since the early 1990's Times Square has been relit, cleaned up and redeveloped under the auspices of the Times Square Business Development District, an organization uniting private enterprises, civic associations and City Hall. The media, the theater world and the hotel business have all reinvested in the area, restoring the old theaters,

pening new theaters, cinemas and shops and building offices, ousing and hotels. The recent building of skyscrapers in the quare and the surrounding area have made this quarter of Manhattan one of the most densely built-up in the world. Notice, for example, the Reuters (1998-2001) and Condé Nast 1996-9) buildings at nos. 3 and 4 respectively. With almost all he buildings covered with advertising boards, giant screens nd electronic displays, Times Square sparkles again, making stunning sight by day or night. Each year a popular tradition ersists: ever since the New York Times first moved here on December 31, 1904, thousands of people have flocked here to ee in the New Year with a fantastic fireworks display.

> "The age of the huge advertising billboards dawned in 1916. The whole district was electrified. Times Square . . . was a new wonderland, an electric city, the Great White Way of Broadway."
>
> Jerome Charyn,
> *Metropolis*

TIMES SQUARE, FORMER TIMES TOWER. (1904, arch. Eidlitz & MacKenzie). *The New York Times* occupied Times Tower or only about ten years before moving most of its operations nto its present premises at 229 West 43rd Street. In 1966 he tower was converted (and renamed the Allied Chemical ower) and its original granite and terracotta facing was eplaced by a marble one, although the electric sign that vraps around the tower is still in place. When first switched n in 1928, it announced the result of the presidential lections with Herbert Hoover's victory.

2ND STREET. The section between Broadway and 8th Avenue vas once nicknamed Theater Row. Left to deteriorate during he 1970's, it has now been given a facelift. The old theaters ave been renovated and two huge complexes comprising novie theaters, restaurants, stores and hotels have been built n either side of the street. Madame Tussaud's Wax Museum, branch of the famous London museum, is also on this street.

TIMES SQUARE VISITORS' CENTER. FORMER EMBASSY HEATER, 1560 7TH AVE., BETWEEN 46TH AND 47TH STS. (1925, rch. Thomas Lamb). This occupies the former Embassy 'heater, a listed building in the middle of the square. In what as the theater's Art Deco auditorium, the Visitors' Center ffers a range of services and information about the Theater District and New York in general. A film tells the history of 'imes Square and there are guided tours of the area.

> **TIMES SQUARE, BUZZING WITH LIFE IN THE HEART OF BROADWAY ☉**
> This small asphalt triangle, surrounded by skyscrapers, at the intersection of Broadway and 7th Avenue is probably the liveliest spot in the city, whatever the time, day or night. Times Square is best visited at night, though, when people are flocking to the theaters and the giant advertising signs plastered over all the buildings on the square are lit up. To see the square at its most spectacular, catch a taxi on Broadway at 57th St. and get out at 42nd St.

LOBBY OF THE FILM CENTER BUILDING
Although the exterior of the Film Center Building is ordinary, its lobby is stunning. The architect, Albert Kahn, was influenced by the Decorative Arts exhibition in Paris (1925) and this building marked the start of his polychromatic phase. For the floor he created a composition combining pinkish marble circles with white and black marble strips; for the walls (above right) a mosaic of blue and orange tiles.

Façade of the Actors Studio.

MURAL PAINTING
The façade of this bicycle store at the corner of 9th Ave. and 47th St. is decorated with a reproduction of a drawing by Sempé, whose *New Yorker* illustrations had caught the eye of the store's owner.

FORMER PARAMOUNT BUILDING. 1501 BROADWAY (1927, arch. Rapp & Rapp). The most eye-catching building on Times Square used to house the offices for Paramount Pictures, as well as the Paramount Theater, which no longer exists. The day after its opening, in 1926, the *New York Times* ran this advertisement: "30,222 spectators in two days! Into the paradise of luxury, color and enchantment they came." The grandiose "movie palace" seating 3,664 people, had a huge lobby, the Grand Hall, larger than that of the Paris Opera House, as well as various lounges and promenades. The movie theater had to close in 1965, as it was not making a profit, and the building was converted into offices. Dolly Down, a singer who once performed there, said of its new occupants: "These kids have no idea what it was and they'll never know because there will not be anything like those theaters again." This building has fourteen symmetrical setbacks, rising to a sphere, formerly illuminated, at the top.

MARRIOTT MARQUIS HOTEL. 1531–49 BROADWAY (1985, arch. John C. Portman & Assocs.). Three theaters were demolished to make way for the Marriott, one of Manhattan's largest hotels. Like many hotels of this period, it is built around a spectacular atrium. Take a dizzying ride in one of the hotel's transparent elevators.

I. MILLER BUILDING. N. E. CORNER OF 46TH ST. AND 7TH AVE. The south façade is decorated with an array of sculptures by A. Stirling Calder (1929), depicting actresses and singers in their most famous roles: Mary Pickford as Little Lord Fauntleroy, Ethel Barrymore as Ophelia, Rosa Ponselle as Norma and Marilyn Miller as Sunny.

FATHER DUFFY SQUARE. The north triangle of Times Square was named after Father Duffy, the "Fighting Chaplain of the 69th regiment". This New York unit served in France during World War I. Later, in his parish church, the Holy Cross Roman Catholic Church (42nd Street), Father Duffy became friendly with many actors and comedians. His statue (1937, Charles Keck) is decorated with a Celtic cross. Father Duffy Square is also the site of the TKTS booth, where one can buy half-price tickets for Broadway shows.

Bicycles

DETOUR TO THE HUDSON RIVER

FORMER McGRAW-HILL BUILDING. 330 W. 42ND ST. (1931, arch. Hood, Godley & Fouilhoux). This New York landmark ● *99*, a fusion of Art Deco and International Style, has a beautifully decorated lobby, whose opaque Carrera glass and stainless steel benefit from a sophisticated lighting system.

FILM CENTER BUILDING ★. 630 9TH AVE. (1929, arch. Ely Jacques). This building is a typical example of 1920's Art Deco ● *99* architecture. Its extraordinary polychromatic lobby is well worth the walk from Broadway.

ACTORS STUDIO. 432 W. 44TH ST. (1858). The famous drama school, founded by Elia Kazan in 1947, moved into this former Presbyterian church in 1955. The Actors Studio became internationally famous through the work of its director, Lee Strasberg, and radically influenced the New York theater scene. The "Strasberg Method", inspired by Stanislavsky and his Art Theater in Moscow, advocated an intensive course of mental exercises to improve actors' self-awareness and their empathy with their characters. Marlon Brando attended classes here.

"HELL'S KITCHEN". The area lying to the west of 6th Avenue,

between 30th and 57th streets was long known as "Hell's Kitchen". This nickname allegedly emerged from a conversation between two policemen who had been called out to deal with a street brawl at the height of summer. One of them apparently exclaimed, "It's as hot as Hell here." The other corrected him, saying "It's cool in Hell. This is Hell's kitchen." Until 1945 the nickname was fairly apt, for the area was then controlled by the underworld. Over the past few decades, however, the inhabitants and real estate developers have done their utmost to revamp its image.

LANDMARK TAVERN. S.E. CORNER 11TH AVE. AND 46TH ST. (1868). This establishment has remained more or less unchanged for years. Inside, the dark wood paneling, the old mirrors, the paved floor and the wood-burning stoves give visitors the impression of having stepped back in time.

INTREPID SEA-AIR-SPACE MUSEUM. PIER 86, W. 46TH ST. The *Intrepid* is an aircraft carrier from World War II which has been converted into a floating museum. Two blocks farther north is the N.Y.C. Passenger Ship Terminal, which belongs to the Port Authority of New York and New Jersey. This was built by the city in 1974 to accommodate the huge luxury cruisers, but with the exception of the *Queen Elizabeth II*, few liners have actually opted to use it.

INTREPID SEA-AIR-SPACE MUSEUM
This museum comprises four units: the *Intrepid* itself, a submarine, a destroyer and a lightship. The aircraft carrier has an exhibition including model ships, satellites and an Apollo space capsule. There is a film archive relating to submarines as well as World War II and the Vietnam War. In the submarine, which, like the *Intrepid*, is a veteran of World War II, visitors can take part in simulated submersions.

GEORGE M. COHAN
This actor-director and author-composer, immortalized in 1959 by Georg John Lober, "gives his regards to Broadway" forever in Father Duffy Square;

"Give My Regards to Broadway" is his best-known song.

For more than a century, Broadway has been almost synonymous with American theater. There is no better yardstick of talent than acting or directing on Broadway. Originally New York's theater district was centered around City Hall ▲ 168, but by the end of the 19th century it had moved to Broadway, around 42nd Street, and it has stayed there ever since. In the 1920's, the movie companies moved here and built huge movie palaces in the vicinity of Times Square. The recession in the movie industry during the 1950's and 1960's led to the closing of several movie theaters. Today the Theater District includes some forty legitimate theaters located between 40th and 57th streets, 6th and 8th avenues.

A subtle hierarchy distinguishes between "Broadway" shows (large-scale productions staged in the Theater District), "Off Broadway" shows (more modest-sized productions) and "Off-off Broadway" productions (avant-garde and fringe theater).

The NEW AMSTERDAM THEATER (1903), at 214 West 42nd Street, is now owned by Disney which has restored it to its baroque glory and stages musicals here. The producer Florenz Ziegfeld was a partial owner and he converted the roof into another theater, AERIAL GARDENS. Ziegfeld's famous revue – the annual Ziegfeld Follies, was performed at the New Amsterdam from 1913 until 1927, when he had his own theater built on the corner of 54th Street and 6th Avenue. Opposite, at 209 West 42nd St., is the New Victory Theater (1898), the oldest existing theater in New York. Its diverse program ranged from the burlesque comedies of Billy Minsky in the 1930's to pornographic

movies in the 1970's. Since 1995, the New Victory has put on shows and workshops for children. THE LYRIC (1903), at 213 West 42nd Street, was the New Amsterdam's main rival and engaged prestigious stars such as Douglas Fairbanks and Fred Astaire and his sister Adele; the Astaires were wooed by both theaters. In 1925 the Lyric staged the first performance by the Marx Brothers of George S. Kaufman's play *The Cocoanuts*, with music by Irving Berlin.

Below, the Majestic Theater, 247 W. 44th St (1927) and the neighboring Broadhurst Theater (1917). Above right, the Biltmore Theater, built by the Chanin brothers.

BOOTH THEATER 222 W. 45th St. (1913) The theater (below, center) owes its name to the actor Edwin Booth ▲ 230. Flanking it are the Shubert and Majestic theaters.

The "Great White Way".

The stretch of 44th Street between 7th and 8th avenues includes five Broadway theaters. The MAJESTIC (1927) at no. 245, the HELEN HAYES (1912) at no. 238 and the BROADHURST (1917) at no. 235 were all the work of Herbert J. Krapp. Krapp was a prolific and talented architect who designed some twenty theaters; all are highly regarded for the quality of their acoustics, their unimpeded sightlines and their decoration. The SHUBERT THEATER (1913) at 225 West 44th Street, was built at the same time as the Booth Theater for

Richard Rodgers' theater: formerly Chanin's 46th St.

BARRYMORE THEATER
243 W. 47th St. (1928). This theater was built in honor of the actress Ethel Barrymore. Fred Astaire appeared in Cole Porter's *The Gay Divorcee* (1932). In 1947, Marlon Brando made his debut, alongside Jessica Tandy, in *A Streetcar Named Desire*.

the Shubert brothers. It runs along the east side of Shubert Alley, a famous passageway formerly frequented by actors who would meet outside the offices of Sam J. J. and Lee Shubert when new productions were being cast. The LAMBS THEATER (1904), situated at 130 West 44th Street, shares the former premises of the Lambs Club with the Manhattan Church of the Nazarene. Many personalities , such as Al Jolson, W. C. Fields, Spencer Tracy and John Barrymore used to meet and stay at the Lambs Club. One block away, at 149 West 45th Street, is the LYCEUM THEATER, the first of the Times Square theaters to be built north of 42nd Street. Completed in 1903, it was considered the height of modernity, for its auditorium had no balcony and there were gift shops inside. The most famous venue for musicals is the IMPERIAL THEATER (1923), 249 West 45th Street; shows by such greats as George and Ira Gershwin, Cole Porter, Irving Berlin and Leonard Bernstein have been staged here. The LONGACRE THEATER (1913), at 220 West 48th Street, had its heyday in the 1930's when the Group Theater staged plays directed by Lee Strasberg.

LYCEUM THEATER
A window in the apartment of producer Daniel Frohman, for whom this theater was built (1903), looked out over the stage, apparently so he could watch his wife Margaret Illington in plays.

From left to right, the Longacre, Neil Simon and Imperial theaters.

**CORNELIUS
VANDERBILT**
(1794–1877)
Vanderbilt's statue
used to grace the
pediment of his
Hudson River
Railroad Freight
Depot, built in 1869.
When the depot
became obsolete in
1927, the statue was
moved to Grand
Central Terminal.

PARK AVENUE TO SUTTON PLACE

PARK AVENUE. In 1888 the city of New York renamed the section of 4th Avenue between
43rd and 96th streets. Although
enjoying the new name of Park
Avenue, it remained a mass of
railroad tracks until the rails
were electrified in 1904 and then
completely covered. This incentive
was part of an overall planning
program which included the
reconstruction of Grand Central
Terminal (1903–13) ▲ 236, as
well as the development of office
buildings, hotels and luxury
apartments along Park Avenue.
FORMER HELMSLEY BUILDING. 230 PARK
AVE., BETWEEN 45TH AND 46TH STS. (1929,
arch. Warren & Wetmore). This was built to
house the headquarters of the railroad company
founded by Cornelius Vanderbilt. "Commodore"
Vanderbilt was, by the
time he died in 1877, the
most famous millionaire in
the United States. By 1810,
at the age of sixteen, he had
bought a sailing ship and
started a ferryboat service
between Staten Island and
Manhattan. He then
assembled a fleet of
transatlantic liners and
coasting vessels. At the age of seventy
he embarked on a career as railroad
magnate, eventually creating the New
York Central Railroad Company.
The building, which later
became part of Leona and
Harry Helmsley's real-estate
empire, has the
distinction of being the
only building in New York
to straddle an avenue. Two
giant portals provide vehicles
with access, one, going
Downtown, along the
Pershing Viaduct, built in
1919, onto Park Avenue

The building site of
Grand Central
Terminal ▲ 239, in
1910, seen from the
north.

**THE HELMSLEY
EMPIRE**
The names Harry and
Leona Helmsley have
taken their place
among New York's
legendary
entrepreneurs. Leona
is now head of the
huge property empire
of her late husband
and a fortune
estimated at $5
billion. Among the
jewels in the crown
are the Empire State
Building and several
luxury hotels such as
the Helmsley Park
Lane and Carlton
House.

South. The building's elegant gilt and white marble lobby is
well worth a visit. The Helmsley Building was sold in 1998.
METLIFE BUILDING, FORMERLY PAN AM BUILDING. 200 PARK
AVE. (1963, arch. Emery Roth & Sons, Pietro Belluschi and
Walter Gropius, 58 stories). Built for Pan Am and bought in
1981 by the Metropolitan Life Insurance Company, this fifty-
eight-story skyscraper is disliked by almost all New Yorkers.
It looms over the Helmsley Building and Grand Central
Terminal ▲ 236, spoiling the view down Park Avenue. In 1977
its roof was the scene of a helicopter crash. Trying to land

1 GRAND CENTRAL TERMINAL
2 MET-LIFE BLDG.
3 HELMSLEY BLDG.
4 FORMER CHEMICAL BANK BLDG.
5 FORMER SHELTON TOWERS HOTEL
6 TURTLE BAY GARDENS AND LESCAZE HOUSE
7 RIVER HOUSE
8 BEEKMAN PLACE
9 U.N. PLAZA
10 FORD FOUNDATION BLDG.
11 TUDOR CITY
12 N.Y. DAILY NEWS BLDG.
13 CHANIN BLDG. AND FORMER BOWERY SAVINGS BANK
14 MOBIL BLDG.
15 GRAYBAR BLDG.
16 GRAND HYATT BLDG.
17 CHRYSLER BLDG.

Five hours

◆ C C3-C4-D3-D4

on the rooftop heliport, the helicopter lost its undercarriage. The debris rained down on the streets below, killing five people and wounding seven others.

FORMER CHEMICAL BANK BUILDING.
277 PARK AVE. (1962, arch. Emery Roth and Sons). When they merged with Chase Manhattan Bank, Chemical Bank sold the building and are now located on the other side of Park Avenue. The new owners removed the Chemcourt Atrium, a public garden extending over three levels that the bank had put in 1982 and which the writer George Chesbro once described in *Bone* as "a wonderful miniature jungle of trees, ferns and plants... a striking counterbalance to the bushes on the pedestrian islands which bisected the elegant thoroughfare."

MARRIOTT EAST SIDE HOTEL, FORMER SHELTON TOWERS HOTEL. 525 LEXINGTON AVE. (1924, arch. Arthur Loomis Harmon). With its 33 stories, this hotel was the tallest in the world when it was built. The building's three-tiered composition and the delicate Romanesque Revival ● 90 detailing at its base are an attractive application of the Zoning Resolution ● 97. The painter Georgia O'Keeffe ● 107 and her husband the photographer, Alfred Stieglitz lived here, when it was built; they occupied Suite 3003, which O'Keeffe also used as a studio until 1934. This suite has magnificent views over the tops of the Chrysler Building ▲ 266 to the south and the former RCA Building ● 98 to the west.

"TAXI"
On 47th Street between Park Avenue and Vanderbilt is a bronze statue of a man hailing a taxi. It was designed by J. Seward Johnson Jr. and built in 1983 to illustrate life on the streets of New York. Similar statues can be found elsewhere in Manhattan – *Out to Lunch* (Exxon Building), *The Commuters* (south wing of the Port Authority Bus Terminal), *The Garment Worker* (opposite 555 7th Ave.).

261

TURTLE BAY

The name of this neighborhood refers to a marshy cove in the East River where turtles once abounded. They – and other creatures – figure as decorative motifs on the walls and the newel posts of the railings of some of the houses in the Turtle Bay Historic District. The area's distinguished residents have included E. B. White, Leopold Stokowski, Tyrone Power and Katharine Hepburn. The U.N. Headquarters ▲ *264* is also located in this neighborhood.

TURTLE BAY GARDENS HISTORIC DISTRICT. 227–247 E. 48TH AND 226–246 E. 49TH STS. (1820, restored in 1920, arch. Dean and Bottomley). In the mid-19th century, Turtle Bay, the site on which the Dutch governor William Kieft had built his farm in 1639, was overrun by factories and slaughterhouses. However, some attractive Italianate rowhouses were also built in this period, and in 1920 an enlightened developer bought a group of them and combined all their back gardens into one common garden. The houses were remodeled so that the living rooms face the garden, thus turning their backs on the surrounding commercial activity.

FORMER LESCAZE HOUSE. 211 E. 48TH ST. (1934, arch. William Lescaze). The style and size of this white house form a contrast with the brownstones of Turtle Bay Gardens. Lescaze designed this International Style ● *100* residence-cum-studio to advertise his own firm. The influence of Le Corbusier is apparent in the judicious use of materials: the glass block panels used in the façade overlooking the street create a bulwark against the city, and the glazed bays at the rear overlook a terrace. This structure fascinated neighbors to such an extent that for a time Lescaze opened his home to visitors.

BEEKMAN PLACE. BETWEEN 49TH AND 51ST STS. This quiet site overlooking the East River is named after a local resident, James Beekman, whose mansion, Mount Pleasant, built in 1765, was used by the British as headquarters during the American Revolution ● *27*. Nathan Hale ▲ *168* was sentenced to death here for spying and hanged on September 22, 1776. The house was destroyed in 1874 when, due to the proliferation of harbor industries, the area became rundown and overcrowded.

RIVER HOUSE. 435 E. 52ND ST. (1931, arch. Bottomley, Wagner & White). Originally, yacht-owning tenants could reach this luxury apartment house from a landing stage on the East River. The residence was cut off from the river in the 1940's when the Franklin D. Roosevelt Drive (also called F.D.R. or East River Drive) was built. The landfill consisted partially of debris from bombing raids on London during World War II, which had been used as ballast for ships carrying American troops back to the United States.

Turtle Bay in 1852.

A DETOUR NORTH: SUTTON PLACE.

BETWEEN 57TH AND 58TH STS. This little enclave, lined with elegant townhouses, owes its name to Effingham B. Sutton, who made his fortune during the California Gold Rush of 1849 and launched the first shipping line operating between New York and San Francisco. He invested some of his profits to develop this neighborhood, but it did not become fashionable until the 1920's. Nearby Riverview Terrace consists of five townhouses, with terrace gardens, overlooking the East River, Queensboro Bridge and Roosevelt Island.

THE UNITED NATIONS

Located along the bank of the East River, between 42nd and 48th streets, the headquarters of the U.N.O. (United Nations Organization) covers more than 15 acres .

THE WORLD'S PARLIAMENT. The U.N.O., created in the aftermath of World War II, succeeded the League of Nations, its fundamental task being to "save succeeding generations from the scourge of war". The General Assembly, which is a true international parliament, is presently made up of delegations from 180 states. It meets every year from September to December, dealing with some 150 cases relating to issues as diverse as disarmament, economic aid and women's rights.

THE ROLE OF NELSON A. ROCKEFELLER. The fifty founding states of the U.N.O. agreed, at the first General Assembly in London, in 1946, that the headquarters should be located in the United States. Several sites were considered: New York, Connecticut, Boston, Philadelphia and San Francisco. Once New York had been chosen, a committee of prominent figures, including Nelson Rockefeller, tried to promote Flushing Meadow, the site of the Universal Exhibition of 1939, as a suitable base. The U.N.O. rejected this proposal (although the General Assembly did meet there between 1946 and 1949).

Construction of the F.D.R. Drive along the East River, viewed from the Queensboro Bridge.

U.N. SECRETARIAT BUILDING
Along 1st Avenue, the multicolored flags of the member nations mark the boundary between the territory of New York and the international enclave of the United Nations. The grayish-blue glass skin of this skyscraper's east and west façades was chosen to minimize the effects of the sun; its north and south façades are clad in Vermont marble. The 38th floor houses the Secretary General's offices.

AN ARCHITECTURAL COMPLEX
A team of ten architects, including Le Corbusier and Oscar Niemeyer, began work on the U.N. headquarters in January 1947. They opted for three self-contained buildings: the Secretariat, the General Assembly and the Conference Building. The first cornerstone was laid on October 24, 1949 (above) and at the end of August 1950 the first civil servants moved into their offices. The library – south of the General Assembly – was added in 1963.

U.N. coat of arms.

THE CONFERENCE BUILDING
This building houses the Security Council Chamber, the Trusteeship Council Chamber, the Economic and Social Council Chamber and a number of smaller rooms. There are daily tours around the U.N. and it is possible to attend public meetings of the General Assembly and the Security Council, here shown (right) in a meeting on January 31, 1992.

As the United Nations was on the point of opting for a headquarters in Philadelphia, Nelson Rockefeller persuaded his father, John D. Rockefeller, Jr, to donate the $8.5 million needed to buy some land along the East River.

TUDOR CITY

SHCHARANSKY STEPS. These steps leading to Tudor City were named in homage to the Soviet Jewish dissident Anatoly Shcharansky. The best view of the United Nations headquarters can be obtained from the top of these steps.

GENERAL ASSEMBLY BUILDING
The curved roof of this building is crowned with a dome, with a nod to important buildings of the past.

A "SELF-CONTAINED CITY". (1925–8, arch. Fred F. French Co.). Tudor City occupies the entire area between E. 40th and E. 43rd streets, 1st and 2nd avenues. Exclusively financed by private funds, and built in a quasi-Tudor style which inspired its name, it was a bold attempt at urban renewal. The aim was to create "a self-contained city" in a then insalubrious neighborhood. There are twelve apartment buildings containing three thousand apartments, a hotel with

FORD FOUNDATION BUILDING ● *100*
Since 1967, this building, at 321 E. 42nd St., has housed the Ford Foundation, which supports the arts, letters and sciences. The elegant brick and glass building has an interior garden (above) which is open to the public. An ornamental pond, replenished by condensation, acts as a self-sustaining irrigation system.

TRUMP WORLD TOWER
843 United Nations Plaza (1999–2001). Overlooking the U.N., this skyscraper (900 feet) built by Donald Trump houses luxury apartments.

1 VISITORS' ENTRANCE
2 LOBBY
3 GENERAL ASSEMBLY HALL
4 DELEGATES' LOUNGE
5 SECRETARIAT BUILDING
6 CONFERENCE BUILDING
7 SECURITY COUNCIL
8 TRUSTEESHIP COUNCIL
9 ECONOMIC AND SOCIAL COUNCIL

six hundred rooms, a post office, various stores and private parks. Around the turn of the 20th century this area was frequented by criminals and gangsters. At one time, it was dubbed "Corcoran's Roost", after the notorious Paddy Corcoran and his "Rag Gang". The neighborhood was also heavily industrialized, filled with factories, breweries and slaughterhouses. The architects designed its buildings so they faced inward, placing very few windows in the walls bordering the surrounding squalor. Today its residents regret being deprived of some stunning views.

Walter Percy Chrysler (1875–1940) began his career as an apprentice in a railroad machine shop; by 1925, he was president of the Chrysler automobile company. In 1928 he resuscitated a project initially conceived by the property developer William H. Reynolds for a skyscraper at the corner of Lexington Avenue and 42nd Street. His architect, William Van Alen, persuaded him to aim at setting a new record for the world's tallest building: in 1930, a stainless steel spire enabled him to achieve his goal, but it was soon surpassed by the Empire State Building.

THE "VERTEX"
The spire, which measures 197 feet in height and weighs about 30 tons, was designed in secret by Van Alen and hoisted in one piece to the top of the tower, an operation that took only an hour and a half.

THE SKY'S THE LIMIT
Chrysler had two goals: to top the Woolworth Building and to snatch the title of the tallest structure in the world from the Eiffel Tower. He was not the only one: the Empire State Building ▲ 242 and the Bank of Manhattan ▲ 161 were also competing in this vertical race.

A CONTEST TO SETTLE ACCOUNTS
What started as simple rivalry turned into an attempt to settle old scores between Van Alen and his former partner and now sworn enemy, H. Craig Severance, the architect of the Bank of Manhattan. Chrysler and Van Alen produced their trump card only after they had led Severance to believe that his building would be the victor. Their "joker" was a spire which Van Alen called "the Vertex". When the building was nearly completed, workers hoisted huge sheets of steel to the 65th story and, with the help of a derrick, raised the spire to the top of the tower.

Once the Vertex was in place, it brought the height of the Chrysler Building to 1,048 feet, higher than the 71-story Bank of Manhattan Company.

"He knew [the Chrysler Building] was really the incarnation of God with its garishly illuminated, multi-faceted roof shaped like a steeple. . . ."

George Chesbro

THE "HIGHEST MAN IN THE WORLD"
A luxurious duplex apartment (left) was built for Walter Chrysler in the building's spire. The triangular windows of the apartment looked out over the vast panorama of Manhattan. The Cloud Club (bottom) was a meeting room for American industrial magnates and is also decorated in the purest Art Deco style. The view is complemented by a painted mural of the city.

"WALKING BUILDING"
The anthropomorphic character of the Chrysler Building is due to the spire, which has been compared to a wildly exaggerated hairstyle. Van Alen himself wore a replica of it to the Beaux Arts Ball in 1931.

▲ CHRYSLER BUILDING

On the 16th floor are classical urns reworked to reflect an Art Deco vision.

A VIRTUOSO DESIGNER

Van Alen, who had been an outstanding student at the École des Beaux Arts, was nicknamed "the Ziegfeld of his profession" by one of his colleagues in *The American Architect*.

In Paris, he had studied under Victor Laloux at the Beaux Arts. He returned to New York in 1911 and formed a partnership with H. Craig Severance.

IN HONOR OF THE AUTOMOBILE

The corners of the main setbacks, designed in compliance with the 1916 Zoning Resolution, are set off by ornamental sculptures made of reflective sheets of steel. The skyscraper's "neck" is adorned by eight stylized eagle heads, modern style gargoyles (below). The thirtieth story, which houses the mechanical equipment and is therefore blind, sports a frieze of two-colored brick representing car wheels with their metal hubcaps and fenders. The corners are decorated with giant Chrysler radiator caps, inspired by Mercury's winged helmet (above).

A BEACON ON THE NEW YORK SKYLINE

The building's visual impact is due partly to the richness of form and partly to the clever use of materials, in particular the plates of stainless steel – evocative of car ornaments – which glitter in the sunshine.

AN EXPRESSIONIST SPIRE

The spire, with its dovetailed arches fitting inside each other like Russian dolls (right), differs markedly from other skyscraper tops of the period, which were inspired mainly by the 1925 Exhibition of Decorative Arts in Paris. The Chrysler Building's spire has more in common with German Expressionism, the utopian drawings of Bruno Taut and movie sets, such as those in Robert Wiene's *The Cabinet of Dr Caligari* (1919).

A SUBTLE BALANCE

Adding the spire of the building – which has been compared to Nijinsky's headdress in a ballet produced by Sergei Diaghilev, or a Balinese dancer's headdress or the crown worn by some exotic monarch – to the main part of the building entailed a subtle arrangement of façades, in which the curved, vertically thrusting shapes rhythmically echo the outline of the three central bays, in turn stabilized by horizontal bands of decoration. The result is as exuberant as New York itself. The complete elevation ▲ *266*, clearly illustrates the use of different motifs.

A door (right) in the main entrance.

'We certainly do lead the world in architecture,' said Professor Timson. 'Architecture, I take it, is the natural artistic expression of a young nation. Youth wants to build, and Manhattan Island kind of looks as though we've done what we wanted.'…
Erik Linklater,
Juan in America

THE LOBBY
The Chrysler Building's décor is eye-catching from top to bottom. The truncated shape of the deeply recessed entrance, which

some critics have compared to that of a coffin, and which rises over three stories, sets the tone for the angular interior polished design. For example, metal triangles are superimposed on the notched strip dividing the doors of a huge stained-glass window. The extraordinary triangular lobby narrows as it rises. Glowing red in the semi-darkness, it is probably the most

spectacular interior to be found in any office building built during the inter-war years. Red Moroccan marble walls, sienna-colored floor, moldings made of amber-colored onyx and bluish marble are orchestrated in a vivid symphony which builds to a climax: the ceiling, painted by Edward Trumbull, symbolizing Energy, Result, Workmanship and Transportation. . . .

ZIGZAG MOTIFS
The lavishness of the décor – even the veins in the huge marble slabs of the walls form zigzag motifs – is breathtaking. The fountain motifs (top left), the palm leaves and the vividly portrayed eagles on

the mailboxes (left) add to the

profusion of images. Taken as a whole, the decoration of the Chrysler Building

represents an apex in Art Deco design, a style which, though created in Europe, became immensely popular in the United States.

GEOMETRIC FRIEZES
& ART DECO STYLE
Art Deco style is
characterized by the
systematic use of simple
geometric shapes in dynamic

compositions. It marks a
break with the Art Nouveau
style popular in the early
20th century, which was
inspired by the sinuous
contours of plants.

A digital clock used
to hang over an
information desk,
opposite the main
entrance, a focal point
like the altar in a
modern-day cathedral,
consecrated to the
worship of
information.

PORTRAIT OF BUILDING
The paintings on the lobby ceiling celebrate the innovation
of air mail and the skyscraper itself, depicting its façade
and scenes from its construction. This sort of narcissistic
"self-portraiture" was one of the most fashionable
themes used by interior designers in skyscrapers of
this period. It also enabled visitors to take in the whole
building and its gigantic dimensions, something
that was impossible
to do from the
boxed-in streets.

MARBLE
AND FINE WOODS
The elevators,
divided from the
lobby by sections
of cathode ray
tubing, creating
the effect of a
theater curtain
in the process
of opening,
comprise four
banks of eight
cars, each decorated
differently with
superb inlays. It took
eight varieties
of wood –
from Japan,

England and Cuba –
to create the fine
marquetry of the
doors (right). These
elevators, whose
splendor and speed
are unsurpassed,
served as models
for the elevators of
recent Postmodern
skyscrapers, such
as the AT&T (now
Sony) Building
▲ 176.

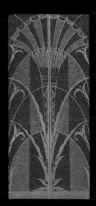

Details of the elaborate radiator grills from the Chanin Building, designed by René Chambellan.

LOBBY OF THE CHANIN BUILDING
This was designed by Jacques Delamarre to celebrate the success of Irwin Chanin in New York and to illustrate "the story of a city in which it is possible for a man to rise from a humble place to wealth and influence by the sheer power of his mind and hands".
New York, 1930

NEW YORK DAILY NEWS BUILDING. 220 E. 42ND ST. (1930, arch. Howells & Hood). Until 1997, this was the headquarter of one of New York's few remaining daily newspapers, which still boasts a wide circulation. It was founded in 1919 as the *Illustrated Daily News* by two army officers, Captain Patterson and Colonel ("Bertie") McCormick. The first issue, on June 26, 1919, proclaimed: "See New York's most beautiful girls every morning in the *Illustrated Daily News…*" The paper was renamed the *Daily News* two years later. When the building was opened, the large GLOBE in the lobby was found to be revolving in the wrong direction. The globe, which is still in the lobby, no longer revolves and has not been renovated for years; it remains a reminder of past days.

AROUND THE CHRYSLER BUILDING

The bronze flooring in the lobby of the Chanin Building ● *98* uses typical Art Deco motifs: boats, planes, trains and cars.

CHANIN BUILDING. 122 E. 42ND ST. (1929, arch. Sloan & Robertson, lobby designed by Jacques Delamarre). Magnificent bas-reliefs, composed of animal motifs, run the length of the façade on the lower part of this 56-story building. The breathtaking Art Deco lobby, with its bronze screens and richly decorated elevator doors and mailboxes, is a "must". The building originally had a scenic roof and a theater on the 50th floor; unfortunately neither is now accessible. You can see the top of the Chanin Building by walking several blocks down Lexington Avenue.

BESTIARY
The carved animal forms that appear on the capitals, cornices and other places in the former Bowery Savings Bank include squirrels, lions and bulls and bears which symbolize respectively thrift, power and the world of finance.

GRAYBAR BUILDING. 420 LEXINGTON AVE. (1927, arch. Sloan & Robertson, 31 stories). When this was built, it was the largest office building in the world, capable of accommodating twelve thousand employees. Lines for Grand Central Terminal ▲ *236* used to run through the basement, and one of the three entrances located on Lexington Avenue still serves as an entrance to the station. One of the arches along this corridor is decorated with frescoes depicting trains, planes and building sites.

FORMER BOWERY SAVINGS BANK. 110 E. 42ND ST. (1923, arch. York & Sawyer). Constructed in the style of a Roman basilica, the former Bowery Savings Bank, now the Cipriani 42nd Street restaurant, has a distinctive arched entrance which opens onto a vast room with a coffered ceiling; today it is used as a space for grand dinners and events. An extraordinary clock is proudly displayed on the south wall, while the huge original solid bronze doors now adorn the east and west walls of this splendid room.

PERSHING SQUARE BUILDING. 100 E. 42ND ST. (1914–23, arch. York & Sawyer). Although the word "square" figures in the building's name, the "square" is actually just an intersection of 42nd Street and Park Avenue South, named in homage to General John J. Pershing, who commanded the American Expeditionary Forces in France in 1917–18. It was the last skyscraper in New York to be built without setbacks, its plans having predated the Zoning Resolution of 1916 ● *97*.

Around
Rockefeller Center

ATLAS
The bronze Atlas by Lee Lawrie, placed at the entrance of the International Building in 1937, faces St. Patrick's Cathedral on 5th Ave. He holds an armillary sphere, decorated with the signs of the zodiac, whose axis points toward the North Star.

THE MODERN AGE. "This Titanesque composition of stone, concrete, glass and steel is symbolic of New York – it embodies its essence, trumpets its pride in the same way as the solemn splendor of cathedrals symbolized the very essence of urban communities in the Middle Ages, handing it down to future generations" (Klaus Mann, 1936). The image of the cathedral seems appropriate for Rockefeller Center, just as it was for the Woolworth Building, since it evokes time-honored tradition, though it fails to take account of the innovative nature of the project. The driving force behind the project, John D. Rockefeller Jr, was not attempting, like Chrysler or John Jakob Raskob – two patrons of the motor car, another symbol of modernity – to feed his ego by building a larger and more magnificent monument than that of his precursors. On the contrary, as Klaus Mann pointed out, his project was the very embodiment of quintessential New York and, more generally, of a type of modernity which was, by definition, American.

A CLASSICAL MODEL. Rockefeller Center is made up of a complex of fourteen buildings, built in the 1930's, plus another five buildings

> "The buildings are a shimmering verticality, a gossamer veil, a festive scene-drop hanging there against the black sky to dazzle, entertain, amaze."
>
> Frank Lloyd Wright

ompleted after 1945, on the other side of 6th Avenue. It is currently home to a number of diverse activities (Radio City Music Hall shows, radio and television production in the studios of NBC General Electric – the former RCA Building), and links to older nations Maison Française and the British Empire Building) which were there from its inception. Its pleasing design provides the city with an open space, dotted with fountains and statues whose transparent symbolism reiterates American values by dint of a great many mythological illusions (*Prometheus* watching over the Lower Plaza, for example). It is a strange mixture of idealism and pragmatism, inspired by functionalist theories similar to those of Le Corbusier but which yield to the constraints of New York's urban fabric. It is also a democratic, liberal American counterweight to the Imperial giganticism of Fascist and Communist totalitarian regimes, as well as an answer to the equally harsh challenge of the Great Depression.

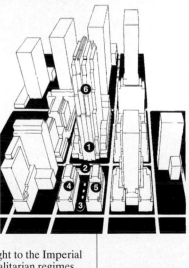

Manhats largest-scale building project was financed by John Davison Rockefeller Jr (1874–1960). He set his heart on three large blocks between 48th and 51st streets, 5th and 6th avenues and, in December 1929, he signed an eighty-year lease with their owner, Columbia University. The lease has since been extended until 2069, much to Mitsubishi's satisfaction, as this company is currently the majority shareholder of Rockefeller Center. The center owes the purity of its design to Nelson Aldrich Rockefeller (1908–79), the financier's second son, who was a collector of modern art, future governor of the State of New York and vice president of the United States.

A COLOSSAL BUILDING SITE
The board of architects, headed by Raymond H and Wallace K. Harrison, who were to be the ch designers for the United Nations building, made the best of continual changes to the plans: the Rockefeller family fortune went through a very rough time which lasted until the end of the 1930's.

RCA BUILDING
(since 1988, General Electric). Opened in 1933, this building took only sixteen months to build. Above, an RCA advertisement.

A DEPTH OF 85 FEET

The parking lots, underground passages and shopping center, around Lower Plaza, were built below ground level, creating space for vast terraces at street level.

AFTER THE CRASH

The collapse of the stock market in 1929 made the realization of the original plans for an opera house impossible and, while demolition work was being completed, in July 1931, the Rockefellers developed the plans for a commercial center. The extension, west of 6th Avenue, was completed in 1973.

Part of the 1999 restoration, the smoking rooms (above) and powder rooms (left) of Radio City Music Hall still contain the original furniture.

RADIO CITY MUSIC HALL

The auditorium, an homage to American Art Deco decoration, was opened on December 27, 1932. The décor was coordinated by Donald Deskey, and many painters contributed to the murals in the lobbies, lounges and stairways (above). These design features are designated as historic landmarks.

IN THE CLOUDS

The restored Rainbow Room, on the 65th floor of the RCA buildings, affords spectacular views of the entire Manhattan skyline. Opposite, a poster from the 1930's, advertising this exceptional view. Today, Rockefeller Center has nearly forty restaurants and several theaters.

A NEW CONCEPT IN TOWN PLANNING
The decoration is mainly restricted to the lower stories because the architects of Rockefeller Center felt it was less important to apply motifs to an architectural mass – which was, in this case, inordinately tall – than to create a landscaped environment whose variety would attract new tenants as well as sightseers. This was a revolutionary attitude for an urban complex composed mainly of office buildings. The Promenade overlooking 5th Ave. was nicknamed "Channel Gardens" because it separates the Maison Française from the British Empire Building. The gardens, which are re-planted several times a year, provide a setting for fountains that have tritons and nereids riding dolphins. The regular gridiron pattern of Manhattan is broken here by other axes, creating a geometrical effect that highlights the feeling of being in a "city within a city".

THE MAJOR ART DECO COMPLEX IN NEW YORK. At the center of Lower Plaza, a gilded bronze *Prometheus* by Paul Manship rises from the waves (opposite). The main entrance of the General Electric Building is crowned by *Genius* by Lee Lawrie which pays homage to the miracle of radio broadcasting. Everything in Lower Plaza – fountains, flags snapping in the wind, sunshades or a huge Christmas tree – combines to create a continual mood of festivity, an atmosphere more in keeping with world fairs than a traditional financial district.

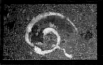
The cladding of Rockefeller Center is white limestone, quarried in Indiana. It contains numerous fossils of tiny animals (left) which lived in the sea 300 million years ago.

LOWER PLAZA
The former RCA Building is reached via the Lower Plaza, originally designed as the entrance to the underground shopping center.

At the height of the Depression, one by one the luxury stores around the plaza folded but, in 1936, an incredible publicity stunt diverted attention away from this commercial failure: the Lower Plaza was transformed into a skating rink or an elegant café depending on the time of year. This was one of the attractions which made Rockefeller Center so popular with all New Yorkers. It was the hub of this cosmopolitan quarter with its travel agencies, shipping companies, consulates, luxury stores and press offices.

A SLENDER SILHOUETTE
"A colossal structure, brazen in its height . . . graceful and monumental, sober and fantastic." (Klaus Mann). The squares and thoroughfares which lead to the General Electric Building provide the perfect vantage point to appreciate the tower's silhouette (above, illuminated at night). The tower's slenderness was dictated by the architect's aim of providing every work station with direct lighting. Each horizontal setback also corresponds to a reduction in the size of the elevator shafts.

A MODERN FORUM

Rockefeller Center marks a return to classical tradition, to a collective style of architecture for use by the whole city, not just an individual (the Prince), a religious order (the Church) or the commercial sector. Its style of decoration also reflects a return to mythology, with its allegorical evocation of the key principles which govern the world it depicts. Inside as well as outside the building, clocks remind passers-by that "Time Is Money"

A FANTASTIC BESTIARY

The treatment of the American eagle (below) irresistibly calls to mind the winged bulls found in Assyrian art, while Hermès, the god of commerce (right), is more in line with Greco-Roman tradition.

THE AMERICAN IDEAL AS SEEN BY A SPANIARD

Even the name of the works that decorate the buildings' interiors show a desire to return to the world of myth; for example, the grandiloquent mural, *Triumph of Man's Accomplishments through Physical and Mental Labor*, by José Maria Sert in the General Electric Building.

FROM EGYPT TO ASSYRIA VIA CLASSICISM

The mural with its shallow-carved characters (right) calls to mind bas-reliefs from Ancient Egypt, while the classical goddess in the allegory (opposite), who is a successful blend of the American eagle and an olive branch, bears an undeniable likeness to *La Marseillaise* by Rude which adorns the Arc de Triomphe in Paris.

AN INTERNATIONAL STYLE OF ARCHITECTURE

Classical antiquity was a rich stylistic source during the 1930's in New York, Moscow, Rome or Berlin. The Allegory of Prosperity and Labor (left and right) are two examples.

THE HAMMER AND THE SICKLE

The tools of the laborer and the peasant still seem to be the time-honored symbols of work, even in New York.

SPACE AND MODERNITY

The imaginative and artistic interior decoration, glimpsed here, links modern and monumental references (as seen in the design and layout of the lobby) with a strong element of symbolism.

THE PEOPLE IN NEW YORK

Pablo Picasso was asked to paint a new mural for the lobby of the RCA Building, but *Man at the Crossroads* was eventually commissioned from the Mexican Communist, Diego Rivera. When the fresco was unveiled the commissioners were stunned to see the face of Lenin, rather than the anonymous figure of the "leader of the worker's movement", as depicted in the sketch they had approved months before. Asked to remove Lenin, Rivera said he would rather see the painting destroyed. The managers of the Center did just that.

▲ ROCKEFELLER CENTER TO THE EAST SIDE

1 ROCKEFELLER CENTER
2 SWISS CENTER
3 SAKS FIFTH AVE.
4 ST. PATRICK'S CATHEDRAL
5 OLYMPIC TOWER
6 NEW YORK PALACE HOTEL
7 WALDORF-ASTORIA HOTEL
8 ST. BARTHOLOMEW'S CHURCH
9 FORMER RCA BLDG
10 SEAGRAM BLDG
11 CITICORP CENTER
12 FORMER LEVER HOU
13 FORMER FULLER BI

⌛ Six hours

◆ **C** B3-B4-C3-C4

DAHESH MUSEUM
601 5th Ave. (48th St.). This small museum, opened in 1995, is named after Doctor Dahesh (1909–1984), a Lebanese writer and philosopher who was an avid collector of 19th-century academic art. His collections included works by Léon Lhermitte, Edwin Long and Lord Leighton.

LOBBY OF THE SWISS CENTER
The gold and silver Art Deco ● *98* elevator doors in the Swiss Center are decorated with floral motifs and nymphs.

Midtown began to develop after the Civil War when new millionaires built luxurious mansions along that stretch of 5th Avenue. In the 1880's, the Vanderbilts, Whitneys, Goulds, Astors and other top families settled here. At the beginning of the 20th century the neighborhood began to change drastically, with many businesses moving into the area, and to escape this invasion the wealthier residents began to migrate northward. Today, Midtown is the second-largest business center in the city after Downtown, with some 750,000 employees flocking into its offices every day. The area has been shaped by magnates such as Trump and Helmsley.

AROUND ST. PATRICK'S CATHEDRAL

FORMER CHARLES SCRIBNER'S SONS BOOKSTORE.
597 5TH AVE. (1913, arch. Ernest Flagg). For more than seventy years this building was the home of Charles Scribner's Sons bookshop. Its huge black wrought-iron and glass storefront is reminiscent of French early 20th century department stores. The listed interior has a vast single-story vaulted space covered in fine wood paneling. Scribner's, founded in 1846, published F. Scott Fitzgerald and E. Hemingway. The bookstore was sold in 1989 and bought by Benetton in 1996.

SWISS CENTER, FORMER GOELET BUILDING. 5TH AVE. AT 49TH ST. (1932, arch. E. H. Faile & Co.). This building occupies the site formerly occupied by the house of the Goelet family, who built up a fortune in real estate. It is a striking example of Art Deco with a façade juxtaposing green and white marble and aluminum. The lobby is worth a visit, especially for its elevator doors. The Swiss Center houses the Swissair offices and the Swiss National Tourist Board.

SAKS FIFTH AVENUE. 611 5TH AVE. BETWEEN 49TH AND 50TH STS. (1924, arch. Starrett & Van Vleck). The first Saks store opened in 1902 on 34th Street. The son of the founder,

CENTRAL PARK

Andrew Saks – who had started his career as a peddler in Washington, D.C. – built this Renaissance-style palazzo when his wealthy clientele moved Uptown. Saks has built up an international reputation as a luxury department store, selling furs, jewelry and designer clothing. The restaurant on the eighth floor has a superb view of St. Patrick's Cathedral, Rockefeller Center ▲ 274 and the Channel Gardens.

CONSTRUCTION
The cathedral was built on a site owned by the Catholic Church since 1828. It was originally bought for a graveyard, but the land proved to be too rocky. At the time the cathedral was built, New York included nearly 200,000 Catholics – mainly Irish immigrants (many from the countryside and unaccustomed to city life, construction and dock workers, and bar owners). Their propensity to drink did nothing to enhance their image with New York's Protestant bourgeoisie, and for this reason Archbishop Hughes added a clause to the building contract for the cathedral stipulating that workers were not allowed to drink during work hours.

ST. PATRICK'S CATHEDRAL ★.
5TH AVE. BETWEEN 50TH AND 51ST STS. (1858–88, arch. James Renwick Jr.). Archbishop John Hughes commissioned James Renwick Jr. to design this church, which was inspired by the Gothic cathedrals of Europe and follows the traditional cruciform plan, enriched with side chapels. When New Yorkers learned that the cathedral was to be built on a site that was then virtually out in the country, they nicknamed it "Hughes' Folly". But as the city expanded north, St. Patrick's was soon enveloped by it. The cathedral was dedicated in 1879, twenty-one years after the first stone was laid. The construction of the building, interrupted by the Civil War, was completed under the aegis of John McCloskey, the first American cardinal. This is the largest Catholic cathedral in the United States. The Lady Chapel, situated behind the altar and completed in 1906, is made of Vermont marble. Its floor includes a mosaic of the arms of Pope Leo XIII and the stained glass windows over the altar depict the mysteries of the rosary.

Statue in St. Patrick's Cathedral.

283

5TH AVENUE IN 1900
"Sunday afternoon
Fifth Avenue filed by
rosily dustily jerkily.
On the shady side
there was an
occasional man in
top hat and frock
coat. Sunshades,
summer dresses,
straw hats were bright
in the sun that glinted
in squares on the
upper windows of the
houses, lay in bright
slivers on the hard
paint of limousines
and taxicabs."
John Dos Passos,
Manhattan Transfer

OLYMPIC TOWER. 645 5TH AVE. (1976, arch. Skidmore, Owings
& Merrill.) This is one of the last "glass boxes" – as they
are dismissively called by New Yorkers – that typifies
the International Style ● *100*. This skyscraper, built at the
instigation of Aristotle Onassis, houses boutiques, offices
and luxury apartments.

FORMER VANDERBILT RESIDENCE. 647 5TH AVE. (1905,
arch. Hunt & Hunt). At the end of the 19th century, several
private mansions belonging to the Vanderbilts were clustered
along the section of 5th Avenue between 51st and 52nd
Streets and were nicknamed the "Vanderbilt Colony".
The only surviving mansion, at number 647, is the former
residence of George W. Vanderbilt. Around 1910, when
the neighborhood was taken over by businesses, the
Vanderbilts moved to the Upper East Side. The former
private mansion is now a Versace store.

VILLARD HOUSES/NEW YORK PALACE HOTEL ● *92* ★.
451–457 MADISON AVE. (1883–1886, arch. McKim,

**THE "VANDERBILT
COLONY"**
The owner of one
"Vanderbilt Colony"
mansion, William H.
Vanderbilt (a son of
the "Commodore"),
created an art gallery
in his home (right and
below) to which the
public was admitted
on Thursdays.

Mead & White). This brownstone building, reminiscent
of a great Renaissance palazzo, actually consists of six
private mansions. Henry Villard, founder of the Northern
Pacific Railroad and owner of the New York Post ● *54*,
began their construction in 1883. When Villard went
bankrupt, he sold the mansions to several
individuals. The Helmsley Corporation
bought them in the 1970s and the highly
controversial plans for the construction
of a hotel (1980) were accepted only after
the corporation agreed to preserve the
courtyard, as well as the interior of the
north and south wings. The hotel now
belongs to the Sultan of Brunei and is called
the New York Palace Hotel. The renowned
restaurant LE CIRQUE moved into the south
wing in 1996, and its celebrated clientele dine
in the two imaginatively designed rooms
downstairs or take in events upstairs.

The north wing houses the Urban Center Bookshop and the Municipal Art Society which advocates excellence in urban design and planning, and the preservation of historic sites. For example, the society saved Grand Central Terminal ▲ 236 and Radio City Music Hall ▲ 277 from demolition. The bookshop, which specializes in books on architecture, design and urban development, also organizes debates, exhibitions and architectural tours of the city.

On Park and Lexington Avenues

Waldorf-Astoria Hotel. 301 Park Ave. between 49th and 50th sts. (1931, arch. Schultze & Weaver). Although it was constructed during the Great Depression, this Art Deco brick- and limestone-faced hotel, with its granite base, is a monument to luxury. It succeeded the first Waldorf-Astoria (5th Avenue and 33rd Street), owned by the Astor family, which had been demolished in 1929 to make way for the Empire State Building ▲ 242. Rising above the hotel (below right) are the forty-two-story Waldorf Towers – which can be seen from several blocks to the north. These private apartments have had some famous tenants, including the Duke of Windsor, President Herbert Hoover, General MacArthur, Frank Sinatra and Mafia boss "Lucky" Luciano ● 40. The lobby of the hotel's Park Avenue entrance is richly decorated with murals and a mosaic by Louis Rigal, *The Wheel of Life.* The clock in the lobby – made by the Goldsmith's Company (London) for the Chicago World's Fair of 1893 – was bought by John Jacob Astor and stood in the first hotel. It is embellished with portraits of heads of state including George Washington, Abraham Lincoln and Queen Victoria. The chimes, which sound every quarter of an hour, are copies of those in Westminster Cathedral. The second-floor Silver Room and Grand Ballroom, which have been restored to their original splendor, are especially worth visiting.

St. Bartholomew's Church ★. Park Ave. and 51st st. (1919, arch. Bertram G. Goodhue). The portico (1912) that graces this Episcopal church came from the first St. Bartholomew's, on Madison Avenue, designed by Stanford White, who modeled it on a French church. The figures were commissioned from Daniel Chester French and Philip Martiny, among others. Inside the stained-glass windows, which were taken from the older church, are worth seeing.

Starlight Roof
In the 1930's and 1940's New York socialites used to dance to the music of Count Basie and Glenn Miller under the vaulted ceiling of the Waldorf-Astoria's famous Starlight Roof. Less fortunate fans of the big band sound tuned in at home to the Starlight Roof's regular radio broadcasts.

FORMER RCA VICTOR BUILDING ★.
570 LEXINGTON AVE. (1931, arch. Cross & Cross) ● *98*, ▲ *275*. This building towers above ST. BARTHOLOMEW'S, its proximity creating a visual shock. It has little in common with the church except for its limestone and pinkish brick, chosen by its architects. Its crown – part Gothic, part Art Deco – is one of the most spectacular sights on the Manhattan skyline. Walk down Lexington Avenue for several blocks to see the FIGURES (below) facing the four cardinal points, which seem to keep watch over the city. Visit the Art Deco lobby with its aluminum-plated ceiling decorated with sunburst motifs.

LEVER HOUSE. 390 PARK AVE. BETWEEN 53RD AND 54TH STS. (1952, arch. Skidmore, Owings & Merrill). Now a designated landmark and extensively restored, this building belonging to the Lever Brothers Company (a major soap manufacturer) is regarded as an exemplar of the minimalist, International Style skyscraper ● *100*. When this ultramodern office block first appeared on Park Avenue – then lined almost entirely with sedate masonry apartment houses – it provoked a storm of protest, but it seems rather subdued now.

SEAGRAM BUILDING. 375 PARK AVE. (1958, arch. Ludwig Mies van der Rohe and Philip Johnson). The design of this building owes much to Phyllis Lambert, the architect daughter of Samuel Bronfman, Seagram's president, who persuaded her father to abandon the original undistinguished design in favor of an innovative one by an internationally renowned architect. Mies' dramatic bronze tower, set back on its open plaza, met with unanimous approval when it was completed and for years it served as a model for skyscraper design.

CITICORP CENTER. LEXINGTON AVE., between E. 53RD AND E. 54TH STS. (1978, arch. Hugh Stubbins & Assocs.). ● *101*. This monumental white aluminum structure, with its top sliced off at an angle (originally designed to accommodate solar panels), has become one of the most distinctive landmarks on the New York skyline. The small building between the tower's pillars is ST. PETER'S CHAPEL.

ON PARK AVENUE
The Four Seasons, one of the best restaurants in New York, is on the ground floor of the Seagram Building (above, center). In the restaurant lobby hangs Picasso's stage backdrop for the ballet *The Three-Cornered Hat* (1919). Opposite the Seagram Building, at 370 Park Avenue, is the Racquet and Tennis Club ● *93* (above), a sports club for affluent New Yorkers. The Florentine Renaissance-style palazzo houses one of the few courts in the United States for playing real (court) tennis – the precursor of lawn tennis.

5TH AVENUE, 52ND AND 53RD STREETS

In the 1940's, at the *Three Deuces* (above, left and right) on 52nd Street, Miles Davis (below) enjoyed top billing for several months.

CARTIER, INC. 651 5TH AVE. AND 4 E. 52ND ST. (1905, arch. Robert W. Gibson). This mansion was built for Morton F. Plant, a banker and "Commodore" of the New York Yacht Club. William Kissam Vanderbilt had sold him the land, stipulating that the site remain residential for twenty-five years. Plant sold it shortly after to Cartier, the Parisian jeweler, for a reputed one million dollars.

TISHMAN BUILDING. 666 5TH AVE. BETWEEN 52ND AND 53RD STS. (1957, Carson and Lundin). Following a controversial renovation, the lobby which used to lead to the waterfall designed by Isamu Noguchi in the former arcade area, has since 1988 been the home of the National Basketball Association and Brooks Brothers Stores. The red limestone accents in the white marble lobby come from a stone quarried in the south of France. On close examination the stone is seen to contain fossils (brachiopods, crinoidea, goniatites). The top-floor bar, The Grand Havana Room, affords panoramic views of Midtown.

SWING STREET. 52ND ST. BETWEEN 5TH AND 6TH AVES. At the end of the 1930's and during the 1940's, this part of 52nd Street (above left and right) was a mecca for jazz ● *60*. Audiences who wanted to hear Charlie Parker or Dizzie Gillespie flocked to such clubs as the Onyx, the Three Deuces, Kelly's Stables and the Famous Door. Performances often lasted all night and ended with jam sessions or occasionally with competitions between musicians.

21 CLUB ★. 21 W. 52ND ST. (1872, arch. Duggin & Crossman). During Prohibition this smart restaurant, now frequented by the New York elite, was a speakeasy called Jack and Charlie's Place. Of the many secret bars on this street, it was the only one to survive. The owners and their customers escaped police raids by disposing of their drinks into trapdoors under the tables and hiding behind concealed doors. The outside staircase and balcony

287

are decorated with cast-iron jockeys wearing the colors of the leading stables in the United States.

CBS BUILDING. 51 W. 52ND ST. AT 6TH AVE. (1965, arch. Eero Saarinen). This building, which was nicknamed "Black Rock" because it was built of dark gray granite, stands as a monument to the success and egocentricity of William S. Paley – founder (in 1929) of the Columbia Broadcasting System – who had a profound influence on media and entertainment in the United States ● *56*.

MUSEUM OF TELEVISION AND RADIO. 25 W. 52ND ST. (1989, arch. Philip Johnson & John Burgee). This museum boasts a collection of 70,000 radio and television programs that can be listened to or viewed.

PALEY PARK, SAMUEL PALEY PLAZA. 3 E. 53RD ST. (1967, arch. Zion & Breen). WILLIAM S. PALEY designed the park in 1965 on the site of the former Stork Club (a popular nightclub in the 1950s) and named it after his father Samuel Paley. Although small, the park is a haven of tranquillity with its lush vegetation and the gentle splashing of its waterfall, which masks the noise of traffic.

AMERICAN CRAFT MUSEUM. 44 W. 53RD ST. (1987, arch. Fox & Fowle). This museum, just opposite MoMA ▲ *290*, is dedicated to American and international crafts. It boasts a collection of objects made in a myriad of different materials including ceramic, plastic, glass, metal, paper and even chocolate.

UNIVERSITY CLUB. 1 W. 54TH ST. (1899, arch. McKim, Mead & White). This Italianate palazzo was built at a time when the club's members included the Vanderbilts and the Rockefellers. The elegant interior has marble halls, high ceilings and wood-paneled walls. Although the club is for members only, some of the rooms can be glimpsed from the street when they are illuminated.

RIZZOLI BUILDING AND COTY BUILDING. 712 AND 714 5TH AVE. (1908, arch. Adolph S. Gottlieb; 1909, arch. Woodruff Leeming). These office buildings were saved from demolition in the 1980s when it was realized that some of the Coty Building's upper windows were the work of René Lalique. The Henri Bendel department store specializing in luxury clothing is now here.

AROUND THE SONY BUILDING

ST. REGIS HOTEL. 2 E. 55TH ST. (1904, arch. Trowbridge & Livingston). Encouraged by the success of the first hotel, the

Waldorf-Astoria ▲ *285*, John Jacob Astor IV decided to build a second luxury establishment. This elegant Beaux Arts-style ● *92* hotel is the height of opulence. Of the hotel's once-famous restaurants, only the King Cole Room remains, named after the fresco *King Cole* painted by the artist Maxfield Parrish, who decorated the room.

SONY BUILDING, FORMER AT&T BUILDING. 550 MADISON AVE. (1984, arch. Philip Johnson & John Burgee). The grayish-pink granite, used here instead of glass as the facing, is one of the elements that mark the advent of Postmodernism ● *102*. An ATRIUM, the Sony Plaza, is on the ground floor.

IBM BUILDING. 590 MADISON AVE. (1983, arch. Edward Larrabee Barnes Assocs.). The best view of this five-sided prism, faced with greenish-black polished granite, is from the corner of 5th Avenue and 57th Street. On the southern side of the building, a huge ATRIUM, planted with a forest of bamboo trees, is open to the public. Concerts are sometimes held here.

The lobby of the St. Regis-Sheraton (top), where Dali stayed on his visits to New York, and (above) the atrium of the IBM Building.

SONY BUILDING AND PLAZA
The construction of this building aroused a great deal of public debate. Certain architecture critics nicknamed the building the "Chippendale Skyscraper" (after the 18th-century English furniture maker ● *66*) because of its unusual pediment, which can be seen from the southwest corner of 5th Ave., and 55th St. Sony Plaza comprises two gallery-stores (Sony Style) that exhibit and sell the company's electronic products, Sony Wonder (an exhibition of the latest technological developments) and an atrium (an open area lined with bars and stores). In 1987, the painter Richard Haas ▲ *112*, depicted the building with the Trump Tower in the foreground (left).

When the Museum of Modern Art (MoMA), designed by Philip Goodwin and Edward Durrell Stone, was founded in 1929, the intention was to make it the largest museum of modern art in the world. Its collections now form one of the most wide-ranging panoramas of modern art: paintings, sculpture, drawings, engravings and photographs, as well as films, architectural models and highstyle functional objects in eye-catching designs.

PABLO PICASSO, *Les Demoiselles d'Avignon* (1907). The rough, almost violent, brushstrokes, the heads turned to the right, their hypnotically staring eyes, the fragmented faces refuting the laws of symmetry and the angular hangings, all contribute to this work's expressive intensity. Picasso initially intended to add two male figures.

PAUL CÉZANNE, *The Bather* (c. 1885). Despite or because of a certain freedom in his treatment of line and scale, this monumental, formal work is extraordinarily powerful.

AUGUSTE RODIN, *Balzac* (1897-8). This bronze statue's full cloak and huge head give it a revolutionary appearance. This colossal being symbolizes much more than the writer – it is the universal embodiment of genius.

VINCENT VAN GOGH, *The Starry Night* (1889) This canvas is simultaneously stormy and transcendent. The stable geometry of the village acts as a foil for the flamelike cypress trees, the roiling sky and the vortex of the planets, rendered with coarse, vigorous brushstrokes, loaded with vision and feeling never before expressed in painting.

THE NEW MoMA
MoMA's original design, an austere, white marble International Style, was a rebuke to museums built like or, in fact, housed in European palaces. In 1951 the museum's first architectural curator expanded the galleries and built the Abby A. Rockefeller Sculpture Garden. Enlarged again in 1984 by Cesar Pelli the museum was nearly doubled in size by Yoshio Taniguchi in 2004, in an acclaimed, classically Modernist style that preserved MoMA's structural DNA but changed the building more significantly than any of his predecessors.

HENRI MATISSE,
The Red Studio (1911) Everything but the painter's works appears in outline.

HENRI ROUSSEAU,
The Sleeping Gypsy (1897). The central figure sleeps near a lion, as she has nothing to fear. The supernatural atmosphere of this scene is typical of this painter's work.

Today an entrance on 54th St allows you, for the first time, to pass through the lobby to 53rd St, and see some artwork without waiting in line to pay for a ticket. Inside the museum, a six-story atrium is crossed with balconies and walkways – Taniguchi's most radical shift. You no longer have to march in a linear fashion through the history of modern art.

Orson Welles' movie *Citizen Kane* (1941), which was suggestive of William Randolph Hearst, caused such a scandal that members of Hearst's empire tried to squash its release. But the film made it to the theater and won popular and critical acclaim.

JOAN MIRÓ, *Hirondelle–Amour* (1933–4). In this painting, the fluid lines of the abstract shapes move against an ethereal blue background, which gives the work a dream-like serenity.

The aerodynamic line of the Cisitalia "202" GT, body designed by Pininfarina (1946), create an impression that the car is moving even when stationary

CONSTANTIN BRANCUSI,
Fish (1930, *right*). The artist is not interested in representing one particular fish but rather has distilled the creature's very essence, reducing it to its natural condition.

THE 2004 METAMORPHOSIS
The entrances to the Sculpture Garden have been reconfigured with black granite, aluminum panels, and white and gray glass for a dramatic and ethereal effect, which along with the translucent white and grey glass on the front and back of the museum give a sense of weightlessness and suspension.

MUSEUM GALLERY

The collection retraces the history of
photography from its invention, around 1840.
Besides works by artists, it shows photographs
taken by journalists, scientists and amateurs.

JASPER JOHNS,
Flag (1954–5).
Flag or painting?
The illusion is almost
perfect. The artist has
blurred the traditional
concept of reality in
painting by merging
the pictorial form and
space of his subject
– here, as often, an
everyday object – with
those of his painting.

WILLEM DE KOONING,
Woman, I (1950–2).
The painter has given
this figure, with its
staring eyes and
artificial grin, a
sinister, ironic look.
This figurative work
was painted at a time
when critics favored
more abstract works.

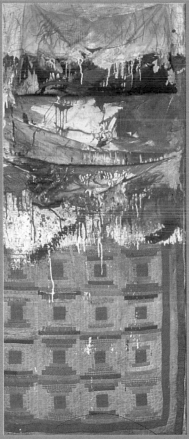

JACKSON POLLOCK, *One (Number 31, 1950)*. Despite the illusion of complete spontancity, Pollock never lost control of his line, thickening, thinning, spreading or layering its applications. The overall effect, although rhythmic and lyrical, is aggressive

ROBERT RAUSCHENBERG, *Bed* (1955). This abstract expressionist work uses the components of a real bed, and is firmly rooted in "the gulf between art and life" – a phenomenon that Rauschenberg was exploring in his work.

ANDY WARHOL, *Gold Marilyn Monroe* (1962). The gold background of this portrait is reminiscent of Byzantine art, which surrounds its subject with an almost mystical aura. Andy Warhol, who painted the actress on many occasions, was clearly aware of the irony of this symbolism.

MERET OPPENHEIM, *Object, Fur Covered Cup* (1936). The Surrealists liked to invent bizarre, nightmarish objects. *Object*, a teacup, saucer and spoon covered in fur, is a good example of the surprise and unease they aimed to create by an unexpected juxtaposition of subject and material.

295

AIR RIGHTS

In Manhattan, each square inch is worth its weight in gold. Historic buildings, even functional buildings, have often been destroyed to make way for taller buildings simply because they were much lower than the permitted height for their surface area. A few years ago, an ingenious scheme was devised, enabling these buildings to be saved: their "air rights" can be transferred to a nearby building project. In other words, the available air space left unused by a low historic building legally can be used by a new building; the latter can therefore exceed current specifications, and the historic building need not be demolished. Thus, Tiffany sold its air rights to Trump Tower, allowing Trump to aim ever higher.

In 1961 Blake Edwards filmed Audrey Hepburn (right) at the prestigious 5th Avenue store Tiffany & Co, for the movie *Breakfast at Tiffany's*.

LVMH TOWER. 21 E. 57TH ST. (1999, arch. Christian de Portzamparc). This 328-foot-high steel and glass tower commissioned by the Louis Vuitton-Moët Hennessy group is considered one of the most striking new buildings. The French architect Portzamparc showed great originality in meeting the challenges represented by the narrow, enclosed plot.

FORMER FULLER BUILDING. 41 E. 57TH ST. (1929, arch. Walker & Gillette). This black, gray and white building, a fine example of restrained Art Deco Style, formerly housed the offices of the Fuller Company, a large building firm that previously occupied the Flatiron Building ▲ *234*. A sculpture by Elie Nadelman on the façade depicts Fuller Company laborers at work.

TRUMP TOWER. 725 5TH AVE. (1983, arch. Der Scutt). This tower, which houses six floors of shops and stores, twenty floors of offices and forty floors of luxury apartments, was named after its real estate developer Donald J. Trump ▲ *161*. When the building was completed in 1983, reactions were mixed, with some critics finding the ATRIUM's waterfall, pink marble and brass trimmings too brash.

TOWARD GRAND ARMY PLAZA

TIFFANY & CO. 727 5TH AVE. AT S. E. CORNER OF 57TH ST. (1940, arch. Cross & Cross). This famous jewelry store was founded by Charles Tiffany in 1837. Above the main entrance there is a carving of Atlas on bronzed wood, commissioned for an earlier store. Tiffany's signature light blue boxes and window displays have become an institution. Charles' son, Louis Comfort Tiffany, was renowned for his designs in jewelry, enamel and glass ● *66*.

CROWN BUILDING ★. 730 5TH AVE. (1921, arch. Warren & Wetmore). This was the first skyscraper to be built on this part of 5th Avenue and the first office block to be built after the 1916 ordinances. It housed the Museum of Modern Art (1929–39), pending the construction of the museum on W. 53rd Street. ▲ *290*. The Crown Building was once owned by Ferdinand and Imelda Marcos.

BERGDORF GOODMAN. 754 5TH AVE., AT S.W. CORNER OF 58TH ST. (1928, arch. Buchman & Kahn). Herman Bergdorf, a

The gilded top of the Crown Building, which conceals a water tower, is an eye-catching feature of Midtown's skyline.

...ailor of Alsatian extraction, founded a store in 1894 and sold his shares to his partner, Edwin Goodman, in 1901. The latter was responsible for assuring the store's reputation for a wide range of top-quality European clothing. In 1928 Bergdorf's moved to its present site.

SOLOW BUILDING. 9 W. 57TH ST. (1974, arch. Skidmore, Owings & Merrill). This is the twin of the Grace Building, opposite Bryant Park ▲ 254. The giant red 9 sculpture on the sidewalk was created by designer Ivan Chermayeff.

GENERAL MOTORS BUILDING. 767 5TH AVE. BETWEEN 58TH AND 59TH STS. (1968, arch. Edward Durell Stone, Emery Roth & Sons). The Savoy Plaza Hotel was demolished to make way for this tower, much to the chagrin of New Yorkers who loved the hotel both for its intrinsic merits and for its contribution to the architectural ensemble of Grand Army Plaza. General Motors cars are on display on the ground floor. The toy store F.A.O. Schwarz, founded in 1862, moved here in 1986.

The original Oak Room (above center) of the Plaza Hotel is named for its oak paneling. This watercolor (above, 1982) of the hotel is by the American artist A. Troubetzkoy.

PLAZA HOTEL. GRAND ARMY PLAZA, W. 58TH AND W. 59TH STS. (1907, arch. Henry Hardenberg). Twenty years after finishing the Dakota Apartments, Henry Hardenberg designed the Plaza Hotel, regarded as a masterpiece of French Neo-Renaissance architecture. Many famous people have stayed at the Plaza including Eleanor Roosevelt, Mark Twain, Groucho Marx, Francis Scott Fitzgerald and Frank Lloyd Wright. The Plaza belonged to Donald Trump between 1988 and 1995.

GRAND ARMY PLAZA. Built in 1912, this plaza was the first European-style square in New York. It takes its name from the Yankee Army in the Civil War, also commemorated by a statue of General William T. Sherman, famous for his victorious march through Georgia to the sea. This work by Augustus Saint-Gaudens is regarded as one of the finest equestrian statues in the United States. The PULITZER FOUNTAIN (1916), which is dominated by the statue of Pomona (goddess of fruit) by Karl Bitter, was financed by the publisher Joseph Pulitzer. In 1919, on learning that his first book had been accepted for publication, F. Scott Fitzgerald joyfully leaped into this fountain.

Statue of William T. Sherman (1820–91), the famous Union general, which stands in Grand Army Plaza.

▲ ROCKEFELLER CENTER TO THE WEST SIDE

7 MANHATTAN LIFE INSURANCE COMPANY
8 HOTEL PARKER MERIDIEN
9 OSBORNE APARTMENTS ET ART STUDENT LEAGUE
10 ALWYN COURT
11 HEARST MAGAZINE BLDG
12 N.Y. ATHLETIC CLUB

1 WORLDWIDE PLAZA
2 ST. MALACHY ROMAN CATHOLIC CHURCH
3 CITY CENTER OF MUSIC
4 PARK CENTRAL HOTEL
6 CARNEGIE HALL

LINCOLN CENTER

CENTRAL PARK

ROCKEFELLER CENTER

DIAMOND DISTRICT

Six hours
◆ C B1-B2-C2-C3

"He blinked . . . and suddenly, he could see. He was crouching in the middle of a large meadow fringed with trees. Beyond the trees, wreathed in fog and mist, dozens of giant buildings were thrusting towards a leaden sky. There was a sign at the top of one of them: Essex House."
George Chesbro, *Bone*

The rapid growth of harbor activity along the Hudson River that started in the early 20th century, created a more varied mix of neighborhoods on the West Side than on the East Side. The Midtown West Side welcomed all manner of businesses and industries – including the entertainment industry – and saw the construction of both tenements and private mansions. After World War II,

298

air transportation became more popular than sea travel, and the decline in harbor activity had a correspondingly adverse effect on this part of town. In the early 1980's the city of New York endeavored to rehabilitate the area west of Broadway and north of Times Square, as can be seen in the recent crop of skyscrapers. The entertainment and arts sectors, long concentrated on the West Side, have undergone a shift to the north. While the mainstream theaters remain clustered in the 1940's, just north of Times Square, and CARNEGIE HALL still stands on West 57th Street, the New York Philharmonic, Metropolitan Opera, New York City Ballet, and other companies are at Lincoln Center ▲ *305* at 65th Street.

THE DIAMOND DISTRICT

DIAMOND AND JEWELRY WAY. W. 47TH ST. BETWEEN 5TH AND 6TH AVES. Four hundred million dollars' worth of precious stones changes hands daily on this block. During the 1920's and 1930's, the diamond trade was concentrated among the Hassidim on the Lower East Side ▲ *194*; it moved to 47th Street around the outbreak of World War II, when more Jewish gem traders and cutters arrived from Europe.

GOTHAM BOOK MART ★ (Formerly at 41 W. 47th St.) 'Wise men fish here" is the motto of this bookshop, founded in 1920 by Frances Steloff, which has now moved to 16 E 46th St. Her customers included T. S. Eliot, Henry Miller and Thornton Wilder, the novelist and playwright, whose most famous play is Our Town. Defying the censors, Frances Steloff stocked copies of Lady Chatterley's Lover, by D. H. Lawrence, a highly controversial work when published in 1928, which she secretly imported from England. She

THE DIAMOND DISTRICT IN THE EARLY 20TH CENTURY At the beginning of the 1920's, about ten bookshops were gathered along this stretch of the street.

employed the poets Everett LeRoi Jones and Allen Ginsberg, as well as the playwright Tennessee Williams, as sales assistants when they were still struggling to make names for themselves. Woody Allen, Saul Bellow and the playwright John Guare, have been frequent visitors to the store. When Frances Steloff died in 1989, at the age of 101, letters and flowers poured in from all over the world. The shop supplies a wide range of books, antique and modern, and literary magazines, in particular those dealing with 20th-century poetry and prose.

Today it is still lined with stores; business transactions are carried out in rooms behind the stores and in clubs such as the Diamond Dealers Club. Until recently, deals were also transacted on the sidewalk, but the murder of two jewelers there in 1977 put an end to this informality.

IN THE VICINITY OF ROCKEFELLER CENTER

Originally Rockefeller Center was intended to include a site between 47th and 52nd streets on the west side of 6th Avenue, but the El, which operated until 1938, checked its development.

Detail of the façade (top right) of St. Malachy's Church on 49th Street.

Construction did not begin until the 1960's, when a Modernist-style complex on 6th Avenue (Avenue of the Americas), including a new McGraw-Hill, Exxon and Time & Life buildings, was built.

ST MALACHY ROMAN CATHOLIC CHURCH. 239-245 W. 49TH ST. (1903). This small neo-Gothic church was the parish church of Broadway's Catholic actors, since its proximity to the theater district enabled them to attend services between performances. In 1926 Rudolph Valentino's funeral took place in this church, attended by thousands of women.

WORLDWIDE PLAZA. 935 8TH AVE. BETWEEN 49TH AND 50TH STS. (1989, arch. Frank Williams). This commercial and residential complex, whose pyramidal top looms above the western side of 8th Avenue, is proof of the recent commercial recovery of this part of Midtown. It was built on the site of the second Madison Square Garden ▲ 249. The northwest corner of 49th Street and Broadway was named JACK DEMPSEY CORNER in memory of the world boxing champion who defended his title at Madison Square Garden. At the end of his boxing career, he opened a restaurant in this district called Jack Dempsey's.

JACK DEMPSEY CORNER

A window of the City Center of Music and Drama.

ROSELAND BALLROOM. 239 W. 52ND ST. BETWEEN BROADWAY AND 8TH AVE. The original Roseland, a club that opened on December 31, 1919, became a mecca for ballroom dancers of all ages; thousands of people came here to learn the new dances: the lindy, shag and jitterbug or, later, the cha-cha and twist. Many top entertainers have performed here, including Ella Fitzgerald ● 61. The first Roseland was on 50th Street and moved in 1956 to the present location. Roseland boasts the largest dance floor in New York.

CITY CENTER OF MUSIC AND DRAMA ★ 135 W. 55TH ST. (1924, arch. Harry P. Knowles). This exotic-looking theater started life as the Mecca Temple of the *Ancient and Accepted Order of the Mystic Shrine* (a branch of Free-masonry). The institution foundered during the 1929 Wall Street crash. Fiorello La Guardia saved the building at the end of the 1930's by converting it into a theater. The City Center was the home of the New York City Ballet and the New York City Opera ● 62 until they moved to Lincoln Center in the 1960's. In recent years the City Center has offered performances by various companies including the Joffrey Ballet, the Paul Taylor Dance Company and the Dance Theater of Harlem.

What's Italian For Carnegie Hall?

PARK CENTRAL HOTEL. 870 7TH AVE. (1927, arch. Groneburg and Leuchtag). Throughout the Prohibition years this hotel was used by bootleggers ● *40* and small-time crooks. One of them, Arnold Rothstein, was thought to be the model for Meyer Wolfsheim in F. Scott Fitzgerald's novel *The Great Gatsby*. He was shot in 1928, in room 349, for refusing to pay a poker debt. In 1957, the gangster Albert Anastasia was murdered in the hotel's barbershop. Both of these murders remain unsolved because, as they say in New York, "nobody saw anything."

TRATTORIA DELL'ARTE. 900 7TH AVE. One wall of this restaurant displays the sculpted noses of famous Italians and Italian-Americans, from Julius Caesar, Dante, and Verdi to Joe DiMaggio, the legendary baseball player and husband of Marilyn Monroe. Enormous sculptures representing different parts of the human body adorn the others.

7TH STREET

Before World War II, this street became one of the most elegant in New York. A concert hall, art galleries, chic boutiques and restaurants abounded. Some of the street's original attractions remain, including several institutions and a great many art galleries.

CARNEGIE HALL. 156 W. 57TH ST. AT THE CORNER OF 7TH AVE. 1891, arch. William B. Tuthill). This Italian Renaissance-style building was financed by the steel magnate, Andrew Carnegie, to house the Oratorio Society, a choir founded by Leopold Damrosch and Carnegie. Tchaikovsky conducted the opening gala concert on May 9, 1891, and paid tribute to the concert hall's "magnificent" acoustics. A year later the New York Philharmonic Orchestra, also founded by Damrosch, took up residence here; it moved to Lincoln Center in 1962. A campaign led by the violinist Isaac Stern saved Carnegie Hall from demolition and it was restored in 1986. Some of the leading figures in the world of music have appeared here. Leonard Bernstein made his debut here in 1943. Duke Ellington, Ella Fitzgerald, Frank Sinatra and the Beatles all performed here. The ROSE MUSEUM AT CARNEGIE, opened in 1991 to mark the hall's centenary, documents the venue's history. On the second floor of the building, near the MAIN AUDITORIUM, there are display cabinets containing treasures such as the baton used by conductor Arturo Toscanini and the program of Bob Dylan's first New York concert given in one of Carnegie Hall's small auditoriums in 1961. Today, Carnegie Hall welcomes the leading performers of orchestral music, opera, pop and jazz. Its halls and corridors are decorated with scores and mementoes of the artists who have helped create its legend.

HOTEL PARKER MERIDIEN. 118 W. 57TH ST. (1981, arch. Philip Birnbaum). The main features of this Postmodern hotel are

Sign from Trattoria Dell'Arte.

ANDREW CARNEGIE (1835–1919) The meteoric rise of the son of impoverished Scottish parents who emigrated to the United States in 1848 is a success story that epitomizes the American dream of the mid-19th century. This child laborer from the suburbs of Pittsburgh became one of the wealthiest men in American and founded an industrial empire that dominated the U.S. steel industry for nearly thirty years. However, Andrew Carnegie is primarily regarded as a great philanthropist, who was deeply concerned about the social inequalities created by the rapid growth of the industrial society. In 1890, he began to undertake a great deal of charitable work, particularly in the fields of culture and education. He opened 2,500 public libraries throughout the world, funded schools, concert halls, and non-profit-making organizations and societies. He ended his days in a fine house on 5th Avenue, now occupied by the Cooper Hewitt Museum ▲ *320*.

HARD ROCK CAFÉ
This New York
establishment displays
electric guitars that
once belonged to Billy
Joel and Brian Jones.

Steinway piano
showroom.

Façade of the New
York Delicatessen.

the breathtaking marble lobby-atrium and the view from the swimming pool terrace on the top floor.

MANHATTAN LIFE INSURANCE BUILDING. 111 W. 57TH ST. (1925, arch. Warren & Wetmore). This neo-classical building, not far from CARNEGIE HALL, used to belong to Steinway, the famous piano manufacturer. The company had to sell the building after the 1929 crash, but they retained the superb ground floor space as a showroom. The MUSEUM OF THE AMERICAN PIANO (211 W 58th St), exhibits 19th-century American musical instruments.

OSBORNE APARTMENTS ★. 205 W. 57TH ST. (1885, arch. James E. Ware). The plain brownstone façade of this building conceals an extravagant marble lobby. Leonard Bernstein, who composed the music for *West Side Story*, was one of the Osborne's illustrious residents. In 1978 the actor Gig Young, who was awarded an Oscar for his role in the film *They Shoot Horses, Don't They?*, with Jane Fonda, was found dead beside his wife in one of the apartments, a revolver in his hand.

ART STUDENTS LEAGUE. 215 W. 57TH ST. (1892, arch. Henry J. Hardenbergh). This French Renaissance-style building originally housed the AMERICAN FINE ART SOCIETY and was built by the Art Students League, founded in 1875. Among the eminent artists who have taught at this school are William Merritt Chase and Robert Henri, who influenced an entire generation of students including Edward Hopper, George Bellows and John Sloane.

HEARST MAGAZINE BUILDING. 959 8TH AVE. (1928, Joseph Urban and George B. Post & Sons). The building was commissioned by William Randolph Hearst (1863-1951), the newspaper tycoon. At the height of his career, in 1935, Hearst – one of the pioneers of "yellow journalism" ● *54* - owned 28 newspapers and 18 magazines. He was immortalized on screen by Orson Welles in *Citizen Kane* (1941). This building, with its over-abundant decoration, including huge columns capped with urns, was intended to have seven more stories, but the 1929 crash forced Hearst to put a stop to the work. However, development plans are once again on the agenda, even though the building is now a listed landmark. The English architect Norman Foster has built a 36-story tower on top of the original building, enabling the newspaper group to house all its offices at the same address.

ALWYN COURT ★. 180 W. 58TH ST. (1909, arch. Harde & Short) This was designed as a luxury apartment building with no more than twenty-two apartments, each containing between fourteen and thirty-four rooms. In 1938 it was divided into seventy-five apartments of three to five rooms. The French Renaissance-

Detail of the French Renaissance-style façade of Alwyn Court.

style façade is covered with sculptures depicting dragons, crowns, leaves, flowers and crowned salamanders, the emblem of Francis I. A large interior courtyard, decorated with a mural by Richard Haas, is situated through the lobby and can be glimpsed through the glass front door.

The Hearst Magazine Building's classical sculptures symbolize music, comedy, tragedy, sport, industry, printing and the sciences.

CENTRAL PARK SOUTH

ESSEX HOUSE. 160 CENTRAL PARK SOUTH (1930, arch. Frank Grad). This Art Deco hotel enjoys a fabulous view over Central Park. Its residents have included such diverse artists as Betty Grable and Igor Stravinsky. Ingrid Bergman stayed here in 1946, when she was performing *Joan of Lorraine* on Broadway.

NEW YORK ATHLETIC CLUB. 180 CENTRAL PARK SOUTH (1929, arch. York & Sawyer). The sculptures decorating the main entrance of this club, founded in 1868, represent athletes in training or playing their sport.

THE GAINSBOROUGH STUDIOS. 222 CENTRAL PARK SOUTH (1908, arch. Charles W. Buckham). Originally this was a building of artists' studios; later converted into apartments. Only the frieze by Isidore Konti and the bust of Gainsborough on the façade point to the building's original purpose. The jazz clarinettist Artie Shaw lived here during the 1940's.

COLUMBUS CIRCLE

This traffic circle was given its present name in 1892 in celebration of the 400th anniversary of Europe's discovery of the New World. The marble column, topped by a statue of Christopher Columbus by Gaetano Russo in 1894, was a gift from America's Italian citizens. The site of the former Coliseum Building, a massive block that extended along one side of the square, is now home to the 55-story, 750-foot twin towers of the Columbus Center, also known as the Time Warner Center. This massive complex of more than 2.8 million square feet was completed in 2004. In two towers, it houses seven restaurants, offices for Time Warner and CNN, a giant Whole Foods grocery and many other stores, a 250-room Mandarin Oriental hotel, 225 super-luxury apartments and Jazz at Lincoln Center ● *63*. The latter is located on the 5th and 6th floors of the building: the Rose Theater seats

MAINE MEMORIAL
The Maine Memorial was erected in 1913 at the behest of William Randolph Hearst, who covered the Spanish-American War extensively in the New York *Journal*.

Plan in perspective for Lincoln Center, displayed in the Avery Library at Columbia University.

1,200 people and is home to the JVC Jazz Festival and the resident Afro-Latin Jazz Orchestra; the Allen Room seats 550 people and hosts well-known touring bands throughout the year; and Dizzy's Club Coca-Cola, with just 140 seats, is the Center's version of a classic jazz club open every night.

MAINE MEMORIAL. S. W. CORNER OF CENTRAL PARK (1913, statue by Attilio Piccirilli and H. Van Bwen Magonigle). This monument commemorates the victims of the sinking of the *Maine*, the American battleship which was blown up in Havana harbor in 1898, an event that helped to precipitate the Spanish-American War.

LINCOLN CENTER CAMPUS OF FORDHAM UNIVERSITY.
COLUMBUS AVE., BETWEEN 60TH AND 62ND STS. This houses the Fordham Law School, part of a Jesuit university based in the Bronx, founded in 1841.

KENT GARAGE. 43 W. 61ST ST. (1930, arch. Jardine, Hill & Murdock). This garage, now converted into apartments, is an Art Deco gem. It was one of the first garages in New York with an elevator that was capable of transporting vehicles.

Some 1.5 million people attended the parade held on the day that the Columbus Circle monument was unveiled. It is situated an the southwest entrance to Central Park.

LINCOLN CENTER ★

The plans for the Lincoln Center for the Performing Arts date from the 1950's, when the Metropolitan Opera and the New York Philharmonic needed new premises more urgently than ever. The work was directed by John D. Rockefeller III and Robert Moses, the New York property developer and parks commissioner. President Eisenhower laid the first stone in 1959. Although most architectural critics have judged it to be conventional and flashy, it has become an important cultural center. It now employs seven thousand people and attracts more than five million patrons to some three thousand performances each year. The construction of Lincoln Center was postponed to allow the slums on 62nd Street to be used as a backdrop for scenes in *West Side Story*. The film's director, Robert Wise, employed some members of neighborhood gangs to play the parts of policemen.

NEW YORK STATE THEATER. (1964, arch. Philip Johnson and Richard Foster). This is the home of the New York City Opera and the New York City Ballet ● 62. Though the theater itself has no central aisle and the design element on the sides of tiers was compared to Cadillac headlights, it has achieved institutional status. The two statues dominating its

Grand Promenade space, *Two Nudes* and *Two Circus Women*, are huge replicas of original works by Elie Nadelman.

METROPOLITAN OPERA HOUSE. (1966, arch. Wallace K. Harrison). This is the centerpiece of Lincoln Center. The Metropolitan Opera House was founded in 1883 by wealthy New Yorkers, such as J. P. Morgan and the Vanderbilts, who wanted to have their own opera house because the "old" New York aristocracy were monopolizing the Academy of Music on 14th Street. Although badly designed and cramped, the old house, on Broadway at 65th Street, was nevertheless used for eighty years, until the opera moved to Lincoln Center in September 1966. The interior, with its red carpeting, gold leaf and marble is a modern version of traditional opera house design. The crystal chandelier was a gift from the Austrian government. The main staircase is

flanked by two huge murals by Chagall, *The Triumph of Music* and *The Sources of Music*, which can best be seen from outside at night (left).

DAMROSCH PARK AND GUGGENHEIM BANDSHELL. (1969, arch. Eggers & Higgins). The park and its open-air theater are used for concerts in the summer.

LINCOLN CENTER
The name of the center was taken from the adjacent Lincoln Square, which marks the intersection of Broadway and Columbus Ave. The layout of Lincoln Center's three main

Every winter, in December, the BIG APPLE CIRCUS raises its tent here. The park takes its name from the conductor and composer Walter Damrosch, who conducted the NEW YORK SYMPHONY ORCHESTRA in the early part of the 20th century.

AVERY FISHER HALL. (1962, arch. Max Abramovitz). This is the home of the New York Philharmonic Orchestra. Originally called Philharmonic Hall, it was renamed in 1973 after its principal patron, Avery Fisher. The acoustics in the hall were so poor that the interior was dismantled and

reconstructed in 1976. The rebuilt hall was greeted warmly by performers and audiences alike. In the lobby areas are the *Tragic Mask of Beethoven* by Antonin Bourdelle and the bronze head of Mahler by Auguste Rodin.

VIVIAN BEAUMONT THEATER. 150 W. 65TH ST. (1965, arch. Eero Saarinen). This building, named after its principal donor, has two theaters, managed

buildings – the Metropolitan Opera, the New York State Theater and Avery Fisher Hall – is modeled on Michelangelo's Piazza del Campidoglio in Rome. Instead of a statue, as in the original, a fountain (above) adorns the center of this plaza. The fountain was financed by a special donation from the Charles Revson Foundation. The huge pool in the northeast plaza contains a sculpture by Henry Moore, *Reclining Figure*. Two other buildings of the center, the Vivian Beaumont Theater and the Juilliard School of Music, are even better examples of the aesthetic trends that dominated architecture in the 1960's.

by Lincoln Center. It has staged extremely successful productions of musicals and plays such as *Anything Goes*, *Six Degrees of Separation* and *Arcadia*.

LIBRARY AND MUSEUM OF THE PERFORMING ARTS. 111 AMSTERDAM AVE. (1965, Skidmore, Owings & Merrill). The library and museum are part of the NEW YORK PUBLIC LIBRARY ▲ *252*. The museum's archives include recordings made at the Metropolitan Opera House since the beginning of the century, the Rodgers and Hammerstein sound archives and several thousand theater programs.

JUILLIARD SCHOOL OF MUSIC. 144 W. 56TH ST. (1969, arch. Pietro Belluschi with Eduardo Catalano and Westermann & Miller). This prestigious school of music, dance and drama, which can take its pick from the most brilliant students in the world, was founded in 1904 by Frank Damrosch and James Loeb and named after its patron, the millionaire Augustus D. Juilliard.

Around
Central Park

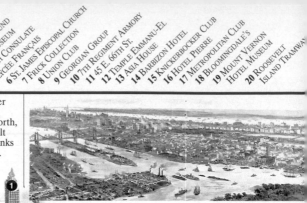

View of the Upper East Side (1907) taken from the north, showing Roosevelt Island and the banks of the East River.

The upper East Side has two natural boundaries – the East River and Central Park, and two urban limits, 60th and 96th streets – where the railroad tracks emerging from the tunnel under Park Avenue form an unmistakable border between one of the most elegant parts of the city and the beginning of Harlem. The first houses in the district were farms, built before 1860, to the east of Park Avenue, which was then named 4th Avenue and marked by above-ground railroad tracks. When the 3rd Avenue El was built in 1878, followed by the 2nd Avenue El ● 36, a crop of tenements sprang up. However, in 1880, to the west, the situation changed again with the completion, finally, of Central Park. The wealthy started to move northward once

E. 77TH ST.
E. 76TH ST.
E. 75TH ST.
E. 74TH ST.
E. 73RD ST.
E. 72ND ST.
E. 71ST ST.
E. 70TH ST.
E. 69TH ST.

▲ Five hours

◆ C A3-A2-B3-B4

AN ATTRACTIVE NEIGHBORHOOD
The sailing ships are long gone, the lawns no longer slope down to the river's edge, a highway runs along the banks, but the neighborhood is still one of the most desirable areas in New York. Its regular streets exude an air of financial ease and security. People still live the good life in this stylish, expensive neighborhood, with its aristocratic houses, luxury apartments, clubs, museums, galleries and churches, liberally interspersed with bars and cafés.

GRAND ARMY PLAZA

MADISON AVE.

308

again and, for the first time in the city's history, they put down roots and stayed in one neighborhood. They did not move again, as they had in 1907. Park Avenue – an attractive and uncluttered thoroughfare lined with sumptuous apartment buildings – was built over the 4th Avenue railroad tracks, which had been sunk beneath a planted center divider. Now the neighborhood extends to the west of Lexington Avenue with a display of residential and commercial prosperity; to the east, a more modest display of wealth dating from the 1950's. When the El was dismantled, the neighborhood regained its tranquility, attracting the middle classes. The side streets, with their carefully renovated houses, are very attractive, while the many bars and movie houses at the foot of modern high-rises contribute to the vibrant bustle of 3rd, 2nd and 1st avenues, making them a favorite haunt for young people.

FROM 5TH AVENUE TO ROOSEVELT ISLAND

Façade of the former Lycée Français. The house is now owned by the Emir of Qatar.

72ND STREET, A MARRIAGE OF OPPOSITES. CORNER MADISON AVE. A profusion of styles and professions is represented by the elegant ROSARIO CANDELA APARTMENT BUILDING (N. W. CORNER, 1936); the Beaux Arts façades of the former LYCÉE FRANÇAIS next door at nos. 7 and 9 (1899, arch. Flagg & Chambers; 1896, arch. Carrère and Hastings), and THE MANSION (S. W. CORNER, 1898, arch. Kimball & Thompson), which houses the Ralph Lauren store – formerly the Olivetti Building, and originally the Gertrude Rhinelander Waldo residence. All are characteristic of this stretch of Madison Avenue.

ST. JAMES EPISCOPAL CHURCH. 865 MADISON AVE., N. E. CORNER 71ST ST. (1884, arch. Robert H. Robertson). Founded in 1810 as a parish church during the summer months, its simple wooden structure was replaced in 1869 by a Victorian Gothic-style building which, in its turn, made way in 1884 for the present church. Note the TIFFANY stained-glass windows.

71ST AND 70TH STREETS. BETWEEN 5TH AND PARK AVES. The elegant streets that flank the Frick Collection ▲ 322, although a little stiff in appearance, still boast a number of neo-classical ashlar mansions dating from the neighborhood's early days: too large to be converted into apartments, they house private colleges, foundations or galleries. The streets to the east of Madison Avenue, which are less ostentatious and more eclectic, still possess some fine residences. The many garages were once stables belonging to the palazzos on 5th Avenue.

LUXURY ON MADISON
The Ralph Lauren boutique (the Mansion) has retained the appearance of a private residence, with its fireplaces and wood-paneled rooms.

UNION CLUB OF NEW YORK. N. E. CORNER OF PARK AVE. AND 69TH ST. (1932, arch. Delano & Aldrich). This is the headquarters of the oldest club in the city, founded in 1836. Clubs have always played an important role in New York society, and membership of specific clubs is taken to provide an accurate gauge of someone's social standing. The UNION CLUB is still quite old-world; the METROPOLITAN (1 E. 60th St., 1893, arch. McKim, Mead & White) places more importance on wealth; and the KNICKERBOCKER (2 E. 62nd St., 1913, arch. Delano & Aldrich) insists on members having one ancestor dating directly back to colonial times. The CENTURY ASSOCIATION (7 W. 43rd St., 1891, arch. McKim, Mead & White) is more concerned with culture ▲ 251. Walk down Park Avenue on the west, to avoid HUNTER COLLEGE's modern buildings, completed in 1940 – the old neo-Gothic style building (1913, arch. C. B. J. Snyder) is on Lexington Avenue.

PARK AVENUE ★. WEST SIDE, BETWEEN 69TH AND 68TH STS. A cluster of Georgian houses provides a glimpse of how Park Avenue would have looked in the early 1900's. These grand buildings now house organisations such as the AMERICAS SOCIETY (1911, arch. McKim, Mead & White), the SPANISH INSTITUTE (1926, same architects) the ITALIAN CULTURAL INSTITUTE (1919, arch. Delano & Aldrich) and the CONSULATE GENERAL OF ITALY (1916, arch. Walker & Gillette).

LUXURY ON "FIFTH"
The doorman, who performs the role of caretaker, doorkeeper and porter, is essential to the Upper East Sider's sense of well-being. The superintendent and back elevator man act as plumbers, electricians and general repairmen, taking care of the residents' continued comfort within the walls of these bastions of wealth.

THE 7TH REGIMENT ARMORY
The huge inner hall (187 feet by 270 feet), once used for military maneuvers, can be rented for private functions, exhibitions or shows. There is also a museum, retracing the history of the unit, which defended Washington, D.C. during the Civil War. Tiffany was the interior designer for two of the rooms, which can be visited by appointment. On the fifth floor, the officers' mess – with its décor devoted to the sport of hunting – has been converted into a restaurant.

THE 7TH REGIMENT

ARMORY ★. 643 PARK AVE. BETWEEN 67TH AND 66TH STS. (1880, arch. Charles W. Clinton). This impressive brick fortress used to be the rallying point for the 7th Regiment of the NATIONAL GUARD.

45 EAST 66TH STREET. (1908, arch. Harde & Short). The façade, a staggering array of double windows separated by terracotta ogives, swelling into a tower at the corner of the avenue, is a monument to the sumptuousness of the first buildings on Madison Avenue.

TEMPLE EMMANU-EL ★. 840 5TH AVE. N. E. CORNER 65TH ST. (1929, arch Robert D Kohn, Charles Butler and Clarence Stein). This SYNAGOGUE, with its Moorish and Romanesque-style decoration, is one of the city's largest places of worship.

ASIA HOUSE, RUSSELL SAGE FOUNDATION AND ROBERT STERLING CLARK FOUNDATION ★. 112 E. 64TH ST. (1959, arch. Philip Johnson). This is one of the architect's great successes, with its tinted glass façade crisscrossed with white steel. It was built to house John D. Rockefeller's collection of art from the Far East, currently at the ASIA SOCIETY (725 Park Ave.).

LEXINGTON AVENUE. CORNER 64TH ST. The view to the north is obstructed by the footbridge straddling the avenue linking the buildings of Hunter College. Further south, it loses its residential character and becomes more commercial.

BLOOMINGDALE'S. LEXINGTON AVE. AND 59TH ST. There is a constant throng of pedestrians around the city's most famous store. Founded in 1870, in a working-class area, it began as a humble store. After the El was dismantled, a middle-class clientele moved into the area and Bloomingdale's supplied them with fashion, food and furniture.

MOUNT VERNON HOTEL MUSEUM. 421 E. 61ST ST. This nine-room museum, set in a property dating from 1799 that once belonged to the daughter of president John Adams, contains an excellent collection of 19th-century furniture. The Federal-style building is one of New York's finest 18th-century townhouses. The small garden was landscaped to a 19th-century design. Concerts are given here in summer.

ROOSEVELT ISLAND. Once owned by a family of farmers, this small island was bought by the city in 1828 to serve as the site for a PENITENTIARY, a MADHOUSE and an ALMSHOUSE. Most of these buildings have now been demolished, and in 1973 mixed rent housing was built. It can be reached by aerial tramway from 2nd Avenue.

ROOSEVELT ISLAND TRAMWAY PLACE ★. S. W. CORNER 2ND AVE. AND 60TH ST. A four-minute ride in the Swiss-made cable car (1976, eng. Prentice & Chan), affords breathtaking views of the eastern part of the city.

Their comfort and speed soon made them indispensable. Furthermore, they afforded a breathtaking view of the city, a fleeting and intimate bird's-eye view of neighboring houses. At night, the spectacle was even more dazzling, due to the myriad lights. But these railways were incredibly noisy and devastated long stretches of the city.

45 EAST 66TH STREET
This eye-catching façade has a twin: Alwyn Court, 180 W. 58th St. ▲ 303.

FROM 5TH AVENUE TO GRACIE MANSION

HOTEL CARLYLE. 35 E. 76TH ST. (1929, arch. Bien & Prince). Crossing Madison Avenue, you can glimpse the Hotel Carlyle's distinctive green, bronze pyramid. This hotel's suites have accommodated a vast number of stars and politicians. President Kennedy used to stay in one of the penthouse suites when he came to New York. There are some fine murals in the two bars, *Bemelmans Bar* and *Café Carlyle*.

UKRAINIAN INSTITUTE. 2 E. 79TH ST. (1899, arch. C. P. H. Gilbert). This residence, encircled by a moat, was built for Isaac D. Fletcher, a reclusive industrialist who donated his collection of paintings to the Metropolitan Museum. There used to be a Renaissance château opposite, on the northeast corner of the street. The demolition of the building caused such a storm of protest that the Landmark Preservation Law was passed (1965).

80TH STREET, A REFUGE. BETWEEN PARK AND LEXINGTON AVES. On this street stand the last private residences dating from before the Depression. They have all been converted into apartments except for the largest, no. 130 (1928, arch. Mott B. Schmidt), sold in 1947 to the JUNIOR LEAGUE, a philanthropic and social organization for young women. The house was built for Vincent Astor, who inherited his father's fortune when he drowned on the Titanic.

UNITARIAN CHURCH OF ALL SOULS. S. E. CORNER 80TH ST. AND LEXINGTON AVE. (1931, arch. Hobart Upjohn). Look up to see small children playing on the terrace. Space on the ground is so expensive that playgrounds are sometimes built on the rooftops. The church, which plays an important role in community life, houses a school, a theater and a soup kitchen.

YORKVILLE BRANCH, N. Y. PUBLIC LIBRARY. 222 E. 79TH ST. The beautiful Palladian façade belongs to the neighborhood's first library. In 1901, Andrew Carnegie founded sixty-five branch libraries.

78TH STREET, A MIXED STREET. BETWEEN 3RD AND 2ND AVES. This street's charm resides in the fact that houses built in the 1860's (numbers 208 to 218 are the most interesting) stand next to tenements built even earlier, but so carefully maintained that the contrast is not jarring.

Beyond 2nd Avenue, leading down to the river, the neighborhood becomes more blue-collar. There are high-rises all along the avenues but the streets still have the five- and six-story apartment buildings occupied by older inhabitants with low incomes, often from abroad, a reminder of the time when the neighborhood was nicknamed "little Europe", due to its many Czech, Hungarian, and German residents.

Until the 1950's, E. 86th St. was the main street in a prosperous German neighborhood.

Over one hundred breweries were built in the surrounding district, including the one owned by Jacob Ruppert, which occupied three blocks between 2nd and 3rd avenues and 90th and 93rd streets.

HELL GATE
The East River used to be more dangerous due to the tides, currents and violent eddies swirling around the rocks. In 1876, dynamite was used to clear these rocks away.

CHEROKEE APARTMENTS. 514 E. 78TH ST. AND 515 E. 77TH ST. (1910–11, arch. Henry Atterbury Smith). This bright, spacious six-story structure was built for families of patients suffering from tuberculosis. External staircases lead up to the apartments which are arranged around large courtyards, reached by paved passageways.

HENDERSON PLACE. 86TH ST. BETWEEN YORK AND EAST END AVES. (1882, arch. Lamb & Rich). This group of Queen Anne-style buildings, with their many towers, turrets and gables ● *90*, was built on the site of a farm that once belonged to JOHN JACOB ASTOR.

CARL SCHURZ PARK ★. EAST END AVE. BETWEEN 84TH AND 90TH STS. (1876, reconstructed 1938, arch. Harvey Stevenson and Cameron Clarke). This park, which is small but has a variety of landscaping effects, affords a splendid view of the river. It was named after a German revolutionary who emigrated to the United States in 1848.

GRACIE MANSION ★. (1799, arch. Ezra Weeks; modern wing, 1966, arch. Mott B. Schmidt). The mayor's private residence can be seen from the park, especially in winter when trees are bare. Built for Archibald Gracie, a Scottish ship-owner whose guests included such famous figures as Louis-Philippe, the future king of France, and Lafayette, it is the only surviving 19th-century country home. Gracie was declared bankrupt in 1812 and his home passed to several owners before the city of New York bought it in 1887. The house was turned into a private residence for mayor Fiorello La Guardia in 1942 and successive mayors have lived here ever since. Note the floor of the entrance, which is decorated with a compass – a reminder of the first occupant's maritime connections.

Above, and opposite page, E. 86th St. in 1939.

GRACIE MANSION
Before the construction of the F.D.R. Drive, the East River was an ideal place for bathing, fishing and mooring boats. Now only the promenade overlooking the river gives an idea of what the view used to be. However, the private and attractive park around Gracie Mansion remains unspoiled, as the F.D.R. Drive passes underneath Carl Schurz Park.

313

▲ CENTRAL PARK

Central Park in spring, its cherry trees
and magnolias laden with blossoms.

"I reached Central Park, level with the street, and decided to walk across it to find Manhattan
... The sky was pale green. Springtime was showering New York with flurries of damp
blossom.... There was a river, boats, ducks ...."

Pierre Bourgeade, *New York Party*

STRAWBERRY FIELD

HECKSCHER PLAYGROUND

SHEEP MEADOW

CHURCH

BANDSHELL

THE MALL

It took
twenty
years
and ten
million
cartloads of
rock and soil to
make this park in
the middle of Manhattan. Its
844 acres comprise gently
sloping meadows, winding paths
and natural-looking lakes,
created from the water which
originally flooded the swampy
site.

Ornamental detail from the stone
staircase of the Terrace, depicting
nature and the seasons.

BOW BRIDGE
The best-known bridge in Central Park links
the Ramble and the Terrace, where the two
arms of the Lake meet.

GREAT HILL

HARLEM MEER

NORTH MEADOW

THE MOUNT

JACKIE ONASSIS RESERVOIR

EAST MEADOW

GREAT LAWN

AKE

THE RAMBLE

GREEN

A VAST OASIS ✪
The best time to visit Central Park is on the weekend, when the road running through the park is closed to traffic and can be used by cyclists, joggers and skaters. If you can only spare half a day, enter the park at 72nd Street, walk to Bethesda Fountain, then follow the lake round to the west. You can then head back up to the Reservoir, passing through one of most unlikely landscapes in Manhattan.

BELVEDERE CASTLE
The castle's terrace overlooks the Shakespeare Garden and the Delacorte Theater, where Shakespeare plays are performed in summer.

State arsenal in Central Park.

Out of the thirty-five plans entered in the competition run by the city in 1858 for the creation of a park, the Greensward Plan by Frederick Law Olmsted (right) and the architect Calvert Vaux was the winning entry.

SHEEP MEADOW
Used for grazing until 1934, this "meadow" is a favorite haunt of New Yorkers in the summer.

THE LAKE
A popular lake, with a bar-restaurant by the water and rowboat trips.

Central Park
in fall.

"They are walking up the Mall in Central Park . . . She is walking in her wide hat in her pale loose dress that the wind now and then presses against her legs and arms, silkily, swishily walking in the middle of the great rosy and purple and pistachiogreen bubbles of twilight that smell out of the grass and trees and ponds, bulge against the tall houses sharp gray as dead teeth round the southern end of the park, melt into the indigo zenith."
John Dos Passos, *Manhattan Transfer*

STRAWBERRY
FIELD

HECKSCHER
PLAYGROUND

SHEEP
MEADOW

THE MALL

WOLLMAN RINK
Renovated with assistance from the developer Donald Trump, the skating rink (below, in 1919) is a popular site.

INFORMATION KIOSKS
Visitor information is provided by Central Park's Administration in these small structures scattered throughout the park. The Dairy is an original, High Victorian Gothic-style structure, which contains a twelve-foot long model showing the park's various points of interest.

13
GREAT HILL

12

JACKIE ONASSIS RESERVOIR

11
GREAT LAWN

10
THE RAMBLE

LAKE

NORTH MEADOW
THE MOUNT

HARLEM MEER
15

14
EAST MEADOW

9

8
7

GREEN

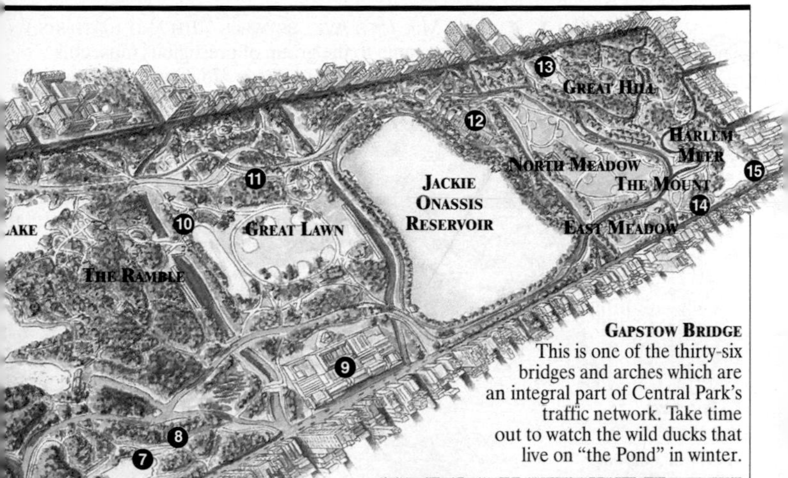

GAPSTOW BRIDGE
This is one of the thirty-six bridges and arches which are an integral part of Central Park's traffic network. Take time out to watch the wild ducks that live on "the Pond" in winter.

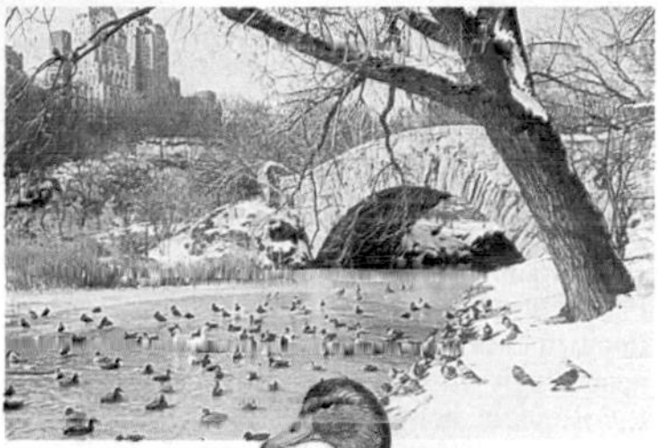

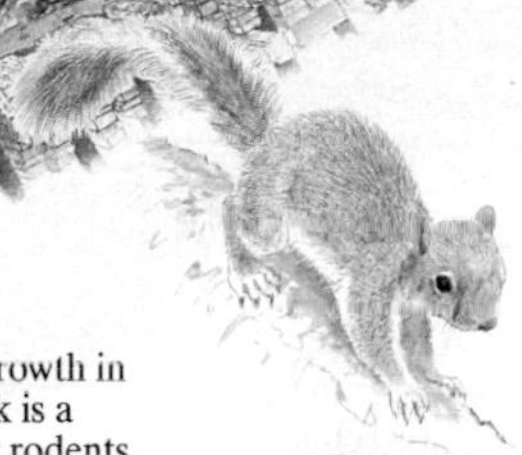

The undergrowth in Central Park is a paradise for rodents. Rabbits, marmots, squirrels – there are nearly fourteen thousand – live on the thirty-seven acres of the Ramble, around the lake.

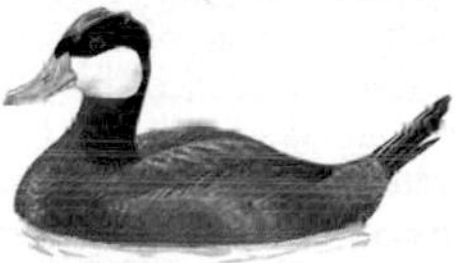

RUDDY STIFF-TAILED DUCK

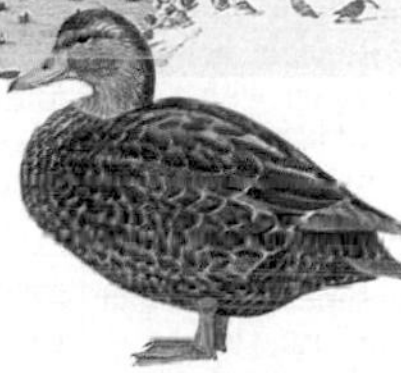

MALLARD

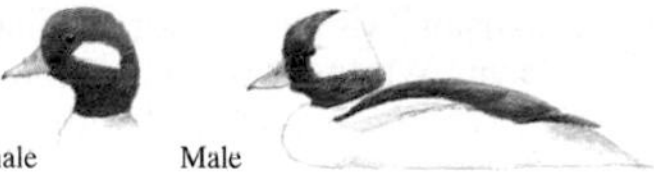

Female   Male   Female   Male

WHITE-FRONTED DUCK   **BUFFEL-HEADED DUCK**

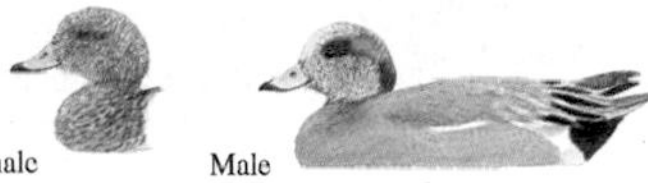

In 1858, Ignaz Anton Pilat, an Austrian gardener, oversaw the planting of nearly four million trees and plants in the park. There are now some 26,000 trees.

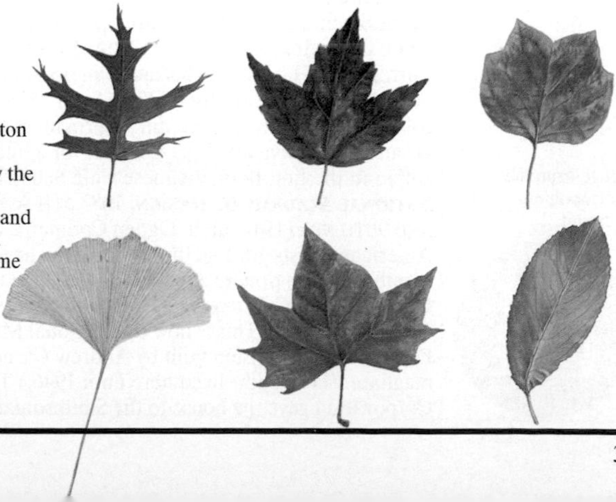

317

M useum Mile (5TH AVE., BETWEEN 70TH AND 104TH STS.) owes its name to the group of prestigious museums (Metropolitan Museum of Art ▲ *328*, Guggenheim Museum ▲ *338*, Frick Collection ▲ *322* and so on) which line the avenue (the Whitney Museum ▲ *326*, a block to the east, is also close by). This part of Upper East Side is a museum in itself, dedicated to the mansions built at the beginning of the 20th century.

E. 105TH ST. E. 104TH ST. E. 103RD ST. E. 102ND ST. E. 101ST ST. E. 100TH ST. E. 99TH ST. E. 98TH ST. E. 97TH ST. E. 96TH ST. E. 95TH ST. E. 94TH ST. E. 93RD ST.

RESERVOIR

⧖ Two days

◆ **C** A3 **E** B3-C3-D3

A CITY OF CULTURE
Although Washington D.C. is the political capital of the US, New York is its cultural capital. Recognizing this phenomenon, the French Embassy has restructured its departments accordingly. In 1952 the Republic bought a mansion, with a curved façade decorated with wave moldings, cherubs and lions' heads. The superb "Venetian room", used by Whitney as a reception room, has been recently restored in line with Stanford White's designs. It is open to visitors on Fridays.

Badge from the Metropolitan Museum.

The Commonwealth Fund (1 E. 75TH ST., 1907, arch. Hale and Rogers), the N.Y.U. Institute of Fine Arts (1 E. 78TH ST., 1912, arch. Horace Trumbauer) and the Duchesne Residence school facility, also known as the Convent of the Sacred Heart, originally the Kahn residence (1 E. 91ST ST., 1918, arch. J. Armstrong Stenhouse and C. P. H. Gilbert), formerly private residences, testify to past glory.

FRENCH EMBASSY CULTURAL SERVICES. 972 5TH AVE. BETWEEN 78TH AND 79TH STS. (1906, arch. McKim, Mead & White). Take a look at the circular entrance hall of Harry Payne Whitney's former mansion, with its border of pillars and marble floor. Harry Payne Whitney was the brother-in-law of Gertrude Vanderbilt Whitney, who founded the Whitney Museum, ▲ *217, 326*.

GOETHE HOUSE. 1014 5TH AVE. BETWEEN 82ND AND 83RD STS (1907, arch. Welch, Smith & Provot). This is the German cultural center. The libraries are open to the public.

NEUE GALERIE. 1048 5TH AVE., CORNER 86TH ST. (1914, arch. Carrère and Hastings). This museum occupies the house once owned by the industrialist William Starr Miller. It has collections of early 20th-century German and Viennese fine art and decorative art. Take time out for a bite to eat or a coffee in the first-floor Viennese Café Sabarsky.

NATIONAL ACADEMY OF DESIGN. 1083 5TH AVE. BETWEEN 89TH AND 90TH STS. (1914, arch. Ogden Codman). In 1825 some American artists got together to form the academy. Each member had to donate a work to the collection.

COOPER-HEWITT MUSEUM ★. 2 E. 91ST ST. (1901, arch. Babb, Cook & Willard). This is now the National Museum of Design, in the mansion built by Andrew Carnegie, the steel magnate. (His widow lived here until 1946.) The Carnegie Corporation gave the house to the Smithsonian Institution in

1972 and the Cooper-Hewitt moved here in 1977, the only branch of the Smithsonian located outside Washington D.C. Taking its inspiration from the Musée des Arts Decoratifs in Paris and the Victoria and Albert Museum in London, the museum was founded in 1897 as the Cooper Union Museum for the Arts of Decoration, by the Hewitt sisters, who amassed an impressive collection of prints, textiles and furniture.

JEWISH MUSEUM. 1109 5TH AVE., N. CORNER 92ND ST. (1908, arch. C. P. H. Gilbert; 1962, arch. Samuel Glazer; 1993, arch. Kevin Roche). The building, which is reminiscent of the Musée Cluny in Paris, was built for the banker Felix Warburg. It has now become the largest American museum devoted to the history and art of the Jewish people: it contains a collection of coins and medals, antique books and valuable manuscripts, objects of worship, and a collection of prehistoric archeological artifacts.

MUSEUM OF THE CITY OF NEW YORK. 1220 5TH AVE. BETWEEN 103RD AND 104TH STS. (1932, arch. Joseph H. Freedlander). This

MUSEUM OF THE CITY OF NEW YORK
Mrs John King van Rensselaer, a socialite who was shocked by how little

New Yorkers knew about the history of their own city, was the driving force behind the founding of this museum with its highly instructive collection.

museum, founded in 1923, was first housed in Gracie Mansion ▲ 313. The city donated the present site in 1928; 5,500 subscribers provided the two million dollars needed for the building. The museum, devoted to the city's history, with period rooms, dioramas, toys, dollshouses and a collection of old fire engines, is equally fascinating for children and adults.

EL MUSEO DEL BARRIO. 1230 5TH AVE. BETWEEN 104TH AND 105TH STS. (1934, arch. Frank N. Maynicke). Very popular with families living in this part of East Harlem, the museum is devoted to the art and culture of Puerto Ricans and other Latin Americans.

Museum Mile meets East Harlem at the Museo del Barrio, which is dedicated to the culture of Latin Americans.

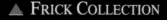

HENRY CLAY FRICK
(1849–1919) This leading Pittsburgh industrialist had been a collector from childhood, but his passion intensified during the last twenty years of his life (bust by Malvina Hoffman).

What is most distinctive about the Frick Collection is that it sets breathtaking works of art against the backdrop of an early 20th-century bourgeois interior. A visit to the museum, unique of its kind in New York, offers a tour of the history of art and taste.

ENTRANCE
This monumental doorway, crowned with a classical inspired relief, has replaced the original *porte-cochère*. This was one of the changes made by the architect John Russell Pope in 1935 to transform Frick's residence into a museum.

Designed in 1913 by Thomas Hastings, the architect of the New York Public Library ● 92, Henry Clay Frick's residence resembles private mansions built in Paris at the end of the 18th century.

VERMEER, OFFICER AND LAUGHING GIRL (1655–60). There are only thirty–five authenticated paintings by the "Delft Sphinx". The Frick collection has three of them, including this radiant interior with its ambiguous subject.

JEAN-HONORÉ FRAGONARD (1771–3), *The Meeting*
One of the four panels that make up "The Progress of Love", painted by Fragonard for Mme du Barry's residence in Louveciennes.

GIOVANNI BELLINI (1480), *Saint Francis in the Desert*
This masterpiece by the *cinquecento* Venetian artist, long considered one of the finest paintings in America. It depicts Saint Francis of Assisi receiving Christ's stigmata in a lyrically rendered landscape in which the details (animals, plants, rocks) reflect the saint's emotions.

JEAN-ANTOINE HOUDON (1741–1828), *Diana the Huntress*
A lifesize terracotta figure whose graceful appearance belies its technical virtuosity.

Wandering through the rooms of Mr Frick's residence, one finds works by Boucher, Bruegel, Chardin, Claude Lorrain, Constable, Drouais, Gainsborough, Goya, Greuze, Ingres, De La Tour, Memling, Monet, Rembrandt, Reynolds, Ruysdael and Watteau.

REMBRANDT, *Self-Portrait* (1658), as an Oriental potentate.

JOHN CONSTABLE, *The White Horse* (1819) "One of my best efforts" said the artist, referring to this tranquil Suffolk landscape.

MAIN STAIRCASE
In response to Mr Frick's desire for a home that would be "simple, comfortable and unostentatious", his architect, Thomas Hastings, and the two interior designers, Sir Charles Allom and Elsie de Wolfe, applied themselves to designing a discreetly luxurious house. The predominantly classical style of decoration contains references to 17th- and 18th-century English decoration, Renaissance and 18th-century French decoration, while incorporating some modern touches, typical of the turn of the century. This residence was designed primarily as a setting for the various works of art collected by its owner. This pink marble staircase acts as a foil for the largest organ ever built for a New York residence, a neo-classical calendar clock (left) and a large sun-drenched painting by Renoir.

HANS HOLBEIN THE YOUNGER. *Portrait of Sir Thomas More* (1527), the great English humanist.

FURNISHINGS
There is a fine collection of tables, armchairs (above, 16th-century French chair), cassoni and carved cabinets from the Italian and French Renaissance, as well as furniture signed by great 18th-century French masters, including a chest of drawers and a secretaire made by Riesener for Marie-Antoinette.

DUCCIO DI BUONINSEGNA, *The Temptation of Christ on the Mountain* (c. 1308). This section of the famous reredos from the Maestà in Siena was one of the first pieces acquired by the museum after Frick's death. The beauty and historic importance of this panel makes it a worthy addition to the founder's collection, especially given his unflagging quest for excellence. His daughter, who took over from him as the museum's influential trustee, encouraged the purchase of works by Bastiani, Castagno, Gentile da Fabriano, Fra Filippo Lippi, Piero della Francesca and Paolo and Giovanni Veneziano.

In 1966 the Whitney Museum moved to its permanent address on the corner of Madison Ave., and 75th St., a building designed by Marcel Breuer, one of great masters of

the Bauhaus. Practically all the leading figures in American art in the last fifty years are represented here. They bear witness to Gertrude Whitney's unremittingly non-conformist stance.

STUART DAVIS, *The Paris Bit* (1959) This is a pastiche made up of remembered fragments of architecture and Parisian life and, according to Stuart, "There was simultaneously so much past and present there, in the same sphere, that you couldn't want for anything more."

The Whitney Museum of American Art, founded in 1931 by Gertrude Vanderbilt Whitney, a sculptor and an enlightened patron of the arts, now houses the largest collection of works by modern American artists in the world.

"Neither symbolism nor calligraphy" is how Franz Kline described his own mature abstract works, exclusively in black and white. In *Mahoning* (1956), as in Kline's later works, the black motifs touch at least two sides of the painting, giving the overall composition an architectural quality.

ANDY WARHOL, *Green Coca-Cola Bottles* (1962) Warhol was the first artist to use silkscreen techniques, hitherto reserved for advertising, in order to produce multiple images of modern life for artistic purposes.

The idea for the Metropolitan Museum of Art was conceived in Paris on July 4, 1866, Independence Day, by a group of Americans, including John Jay, grandson of the famous jurist. In 1880 the first building was opened on 5th Avenue and 82nd Street. Completed in 1902, the lavish Beaux Arts-style façade incorporated the original Renaissance Revival frontage to give the building the appearance of a true civic institution.

ONE OF THE LARGEST ART MUSEUMS IN THE WORLD ✪
You need at least three days to properly explore the "Met". Pick up a floor plan at the entrance to help you decide which of the eighteen departments you have time to visit. The Temple of Dendur (Egypt), enclosed in a glass extension which overlooks Central Park, is a must, as is a visit to the sculpture on the Roof Garden, between May and October, which affords superb views of the park. The entrance fee to the Met also includes admission to the Cloisters Museum ▲ *362* on the same day. To get there, catch bus M4 on Madison Avenue; the journey will take an hour.

GREAT HALL
Richard Morris Hunt, who designed the Great Hall, worked with monumental proportions and a wealth of Beaux Arts styling to create an effect of imposing grandeur. On his death, his son, Richard Howland Hunt, took over and completed the original project. There are extraordinary floral arrangements decorating the four symmetrical side niches and the information desk, which are changed regularly.

HALL OF ARCHITECTURE CASTS
Built by Calvert Vaux and opened in 1880, this Hall used to house plaster casts. Now, after extensive remodeling, some of the medieval collections are exhibited here.

ENGELHARD COURT
The fine examples of sculpture, architecture and decorative arts at Engelhard Court serve as a microcosm of the diversity of American art, from the severe Classicism of the 1820's to the Modernism of the 20th century.

A STRING OF ARCHITECTS
Around 1906, McKim, Mead & White built the North and South wings, and Kevin Roche John Dinkeloo & Associates were responsible for the additions after 1975.

JACQUES-LOUIS DAVID, *Antoine Lavoisier et sa femme* (1788). This double portrait, one of the painter's most remarkable, depicts the intellectual and emotional closeness between Lavoisier, the master chemist, surrounded by his scientific instruments, and his wife, who studied under David and illustrated her husband's works.

PENDANT MASK
(early 16th century)
This extraordinary ivory and metal object is a typical example of the highly elaborate works of art which came out of the kingdom of Benin in Nigeria, usually from the royal court, and which astounded European travelers. The king probably wore this mask on his belt for ceremonies honoring the dead Queen Mother, of whom this may be a portrait.

HEADDRESS
(Nigeria)
Carved out of a single block of wood, this was worn by the Yorubas during masked invocations of the water spirits.

YAISUHASHI SCREEN
(Edo period, 1603–1867)
This screen is the work of the Japanese artist, Ogata Korin. Its design – a composition of irises, massed against a bridge made of eight planks of wood, and set against a gold background – unfolds across six sections.

Astor Court

The court of the famous Garden of the Master of the Fishing Nets at Suzhou, was reproduced by Chinese craftsmen (left) who used the original techniques and materials to recreate this perfect microcosm of the natural world: water, rocks and plants, where the contrast of light and shade, softness and hardness, creates a feeling of serenity.

Reception Room from the Nur Ad-Din House (1707)

This room (right) is from a residence in Damascus built during the reign of the Ottoman empire and its magnificent marble inlays, gilded and painted wood paneling, stained-glass windows and ceramic tiles encapsulate that period's harmonious luxury.

Michael C. Rockefeller Wing

This wing (below) was inaugurated in 1982 and houses collections of African, Pacific and American art. Nelson Rockefeller donated the wing to the museum, in memory of his son, an explorer who died during a trip to New Guinea.

Mbis Totem

(20th century) The Asmat tribe in New Guinea produces wood carvings, especially totem poles, which are reserved for ritual ceremonies associated with death.

▲ METROPOLITAN MUSEUM

TEMPLE OF DENDUR
A gift to the United States from the Egyptian government in recognition of American assistance in saving the monuments of Nubia, this small temple dedicated to Isis, built by Augustus around 15 BC, was reconstructed to look as it did on the banks of the Nile, with a pool in the foreground. It can be seen from the park and is illuminated at night.

FUNERARY STELE
(6th century BC)
This Attic sculpture shows a female sphinx watching over the tomb of two hieratic young men.

"PORTRAIT OF A MAN"
(Fayum, 2nd century BC)
Funerary portrait in the Egyptian tradition influenced by Greco-Roman art.

"SEATED HARP PLAYER"
(3rd millennium BC)
This Cycladic marble statue is beautifully simple and represents a male musician – a highly unusual subject.

BOSCOREALE
This town, which was buried by the eruption of Vesuvius in AD 79, left, like Pompeii, a superb legacy, including trompe-l'oeil paintings.

"KING'S HEAD"
(4th century AD). This engraved and embossed silver head shows the talent of Sassanian artists.

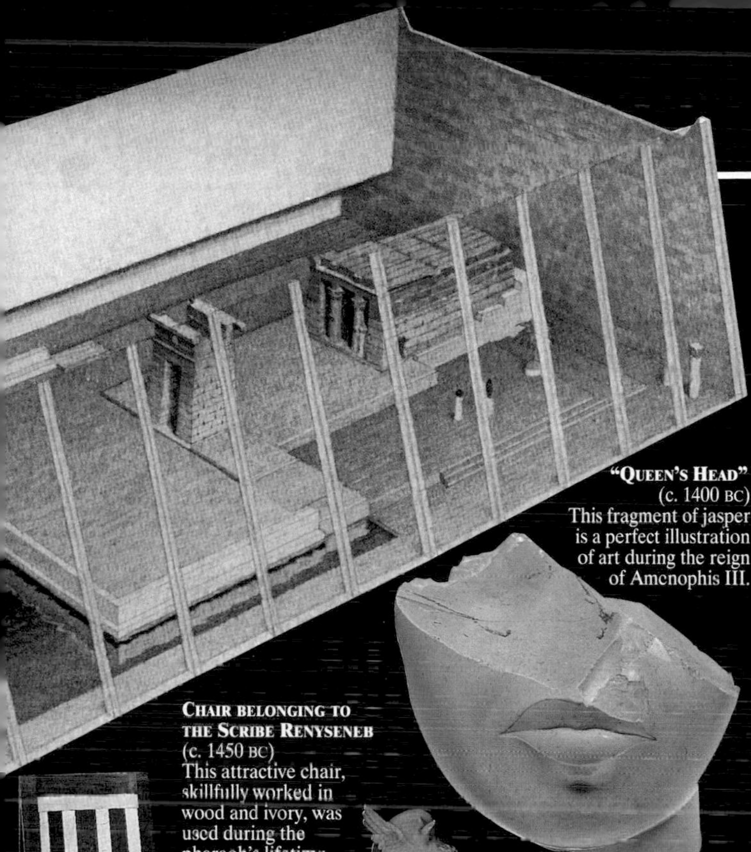

"QUEEN'S HEAD"
(c. 1400 BC)
This fragment of jasper
is a perfect illustration
of art during the reign
of Amenophis III.

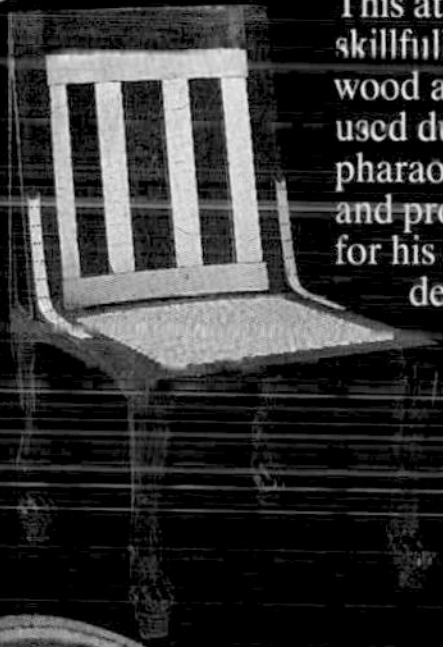

**CHAIR BELONGING TO
THE SCRIBE RENYSENEB**
(c. 1450 BC)
This attractive chair,
skillfully worked in
wood and ivory, was
used during the
pharaoh's lifetime
and probably engraved
for his tomb after his
death.

KNEELING MAN
(6th century)
This Mayan wooden statue, from
the border between Mexico and
Guatemala, has miraculously
survived the tropical climate.

"PERSEUS WITH THE HEAD OF MEDUSA"
(1808) Inspired by the *Apollo of the
Belvedere* in the Vatican, this marble
statue displays Antonio
Canova's perfect mastery of
the neo-classical style.

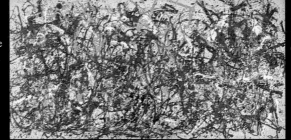

JACKSON POLLOCK,
Autumn Rhythm
(1950)
This painting was the last in a series of large "drip" paintings, an innovative technique which contributed to the development of Abstract Expressionism.

LIVING ROOM FROM THE LITTLE HOUSE
In 1914 Frank Lloyd Wright (1867–1959) designed a summer house for Francis W. Little in Wayzata, a suburb of Minneapolis. The ocher-colored walls, natural oak floor and brick fireplace contribute to the harmonious feeling of this room. The oak furniture, and even the way it is arranged, form an integral part of the overall architectural composition.

CHARLES DEMUTH,
I Saw the Figure 5 in Gold (1928)
This abstract impression of urban life is typical of the modernist American painter.

ROOM FROM THE HEWLETT HOUSE
(c. 1739)
The furniture and paneling of this room came from a farmhouse on Long Island at a time when English and European styles were being mixed. The large cupboard painted in grisaille, is typical of the Dutch colonial period.

MARSDEN HARTLEY,
Portrait of a German Officer
This powerful canvas was painted in November 1914, during a visit to Berlin.

Hartley's treatment of the military themes shows the influence of German Expressionism, as well as Cubism. This painting of an officer with its dense mass of symbols, insignias, medals and flags, enhanced by more personal references – letters and numbers – to a friend who had just been killed at the front, is intended to be a collective physical and psychological portrait.

THOMAS EAKINS,
Max Schmitt in a Single Scull (1871)
Between 1870 and 1874 Eakins painted a series of canvases devoted to rowing – clear evidence of his passion for sport. Note his treatment of light and space, as well as his great technical virtuosity and his immediate, analytical approach to the subject matter.

WINSLOW HOMER,
The Gulf Stream
Homer painted this canvas from sketches done during a trip to the Bahamas. It is a fine example of one of his favorite themes, the reciprocal relationship between man and nature, a subject that is most powerfully expressed in his seascapes.

(1506–15)
This inner courtyard
came from a castle
near Almería (Spain).
It is lavishly sculpted
and a gem of
Renaissance-style,
Italo-Hispanic
architecture.

JAN VAN EYCK,
The Last Judgment
(c. 1425)
This painting, one of
the earliest by the
Flemish painter and a
masterpiece of the
new technique of oil
painting, foreshadows
Northern Realism.

GEORGES DE LA TOUR, *The Fortune*
(1616–39).This is one of the painter's rare
daylight scenes, depicting betrayed innocence.

EL GRECO,
View of Toledo (c. 1595)
This is one of the few surviving
landscapes by El Greco; he
limited himself to the use of
greens, grays and a dazzling
white, which gives the
painting an inner luminosity
and a mystical aura.

PARADE ARMOR
(c. 1550). Decorated
by the engraver
Étienne Delaune,
for Henry II, of
France, its superb
engravings depict
the themes of
Victory and Fame.

PICASSO, *Woman in White* (1923). This is a classical, monumental and monochromatic portrait of Olga.

SEURAT, *The Side Show*) (1887–8). This painting is the artist's first magical evening scene depicting a popular entertainment.

MANET, *Boating* (1874). All the elements of the burgeoning Impressionist movement are here: an open-air setting, color and atmosphere.

MADONNA WITH CHILD (Auvergne, 1200). Mary, Throne of Wisdom, holds Jesus, Divine Wisdom, depicted full-face with stylized features.

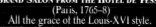

GRAND SALON FROM THE HOTEL DE TESSÉ (Paris, 1765–8)
All the grace of the Louis-XVI style.

Fernande with Black Mantilla (1905) by Pablo Picasso.

The baroness Hilla Rebay von Ehrenwiesen, who inspired Solomon Guggenheim's collection and was also its director, commissioned the architect Frank Lloyd Wright to build a museum to house it, with the instruction: "I want a temple of spirit." Solomon Guggenheim, a copper magnate and enlightened patron of the arts, was already the proud owner of a collection of Old Masters and had been introduced to modern art twenty years before when he met the baroness, who had opened his eyes to the work of

Mountains at Saint-Rémy (1889) by Vincent van Gogh, left to the museum in 1976 by Justin K. Thannhauser.

King of Kings (c. 1930), oak carving by Constantin Brancusi, and *Femme cuiller* (*Spoon in the form of a woman*), (1926), a bronze by Alberto Giacometti.

Delaunay, Gleizes, Chagall, Kandinsky and Bauer. He set up an award for modern artists and founded the Solomon Guggenheim Foundation, whose aim was "the promotion and encouragement of education in art". "I do not want to found another museum such as now exists in New York . . . No such building as is now customary for museums could be appropriate for this one."

A MUSEUM ILLUMINATED BY NATURAL LIGHT.
The architect drew up plans which focused on the importance of natural light. As well as the glass dome over a central court – which figured in all the early proposals – Wright recommended a strip running along the walls, providing a constant source of daylight, modeled on his own studio in Wisconsin. Another concept which figured prominently in Wright's plans was that of an open space, without partitions, which a wheelchair could traverse from one end to another. In his original plans, Wright wrote the words "constant ramp" – and the idea of a building with a spiral ramp was born.

Preparedness (1968), triptych by Roy Lichtenstein.

View of the dome from inside the museum.

A UNIQUE BUILDING FOR A UNIQUE COLLECTION ✪
This is a good museum to visit before or after a stroll in Central Park, as its entrance is just opposite the Reservoir ▲ *314*, at 89th Street. The remarkable helical structure designed in the 1950s by Frank Lloyd Wright has lost none of its striking originality. The famous spiral ramp and the adjacent galleries, which exhibit collections ranging from the Impressionists to the present day, should be viewed from top to bottom. Allow two to three hours.

A CONTROVERSIAL PROJECT. It took sixteen years from the first plans to the final building. This was due to clashes with the building authorities and with the director of the Foundation, James Johnson Sweeney, who succeeded Baroness Rebay in 1952 and who felt that Wright's proposals might cause grave problems in terms of conserving and hanging the collections. Not only was Wright keen on having the paintings illuminated by natural light, which would change with the movement of the sun and the seasons, but he he also wanted them to be displayed at an angle, as if on an easel. The following scheme was finally adopted: a spiral ramp, 1416 feet long, gently climbing up to a glass dome, about 92 feet higher, showering the whole building with light. Along the ramp, artificial lighting was used. In keeping with Wright's intentions, the paintings are exhibited without frames or with very simple frames, and are hung, "as if in an artist's studio", on the curved walls and partitions.

Painting with White Border (1913) by Wassily Kandinsky

MUSEUM

A Main entrance to the Solomon
R. Guggenheim Museum, 1071
5th Ave.

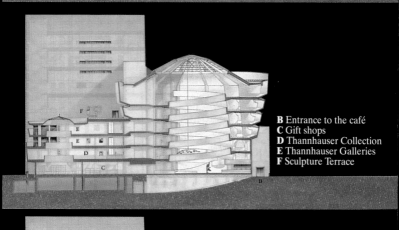

B Entrance to the café
C Gift shops
D Thannhauser Collection
E Thannhauser Galleries
F Sculpture Terrace

G High Gallery
I Auditorium
K Rotunda

H Offices
I Auditorium
J Tower Gallery
K Rotunda

"A Ship within the City". Work started in August 1956. Wright visited his building site for the last time in January 1959 and died three months later,

Composition I A (1930), oil painting by Piet Mondrian.

without seeing his work completed.

The museum opened in October of the same year and caused a storm of protest: people were considerably taken aback, not only by the concrete used for the façade (instead of marble as Wright had wanted) and the upended spiral defying the laws of balance, but also by the abstract works on display inside. Wright had already answered those who, well before it was completed, had called the museum a "washing machine" or a "monstrous mushroom" by saying: "One should no more judge a building from the outside than a car by its color."

THE COLLECTION. The Guggenheim Museum is essentially made up of five major private collections: SOLOMON

Terremoto (1981) Installation by Joseph Beuys composed of eighteen objects:

GUGGENHEIM'S COLLECTION OF NON-OBJECTIVE PAINTINGS – Kandinsky, Bauer, Moholy-Nagy, Léger, Delaunay, Chagall, Modigliani; JUSTIN K. THANNHAUSER'S COLLECTION OF IMPRESSIONIST AND MODERN ART – including a large number of Picasso's early works; KARL NIERENDORF'S GERMAN EXPRESSIONIST PAINTINGS (including over 100 works by Paul Klee); KATHERINE S. DREIER'S HISTORIC AVANT-GARDE PAINTINGS AND SCULPTURES – Brancusi, Mondrian; COUNT GIUSEPPE PANZADI BIUMO'S

a typewriter, a flag, some felt, nine paintings covered in chalk drawings and diagrams, a cask, a tape-recorder, a cassette and some brochures.

Morning in the Village after a Snowstorm (1912) oil painting by Kazimir Malevich.

COLLECTION OF AMERICAN "MINIMAL ART" FROM THE 1960's AND 1970's – Robert Ryman, Dan Flavin; as well as successive acquisitions by the museum's directors and curators – including works by Roy Lichtenstein and Joseph Beuys. Currently the Museum owns more than 5,000 paintings, sculptures and sketches ranging from the Impressionists to the present day. Many works have never been shown due to lack of space. An annex designed by Gwathmey Siegel and Associates was opened in 1992, inspired by the plans drawn up by Wright for artists' studios, intended to occupy the same site. A new annex of the museum is planned in South Manhattan on the banks of the East River.

Luminous Object by Dan Flavin, exhibited from June 28, to August 27, 1992.

▲ UPPER
WEST SIDE

1 JOAN OF ARC STATUE
2 SOLDIERS' AND SAILORS' MONUMENT
3 YESHIVA CHOFETZ CHAIM
4 RIVERSIDE DRIVE
5 APTHORP APARTMENTS
6 COLLEGIATE CHURCH AND SCHOOL
7 ANSONIA HOTEL
8 THE PYTHIAN TEMPLE
9 LINCOLN CENTER
10 CENTURY APARTMENTS

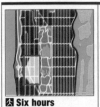

☒ Six hours

◆ **C** A1-A2-B1-B2 **E** C1-D2

The Upper West Side did not actually become a popular residential area until 1879, when the El was built on 9th Avenue (Columbus Avenue). The section of 8th Avenue between 59th and 110th streets was called Central Park West to encourage property developers to build quality residences there. It is now the most prestigious area in the district, its arresting skyline forming a contrast with that of 5th Avenue when seen from the east side of Central Park. At the same time as the extensive Riverside Park was opened along the Hudson River, another

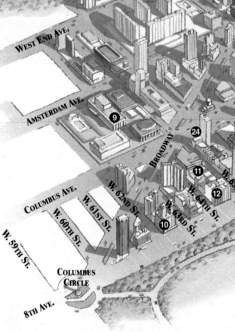

YACHTING HARBOR

HUDSON RIVER

THE SOCIETY FOR ETHICAL CULTURE FOUNDED IN THE CITY OF NEW YORK MAY 1876

WEST END AVE.

AMSTERDAM AVE.

COLUMBUS AVE.

BROADWAY

W. 62ND ST.
W. 61ST ST.
W. 60TH ST.
W. 59TH ST.
W. 63RD ST.
W. 64TH ST.
W. 65TH ST.

COLUMBUS CIRCLE

8TH AVE.

N.Y. SOCIETY FOR ETHICAL CULTURE
This society, founded by Felix Adler, made a name for itself primarily for its highly progressive teaching methods. It has established several schools (Ethical Culture Schools), one of which is nearby, at 33 Central Park West, on the corner of 63rd St. The N.Y. Society for Ethical Culture founded New York's first free kindergarten in 1878 and the first social work center in the United States.

stylish enclave was created in the west, along Riverside Drive and West End Avenue. Some of the finest examples of former "residential hotels" (apartment buildings that provided hotel facilities) can still be seen on the Upper West Side and some superb groups of rowhouses ● 90 in the side streets. In the early 20th century, this neighborhood acted as a magnet for intellectuals and artists, a trend that became even more marked when the Lincoln Center was built in the 1960's. The Upper West Side is now a fashionable residential neighborhood. Its institutions, the New York Historical

RIVERSIDE PARK

W. 90TH ST.
W. 89TH ST.
W. 88TH ST.
W. 87TH ST.
W. 86TH ST.
W. 85TH ST.
W. 84TH ST.
W. 83RD ST.
W. 82ND ST.
W. 81ST ST.

CENTRAL PARK WEST

W. 77TH ST.
W. 76TH ST.
W. 75TH ST.
W. 74TH ST.
W. 73RD ST.
W. 72ND ST.
W. 71ST ST.
W. 70TH ST.

MUSEUM OF AMERICAN FOLK ART
2 Lincoln Square, between 65th and 66th streets. This museum, founded in 1961 by a group of collectors, mounts temporary exhibitions in its galleries which showcase a wide range of craft traditions from all over America.

Society, the Museum of Natural History and the Children's Museum of Manhattan, on 83rd Street, are popular tourist attractions. Its streets are lined with stores, including the famous Zabar's (80th Street), where you can buy gourmet food and kitchenware from all over the world.

AROUND CENTRAL PARK WEST

CENTURY APARTMENTS. 25 CENTRAL PARK WEST (1931, arch. Irwin Chanin). This is the southernmost apartment building that has twin towers of the five that run along Central Park West and give it its unique and impressive skyline. The others are, the MAJESTIC, the SAN REMO, the BERESFORD (which actually has three towers) and the ELDORADO.

NEW YORK SOCIETY FOR ETHICAL CULTURE. 2 W. 64TH ST. (1910, arch. Robert D. Kohn). Founded in 1876, the aim of this humanist society was to encourage morality irrespective of religious principles and dogma. It now has twenty-three branches throughout the United States and three thousand members.

THE ELDORADO
300 Central Park West (1931). This building was designed by Margon & Holder in collaboration with

Emery Roth, who was also responsible for the SAN REMO and the BERESFORD. Below, one of the three murals from the lobby.

343

When it opened the Hôtel des Artistes had a communal kitchen, a squash court, a swimming pool, a ballroom and . . . the Café des Artistes.

Café des Artistes

AMERICAN BROADCASTING COMPANY TELEVISION STUDIOS. 56 W. 66TH ST. (1901, arch. Horgan & Slattery). ABC restored the former First Battery Armory of the New York National Guard in 1978. Its television studios now occupy the building and many features have been filmed here.

TAVERN ON THE GREEN. CENTRAL PARK WEST AND 67TH ST. (c. 1870). This restaurant is in Central Park. It started life more modestly as a fold for the sheep grazing nearby in Sheep Meadow. Since first opening, in 1934, it has become a favorite haunt of celebrities. At night the surrounding trees are spectacularly festooned with lights.

TAVERN ON THE GREEN
Every year since 1970 the illuminated trees of the Tavern on the Green (below) have marked the finishing line of the New York marathon. This 26.2 mile long race starts from Staten Island, at the entrance to the Verrazano Bridge, and takes in the city's five boroughs.

HÔTEL DES ARTISTES, CAFÉ DES ARTISTES. 1 W. 67TH ST. (1918, arch. George Mort Pollard). This was one of a number of residences built along this street at the beginning of the 20th century by groups of artists who had pooled their finances. The buildings contained studios as well as apartments which could be rented out. The revenues from rents helped the artists to eke out a living and to pay back the money they had borrowed for the construction work. Isadora Duncan, Noel Coward, Norman Rockwell and John Lindsay, one of New York's former mayors, were among the many celebrities who lived here. The painter, Howard Chandler Christy, one of the first residents, painted murals in the charming Café des Artistes which can be reached via the hotel lobby. They depict thirty-six willowy, naked beauties in a woodland setting. Most of the artist's models were well-known by the hotel's other residents.

CONGREGATION SHEARITH ISRAEL. 99 CENTRAL PARK WEST (1897, arch. Brunner & Tryon). The oldest Jewish congregation in New York, whose name means "remnant of Israel", was formed in 1655 by refugees from Brazil who were fleeing persecution. The Dutch governor, Peter Stuyvesant, wanted to prevent them from settling here, but was informed by his employer, the Dutch West India Company, that the company's Jewish shareholders would not tolerate such an attitude. The group was allowed to stay and build its first synagogue in 1730 on Mill Street, in Lower Manhattan. That small Georgian-style synagogue has been recreated within the present building, containing two millstones from a Dutch windmill that used to stand nearby.

"CAFÉ DES ARTISTES"
Right, murals by Howard Chandler Christy, a long-time resident at the Hôtel des Artistes. Christy, nicknamed the "pin-up artist", was renowned for paintings of naked women and his pin-ups were often used as magazine illustrations. This was why he was asked to be one of the judges for the first Miss America beauty contest

THE PYTHIAN CONDOMINIUM, FORMER PYTHIAN TEMPLE. 135 W. 70TH STREET (1927, arch. Thomas W. Lamb). This eye-catching building, west of Columbus Avenue, is worth making a detour to visit. It was created by Thomas Lamb, the theater designer, to house the headquarters of the brotherhood, the *Knights of Pythias*. In 1986 the building, whose décor evokes Hollywood epics of the 1920's, was remodeled and converted into apartments. Note the inscription above the front door: "If fraternal love held all men bound how beautiful this would be."

WEST 71ST STREET. BETWEEN CENTRAL PARK WEST AND COLUMBUS AVENUE (1890's). The rowhouses that line this stretch of 71st Street date from the time when the Upper West Side was just becoming established. Most of them were private houses.

MAJESTIC APARTMENTS. 115 CENTRAL PARK WEST (1930, arch. Jacques Delamarre). This apartment building was the successor to the sumptuous Majestic Hotel, built in 1893 and renowned for its roof garden. These hanging gardens, resplendent with fountains and waterfalls, were one of the fashionable haunts of New York's high society at the beginning of the 20th century. Fred Astaire stayed at the *Majestic Hotel* in 1919. Its successor, the Majestic Apartments accommodated residents such as the gangsters Lucky Luciano and Meyer Lansky. More recently, Frank Costello lived here in a seventeen-room penthouse suite. In 1957, a man waiting in the lobby took a shot at him, grazing his head. This led to Costello's "retirement" from the world of crime.

WEST 71ST STREET
The façade and main entrance of the houses lining the two sides of this street are decorated with carved ornamental motifs, including lions' heads, cupids and shells. The carved bas-relief of the first bay window of the house at no. 33 shows a fox holding a rabbit in its jaws, among other motifs.

"Once again, Stillman retreated to Riverside Park, this time to the edge of it, coming to rest on a knobby outcrop at 84th Street known as Mount Tom. On this same spot, in the summers of 1843 and 1844, Edgar Allan Poe had spent many long hours gazing out at the Hudson."
Paul Auster,
City of Glass

THE FORMER PYTHIAN TEMPLE
This building is one of the area's most interesting sights. Its façade offers a carefree mixture of ancient decorative styles (Sumerian, Assyrian, Egyptian) and has an unusual top, dominated by two colorful pharaohs.

345

DAKOTA APARTMENTS
Designed by the architect who later designed the Plaza, the Dakota is regarded as an architectural gem and one of the city's most desirable addresses. It used to house an army of servants and provide a huge range of services to its rich residents. Roberta Flack, Leonard Bernstein and Judy Garland all lived here. Roman Polanski used it as the setting for his film *Rosemary's Baby* (1968). The Dakota (right) was John Lennon's last address. In 1980 he was shot dead by a misfit just in front of the building. His wife, Yoko Ono, still lives at the Dakota. The section of Central Park just opposite the hotel was landscaped at her request, including this mosaic (right) and is called Strawberry Fields, after the title of a Beatles song written by Lennon.

He died here of a heart attack sixteen years later.

DAKOTA APARTMENTS. 1 W. 72ND ST. (1884, arch. Henry J. Hardenbergh). This was the first residential luxury apartment house in New York, built by Edward Clark, president of the Singer Sewing Machine company. When people found out that he had decided on an Uptown site, many nicknamed the project, "Clark's folly". Why not in Dakota, in the remote Far West? asked one of his friends. Clark kept the name and had the building decorated with arrowheads, ears of corn and an Indian head over the main entrance.

SAN REMO APARTMENTS. 77TH STREET AND CENTRAL PARK WEST (1930, arch. Emery Roth). The actress Rita Hayworth lived in this luxury apartment building until she died in 1987. A boat trip on Central Park lake probably affords the best view of the *San Remo* and its spectacular towers, each topped with a cupola (right).

NEW YORK HISTORICAL SOCIETY. 77TH ST. AND CENTRAL PARK WEST (1908, arch. York & Sawyer). Founded in 1804 by a group of New Yorkers who were keen to preserve the history of their city, the New York Historical Society is a museum and reference library. Its permanent collections include three hundred watercolors by John James Audubon ▲ *361*, works by Thomas Cole and other members of the Hudson River School as well as a large collection of Tiffany glass and lamps ▲ *296*. The museum mounts temporary exhibitions on the history of the city and of the United States.

IMAGINE

> "Huddled together on the narrow island, the buildings with their thousand windows will soar, sparkling ... tops surrounded by white clouds, rising above the storms. ..."

John Dos Passos

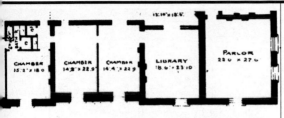

Plans of the Dakota.

AMERICAN MUSEUM OF NATURAL HISTORY. CENTRAL PARK WEST, BETWEEN 77TH AND 81 STS. (original wing 1872–7, arch. Calvert Vaux and J. Wrey Mould). Opened by President Ulysses S. Grant, the museum's original wing is now lost among an array of twenty-one later buildings. The THEODORE ROOSEVELT MEMORIAL

THE MUSEUM OF NATURAL HISTORY
This vast museum's collections range from butterflies to dinosaurs, which are also shown in murals.

(1936, arch. John Russell Pope) now forms the main entrance of the museum, on Central Park West. The interior is decorated with murals depicting scenes from the life of the former president, a great explorer who campaigned for the preservation of natural sites in the United States (such as the Grand Canyon). An equestrian statue standing outside (1940, James Earle Fraser)

shows Roosevelt flanked by an Indian and an African to symbolize his "friendship for all races". This is one of the most visited museums in New York. The collections documenting Indian, African and Pacific civilizations, the dioramas of animal habitats, the lifesize reproduction of a blue whale and the Dinosaur Hall are particularly popular. Opened in 2000, the Rose Center for Earth and Space is an impressive high-tech science museum with interactive displays. Designed by James Stewart Polshek, it is devoted to space and the origins of life.

ROSE CENTER FOR EARTH AND SPACE
This remarkable museum with a metal sphere enclosed in a spectacular glass and steel box-like structure has permanent and temporary exhibits. Inside the two theaters you can see amazing films with special effects.

THE BERESFORD. 211 CENTRAL PARK WEST (1929, arch. Emery Roth). This huge luxury apartment building, designed by the architect who was responsible for the *San Remo* replaced a hotel of the same name on this site. Its main distinguishing characteristics are its three Baroque-style towers, which loom above Central Park.

FROM BROADWAY TO RIVERSIDE PARK

ANSONIA HOTEL. 2109 BROADWAY (1904, arch. Graves and Duboy) ● 95. This Beaux Arts building has an extremely ornate exterior, designed primarily by the French architect and sculptor Paul E. Duboy. Note the corner towers topped with domes and the many balconies. As a luxury hotel, it represented the height of modernity and was the first air-conditioned building in New York. Its excellent sound-proofing has attracted many musicians, including Stravinsky, Toscanini, Caruso, Chaliapin and Menuhin. See the display of photos in the lobby tracing the Ansonia's glamorous history. These show that it once had two swimming pools, several stores, a fountain in the lobby with seals and a roof garden with a henhouse built by the owner who provided his guests with fresh eggs.

RIVERSIDE PARK
Riverside Drive, first developed in the 1880's, has never seriously rivaled 5th Avenue as a fashionable address, but the proximity of Riverside Park (right, at the beginning of the 20th century) and its magnificent views of the Hudson River, have ensured its appeal for many New Yorkers.

STATUE OF JOAN OF ARC
Riverside Drive and W. 93rd St. This statue, designed in 1915 by Anna Vaughn Hyatt Huntington, stands at the center of Joan of Arc Park. Some of the stones of its pedestal come from Rheims Cathedral and others from the tower in Rouen where Joan of Arc was imprisoned.

COLLEGIATE CHURCH AND COLLEGIATE SCHOOL. 241 W. 77TH ST. (1893, arch. Robert W. Gibson). The Collegiate Church's gables, steeples and intricately worked dormer windows are a reminder that it used to belong to the Dutch Reformed Church, established in the United States in 1628. The Collegiate School is no longer directly connected with the church. This prestigious private boys' school is one of the oldest schools in the United States.

APTHORP APARTMENTS. 2211 BROADWAY (1908, arch. Clinton & Russell). Built by William Waldorf Astor, this Italian Renaissance-style apartment building, which covers an entire block, has had such famous tenants as Nora Ephron, actor and director Bob Balaban, and Broadway set designer, Tony Walton. Its two large arched gateways lead into a vast inner court with a decorative central fountain.

RIVERSIDE DRIVE WEST 80TH–81ST STREETS HISTORIC DISTRICT (c. 1890). The thirty-two rowhouses that make up this historic district were built by developers who were reluctant to emulate the prevailing trend for residential hotels. Note the embellishment of the ridgepoles and the varied array of bow windows.

RIVERSIDE PARK. RIVERSIDE DRIVE, FROM 72ND TO 153RD STS. (1873–1910, Frederick Law Olmsted). This is Manhattan's other major park, after Central Park, designed by the same landscape gardener. It covered the disused tracks of the New York Central Railroad for a stretch of seventy blocks. The riverside promenade, with its small marina at 79th Street, running along the Hudson between 72nd and 86th streets, is a worth a visit.

YESHIVA CHOFETZ CHAIM/FORMER VILLA JULIA. 346 W. 89TH ST. (1901, arch. Herts & Tallant). The former home of Isaac L. Rice, who called it Villa Julia after his wife, is one of the few private mansions still standing on Riverside Drive. Rice made his fortune selling electric batteries and made a name for himself, in his later years, as a first-rate chess player. His house is now occupied by a Jewish seminary (*yeshiva* in Hebrew).

Harlem and
Brooklyn

⚡ **Four hours**
◆ **E** A1-B1

"I remember …
when you had to
change trains at
Washington and had
to travel in a car for
Blacks only – when
you could not go to
the dining car until
all the Whites had
finished. . . . I don't
mean that I want to
eat with the Whites.

It just makes life a
little easier – it may
make my children's
life a little easier.
Perhaps that is all I
want."
James Baldwin,
Harlem

This itinerary includes
Morningside Heights and
Harlem – two adjacent neighborhoods
that lie north of 110th Street and together run the width of
Manhattan. Morningside Heights has various educational
and religious establishments, notably Columbia University,
Barnard College, Riverside Church
and the huge and splendid Cathedral
of St. John the Divine, reflecting the
movement that began in the 1890's to
make this part of town a spiritual and
intellectual center. Harlem's history is
more checkered; it has a rich and varied
past which dates back to the 17th century.
HISTORY. In 1658 Dutch farmers built the
village of Nieuw Haarlem – named after
a town in Holland – about 10 miles north of the main
settlement, New Amsterdam. In the next century wealthy New
Yorkers built country residences here. In 1837 the New York
and Harlem railroad opened on 4th Avenue and transformed
the village into a thriving suburb, whose western area acquired
some fine rowhouses. The building of the 3rd- and 2nd-
Avenue elevated railways in 1879 then, in 1901, that of the
Lenox Avenue IRT subway, led to an influx of immigrants
who wanted to leave the Lower East Side ▲ *189*.

The trompe l'oeil façade of this Harlem house is a remnant of the elegance that prevailed here at the beginning of the 19th century.

"Harlem, in New York, soon became the largest black community in the world; it became the symbol and the model of the city lifestyle that the Blacks, victims of segregation, were creating within their new group. Harlem . . . formed a sort of urban frontier zone."

Daniel J. Boorstin

THE BLACK COLONIZATION OF

HARLEM. Toward the end of the 1880's plummeting prices, caused by overly optimistic speculation by real estate developers, attracted an influx of poor Blacks. By 1920 200,000 Blacks were living in Harlem. This decade was the neighborhood's golden age, known to many as the "Harlem Renaissance" – Black musicians, intellectuals and writers came here in droves – but the 1929 stock market crash put an end to this revival.

THE 1960's. During this period Harlem became a center of political and social activism. The Black Muslims, led by Elijah Mohammed, founded the Temple of Islam on Lenox Avenue at 116th Street where Malcolm X worked until 1964 before setting up his own organization. He was assassinated in February 1965 at the Audubon Ballroom on 165th Street. In 1968 the residents of Harlem began rioting for social and economic justice. In the mid 1970s, various New York landowners burned down their apartment buildings to claim the insurance – 300,000 apartments were destroyed in Harlem and South Bronx. Harlem is now flourishing, having been given a boost by the influx of wealthy young Blacks who are restoring the many rowhouses. Various stores and leading brand names have moved into the area, as has Bill Clinton, the former US president, who has offices here. A growing number of young white Americans are also moving in for the cheaper rents.

351

STATUE OF THE ALMA MATER
Daniel Chester French's statue, completed in 1903, presides over the majestic staircase outside the Low Memorial Library.

SETH LOW
(1850–1916)
He was the Mayor of Brooklyn and, from 1890, President of Columbia University. He built the Low Memorial Library. In 1901, he was elected Mayor of New York.

Columbia University at the beginning of the 20th century.

COLUMBIA UNIVERSITY

HISTORY. Founded in 1754 as King's College and renamed Columbia College after the American Revolution, Columbia University is now one of the oldest and largest universities in the country and one of the largest private landowners in New York, after the Catholic Church. Even in its infancy the college produced some distinguished citizens. Alexander Hamilton, the first secretary of the treasury; John Jay, the first chief justice of the Supreme Court, and Robert Livingston, the first secretary of foreign affairs, all graduated from King's College. More recently, both Theodore and Franklin D. Roosevelt attended the university's Law School. Dwight D. Eisenhower was president of the university from 1948 to 1953, before becoming President of the United States.

Columbia University now has nearly 20,000 students and a faculty of 5,000. The campus is open to the public and guided tours can be arranged.

SEVERAL SITES. The first site of King's College was near Trinity Church ▲ *154* in Lower Manhattan. In 1857, it moved to Madison Avenue between 49th and 50th streets. It moved to its present site, bounded by 114th and 121st streets, Broadway and Amsterdam Avenue, in 1897. The plan and most of the original buildings on the campus were designed by McKim, Mead & White.

LOW MEMORIAL LIBRARY ● *93*. (1897, arch. McKim, Mead & White). Low Memorial Library, standing in the middle of the campus and built in

> "It was really Harlem, and all the stories I had heard about the city within the city flashed into my mind."
>
> Ralph Ellison

"OUR COUNTRY AND OUR CULTURE"
In the 1950's, the universities, and primarily Columbia University, were the driving force behind intellectual activity. In 1952, the *Partisan Review* published a synthesis of the new approach adopted by thinkers, defined during a symposium called "Our Country and Our Culture". It forecast America's intellectual emancipation from Europe and the birth of an American intellectual hegemony.

the shape of a Greek cross, was the first building to be constructed on the campus. It has an exquisite Beaux Arts interior, featuring a vast rotunda capped with a dome, reminiscent of the Pantheon in Rome. The library was superseded by the Butler Library in 1934, and the building now houses the university's central administrative offices, as well as the COLUMBIANA LIBRARY COLLECTION, an archive of documents, books and portraits relating to the university's history.

BUTLER LIBRARY. (1934, arch. James Gamble Rogers). Columbia University's main library is opposite the Low Memorial Library, on the southern side of the campus. Butler Library owes its name to Nicholas Murray Butler, president of the university from 1902 to 1945. With more than six million volumes, it is one of the largest libraries in the United States. Rogers was inspired by the Bibliothèque Sainte-Geneviève in Paris, designed by Henri Labrouste.

ST. PAUL'S EPISCOPAL CHAPEL. (1907, arch. Howells & Stokes). This nondenominational (formerly Episcopal) chapel, in the shape of a Greek cross, is situated east of Low Memorial Library. Its construction was financed by the family of Anson Phelps Stokes, a wealthy financier and philanthropist. Below the chapel, there is the Postcrypt, a small café-concert hall where students in the 1960's discovered the *Beat Generation* poet Jack Kerouac and the songs of the young Robert Zimmerman (Bob Dylan).

EAST HALL. BETWEEN LOW LIBRARY AND ST. PAUL'S EPISCOPAL CHAPEL (1878). This building, part of a former insane asylum, now houses the TEMPLE HOYNE BUELL CENTER FOR THE STUDY OF AMERICAN ARCHITECTURE as well as the MAISON FRANÇAISE OF COLUMBIA. On the lawn between East Hall and the Philosophy Department stands a replica of Rodin's *Thinker*, executed in 1930. Opposite stands Avery Hall and AVERY LIBRARY, the largest architecture library in the country. Although the campus as a whole is open to the public, you must have a Columbia University student card to get into the Butler and Avery libraries.

A FRENCH CULTURAL CENTER
Columbia University's Maison Française, established in 1910, is the oldest foreign language study center attached to an American university. Its artistic and literary events attract a lively French contingent. Jean-Paul Sartre and Eugene Ionesco, among others, have given lectures here.

1 GREEK AMPHITHEATER
2 GRAPHIC ARTS STUDIO
3 OMEGA LITURGICAL DANCE COMPANY
4 ENSEMBLE FOR EARLY MUSIC
5 HORIZON CONCERTS
6 SCULPTURE STUDIO
7 BIBLICAL GARDEN

St. John the Divine ★

At the beginning of the 20th century, people were already impressed by the size of the cathedral, shown (below) under construction. When finished, Saint John the Divine will be the largest Gothic cathedral in the world, 601 feet long and 177 feet high under the nave.

THE EPISCOPAL CATHEDRAL OF NEW YORK. This majestic cathedral stands on Amsterdam Avenue at 112th Street in Morningside Heights. Near this spot, on September 16, 1776, the patriot forces, under George Washington, defeated the British in the Battle of Harlem Heights, which took place during the American Revolution. In 1887, wishing to build a cathedral on a par with the finest in Europe, the Episcopal Diocese of New York paid an exorbitant sum of money for 15 acres of land and launched a competition for its design. Of the sixty entries, the winning plan was one for a Romanesque-style building submitted by the firm of Heins & La Farge.

A LONG AND DIFFICULT TASK. A century after work began in 1892, under the guidance of Bishop Henry Codman Potter, the cathedral still remains unfinished. The first phase, constructing the choir and the four arches of the great dome, took nearly twenty years. In 1916 the plans underwent radical changes; following the death of the two architects and Bishop Potter, it was decided to adopt plans by Cram & Ferguson for a Gothic-style cathedral. The construction of the nave did not start until 1925 after an appeal for contributions from the public, which raised $15 million. The first service was

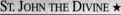

The stonecutters have continued the Gothic tradition of depicting the world in which the cathedral exists by carving buildings on the pedestal of one of the central portal's statues.

held in 1939.

The work, disrupted by the war in 1941, was not resumed until 1979, under the guidance of Reverend Dean Morton. Today, the north and south transepts, the two west towers, the crossing, the roof of the choir and the sculptures for the central and south portals are still under construction. Young apprentices, many from the surrounding neighborhood, cut and carve the stone using techniques employed in the Middle Ages for building European cathedrals. One apprentice has carved the Manhattan skyline at the feet of one of the central portal's statues.

THE INTERIOR. The nave's fourteen bays symbolize the various spiritual and terrestrial vocations of mankind, while the seven chapels of the ambulatory, behind the choir, are each dedicated to a different ethnic group. The cathedral contains many works of art, including two 17th-century Gobelin tapestries. Before leaving the cathedral, be sure to visit the stoneyard, where you can watch the work in progress, the Biblical Garden and the Peace Fountain, which was created in 1985 by Greg Wyatt.

PEACE FOUNTAIN
This work illustrates the struggle between good and evil, embodied in the Archangel Michael and Satan. The giant crab symbolizes the sea and the origins of life, while the pedestal's double helix represents DNA, the genetic chain. The fountain is decorated with sixty small bronze animals, cast from children's works selected by competition.

"But when I opened my eyes we were turning into Riverside Drive. . . . To my right and ahead the church spire towered high, crowned with a red light of warning. And now we were passing the hero's tomb (Grant's Tomb) and I recalled a visit there. You went up the steps and inside and you looked far below to find him, at rest, draped flags . . ."
Ralph Ellison, *Invisible Man*

BARNARD COLLEGE.

BETWEEN BROADWAY AND CLAREMONT AVE., 116TH AND 120TH STS. The campus of Barnard College, located west of the Columbia University campus, consists of nine buildings built between 1896 and 1988. The oldest wing is at 606 West 120th Street. Founded in 1889 as a women's college, Barnard College was affiliated with Columbia, which was at that point exclusively male (the first female students were admitted in 1983). Although Columbia now welcomes members of both sexes, Barnard College has proudly preserved its status as a women's college. It owes its name to Frederick A. P. Barnard, one of the first champions of equal rights for women in higher education.

NORTHERN MORNINGSIDE HEIGHTS

UNION THEOLOGICAL SEMINARY. BROADWAY, BETWEEN 120TH AND 122ND STS. (1910, arch. Allen & Collens). Some of the most eminent Protestant pastors in the United States – including Reinhold Niebuhr, who was professor of Christian ethics here between 1928 and 1960 – have been associated with this seminary, which was founded in 1836. Ask to visit the small garden within the cloisters and see the magnificent staircase.

JEWISH THEOLOGICAL SEMINARY. 3080 BROADWAY (1930, arch. Gehron, Ross, Alley). This seminary, founded in 1886 to train rabbis and theologians, has become the central institution of the American Jewish conservative movement. It boasts an immense Hebrew and Jewish library, a collection of rare books and documents relating to the Jewish community during the colonial period.

RIVERSIDE CHURCH ★. 490 RIVERSIDE DRIVE AND W. 120TH ST. (1930, arch. Allen & Collens, Henry C. Pelton). This neo-Gothic ● 86 church was founded by a Baptist congregation. It is now interdenominational and renowned for its liberalism and active involvement in community affairs. It was here, in 1967, that the Rev. Martin Luther King, Jr, gave his famous sermon, "It is time to break the silence", protesting against American intervention in Vietnam. Nelson Mandela was

UNION THEOLOGICAL SEMINARY. This building, designed by the architect of Riverside Church and Teachers College (on 120th Street), is based on the same theme with neo-Gothic ● 86 variations. It is one of the finest examples of the English Gothic style in New York.

> "The beauty of Riverside Drive, overlooking the Hudson, makes you wish that New York could once again be what it was during Dutch occupation, a site surrounded by water, whose finest residences stood on the riverside".
> P. Morand

The Baptist Church, introduced in North America in the 17th century, became very popular, especially among Blacks. Here (left) a baptism in 1834 in the waters of the Hudson River.

CARILLON OF RIVERSIDE CHURCH

At the top of the church's bell tower is the Laura Spelman Rockefeller Memorial Carillon. Its 20-ton great bell,

the largest in the world, and its 74 other bells cover a range of more than five octaves.

BLACK LEADERS

The clergy has often provided political leaders for the Black community, such as, in New York, Adam Clayton Powell Jr. of the Abyssinian Baptist Church in Harlem and, more recently, Reverends Calvin O. Butts, Al Sharpton and Herbert Daughtry (below).

honored here in 1990, for his work in bringing an end to apartheid in South Africa. The interior of the church contains many remarkable works of art including some fine stained glass and a huge sculpture, *Christ in Majesty* by Jacob Epstein.

GENERAL GRANT NATIONAL MEMORIAL. RIVERSIDE DRIVE, NEAR W. 122ND ST. (1891–7, arch. John H. Duncan). Erected with funds raised by subscription, this tomb is the final resting place of Ulysses S. Grant (1822–85), commander-in-chief of the Union Armies during the Civil War and President of the United States from 1869 to 1877, and of his wife Julia. This shrine is a reconstruction of the tomb of King Mausolus in Halicarnassus (in modern-day Turkey), one of the seven wonders of the ancient world. The words spoken by Grant when he was nominated for President ("Let us have peace") are engraved above the entrance, flanked by allegories of Victory and Peace. The design of the tomb itself, clad in red marble, was modeled on Napoleon's tomb at the Hôtel des Invalides in Paris. The five busts on the colonnade, carved in 1938, portray the generals who served under Grant during the Civil War: Sherman, Thomas, McPherson, Ord and Sheridan. Three mosaics (1966, Allyn Cox) represent the Battle of Vicksburg, his first great victory; the Battle of Chattanooga, his first as commander of all the armies in the West and, between them, Grant and Lee shaking hands to seal the surrender of the Confederacy at Appomattox. More than one million people followed Grant's funeral procession on August 8, 1885. He has gone down in history as the man who saved the nation and restored peace; but he was more successful as a general than as President. He failed in his attempts to rebuild the South and integrate Blacks into society, and his term of office was tainted by corruption.

Tom-toms in the African Market, on the corner of 116th Street on Lenox Avenue.

THE HEART OF HARLEM

APOLLO THEATRE. 253 W. 125TH ST. (1915, arch. George Keister). When this theater first opened it was a burlesque house for Whites only. In 1934, when its new owners, Leo Brecher and Frank Schiffman, opened it to Blacks, it became extremely popular, with such top entertainers as Bessie Smith, "the Empress of the Blues", and Billie Holiday who performed there in the 1930's; Duke Ellington and Count Basie played there in the 1940's, as did Charlie Parker and Dizzie Gillespie, the fathers of bebop ● *60*. Many other artists, including Aretha Franklin and the Jackson Five, have since appeared on the bill.

THERESA TOWERS, FORMER THERESA HOTEL. 2090 ADAM CLAYTON POWELL JR. BLDG. (1910, arch. George and Edward Blum). Built at a time when racial segregation was still widely practiced in New York, this establishment was reserved for Black customers, since Blacks, however wealthy, could not stay at most other New York hotels. It soon became one of the most popular haunts in Harlem. Fidel Castro stayed here in 1960, when he came to New York to speak before the United Nations General Assembly. Nikita Khrushchev also stayed here. Malcolm X moved his offices into the hotel in 1965. The hotel was converted into offices in 1971.

THE STUDIO MUSEUM IN HARLEM. 144 W. 125th ST. This museum is devoted to Black artists from the United States, the Caribbean and the African Diaspora. Its collections include works by Norman Lewis, Hale Woodruft and Jacob Lawrence. It is the only accredited African-American museum in the US.

MARCUS GARVEY PARK. BETWEEN MOUNT MORRIS PARK W. AND MADISON AVE., 120TH AND 124TH STS. This was called Mount Morris Park when it was opened in 1839, and renamed in 1973 in homage to Marcus Garvey, the West Indian leader of the *Back to Africa* movement in the early 20th century. This park was built when it proved impossible to move the enormous central rock obstructing 5th Avenue. A fire watchtower was built in 1855 on top of this promontory. This is the last of the city's many fire towers.

SYLVIA'S RESTAURANT. 328 LENOX AVE. This Harlem institution serves African-American cuisine. Its walls are covered with photos of famous Black Americans and with murals. The riot of August 1, 1943 broke out in this area when a White policeman shot a Black soldier. Thousands of Blacks poured into the streets, overturning cars, ransacking stores belonging to Whites and starting a number of fires.

Below, the stores and stalls on 125th Street.

125TH STREET
125th Street, Harlem's main shopping center, is constantly teeming with activity. Bazaars and stores selling clothes, furniture and electronic goods abound and there are all kinds of itinerant street vendors on the sidewalks. The western end of the street is the site of the African Market where African immigrants buy fabrics, crafts and foodstuffs from their homeland. In recent years many chain stores have opened, such as Lane Bryant, Old Navy, Foot Locker and The Body Shop.

SCHOMBURG CENTER FOR RESEARCH IN BLACK CULTURE. 515 LENOX AVE. (1978, arch. Bond Ryder Assocs.). This is one of the largest branches of the New York Public Library ▲ *252* . It owes its name to Arthur A. Schomburg (1874–1938), a Black Puerto Rican who collected documents on African-American culture after being told at school that the Blacks had no history. THE CARNEGIE CORPORATION OF NEW YORK bought his collection in 1926 and employed him as the curator. The Schomburg Center is now – with some 75,000 books, 300,000 photographs and a collection of musical recordings – the largest historical collection devoted to all peoples of African descent in the world.

ABYSSINIAN BAPTIST CHURCH. 132 W. 138TH ST. (1923, arch. Charles W. Bolton). The church, whose name is a constant reminder to parishioners of their African heritage, was founded in 1808 on Worth Street, and was moved when the congregation migrated northward. Its main claim to fame is its former preacher, Adam Clayton Powell Jr (1908–72), elected to the House of Representations in 1945. He presented bills in favor of education and civil rights, campaigning in particular for a minimum wage and the abolition of racial segregation in the army. This church boasts one of the finest gospel choirs in Harlem.

ST. NICHOLAS HISTORIC DISTRICT. 138TH AND 139TH STS., BETWEEN ADAM CLAYTON POWELL, JR, AND FREDERICK DOUGLASS BLVDS. These rowhouses from 1891, grouped around a communal backyard, were built for middle-class Whites, but began to be occupied by Black middle-class families from 1919. As a result the district was nicknamed "Striver's Row". W. C. Handy, Noble Sissle and Eubie Blake – all famous jazz musicians – lived here.

THE AMERICAN NEGRO THEATRE
PRESENTS

"ANGEL STREET"
by Patrick Hamilton
Staged and Directed by Stanley Greene

"ANGEL STREET"
In 1943, at the same time as rioting broke out in the Black ghettos, a new style of music was born. It spread throughout the country and all over the world. Below, from left to right: Coleman Hawkins, Benny Harris, Don Byas, Thelonius Monk, Denzil Best, Eddie Robinson, photographed in 1944.

HARLEM, THE CULTURAL AND POLITICAL HUB OF BLACK AMERICA ✪
Fans of gospel should visit Harlem on Sunday mornings, as the masses here begin around 11am. If you can only spare a few hours, visit the St. Nicholas Historic District to appreciate Harlem's architectural treasures, then stroll along 125th Street, the most colorful street in the neighborhood. Finally, walk back down towards Morningside Heights, stopping off at the campus of Columbia University and the Cathedral of St. John the Divine.

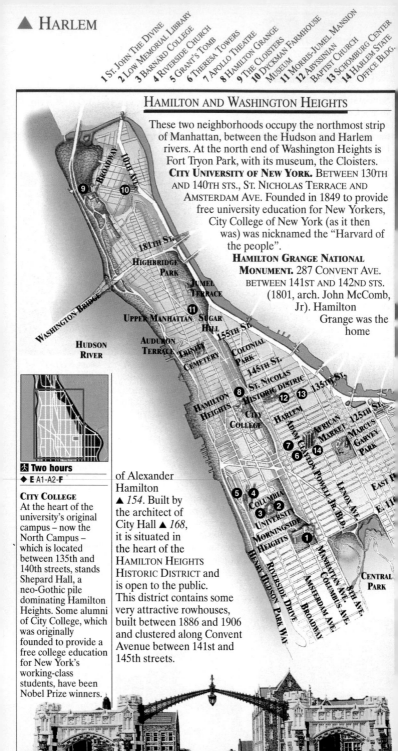

HAMILTON AND WASHINGTON HEIGHTS

These two neighborhoods occupy the northmost strip of Manhattan, between the Hudson and Harlem rivers. At the north end of Washington Heights is Fort Tryon Park, with its museum, the Cloisters.

CITY UNIVERSITY OF NEW YORK. BETWEEN 130TH AND 140TH STS., ST. NICHOLAS TERRACE AND AMSTERDAM AVE. Founded in 1849 to provide free university education for New Yorkers, City College of New York (as it then was) was nicknamed the "Harvard of the people".

HAMILTON GRANGE NATIONAL MONUMENT. 287 CONVENT AVE. BETWEEN 141ST AND 142ND STS. (1801, arch. John McComb, Jr). Hamilton Grange was the home

🏃 **Two hours**

◆ **E** A1-A2-**F**

CITY COLLEGE

At the heart of the university's original campus – now the North Campus – which is located between 135th and 140th streets, stands Shepard Hall, a neo-Gothic pile dominating Hamilton Heights. Some alumni of City College, which was originally founded to provide a free college education for New York's working-class students, have been Nobel Prize winners.

of Alexander Hamilton ▲ *154*. Built by the architect of City Hall ▲ *168*, it is situated in the heart of the HAMILTON HEIGHTS HISTORIC DISTRICT and is open to the public. This district contains some very attractive rowhouses, built between 1886 and 1906 and clustered along Convent Avenue between 141st and 145th streets.

> "I will buy you the finest house
> At the top of the Fifth
> And we will get merry
> Through the streets of Harlem." George Gershwin

SUGAR HILL. SUGAR HILL BETWEEN ST. NICHOLAS AND EDGECOMBE AVES., 143RD TO 155TH STS. This district used to be called Sugar Hill because its affluent Black residents had finally earned their place in the sun and the right to a "sweet life in Harlem". Duke Ellington and Cab Calloway, the Black leader W. E. B. DuBois and the writer Langston Hughes all lived along Edgecombe Avenue.

FROM AUDUBON TERRACE TO THE CLOISTERS

TRINITY CEMETERY. BETWEEN AMSTERDAM AVE. AND RIVERSIDE DRIVE, 153RD AND 155TH STS. This cemetery ▲ *154*, straddles Broadway. The entrance, on Riverside Drive, leads into the western part, which affords a magnificent view of the Hudson River and the George Washington Bridge. Clement Clarke Moore, author of "A Visit from Saint Nicholas", is buried in the eastern part of the cemetery and every Christmas Eve a children's choir sings carols around his tomb.

TRINITY CEMETERY
This covers a section of the land that once belonged to artist and naturalist John James Audubon (1785–1851), who is buried in the eastern part, behind the Church of the Intercession.

AUDUBON TERRACE HISTORIC DISTRICT. BROADWAY, BETWEEN 155TH AND 156TH STS. (1908–30, arch. Charles Pratt Huntington and others). This is a group of museums clustered around a central courtyard in which stands a statue of El Cid (1927, Anna Hyatt Huntington). The AMERICAN ACADEMY OF ARTS AND LETTERS houses manuscripts, paintings, sculpture, and musical scores by its members, who are some of America's most respected artists. The HISPANIC SOCIETY OF AMERICA, devoted to the art, culture and history of Spain and Latin America, contains works by El Greco, Velázquez, Goya and Picasso. The AMERICAN NUMISMATIC SOCIETY is a museum of coins and civil and military decorations. Audubon Terrace was once the site of the MUSEUM OF THE AMERICAN INDIAN, founded in 1916, which possesses a magnificent collection of art and crafts; it has moved to Bowling Green, Downtown.

MORRIS-JUMEL MANSION
This house has one of the finest Georgian interiors in New York. In 1810 Stephen Jumel, a wealthy merchant of French origin, related to Bonaparte's family, bought the house and remodeled it. In particular, he added the Federal-style entrance. After his death, his widow, Eliza Jumel, married Aaron Burr. She lived here until her death in 1865.

MORRIS JUMEL MANSION ● *82* ★. N.W. CORNER OF 160TH ST. AND EDGECOMBE AVE. (1765, remodeled in 1810). This superb residence gives an impression of the way rich New Yorkers would have lived two centuries ago. It was built in the Georgian style ● *82* by a British colonel, Roger Morris. During the American Revolution Washington used it briefly as his headquarters before it fell into British hands. SYLVAN TERRACE, a pretty lane to the west of the house, dates from 1882.

DYCKMAN FARMHOUSE MUSEUM ● *82* ★. 4881 BROADWAY AT N. W. CORNER OF 204TH ST. (1784). East of the Cloisters stands the last remaining colonial farmhouse in Manhattan. It once belonged to a family of Dutch settlers, the Dyckmans, who settled here in 1661. After the American Revolution, during which the British burned down the original farmhouse, the Dyckmans constructed the house that stands today. This building was saved from demolition in 1916, and has since been transformed into a museum, evoking rural life during the colonial period.

Part of the Metropolitan Museum of Art, the Cloisters was established in 1938 and is devoted exclusively to European art of the Middle Ages. On entering this complex of buildings, the visitor is immediately immersed in the past: medieval treasures – including architectural fragments of monasteries and churches – have been cleverly incorporated into the new structure.

The flexible plan enabled the architects to incorporate the Romanesque apse from the church of Fuentadueña in Spain. Composed of nearly three thousand slabs of pale limestone, it was dismantled stone by stone, brought back to New York and carefully reassembled.

This 14th-century Italian diptych, entitled *Crucifixion and Lamentation*, is one of the many works of medieval painting in the Cloisters.

The museum has many precious works of art such as *Saint John the Evangelist*, a Carolingian ivory (c. 800).

This silver ewer is a gem of medieval decorative art. (German, c. 1500).

COLLECTOR AND PATRON OF THE ARTS John D. Rockefeller, Jr. financed this building, which stands on top of a hill in Fort Tryon Park, (above), in Upper Manhattan. His own gifts and the acquisition, in 1925, of the collection owned by George Grey Barnard, an American sculptor living in France, formed the initial core of the museum's collection, which has grown considerably since then.

Another masterpiece of European art, a *Virgin and Child* from 12th-century Burgundy.

The museum is so called because fragments of four medieval cloisters have been incorporated into the modern structure. The floral gardens in the cloisters of Cuxa, Bonnefont and Trie include the same plants as those listed in inventories compiled in the Middle Ages. The cloister of Saint-Guilhem-le-Désert encloses a winter garden.

THE ANNUNCIATION

The Annunciation, a triptych by Robert Campin (c. 1425), illustrates the convergence of religious and secular themes.

Although the symbolism of the *Annunciation* is still medieval, the treatment anticipates the Renaissance.

Manuscript from the end of the 15th century (below).

The 12th-century cloister from Saint-Michel-de-Cuxa (left), in the Pyrenees, is completely made of marble.

The rosary bead above, made of boxwood, dates back to the early 16th century.

John D. Rockefeller's generosity was not limited to financing the construction of the Cloisters; he also endowed the museum with more than forty pieces from his own collection. Among the most important are the Unicorn Tapestries (right).

The famous Unicorn Tapestries, seven hangings (above, the *Unicorn at the Fountain*) probably designed in Paris and woven in Brussels c. 1500, represent the symbolic quest for this mythical animal.

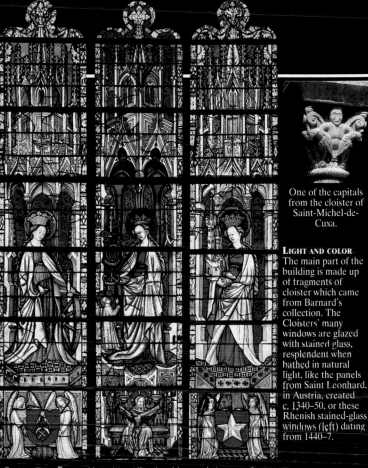

One of the capitals from the cloister of Saint-Michel-de-Cuxa.

LIGHT AND COLOR
The main part of the building is made up of fragments of cloister which came from Barnard's collection. The Cloisters' many windows are glazed with stained glass, resplendent when bathed in natural light, like the panels from Saint Leonhard, in Austria, created c. 1340–50, or these Rhenish stained-glass windows (left) dating from 1440–7.

George Grey Barnard bought medieval architectural elements from farmers and magistrates who had salvaged them in monasteries and churches damaged during the 16th-century wars of religion, then abandoned during the French Revolution. Although Barnard sold some of his acquisitions to subsidize his work as a sculptor, he exhibited the others in New York to introduce Americans to the mastery of what he called the "patient Gothic chisel".

"...those who come under the influence of this place go out to face life with a new courage and restored faith because of the peace, the calm, the loveliness they have found here . . . those who have built here will not have builded [sic] in vain."   John D. Rockefeller

View of the Fulton Ferry Building
in Brooklyn, in June 1857.

**BROOKLYN
HISTORICAL SOCIETY**
This society was
founded in 1863 and
opened to the public
in 1880. It contains a
remarkable collection
documenting the
history of Brooklyn,
the city and the State
of New York, and has
one of the best
genealogical research
libraries in the
country. Busts of
Christopher
Columbus and
Benjamin Franklin
decorate the façade.
It is located at 128
Pierrepont Street.

**BROOKLYN HEIGHTS
ESPLANADE** (1951)
Built to cover the
Brooklyn-Queens
Expressway and lined
with houses and
gardens, this
promenade affords a
magnificent view of
Manhattan, the Bay
of New York and the
Brooklyn Bridge.

Founded in 1645 by Dutch settlers, Brooklyn (after Breuck-elen, a small town in the Utrecht region) is now the most populated borough of New York. Like a city within a city, it has its own history, its own multi-ethnic communities, its own museums, architecture, ports and parks. Although Brooklyn's own neighborhoods were once inhabited mainly by working- or middle-class families and the dream of most Brooklynites was to escape to the suburbs, the socio-economic character is changing rapidly in many parts of the borough because of an influx of younger, more well-heeled residents.

BROOKLYN HEIGHTS

A headland that overlooks the East River, Brooklyn Heights grew considerably after 1814, when Robert Fulton established a steam ferry service, which allowed people to cross the river more quickly than via the existing boats. The wealthy inhabitants moved out of Brooklyn Heights after the Brooklyn Bridge was opened in 1883; a legislative act merged Brooklyn with the other four boroughs, to form a single city on January 1, 1898. The first subway line to Brooklyn Heights began running in 1908 and many of the elegant mansions of the neighborhood were converted into apartments, although the area lost none of its charm. It is still today one of the city's most highly coveted – and most expensive – neighborhoods.

MONTAGUE STREET ★. Once nicknamed "Bank Avenue" because of the predominance of financial establishments, Montague Street now has all the charm of a European shopping street with its restaurants, stores, brownstones and the Church of St Ann and the Holy Trinity at no. 157. Note in particular, at no. 185, the former National Tile Guaranty Building, in Art Deco style (1929, arch. Corbett, Harrison and MacMurray).

DUMBO. Just to the north of Brooklyn Heights is DUMBO (Down Under the Manhattan Bridge Overpass). It's an area of factory buildings and warehouses converted first to artists' studios and galleries, more recently to condominiums. The views of the Manhattan skyline are spectacular and the feel

is relaxed and removed from the bustle of the city.

RED HOOK. Further west and under the Brooklyn-Queens Expressway is Red Hook, the former home of the container ships and made famous by Marlon Brando in *On the Waterfront*. Long in disrepair, if not total abandonment, this area is set for massive rejuvenation when the piers are repaired and begin to accept cruise ships, including the Queen Mary 2, in 2006. Currently, the low-slung former rope factories house artists and the long-shut longshoremen's bars give the area the edgy feel of the Lower East Side in the 1970s.

WILLIAMSBURG

In the space of about ten years, cafés, design stores and art galleries have sprung up in this trendy Brooklyn neighborhood.

WILLIAMSBURG SAVINGS BANK. This skyscraper, which was erected during the 1929 crisis and is the tallest building in Brooklyn, is reminiscent of a Byzantine church, with its mosaics, carved capitals and its vault three stories high. The counters on the first floor are small votive chapels. Where the altar would be, a large mosaic depicts an aerial view of the city with Brooklyn and the Williamsburg Savings Bank Tower in the center.

PARK SLOPE

Park Slope, southeast of Brooklyn Heights, is a leafy residential neighborhood full of brownstones settled after the opening of the Brooklyn Bridge. There are many restaurants and shops along Seventh and Fifth aves. The neighborhood went into decline after the World War II, but was gentrified starting in the 1970s. Park Slope can feel a bit like Berkeley, California; it is a haven for hippies and gays and lesbians.

CARROLL GARDENS. This neighborhood, to the south of Brooklyn Heights and the west of Park Slope, has cleaned itself up to a remarkable degree. Fashionable shops, restaurants and bars line Smith and Carroll Streets that all

WILLIAMSBURG, AN UP-AND-COMING NEIGHBORHOOD ★
Since the late 1990's, Williamsburg, Carroll Gardens and Park Slope have attracted young artists and yuppies from Manhattan looking for cheaper rents, a lively neighborhood, and a village atmosphere that makes a pleasant change from the hustle and bustle of Manhattan. Williamsburg is very popular with those who enjoy a bohemian lifestyle. The area is at its liveliest around the Bedford Avenue subway: come here during the day for a stroll or in the evening to listen to live music.

Below,
Park Slope

**BROOKLYN MUSEUM
OF ART**

cater to the neighborhood's newest residents: hip twenty-somethings.

PROSPECT PARK. A number of mansions line Prospect Park West, the avenue that runs along Prospect Park, 526 acres designed by Frederick Law Olmstead and Calvert Vaux in the early 1880s. The park itself is has a three-mile loop for walking, jogging, or bike-riding. Horseback riding is popular in summer, as are picnics and Frisbee in the Long Meadow.

BROOKLYN MUSEUM OF ART

EASTERN PARKWAY AND WASHINGTON AVE. (arch. McKim, Mead & White, 1897 and 1924). This museum is housed in a huge Beaux Arts-style building just to the east of Prospect Park. The new 17,000 square-foot glass entrance, designed by James Stewart Polshek, opened in 2004. The museum's Egyptian collection, which also reopened in 2004 after a huge renovation, is considered the best in the US. The museum hosts many major traveling exhibitions and has works by American painters and sculptors such as Georgia O'Keeffe, Winslow Homer, John Singer Sargent and Milton Avery.

BROOKLYN BOTANICAL GARDEN. The 40-acre gardens are accessible through gates on either side of the Brooklyn Museum of Art, and include the massive Steinhardt Conservatory, a Japanese hill-and-pond, a Shakespearean, a large rose, and rock gardens. The Cherry Esplanade is particularly beautiful in spring.

Below, Brooklyn
Botanical Garden

CONEY ISLAND

It wasn't until 1877 that the first beach-front hotel opened in Coney Island, but in quick succession a horseracing track and the world's first roller-coaster were built there, and one of the world's great popular resorts was born. Coney Island remained a place for the well-to-do until 1920, when the subway connected it to the rest of the city, meaning anyone, rich and poor, could spend the a weekend at the beach. Coney Island fell on hard times more recently, but you can still enjoy a ride on the Cyclone, a Nathan's hot dog, body surfing, and salsa dancing at a boardwalk bar all in one day. Just to the east of the amusement parks (and the New York Aquarium – a favorite with children) is Brighton Beach, the center of New York's immigrant Russian community. Bookstores, delicatessens, restaurants and bars line the main avenue and a stroll on the beach itself will make you think you're back in Svetlogorsk.

Practical information

TIME DIFFERENCE

New York is on Eastern Standard time (EST), which is behind Greenwich Mean Time by five hours (Nov–March) or six hours (April–Oct). New York is three hours ahead of Los Angeles and one ahead of Chicago.

USEFUL ADDRESSES

→ **US EMBASSY IN LONDON**
24 Grosvenor Square
London W1A 1AE
Tel. 020 7499 9000
Visa information:
Tel. 09055-444-546
(£1.30/min.)
Mon-Fri 8am–8pm;
Sat 9am–4pm)
www.usembassy.org.uk

→ **US EMBASSY IN CANADA**
■ CONSULAR SECTION
490 Sussex Drive
Ottawa, Ontario
Tel. 613-238-5335
For consulates in other Canadian cities or general information:
Tel. 1-900-451-2778
(CA$2/min.)
www.amcits.com

FORMALITIES

→ **PASSPORT**
Overseas visitors must have a valid passport and a return ticket (except for those travelers entering the country overland), as well as proof of sufficient resources to cover your stay in the country.

→ **VISA**
For Europeans, no visa is necessary for stays of up to 90 days. For travelers from the Middle East, Asia and Africa, a visa is necessary, and following 9/11 takes longer to obtain so plan well ahead.

HEALTH

Health care is very expensive and hospitals will not treat uninsured patients. It is essential that you purchase a health insurance policy before traveling to the US. Check with your travel agents or with your bank or credit card company whose various services may include health coverage abroad.

MONEY

→ **CURRENCY**
The dollar ($), divided into 100 cents (¢). Coins are: penny (1¢), nickel (5¢), dime (10¢) and quarter (25¢).

→ **TRAVELER'S CHECKS**
Traveler's checks in dollars are very handy as they are accepted as cash by most hotels, restaurants and stores. They are also refunded in case of loss or theft.

TELEPHONE

→ **FROM UK TO US**
Dial 00 1, followed by one of New York's area codes: 212, 949, 646, 718 or 347), followed by the 7-digit number.

TRAVELING TO NEW YORK BY AIR

→ **FROM ABROAD**
Regular flights from London and most other major cities direct to New York JFK, LaGuardia or Newark airports. Check with the following airlines for details of fares and conditions:
■ BRITISH AIRWAYS
www.ba.com
■ VIRGIN ATLANTIC
www.virginatlantic.com
■ AMERICAN AIRLINES
www.aa.com

■ WEBSITES
www.cheapflights.com (or .co.uk)
www.expedia.co.uk
www.travelocity.com
www.orbitz.com

→ **INTERNAL FLIGHTS**
The following major domestic carriers offer flights to and from Kennedy, Newark and LaGuardia airports.
■ AMERICAN AIRLINES
Tel. 1 800-433-7300
■ DELTA AIRLINES
Tel. 1 800-221-1212
■ UNITED AIRLINES
Tel. 1 800-UNITED-1

TRAVELING TO NEW YORK BY TRAIN

You will arrive in one of Manhattan's two stations: Grand Central Terminal or Pennsylvania Station. See under Rail Stations ◆ 374.

TRAVELING TO NEW YORK BY COACH

All "long distance" buses terminate at the Port Authority Bus Terminal, 8th Ave. (between 40th and 42nd Sts; map **C** D2)
Tel. 1 800-221-9903
■ GREYHOUND BUS
Tel. 1 800-231-2222
www.greyhound.com

TRAVELING TO NEW YORK BY SEA

→ **FROM THE UK**
There are many sailings a year from Southampton on the Queen Elizabeth II

and the Queen Mary 2. The journey takes about six nights. Roundtrip prices from around £900.
■ CUNARD LINE
UK reservations:
0845 071 0300
US reservations:
1 800-7-CUNARD
www.cunard.com

CLIMATE

■ WINTER
December: 30°/40°F
January: 30°/40°F
February: 30°/42°F
■ SPRING
March: 30°/45°F
April: 42°/60°F
May: 53°/70°F
■ SUMMER
June: 64°/82°F
July: 70°/84°F
August: 66°/80°F
■ FALL
September: 62°/74°F
October: 54°/64°F
November: 43°/52°

VOLTAGE

110 Volts and 60 Hz. Plugs have two flat pins. Adapters and power converters are necessary for all European appliances.

NEW YORK ON THE NET

– www.ci.nyc.ny.us
Official city website.
– www.nycvisit.com
Official site of the New York tourist Office.
– www.newyork.city search.com
What's on in the city and general advice.
– www.iloveny.com
Official tourist website of the State of New York.

STAYING IN NEW YORK FROM A TO Z ◆

Accommodation, Airports and city links, Alcohol, Bicycle rental, Boats

Topics are arranged alphabetically.

ACCOMMODATION

→ RESERVATIONS
Some reservation agencies offer rooms at very reasonable prices.
From the UK dial 880 instead of 800.
Hotel Reservations Network
Tel. 1 800-964-6835
Delta Vacations
Tel. 1 800-654-6559

→ RATES
Rates vary according to season, days of the week and availability. Many hotels offer special weekend and low-season (July–Aug.) rates, depending on availability. Most hotels charge according to the number of persons in a room (add 8–10% per person to single rates). Most hotels do not charge for children sleeping in the same room as their parents, but the age limit may be different from one place to another (under 12's to under 18's).

AIRPORTS AND CITY LINKS

There are two international airports, JFK and Newark, and one airport for domestic flights, LaGuardia.
■ **JFK**
Tel. (718) 244-4444
■ **NEWARK**
Tel. (973) 961-6000
■ **LAGUARDIA**
Tel. (718) 533-3400
■ **GROUND TRANSPORTATION CENTER**
It is found in the three airports, and gives information on all links to the city.

→ BY TAXI
■ **JFK**
Approx. $35 (around 60 mins)
■ **NEWARK**
Approx. $45 (around 60 mins)

■ **LAGUARDIA**
Approx. $30 (around 30 mins). A toll fee of $6 and a tip must be added to the above-mentioned prices.

→ BY BUS
■ **FROM JFK AND LAGUARDIA**
Buses run every 30 mins from 6.05am until 11.40pm daily, stopping at Grand Central Terminal (Park Ave and 42nd St), Port Authority Terminal (8th Ave and 42nd St), Penn Station (7th Ave. and 34th St), Bryant Park as well as stopping at hotels between 27th and 59th Sts.
New York Airport Service
Tel. (718) 875-8200
www.nyairportservice.com
One-way fares to city center: $15 from JFK, $12 from LaGuardia.
■ **FROM NEWARK**
Buses run daily every 15–30 mins to Grand Central station, Pennsylvania Station, Port Authority Terminal, and many midtown hotels.
Olympia Trails
Tel. 877-8-NEWARK or 908-354-3330
www.coachusa.com/olympia
One-way fare: $13 from Newark.

→ BY AIRTRAIN
■ **FROM JFK**
A $5 fee will take you from JFK to Howard Beach station (to connect to the A line subway) or Jamaica station (to connect to the Long Island Rail Road). From there, the train or subways will take you anywhere in New York.
www.jfkairtrain.com
■ **FROM NEWARK**
A free monorail system connects Amtrak, PATH or New Jersey transit trains to New York City.
www.airtrainnewark.com

→ BY MINIBUS
Request stops between 23rd and 125th Sts. Roundtrip prices: $28 from JFK, $26 from LaGuardia, $28 from Newark.
Gray Line Air Shuttle
Tel. 1 800-451-0455 and (212) 315-3006

→ BY SUBWAY (LINE A)
■ **FROM JFK ONLY**
Take the Long Term Parking Lot Shuttle Bus (free) from any terminal to the Howard Beach Subway Station to board a train. Cheapest form of transportation ($2). 60–75 minutes.

→ BY LIMOUSINE
Limousines do not necessarily cost more than taxis and are good value for large parties. The price varies according to the size of the car. From $60 per hour, plus toll fee. You will also need to give the driver a 15% tip.
Carmel Limo
Tel. 1 800-922-7635 and (212) 666-6666
AA Executive Town Car & Limo
Tel. 1 800-716-2799 and 516-538-8551

ALCOHOL

You must be over 21 to be allowed to purchase alcohol or to drink alcohol in a bar. Proof of age is often required. Restaurants that display a *no-liquor license* sign are not allowed to serve any alcohol, but you can bring your own wine or beer (or *brownbag* it).

BICYCLE RENTAL

Loeb Boat House
E. 72nd St, west of 5th Ave.
Tel. (212) 517-2233
$10 per hour.

Bite of Apple Tours
59th St at Broadway
Tel. (212) 541 8759
Bike tours of Central Park and bike hire.

BOATS

→ CRUISES
Boat trips around Manhattan with commentary.
■ **CIRCLE LINE**
Pier 83, W. 42nd St. and 12th Ave. and Pier 16, South Street Seaport
Tel. (212) 563-3200
www.circleline.com
Circle Line–Statue of Liberty Ferry, Inc
The Statue of Liberty and Ellis Island are accessible only with the above ferries.
Round-trip to both: $10 adults ($8 senior citizens, $4 children). Ferries depart from Battery Park or Liberty State Park in Jersey City, New Jersey.
Tel. 1 866-STATUE-4
www.statueofliberty ferry.com
■ **NEW YORK WATERWAYS**
Pier 78, W 38th St and 12th Ave. and Pier 17, South Street Seaport St (Weschester)
Tel. 1 800-533-3779
■ **SPIRIT CRUISES**
Pier 61, Chelsea Piers (Hudson River and W 23rd St.)
Tel. (212) 727-7735

→ FERRY
From Staten Island to Manhattan.
Staten Island Ferry
(Battery Park), Whitehall Terminal, South Ferry
Tel. (718) 876-8441

BUSES

Buses run along avenues in a north–south direction, stopping every two or three blocks, as well as along the main streets across town in an east– west direction. Buses run 24 hours a day.

◆ STAYING IN NEW YORK FROM A TO Z

Buses, Cabs, Cars, Finding your way, Health, Helicopter tours

→ BUS SIGNS

Bus stops show a stylized bus on a blue and red background and the line number.

→ FARES AND TRANSFERS

The fare ($2) is the same regardless of the journey's length or duration, and can be paid directly to the driver when boarding the bus.

■ METROCARDS
MetroCards ($2) are rechargeable magnetic card which enables you to travel any distance. They are sold for single rides or many rides, or as weekly or monthly passes.

■ REDUCTIONS
Children shorter than 3½ feet travel free. For $7 per day the Fun Pass gives unlimited access to the subway and buses.

■ TRANSFERS
A MetroCard allows you to transfer buses or subways on different routes within 2 hours of the first use (free).

CABS

The yellow cars are easily spotted. You can flag them when their roof light is on.

→ RIDE

A base $2.50 is charged; additional 40¢ for each 0.2 mile and an additional 50¢ between 8pm and 6am.

→ TIPS

No more than 10% of the price indicated by the meter and any relevant toll fees.

→ COMPLAINTS AND LOST PROPERTY

The car's identity number (4 digits at the side of the meter) can be used to track down lost objects or file a complaint.

Taxi & Limousine
Commission
Tel. 311

CARS

→ PARKING
Difficult and expensive.
■ PRIVATE PARKING LOTS
Displays their rates at the entrance.
■ ON THE STREET
Metered parking places are limited to one hour.
■ IN FREE ZONES
On some streets there is an alternate side for parking. You can leave your car parked there all day and all night, but you must move it and park it on the other side before 8am the following morning.

→ CAR IMPOUNDING
$150 plus $15 per day. Open 24 hours, except Sundays.
Tow Pound
Pier 76, W 38th St (12th Ave.)
Tel. (212) 971-0772

→ CAR RENTAL
In Manhattan, allow approximately $65–$80 per day.
■ AVIS
Tel. 1 800-230-4898
■ HERTZ
Tel. 1 800-654-3131
■ NATIONAL
Tel. 1 800-328-4567
■ DOLLAR
Tel. 1 800-800-3665

FINDING YOUR WAY

→ AVENUES
Most avenues bear numbers rather than names.
■ BUILDING NUMBERS
They increase from south to north. The length of the avenues means that it is useful to mention the name of the street that the avenue crosses: *201 Park Avenue South (at 17th St)* or even *56 Irving Place (between 17th and 18th sts)*.

→ STREETS
Streets run one way as marked. With the exception of the Financial District and Greenwich Village, they are given numbers from 1st to 215th starting from the south. The numbering system starts from 5th Ave.

→ STREET SIGNS
Most street names are indicated in white against a green background. The streets or squares bearing the names of famous people or particular activities may also be indicated by blue or brown signs.

→ BLOCKS
The distance between two streets or two avenues is usually refered to as a block.

→ DISTRICTS AND ZONES
Every district in Manhattan has a name (Harlem, Chelsea, East Village...), and is part of one of three large zones: downtown, midtown and uptown. The island stands directly in a north–south line, while 5th Avenue and Central Park divide Manhattan east–west.
■ DOWNTOWN
The area south of 14th St (from Greenwich Village to the Financial District). To go downtown means going to the south of Manhattan.
■ MIDTOWN
The zone between 14th and 59th Sts. Beyond 59th St, 5th Avenue marks the division between East and West sides.
■ UPTOWN
North of 59th St, the Upper East Side and Upper West Side are separated by Central Park to 110th St.

HEALTH

Doctors are listed in the Yellow Pages under *Physicians*.

→ 24-HOUR PHARMACIES
■ ECKERD
2nd Ave. (68th St)
Tel. (212) 772-0104
■ DUANE READE DRUGSTORES
– 300 Park Ave. South (22nd St)
Tel. (212) 533-7580
– 224 W. 57th St (Broadway)
Tel. (212) 541-9708

HELICOPTER TOURS

See New York from the air. Most hotels can make the bookings for you.

■ LIBERTY HELICOPTER TOURS
Tel. (212) 967-6464
Departure points:
VIP heliport
12th Ave. and 30th St (Hudson River).
Daily 9am–9pm
Downtown Manhattan heliport
Pier 6, near South Street Seaport (East River)
Mon.–Fri. 9am–6pm

LIMOUSINES

A private chauffeur-driven car can be hired by the hour, by contract, and to go to the airport.
City Ride and Limo Service
Tel. (212) 861-1000 or 1 800-CITYRIDE

MONEY

→ BANKS
Most banks are equipped with ATMs (Automatic Teller Machine) and change foreign currencies.
■ OPENING HOURS
Mon.–Fri. 9am–3pm, Sat. 9am–1pm

→ EXCHANGE RATE
$1 = £0.56 / €0.82 (at the time of writing)

■ **TRAVELEX CURRENCY SERVICE**
Tel. (212) 265-6063
1590 Broadway (at Times Square) Daily 9am–7pm (5pm Sun)

→ **AUTOMATIC TELLER MACHINES**
The main ATM machines are Cirrus, linked to Visa, and Plus, linked to MasterCard.

→ **CARDS**
Cash or credit cards are widely accepted.
■ **LOST CARDS**
Mastercard
Tel. 1 800-MC-ASSIST
Visa
Tel. 1 800-847-2911
American Express
Tel. 1 800-992-3404

MUSEUMS

→ **OPENING TIMES**
Usually 10am–5pm. Many are closed on Monday or Wednesday.

→ **DISCOUNTS**
Available to students and the over-60s. They vary depending on the museum.

→ **MUSEUM MILE**
The nine major New York museums are free 6–9pm the 2nd Tuesday in June.

→ **CITYPASS CARD**
From ticket offices of participating monuments and museums. Price $53 adults, $41 youth, valid 9 days. Free access to: American Museum of Natural History, Guggenheim Museum, Empire State Building, MoMA, Intrepid Sea Air Space Museum and Circle Line Harbor Cruise.
http://citypass.com

NIGHTLIFE

→ **LISTINGS**
For details of theaters, concerts, opera, cabarets, nightclubs, movie theaters, etc.:
■ **NEW YORK TIMES**
www.nytimes.com
Check the weekend section in the Friday issue and the Arts & Leisure section on Sundays.
■ **THE VILLAGE VOICE**
www.villagevoice.com
Free weekly newspaper, out on Wednesdays.
■ **TIME OUT NEW YORK**
www.timeoutny.com
Weekly magazine, out on Tuesdays.
■ **BROADWAY LINE**
Tel. (212) 302-4111
(information on Broadway shows).

→ **RESERVATIONS**
Tickets can be purchased directly from the theaters, or from central agencies.
■ **TICKET MASTER**
Tel. (212) 307-7171
■ **HMV RECORDS**
565 5th Ave. (46th St)
For nearly all shows, concerts and sports events.
■ **TICKET CENTRAL BOX OFFICE**
416 W 42nd St.
(between 9th and 10th aves)
Tel. (212) 279-4200
www.ticketcentral.com
■ **TIMES SQUARE VISITORS CENTER**
1560 Broadway
(between 46th and 47th sts).
Open daily 8am–8pm
■ **TKTS**
www.tdf.org/tkts/
Tel. (212) 221-0013
Same-day tickets to broadway, off-Broadway and other art events at up to 50 percent off their original prices.
TKTS booth in Duffy Square
47th St (corner of Broadway). Aim to start queuing from 5pm (or 2pm for popular shows).
TKTS booth in South Street Seaport
199 Water St
(corner of Front and John sts). Open Mon–Sat 11am–6pm; Sun 11am–3.30pm.

POST OFFICES

→ MAIL BOXES
Boxes are colored blue and bear the inscription *U.S. Mail*.

→ CENTRAL POST OFFICE
8th Ave. (33rd St.)
Tel. 1 800-275-8777

→ INLAND MAIL
It costs 37 cents to send a one-ounce (28g) letter. Each additional ounce costs 23 cents.

→ SENDING MAIL
Depending on the country of destination, a letter costs 60–80 cents, and a postcard 50–70 cents.

→ EXPRESS MESSENGER SERVICES
■ FEDERAL EXPRESS
New York–London in two days maximum, from $25.50.
Tel. 1 800-463-3339

→ TELEGRAMS AND MONEY TRANSFERS
Service run by private companies.
■ WESTERN UNION
Tel. 1 800-325-6000

PUBLIC HOLIDAYS AND SPECIAL EVENTS

→ PUBLIC HOLIDAYS
■ New Year's Day Jan. 1
■ Martin Luther King Jnr. Day (3rd Monday in Jan.)
■ President's Day (3rd Monday in Feb.)
■ Memorial Day (last Monday in May)
■ Independence Day July 4
■ Labor Day (1st Monday in Sep.)
■ Columbus Day (2nd Monday in Oct.)
■ Veteran's Day Nov. 11 (Armistice)
■ Thanksgiving Day (4th Thursday in Nov.)
■ Christmas Dec. 25

→ SPECIAL EVENTS
■ DECEMBER 31
New Year's Eve, Times Tower illuminations at midnight (Times Square).
■ END JANUARY–BEG. FEBRUARY
Chinese New Year (Chinatown)
■ MARCH 17
St Patrick's Day Parade (down 5th Ave., from 86th to 44th sts)
■ EASTER
Easter Parade (down 5th Ave., from 59th to 44th sts)
■ JULY 4
Fireworks on the East River (can be watched from Battery Park)
■ OCTOBER 31
Halloween Parade (Greenwich Village)
■ 4TH THURSDAY IN NOVEMBER
Macy's Thanksgiving Day Parade (down Broadway, from Central Park West to Herald Square)

RAIL STATIONS

→ GRAND CENTRAL TERMINAL
Park Ave. and 42nd St (map **C** C3)
Tel. (212) 532-4900
Trains to the suburbs (Metro-North), upstate New York and Connecticut; also provides subway, bus and airport bus services.
■ METRO-NORTH
Fast suburban trains to the Hudson Valley, New Haven, eastern New York and Weschester County.

→ PENNSYLVANIA STATION
7th Ave. and 33rd St (map **C** D2)
Penn Station serves commuters from Long Island and New Jersey. It also has trains to many cities in the United States (Boston and Washington, D.C., Chicago etc) and Canada.

■ LONG ISLAND RAIL ROAD (LIRR)
Tel. (718) 217-5477
Trains to Long Island.
■ AMTRAK
Tel. 1 800-872-7245
www.amtrak.com
National railway company linking New York to cities in the US and Canada.
■ NJ TRANSIT
Tel. 1 800-772-2222
www.njtransit.com
Trains to New Jersey.

SHOPPING

→ AREAS
■ CHINATOWN
Canal Street is the main market for counterfeit watches, pens, handbags, shoes, scarves and perfume. Bargain and buy at your own risk. Small Chinese stores and bazaars on Mott, Pell, Mulberry and Doyers sts.
■ ORCHARD STREET
In the heart of the Lower East Side: clothes and leather goods, designer-inspired fashions, household linen and luggage at unbeatable prices. Check out the neighboring streets as well: Grand, Delancey, Bowery and Ludlow sts. Some stores closed Saturdays, but there is a lively atmosphere on Sundays.
■ NOLITA
NoLita (North of Little Italy), which includes Lafayette, Mulberry, Mott and Elizabeth sts, between Spring and Houston sts, is the new shoppers' paradise with fashion boutiques and unusual decoration goods. Most of them do not open until noon.
■ SOHO
You'll find everything here: second-hand clothes, jeans, ready-to-wear and designers' clothes, cosmetics, household goods and furniture, delicatessens, etc. SoHo is becoming a huge commercial center, and has many art galleries and restaurants.
■ CHELSEA AND FLATIRON DISTRICT
The former *Ladies' Mile* has got its second wind with large chains such as Barnes & Noble, Bed Bath & Beyond, Pottery Barn, Old Navy, etc., on 6th Ave., and cheap electronic goods between Broadway and 6th Ave., and between 14th and 23rd sts. There has recently been a phenomenon of smart new fashion stores springing up on 14th St., such as Jeffrey's, Alexander McQueen and Stella McCartney.
■ GARMENT DISTRICT
Sample sales from stores and workrooms on 7th Ave. (Fashion Avenue), between 42nd and 34th sts. Collect addresses from the advertising leaflets handed to you on the avenue.
■ 5TH AVENUE
Prestigious stores (Tiffany, Chanel, Saks, etc.) now stand shoulder to shoulder with show business as well as sports and electronic goods stores such as Nike, Disney, Sony or NBA.
■ MADISON AVENUE
The select world of haute couture and luxury prêt-à-porter, between 57th and 79th sts.
■ 125TH STREET
For hip-hop and African-fabric clothes, jeans, T-shirts at very low prices.

→ OPENING TIMES
Stores are usually open from 9am to 6pm. For Christmas shopping (from the end of Nov. to Christmas Eve) stores stay open later. Some stores in

STAYING IN NEW YORK FROM A TO Z ◆

Smoking, Subway, Taxes, Telephone, Tipping, Useful addresses

WOMEN'S SIZES

CLOTHES

US 8 = UK 10
US 10 = UK 12
US 12 = UK 14

SHOES

US 7½ = UK 4
US 8½ = UK 5
US 9½ = UK 6

MEN'S SIZES

SHIRTS

UK and US jacket, trouser and shirt sizes are the same.

SHOES

US 8½ = UK 8
US 9½ = UK 9
US 10½ = UK 10

the Lower East Side and the Diamond District are closed on Friday afternoons and Saturdays, for the Jewish Sabbath, and other Jewish holidays. Opening and closing times in Chelsea, SoHo and Greenwich Village vary.

→ SALES

On special public holidays such as President's Day (3rd Monday in Feb.), Memorial Day (last Monday in May) and Columbus Day (2nd Monday in Oct.)

SMOKING

Smoking is not allowed in any public places, nor in certain open-air public places such as stadiums, in public transportation carriages, theaters, stores and office lobbies. New York State also prohibits smoking in most restaurants and bars.

SUBWAY

The fastest means of transportation, especially during rush hour.

→ LOCAL AND EXPRESS LINES

These lines are referred to by letters or numbers.
■ EXPRESS LINES
Express trains stop only at the larger stations.
■ LOCAL LINES
Local trains make all the stops.

→ STATIONS

In general, the stations bear the names of streets. Usually a subway entrance is for one direction only (uptown for the north, or downtown for the south) and is designated by a green or a red globe.
■ GREEN GLOBE
Ticket office open 24 hours.
■ RED GLOBE
Limited opening times.
■ FINDING YOUR WAY
As soon as you enter the subway system, the lines, directions and destinations are indicated by signs. Usually there will be a separate entrance for uptown and one for downtown, on one or the other side of the street.

→ FARES AND TRANSFERS

The fare ($2) is the same, regardless of the journey's length or duration, and is paid by tokens (which are sold individually or 10 at a time), or by MetroCard (minimum $2), a rechargeable magnetic card which enables you to travel any distance.
■ REDUCTIONS
Children shorter than 3½ feet travel free. For $7 per day the Fun Pass gives unlimited access to subway and buses.

TAXES

Goods purchased in Manhattan usually carry a sales tax of 8.25% which is not included in the marked price, but added at the time of payment. In hotels, an additional 13.25% must be added to the fixed hotel tax of $2.

TELEPHONE

→ FROM NEW YORK TO OTHER STATES

Dial the state code followed by the number you wish to call.

→ CODES

Manhattan: 212, 917 and 646. Other boroughs: 718, 347.

→ FREE CALLS

Numbers preceded by 1 800, 866, 877 or 888 are free of charge.

→ PHONING THE UK

Dial 011 44 followed by the number you want without the initial 0.

→ CARDS

Calling from your hotel may result in high charges. With an international card your calls will be charged directly to your bank account.

→ PUBLIC TELEPHONES

50¢ for 3 mins. The cost of calls other than local ones is indicated.

→ USEFUL NUMBERS

■ POLICE, FIRE
Tel. 911 (free)
■ TRAVELER'S AID SOCIETY
(JFK Airport only)
Tel. (718) 656-4870
■ INFORMATION
Tel. 411 (free)

TIPPING

Between 15 and 20% (as a quick reckoning, just double the 8.25% sales tax).

Service is never included in a bill and must therefore be added. No tipping is required in gas stations, theaters or cinemas.
■ PAYMENT
If paying by credit card, add the amount you wish to leave as a tip to the amount you have to pay, enter the total sum to pay and sign.

USEFUL ADDRESSES

→ CONSULATES

■ CANADA
1251 Ave. of the Americas
New York, NY 10020
Tel. (212) 596-1628
www.canada-ny.org
■ UK
845 3rd Ave.
New York, NY 10022
Tel. (212) 745-0200
www.britainusa.com/consular/ny

→ TOURIST OFFICE

■ NEW YORK CONVENTION AND VISITOR'S BUREAU
810 7th Ave.
(between 52nd and 53rd sts)
Tel. (212) 484-1222
Open daily Mon–Fri 8.30am–6pm;
Sat–Sun 9am–5pm.

→ BIG APPLE GREETER

A New Yorker can be assigned to you for 2–4 hrs to help you find your way around the city or to visit a particular area.
Tel. (212) 669-8159

375

▫	< $100
▣	$100 to $150
▦	$150 to $200
▥	> $200

FINANCIAL DISTRICT

HOTELS

EMBASSY SUITES HOTEL NEW YORK
◆ **A** A1
102 North End Ave.
(at Murray St)
Tel. (212) 945-0100
Fax (212) 945-3012
www.embassysuites.com
This hotel is a relative bargain. Every guest is given a living room and bedroom, and many have views of New York Harbor. There are lots of amenities, including a health club, movie theater, four restaurants, and an 11-story atrium painted by Sol Lewitt.
▫

RITZ-CARLTON NEW YORK
◆ **A** C2
2 West St
(at Battery Pl.)
Tel. (212) 344-0800
or 1-800-241-3333
Fax (212) 344-3801
www.ritzcarlton.com/hotels/new_york_battery_park
The incredible views of the Statue of Liberty and New York harbor you get from most of the rooms made the Ritz-Carlton New York an instant classic the day it opened in 2002. It's a little bit remote, at the southern tip of downtown, but you can step out of the hotel in the morning for a jog around Battery Park and the Manhattan waterfront. The 14th-story Rise bar, with a terrace, has perhaps the best view in the city.
▥

RESTAURANTS

AMERICAN PARK
◆ **A** D2-3
Battery Park
(at State St)
Tel. (212) 809-5508
Closed Sat. lunch, Sun.
Ideal location at the tip of Battery Park, facing the bay of New York. It is particularly nice in the summer when the terrace is open. Fish specialties.
▥

BAYARD'S
◆ **A** C3
1 Hanover Square
(between Pearl and Stone sts)
Tel. (212) 514-9454
www.bayards.com
A temple of French gastronomy in a beautifully restored building. Eberhard Müller, former chef at Lutèce and Bernardin, is in charge, so expect hefty prices and a truly special meal.
▥

BRIDGE CAFÉ
◆ **A** A4
279 Water St
(at Dover St)
Tel. (212) 227-3344
Closed Sat. lunch
Fish restaurant at the foot of the Brooklyn Bridge, near the former Fulton Fish Market. Excellent brunch on Sundays.
▥

14 WALL STREET RESTAURANT
◆ **A** C-3
14 Wall St
(between Broad St and Broadway)
Tel. (212) 233-2780
Worth it for the view. This elegant restaurant, on the 31st floor, used to be J.P. Morgan's private penthouse and the place is packed today with banking movers and shakers.
▥

LES HALLES
◆ **A** B3
15 John St
(between Broadway and Nassau sts)
Tel. (212) 285-8585
This is the more sedate downtown outpost of the Park Avenue South original. Chef Anthony Bourdain, who wrote the best-selling Kitchen Confidential, *serves the best hangar steak in New York. Both locations also serve as butcher shops.*
▥

HARRY'S AT HANOVER SQUARE
◆ **A** C3
1 Hanover Square
(between Pearl and Stone sts)
Tel. (212) 425-3412
A typical Wall Street scene where brokers eat hamburgers with their eyes glued to an electronic display board in the center of the restaurant, with its relentless stream of stock exchange prices at breakneck speed.
▥

TRIBECA

HOTELS

TRIBECA GRAND HOTEL
◆ **B** D2
2 Avenue of the Americas (between Walker and White sts)
Tel. (212) 519-6600
or 877-519-6600
www.tribecagrand.com
Latest in elegant accommodation in eight-story atrium building from the same people responsible for the luxurious SoHo Grand. Convenient downtown location. There's a lobby restaurant and a large screening room downstairs.
▦

RESTAURANTS

BOULEY BAKERY & MARKET
◆ **B** D2
130 W. Broadway
(at Duane St)
Tel. (212) 608-5829
Bouley Bakery & Market, located directly across the street from the gastronomic Bouley Restaurant, is the latest, three-level venture to come from chef-owner David Bouley. You can shop for fish, cheese, quiches, homemade ice cream and more in the basement (to take out or eat on one of the tables outside) and buy bread at the bakery on the main floor. One floor up is a sushi bar, where the two chefs also mix delicious exotic cocktails (try the one with black truffles and fresh fruits), and the intimate Upstairs restaurant, where chef-owner David Bouley and his team regularly give cooking classes (call 219-1011 well in advance to reserve a place).
▥

BUBBY'S
◆ **B** D2
120 Hudson St
(at N. Moore St)
Tel. (212) 219-0666
Open until 3am Wed.–Sat.
Neighborhood restaurant, popular for breakfasts and country brunches on Sunday.
▥

CHANTERELLE
◆ **B** D2
2 Harrison St
(at Hudson St)
Tel. (212) 966-6960
Closed Sun. and Mon. lunch
An elegant, stately room with wide-spread tables and very serious food served with great reverence. The lunchtime set-price menus make this gastronomic restaurant affordable.
▥

DANUBE
◆ **B** D2
30 Hudson St
(at Duane St)
Tel. (212) 791-3771
David Bouley has created a gloriously beautiful, romantic and fun space for his

❶ < $20
❷ $21 to $34
❸ $35 to $49
❹ > $50

excellent Viennese cuisine: bone-marrow dumplings, braised beef cheeks and Wiener Schnitzel, of course.
⊞

THE HARRISON
◆ **B** D2
355 Greenwich St (at Harrison St)
Tel. (212) 274-9310
Chic meets down-home charm here and the food is seasonal American with a Mediterranean twist – cod with artichoke stew, calf's liver with an onion-bacon frittata. They offer more desserts than vegetables (pistachio semifredo, frozen banana mousse, green apple sorbet with cinnamon beignets), so you have no chance of leaving hungry.
⊞

NOBU
◆ **B** D2
105 Hudson St (at Franklin St)
Tel. (212) 219-0500
When chef Nobu Matsuhisa hit New York with his innovative Japanese-Peruvian nouvelle cuisine, it was an instant success – one food critic hailed him as 'perhaps the best Japanese chef in the world'. Reserve well in advance and if you cannot get a table here, try Nobu on 57th St (between 5th and 6th aves; tel 757-3000).
⊞

LE ZINC
◆ **B** D2
139 Duane St (between Church and W. Broadway)
Tel. (212) 513-0001
A casual, rather noisy bistro run by the team from the high-end Chanterelle. Delicious steak frites and roast chicken, Le Zinc has an excellent

wine list and can accommodate large groups.
❸

ODEON
◆ **B** D2
145 W. Broadway (between Duane and Thomas sts)
Tel. (212) 233-0507
Made famous by it's art-world clientele in the 1980's, it still attracts the terminally hip until late at night for its hamburgers, steak frites, or simply its huge martinis and a plate of oysters. The red banquets, tile floors and crowded tables haven't changed a whit, all of which keeps people coming back.
❸

FORLINI'S
◆ **B** D3
93 Baxter St (at Canal St)
Tel. (212) 349-6779
Forlini's serves traditional family cuisine from northern Italy. Try the homemade pasta.
❸

JOE'S SHANGAÏ
◆ **B** D3
9 Pell St (between Bowery and Mott St)
Tel. (212) 233-8888
Specialties include steamed buns (stuffed with pork or crab meat in steaming hot soup) and braised pork shoulder in malt sauce. It's overlit and rather tatty, like most Chinatown spots, but the line outside attests to the high-quality food and low prices. There's a new midtown location, at 24 W. 56th St, and the original in Flushing, Queens, but the Pell St Joe's is the most popular restaurant in Chinatown.
❷

MERCER HOTEL
◆ **B** C2
147 Mercer St (at Prince St)
Tel. (212) 966-6060 or 888-918-6060
www.mercerhotel.com
This hotel in the heart of Soho, favored by the worlds of fashion and show biz, has loft-style rooms with a minimalist décor and huge, well-designed, oversized bathrooms. The restaurant, Mercer Kitchen, is very popular.
❹

OFF SOHO SUITES
◆ **B** C3
11 Rivington St (between Chrystie and Bowery)
Tel. (212) 979-9808 or 1-800-633-7646
www.offsoho.com
Nestled on the border between SoHo and the trendy Lower East Side, this small hotel offers great value to match its location. Many rooms have kitchenettes, but there's a café as well.
❶

60 THOMPSON
◆ **B** C2
60 Thompson St (between Spring and Broome sts)
Tel. 877-431-0400
www.60thompson.com
This hotel caters to the film world and other creative types who make the bar off the lobby bustle. The taupe and beige rooms are spacious and the bathrooms, in brown marble, are gorgeous. Its rooftop bar, open in late spring and summer, has a 360-degree view over downtown. Don't miss the Thom bar and the restaurant, Kittichai, popular for its delicious Thai food.
❹

SOHO GRAND HOTEL
◆ **B** D2
310 West Broadway (between Canal and Grand sts)
Tel. (212) 965-3000 and 1-800-965-3000
Fax 212-965-3244
www.sohogrand.com
This is an unusual hotel in a magnificent cast-iron SoHo building with a transluscent staircase. The Soho Grand is the best place in New York to have breakfast but the huge bar is also well worth a visit. The 369 rooms and suites are modern and luxurious: the sheets are Bergamo, the mini-fridge is stocked by Dean & Deluca, and pet goldfish are available on request.
❹

RESTAURANTS

BALTHAZAR RESTAURANT AND BAKERY
◆ **B** C2
80 Spring St (between Broadway and Crosby St)
Tel. (212) 965-1414
Keith McNally's beautiful and authentic-looking French brasserie offers some of the city's best seafood, steak and French fries (and bread) in a lively, noisy setting of downtown trendsetters.
⊞

FANELLI'S CAFÉ
◆ **B** C2
94 Prince St (at Mercer St)
Tel. (212) 226-9412
This calm neighborhood burger and beer joint has been in business since 1872. A dark hideaway from the SoHo crowds on an afternoon, it becomes pretty raucous (and hard to get a table) in the evenings.
❷

⊡	< $100
⊡	$100 to $150
⊡	$150 to $200
⊞	> $200

HONMURA AN
◆ **B** C2
170 Mercer St
(between Houston
and Prince sts)
Tel. (212) 334-5253
*Great soba and udon
in an elegant, loft-like
space with perfect
service.*
⊞

JERRY'S
◆ **B** C2
101 Prince St
(at Greene St)
Tel. (212) 966-9464
Closed Sun. eve.
*Jerry's is a busy,
lively neighborhood
institution and a
favorite with SoHo
gallery owners,
where the delicious
sandwiches and
salads are whole
meals in themselves.*
⊡

OMEN
◆ **B** C2
113 Thompson St
(at Prince St)
Tel. (212) 925-8923
Closed lunch
*Traditional Kyoto
dishes in calm
atmosphere. Highly
recommended*
⊞

PROVENCE
◆ **B** C2
38 MacDougal St
(between Houston
and Prince sts)
Tel. (212) 475-7500
*A lively bistro, serving
authentic Provençal
cuisine. The garden is
a particular joy in
fine weather.*
⊞

LOWER EAST
SIDE
RESTAURANTS

BASSO EST
◆ **B** C3
198 Orchard St
(at Stanton St)
Tel. (212) 358-9469
*A low key hole in
the wall with
delicious Northern
Italian cuisine and
a very friendly
atmosphere.
Daily specials and the
best Bucatini All'*

*Amatriciana this side
of Rome.*
⊡

'INOTECA
◆ **B** C3
98 Rivington St
(at Ludlow St)
Tel. (212) 614-0473
*This stylishly rustic
Italian café serves
a variety of panini,
cheeses, sausages
and salad with more
than two hundred
wines to a young
and lively crowd.*
⊡

SCHILLER'S
◆ **B** C3
131 Rivington St
(at Norfolk St)
Tel. (212) 260-4555
*Keith McNally's noisy,
lively riff on French
working class bistro.
Great roasted
chicken and steak.
Not too pricey, but
sometimes too
crowded for comfort.*
⊡

**71 CLINTON FRESH
FOOD**
71 Clinton St
(between Rivington
and Stanton sts)
Tel. (212) 614-6960
*This is the restaurant
that started the
Lower East Side's
high-end restaurant
craze in 2000. Try the
braised sweetbread
and crayfish gratin
and the crispy skate
with sweet and sour
rhubarb. The original
chef, Wylie Dufresne
(who before that
worked at
Jean-Georges), has
left to open his own
restaurant, WD-50,
down the street
(see below).*
⊞

WD-50
◆ **B** C3
50 Clinton St
Tel. (212) 477 2900
www.wd-50.com
*A stylishly modern
restaurant serving
eclectic American
cuisine. The very
innovative dishes are
seasonal and include*

*shrimp couscous
with avocado, papaya
and crispy kaffir, or
mussel-olive oil soup
with coconut, water
chestnut and orange
powder as starters;
scallops with celery
noodles, hazelnut-
potato and pine
needle oil as a main
course. There is also
a nine-course tasting
menu.*
⊡

RESTAURANTS

BAO 111
◆ **B** B1
111 Ave. C (at 7th St)
212-254-7773
*A small, stylish
Vietnamese
restaurant that places
a premium on
innovative dishes and
excellent service.
Very popular with
East Village locals
and gourmands alike,
so book ahead if you
must have lobster
and lotus root salad
or frog legs in a spicy
lemongrass and
coconut curry sauce.*
⊡

ISO
◆ **B** B3
175 2nd Ave.
(at 11th St)
Tel. (212) 777-0361
*One of the finest
Japanese restaurants
in the city offering
really fresh sushi.
There's nothing
surprising about this
husband and wife-
run spot, but the
service and quality
have made a
neighborhood
institution.*
⊡

MERMAID INN
◆ **B** B3
96 2nd Ave. (between
5th and 6th sts)
Tel. (212) 674-5870
*A simply decorated
sea food spot that
makes an excellent
lobster roll. Reserve
in advance or you
might wait two hours
at the bar for a table.*
⊡

MITALI EAST
◆ **B** B3
334 E. 6th St
(between 1st
and 2nd aves)
Tel. (212) 533-2508
*The décor might be
uninteresting, but the
good northern Indian
cuisine has
unbeatable prices.
Brunch on Sundays.*
⊡

VESELKA
◆ **B** B3
144 2nd Ave.
(at 9th St)
Tel. (212) 228-9682
*An East Village
institution, this
Ukrainian blintz and
borscht spot is open
twenty four hours a
day and extremely
inexpensive.*
⊡

GREENWICH
VILLAGE
HOTELS

**THE HOTEL
GANSEVOORT**
◆ **B** B1
18 9th Ave.
(at 13th St)
Tel. (212) 206-6700
or 1-877-426-7386
Fax. (212) 255-5858
www.hotelgansevoort.
com
*A new, hyper-trendy
addition to the
Meatpacking District,
directly across the
street from Soho
House, the private
club. A heated
rooftop swimming
pool is open all year
round and has views
of the Hudson River.
There's an outdoor
bar that's popular in
summer, and a well-
regarded sushi
restaurant, Ono,
downstairs.*
⊞

THE MARITIME HOTEL
◆ **B** B1
363 W. 16th St
(at 9th Ave.)
Tel. (212) 242-4300
Fax (212) 242-1188
www.themaritimehote
com
*A new hotel just to
the north of the*

■ < $20
■ $21 to $34
■ $35 to $49
⊞ > $50

Meatpacking District that may be better known for its restaurants than its cramped rooms with porthole windows. Matsuri (see further down) is an elegant and pricey sushi spot, while La Bottega is a more casual bistro with a huge terrace that is invariably crowded on warm evenings. ▣

WASHINGTON SQUARE HOTEL
◆ **B** B2
103 Waverly Pl. (between 5th and 6th aves)
Tel. (212) 777-9515 or 1-800-222-0418
Fax (212) 979-8373
www.wshotel.com
Ideal for young travelers who are not too fussy about accommodation. In the heart of Greenwich Village. Reserve in advance. ▣

RESTAURANTS

BABBO
◆ **B** C2
110 Waverly Place (between 6th Ave. and MacDougal St)
Tel. (212) 777-0303
Black spaghetti with rock shrimp and spicy soppressata, beef-cheek ravioli and fennel-dusted sweetbreads are just three of chef-owner Mario Batali's creative Italian dishes. An unusual wine list and you must book well in advance. ⊞

BLUE RIBBON
◆ **B** C2
97 Sullivan St (between Prince and Spring sts)
Tel. (212) 274-0404
This restaurant is incredibly popular, with an excellent raw bar and serving American comfort food – cheese-burgers, rack of lamb,

---

hanger steak. No reservations are accepted, so you may wait up to two hours on a weekend, but the kitchen stays open until 4am, so you won't miss out. Also, Blue Ribbon Sushi, 119 Sullivan, serves some of the freshest fish available and has a huge sake menu, and the Blue Ribbon Bakery, at 33 Downing St, serves a delightful weekend brunch. ▣

CAFÉ LOUP
◆ **B** B1-2
105 W. 13th St (between 6th and 7th aves)
Tel. (212) 255-4746
Unpretentious and extremely popular with locals. Good bistro fare.

CORNER BISTRO
◆ **B** B1
331 W. 4th St (at Jane St)
Tel. (212) 242-9502
Famous for its specialty; juicy hamburgers with huge garnish for those with large appetites (and mouths!).

DA SILVANO
◆ **B** C2
260 6th Ave. (at Bleecker St)
Tel. (212) 982-2343
You may see famous faces from the worlds of fashion, film and art at this cozy, but pricey Italian café with a large outdoor area popular in summer. ⊞

ENNIO & MICHAEL
◆ **B** C2
539 La Guardia Pl. (at Bleecker St)
Tel. (212) 677-8577
Basic Italian dishes, such as fried zucchini, seafood salad, gnocchi in tomato sauce and

---

gamberi à la diable. Outdoor café in summer. ▣

GOTHAM BAR & GRILL
◆ **B** B2
12 E. 12th St (between 5th Ave. and University Place)
Tel. (212) 620-4020
Closed lunch Sat.–Sun.
This attractive restaurant is not to be missed, if only for the calf sweetbreads, the seafood salad and the lemon dessert. Fixed-price lunch menu. ⊞

HOME
◆ **B** C2
20 Cornelia St (at Bleecker St)
Tel. (212) 243-9579
Small restaurant in the West Village popular for its regional cuisine and the quality of its hamburgers. Even the ketchup is homemade. Brunch on the garden-terrace in summer. Reservations recommended. ▣

JOHN'S PIZZERIA
◆ **B** C2
278 Bleecker St (at 6th Ave.)
Tel. (212) 243-1680
The best Neapolitan pizza house—only whole pies sold—in Manhattan. Brunch. No credit cards. Other locations at 408 E. 61st, between 1st and York avenues, and 260 W. 44th St, between Broadway and 8th Avenue. No credit cards. ▣

MATSURI
◆ **B** B1
369 W. 16th St (at 9th Ave.)
Tel. (212) 243-6400
All eyes will be on you as you walk down the stairs into this glamorous room where paper lanterns

---

hang from the wood-ribbed ceiling. Try the black cod cooked in sake and the lotus root. Don't miss the celebrity clientele mixed in among the downtown crowd. Reservations necessary. ⊞

PASTIS
◆ **B** B1
9-11 Little W. 12th St (at 9th Ave.)
Tel. (212) 929-4844
The Meatpacking District's trendsetter, by Keith McNally who also brought New York Balthazar, in Soho. This French-style bistro has lower prices and a lower key than its Soho cousin. ▣

SPICE MARKET
◆ **B** B2
403 W. 13th St (at 9th Ave)
Tel. (212) 675 2322
Malaysian wall carvings, colonial furniture, teak floors and Vongerichten's nod to Vietnamese, Indian, Thai street food make this an exotic dining experience. Chicken samosas or chili-garlic egg noodles with shrimp are not to be missed. Book well in advance. ⊞

VILLAGE
◆ **B** B2
62 W. 9th St. (between 5th and 6th aves)
Tel. (212) 505-3355
A local standby, this bistro-style eatery serves a perfect steak-frites and interesting fish dishes. It has a lively bar and an airy dining room that is jammed every night. ▣

WALLSÉ
◆ **B** B1
344 W. 11th St (at Washington St)

◆ HOTELS AND RESTAURANTS

Gramercy area, Chelsea area

Tel. (212) 941-0142
This is a spare and small Austrian restaurant known for its nouvelle-style Wiener schnitzel and hip clientele.
⊡

GRAMERCY AREA
HOTELS

THE INN AT IRVING PLACE
◆ **B** A2
56 Irving Place
(between 17th and 18th sts)
Tel 212 533-4600 or 1-800-685-1447
Fax (212) 533-4611
www.innatirving.com
On a tree-lined street in the historic area of Gramercy Park, this small but luxurious and discreet hotel (the name is not displayed anywhere outside) is one of the most romantic in Manhattan. It occupies two adjacent townhouses dating from 1834. Only 12 exquisitely furnished rooms (period furniture, parquet flooring, fireplaces, four-poster beds), charming tea rooms (Lady Mendel Tea Salon), and a restaurant (Verbena) that offers new American cuisine and looks out onto the garden.
⊞

HOTEL 17
◆ **B** B3
225 E. 17th St
(between 2nd and 3rd aves.)
Tel. (212) 475-2845
Fax (212) 677-8178
www.hotel17ny.com
The early-20th-century ornaments and old elevator give this cheap hotel a certain retro atmosphere. That may explain why it is so popular among celebrities: Woody Allen shot Manhattan Murder Mystery and Madonna held a

photo session here. Its location, in the quiet area of Gramercy Park opposite Stuyvesant Park, is also excellent. The rooms have been renovated in a 1950's eclectic style.
⊡

W NEW YORK – UNION SQUARE
◆ **B** B2
201 Park Avenue South (at 17th St)
Tel. (212) 253-9119
www.starwoodhotels.com/whotels
A large, stylish hotel between Greenwich Village and Gramercy Park. With 24-hour concierge service and a pet spa, two restaurants and a large lobby bar, the W is a welcome addition to an area underserved by hotels. There are three other W Hotels in New York.
⊞

RESTAURANTS

CASA MONO
◆ **B** B2
52 Irving Place
(between 17th and 18th sts)
Tel. (212) 253-2773
Mario Batali's take on tapas. This is a tiny place, so expect a wait at the bar, but the small dishes are excellent as is the wine list.
⊡

CRAFT
◆ **B** A2
43 E. 19th St
(between Broadway and Park Avenue South)
Tel. (212) 780-0880
In a great looking, 19th century American space , innovative delicious cooking and simply one of the best restaurants in the city. Make reservations one month in advance. Also, next door at 47

E. 19th is Craftbar, a cheaper, but no less stellar, spin-off.
⊞

ELEVEN MADISON PARK
◆ **B** A2
11 Madison Ave.
(at 24th St)
Tel. (212) 889-0905
Closed Sun. lunch
Expensive but delicious Franco-American cuisine in a soaring, Deco setting, with black leather banquettes and two-story windows looking out at the park.
⊞

GRAMERCY TAVERN
◆ **B** A2
42 E. 20th St
(between Park Avenue South and Broadway)
Tel. (212) 477-0777
Eat this refined cuisine at the bar or in the main room. Remember to save space for the spectacular desserts. Reservations necessary.
⊞

PERIYALI
◆ **B** A2
35 W. 20th St
(between 5th and 6th aves)
Tel. (212) 463-7890
Closed Sat. lunch and Sun.
The most quietly elegant Greek restaurant in the city has a mean Feta and onion salad and barbecued octopus.
⊞

PUNCH
◆ **B** A2
913 Broadway
(between 20th and 21st sts)
Tel. (212) 673-6333
Reasonably-priced American fusion food in a cozy, lively neighborhood setting. You can also eat at the bar and don't miss the desserts.
⊡

TAMARIND
◆ **B** A2
41–43 E. 22nd St
(between Park Avenue South and Broadway)
Tel. (212) 674-7400
This sleek modern space is soothing for lunch and packed at dinner. Delicious traditional Indian cuisine with a twist including shrimp in chili masala and lamb marinated in lemon and garlic. Try their tea room next door.
⊞

UNION SQUARE CAFÉ
◆ **B** B2
21 E. 16th St
(between 5th Ave. and Union Square West)
Tel. (212) 243-4020
Closed Sun. lunch
Great salads, sandwiches, crispy lemon pepper duck are among the favorites at this very popular spot. Book in advance.
⊞

ZEN PALATE
◆ **B** B2
34 Union Square East (at E. 16th St)
Tel. (212) 614-9291
This restaurant serves some of the best vegetarian dishes in New York. Two other locations: 2170 Broadway, between 76th and 77th sts, and 663 9th Avenue, at 46th St.
⊡

CHELSEA AREA
RESTAURANTS

BOTTINO
◆ **B** A1
246 10th Ave.
(at 24th St)
Tel. (212) 206 6766
Closed Sun. and Mon. lunch
Located in a former hardware store, with a rustic décor, this Tuscan restaurant has a charming garden in the summer.
⊡

■ < $20
■ $21 to $34
■ $35 to $49
⊞ > $50

EMPIRE DINER
▲ 220 ◆ B A1
210 10th Ave.
(at 22nd St)
Tel. (212) 924-0011
Open 24 hours
Magnificent restored Art Deco monument. The menu has been designed for eclectic tastes, ranging from chicken wings, nachos and Chinese wontons to bacon, lettuce and tomato sandwiches and ice cream sundaes seasoned with chilli.
■

LA LUNCHONETTE
◆ B A1
130 10th Ave.
(at 18th St)
Tel. (212) 675-0342
This French bistro has a traditional menu menu: leek and lentil salad, snails in cognac, grilled lamb sausages and brains in black butter.
■

LOLA
◆ B A2
30 W. 22nd St
(between 5th and 6th aves)
Tel. (212) 675-6700
Closed Mon. lunch
Sample the Cajun-style onion-rings or 100-spiced chicken. The atmosphere tends to be noisy. Gospel brunch on Sundays.
■

LE MADRI
◆ B A1
168 W. 18th St
(at 7th Ave.)
Tel. (212) 727-8022
Delicious pizzas cooked in traditional wood-fired oven, imaginative pasta dishes and generous daytime specials.
⊞

THE PARK
◆ B B1
118 10th Ave.
(between 17th and 18th sts)
Tel. (212) 352-3313
A beautifully decorated spot with a lovely garden open in summer. A Mediterranean menu and a lively bar scene.
■

MIDTOWN EAST
HOTELS

BEEKMAN TOWER
◆ C C4
3 Mitchell Pl.
(49th St and 1st Ave.)
Tel. (212) 355-7300
or 1-800-ME-SUITE
Fax (212) 753-9366
www.mesuite.com
In a very pleasant neighborhood near the UN. Superb views from some of the rooms. Handy for families and long stays.
⊞

THE BENJAMIN HOTEL
◆ D B4
125 E. 50th St
(at Lexington Ave.)
Tel. (212) 715-2500
Fax (212) 715-2525
www.thebenjamin.com
All suites have office centers at this recently refurbished, quiet sanctuary in a 1927 Emery Roth-designed beauty. Choose from among ten types of pillow.
⊞

CROWNE PLAZA UN
▲ 264 ◆ C C4
304 E. 42nd St
(between 1st and 2nd aves)
Tel. (212) 986-8800
Fax (212) 986-1758
www.ichotelsgroup.com
A comfortable red-brick hotel in the business district, between Grand Central and the United Nations. Well-equipped rooms, business facilities, a sports club and a sauna.
⊞

70 PARK AVENUE HOTEL
◆ C D3
70 Park Ave.
(at 38th St)
Tel. (212) 973-2400
or 1-800-546-7866
Fax (212) 973-2479
www.70parkave.com
A chic hotel with an intimate, secluded atmosphere. Marble bathrooms and Scandinavian-style furniture. European clientele.
⊞

HOTEL ELYSÉE
◆ D B4
60 E. 54th St
(between Park and Madison aves)
Tel. (212) 753-1066
Reservations:
1-800-535-9733
Fax (212) 980-9278
www.elyseehotel.com
Small, well situated, luxurious hotel, well worth the relatively high prices. Marble and mahogany in the lobby, recently renovated rooms, conference rooms. Trendy bar-restaurant (Monkey Bar).
⊞

HOTEL QT
◆ D D1
125 W 45th St
Tel. (212) 354 2323
www.hotelqt.com
Andre Balazs' small, chic, ultramodern budget hotel with platform or bunk beds in the 140 rooms, Egyptian cotton sheets, a pool with underwater music and instead of room service, take-out fliers from local restaurants.
■

FOUR SEASONS
◆ D A4
57 E. 57th St
(between Madison and Park aves.)
Tel. (212) 758-5700
Fax (212) 758-5711
www.fourseasons.com/newyorkfs
A grand-scale hotel designed by I.M. Pei in 1993 (who also designed the glass pyramid by the Louvre museum in Paris) and decorated with exquisite materials (onyx and sycamore wood) in predominantly neutral tones. Breathtaking views over the city from rooms in this 52-story hotel. Restaurant: the FiftySevenFiftySeven.
⊞

HELMSLEY MIDDLETOWNE
◆ C C3
148 E. 48 St
(between Lexington and 3rd aves)
Tel. (212) 755-3000
or 1-800-221-4982
Fax (212) 832-0261
www.helmsleyhotels.com
Simple but spacious rooms, some with kitchenettes.
■

LOMBARDY HOTEL
◆ C B3
111 E. 56th St
(between Park and Lexington aves.)
Tel. (212) 753-8600
or 1-800-223-5254
Fax (212) 754-5683
www.lombardyhotel.com
A small boutique hotel built in 1926 with all the amenities of the major hotels – restaurants, a cigar bar, microwave ovens in the room – at a lower price.
⊞

MORGANS HOTEL NEW YORK
◆ C D3
237 Madison Ave.
(between 37th and 38th sts)
Tel. (212) 686-0300
Fax (212) 779-8352
Reservations
(800) 606-6090
www.morganshotel.com
A quiet hotel near the Empire State building and named for the Pierpont Morgan library, one block north. Asia de Cuba is a restaurant popular with visiting Hollywood types, but the intermittent crowds don't spoil the restrained elegance of the

◆ HOTELS AND RESTAURANTS

André Putnam-designed gem.
▦

NEW YORK PALACE HOTEL
▲ 284 ◆ **D** C3
455 Madison Ave.
(at 50th St)
Tel. (212) 888-7000
or 1-800-NY-PALACE
Fax (212) 303-6000
http://newyorkpalace.com
Totally renovated and owned by the Sultan of Brunei, this very beautiful hotel is located in the former Villard Houses designed by the architect Stanford White. Restaurants (Le Cirque 2000 and Istana).
▦

OMNI BERKSHIRE PLACE
◆ **D** B3
21 E. 52nd St
(between 5th and Madison aves)
Tel. (212) 753-5800
or 1-800-843-6664
Fax (212) 754-5018
www.omnihotels.com
Large, comfortable rooms in a well-situated hotel. Friendly service.
▦

PICKWICK ARMS HOTEL
◆ **C** C3–4
230 E. 51st St
(between 2nd and 3rd aves)
Tel. (212) 355-0300
Fax (212) 755-5029
www.pickwickarms.com
Basic comforts and services at very competitive prices.
▣/▣

ROGER SMITH
◆ **D** C4
501 Lexington Ave.
(at 47th St)
Tel. (212) 755-1400
or 1-800-445-0277
Fax (212) 758-4061
www.rogersmith.com
Renovated hotel, with a friendly atmosphere. Piano-r decorated with mic strips.

ROOSEVELT HOTEL
◆ **D** D3
45 E. 45th St (at Madison Ave.)
Tel. (212) 661-9600
Fax (212) 885-6161
Reservations:
1-888-TEDDY-NY
www.theroosevelthotel.com
Opened in 1924, this beautiful neo-Renaissance hotel, named after President Theodore Roosevelt, has just been scrupulously restored. The huge lobby with its columns and the Palm Room with its decorated ceiling are particularly stunning. Two restaurants, Madison Cigar Bar Lounge (restaurant-bar) and Teddy's Table (American food).
▦

ST REGIS
▲ 288 ◆ **D** B3
2 E. 55th St
(between 5th and Madison aves)
Tel. (212) 753-4500
or 1-800-325-3535
Fax (212) 787-3447
www.starwood.com/stregis
In a 1904 edifice built by Jacob Astor and restored at great cost, the St Regis is one of the most opulent hotels in the city. Financial information service and secretarial facilities. Majordomo attached to each floor.
▦

SWISSHOTEL DRAKE PARK AVENUE
◆ **C** B3
440 Park Ave.
(at 56th St)
Tel. (212) 421-0900
Fax (212) 371-4190
http://newyork.swissotel.com
A stately, quiet hotel popular with business travellers. With more than 400 rooms and 100 suites, this hotel will meet the needs of any executive with an expense account.

The French chocolate shop Fauchon is connected to the lobby and has a café.
▦

VANDERBILT YMCA
◆ **C** C3-4
224 E. 47th St
(between 2nd and 3rd aves)
Tel. (212) 756-9600
Fax (212) 752-0210
www.ymcanyc.org/ygny/index.html
For the over 18's. Friendly, up-beat atmosphere. Shared bathroom facilities.
▣

WALDORF ASTORIA & THE WALDORF TOWERS
▲ 285 ◆ **D** C4
301 Park Ave.
(between 49th and 50th sts)
Tel. (212) 355-3000 or 1-800-WALDORF
Fax (212) 872-7272
www.waldorfastoria.com
World-famous. The building dating back to 1931 has been restored and now basks in its original elegance. Each of the rooms has a different décor. Very good Japanese restaurant.
▦

▬▬▬ **RESTAURANTS** ▬▬▬

AQUAVIT
◆ **C** B3
65 E. 55th St
(between Park and Madison aves)
Tel. (212) 307-7311
Nouvelle-Scandinavian cuisine includes a mini-lobster roll, lemon cured duck breast and in the café, diced sirloin with onion and a raw egg and open-faced sandwiches. All in a stark new setting.
▦

BLT STEAK
◆ **C** B3
106 E. 57th St
(between Park and Lexington aves)
Tel. (212) 752-7470
Chef Laurent Tourandel whips up

40 oz. Porterhouse (for two), Kobe beef, salads, and three-pound lobsters in a room done in suede and mahogany. The desserts should not be missed.
▦

BRASSERIE
◆ **C** C3
100 E. 53rd St
(between Park and Lexington aves)
Tel. (212) 751-4840
This sleek and translucent green modern space in the Seagram Building, offers an imaginative and delicious take on classic bistro fare.
▦

DAWAT
◆ **C** B3-4
210 E. 58th St
(between 2nd and 3rd aves)
Tel. (212) 355-7555
Closed Sun. lunch
Indian actress and cook book writer Madhur Jaffrey has overseen the traditional menu of this well-located midtown Indian restaurant.
▣

FOUR SEASONS
▲ 286 ◆ **D** B4
99 E. 52nd St
(between Lexington and Park aves)
Tel. (212) 754-9494
Closed Sat. lunch and Sun.
This now iconic space designed by Philip Johnson includes the Grill Room, popular for high-powered business lunches and the Pool Room which is, however, more romantic.
▦

LA GRENOUILLE
◆ **D** B3
3 E. 52nd St
(between 5th and Madison aves)
Tel. (212) 752-1495
Closed Sun.
Perfect, old-fashioned service,

superb, classic French cooking in one of the most elegant rooms in the city filled with giant flower arrangements. Expensive and need to reserve.
⊞

GUASTAVINO'S
◆ **C** B4
409 E. 59th St
(between 1st and York aves)
Tel. (212) 980-2455
Built under the 59th St Bridge and named after the designer of the elaborate brick work that makes up the beautiful ceiling, this lively Terence Conran restaurant has a good menu but so-so service.
⊞

LEVER HOUSE RESTAURANT
◆ **C** C3
390 Park Ave.
(at 53rd St)
Tel. (212) 888-2700
Marc Newsom designed this futuristic-looking space in the celebrated 1952 Gordon Bunschaft modernist landmark building (you'll never find the bathroom on your own). Dan Silverman's seafood dishes are inventive – and expensive. Try the lobster tails in saffron sauce with root vegetables or the black trumpet mushroom risotto. But leave some room for the warm chocolate cake with coffee ice cream.
⊞

OYSTER BAR
▲ 239 ◆ **D** D4
Grand Central Station, Lower Level
Tel. (212) 490-6650
Closed Sun.
This dramatic and cavernous underground space under Grand Central station is famous for its exceptionally fresh fish and

seafood dishes.
⊞

PALM
◆ **C** C4
837 2nd Ave.
(at 44th St)
Tel. (212) 687-2953
Closed Sat. lunch and Sun.
This sawdust-on-the-floor quintessential American steakhouse offers giant portions of steak, chicken, lobster, onion rings and cheesecake. Book in advance.
⊞

PETROSSIAN
◆ **C** B2
182 W. 58th St
(at 7th Ave.)
Tel. (212) 245-2214
This restaurant's claim to fame is its excellent caviar and smoked salmon (which are also on sale to take out). The lunch menus are more reasonably priced.
⊞

P.J. CLARKE'S
◆ **C** B3
915 3rd Ave.
(at 55th St)
Tel. (212) 317-1616
A lively bar, simple menu, checkered tablecloths and wood floors as well as the best hamburgers in town have made this East Side institution popular with celebrities and locals alike.

ROSA MEXICANO
◆ **C** B4
1063 1st Ave.
(at 58th St)
Tel. (212) 753-7407
Closed for lunch
This favorite is famous for its guacamole prepared in front of the clients. Incredible chilli-and-chocolate dessert.
❑

SARGE'S DELI
◆ **C** D3
548 3rd Ave.

(at 36th St)
Tel. (212) 679-0442
Open daily 24 hours
This Murray Hill deli takes care of big appetites at any hour of the day with huge pastrami sandwiches and enormous bowls of chicken soup.
❑

SHUN LEE PALACE
◆ **D** B4
155 E. 55th St
(at Lexington Ave.)
Tel. (212) 371-8844
The wonderful Cantonese dishes make up for the fact that you are being jostled on all sides as you eat.
⊞

SMITH & WOLLENSKY
◆ **C** C3
797 3rd Ave.
(at 49th St)
Tel. (212) 753-1530
Typical New York fare (steaks and lobster). Wide selection of fine wines.
❑

SPARKS STEAKHOUSE
◆ **C** C3-4
210 E. 46th St
(between 2nd and 3rd aves)
Tel. (212) 687-4855
Closed Sat. lunch and Sun.
One of the best steakhouses in New York, also famous for being the restaurant outside of which mob boss Paul Castellano was shot and killed by John Gotti.
⊞

SUSHI YASHUDA
◆ **C** C3-4
204 E. 43rd St
(between 2nd and 3rd aves)
Tel. (212) 972-1001
Closed Sun.
In this elegant floor-to-ceiling bamboo-covered space with an airy feel you'll have the best sushi you've ever tasted. Fresh and exotic fish flown in from around the world. Eat at the

sushi bar near chef Yasuda.
⊞

VONG
◆ **C** C3
200 E. 54th St
(at 3rd Ave.)
Tel. (212) 486-9592
Closed Sat. lunch and Sun.
Virtuoso chef-owner Jean-Georges Vongerichten combines French and Thai cuisine to create sophisticated and exotic dishes created in a stunning setting. You should book well in advance.
⊞

ZARELA
◆ **O** C4
953 2nd Ave.
(at 50th St)
Tel. (212) 644-6740
Closed Sat. and Sun. lunch
Owner-chef Zarela Martínez is often around in this crowded and popular spot serving traditional Mexican food.
❑

▬ MIDTOWN WEST ▬

▬ HOTELS ▬

ALGONQUIN HOTEL
▲ 252 ◆ **D** D3
59 W. 44th St
(between 5th and 6th aves)
Tel. (212) 840-6800
or 1-888-304-2047
Fax (212) 944-1618
www.thealgonquin.net
A host of writers have stayed here, assuring its fame. The worlds of literature and publishing still use this hotel. Renovated in 1996. Small rooms with an Edwardian décor.
⊞

CASABLANCA HOTEL
◆ **C** C2
147 W. 43rd St
(between 6th Ave. and Broadway)
Tel. (212) 869-1212 or
1-888-299-7225
www.casablancahotel.com/index3.htm

Situated in the heart of Times Square, this hotel has a Moroccan-style décor. Continental breakfast included.
⊞

CHAMBERS
◆ **C** B3
11 W. 56th St
(between 5th and
6th aves)
Tel. (212) 974-5656
Fax. (212) 974-5657
www.chambershotel.
com
A boutique hotel ideally located close to MoMA and Central Park. The rooms and public spaces are lined with original art and the beautifully designed restaurant, Town, which serves contemporary French cuisine, was given three stars by the New York Times.
⊞

CITY CLUB HOTEL
◆ **C** C3
55 W. 44th St
(between 5th and
6th aves)
Tel. (212) 921-5500
Fax (212) 944-5544
www.cityclubhotel.com
A luxury hotel with 65 well-appointed rooms and two duplex suites with terraces. Daniel Boulud's chic restaurant, DB Bistro Moderne, serves a famous (or infamous) foie gras, short rib, and truffle-stuffed burger (see further down under 'restaurants').
⊞

DOUBLETREE GUEST SUITES TIMES SQUARE
◆ **D** C2
1568 Broadway
(at 47th St)
Tel. (212) 719-1600
Fax (212) 921-5212
Reservations:
1-800-222-TREE
www.doubletree.com
Well equipped for business people and practical for families. Two-room

suites fitted with self-catering facilities. Its Kid's Club organizes artistic and craft activities as well as guided tours.
⊞

EDISON HOTEL
◆ **D** C1-2
228 W. 47th St
(between Broadway
and 8th Ave.)
Tel. (212) 840-5000
or 1-800 637-7070
Fax (212) 596-6850
www.edisonhotelnyc.
com
Cheap hotel in Art Deco style building near Times Square. Spacious rooms.
⊡

ESSEX HOUSE
▲ 303 ◆ **D** A2
160 Central Park
South (between 6th
and 7th aves)
Tel. (212) 247 0300
Fax (212) 315 1839
www.starwood.com/
westin
Elegant Art Deco building, opposite Central Park. Luxurious rooms with superb views over the park. Two good restaurants.
⊞

THE GORHAM
◆ **D** B2
136 W. 55th St
(between 6th
and 7th aves)
Tel. (212) 245-1800
or 1-800-735-0710
www.gorhamhotel.
com
Intimate and congenial atmosphere. Art Deco style. Suites for families.
⊡

HELMSLEY PARK LANE
◆ **D** A3
36 Central Park
South (between 5th
and 6th aves)
Tel. (212) 371-4000
or 1-800-221-4982
Fax (212) 750-7279
www.helmsley
hotels.com
Breathtaking view over Central Park from the upper floors

of this 46-story hotel. Bright rooms. Pleasant hotel restaurant. This is also the home of the celebrated Harry's Bar.
⊞

CROWNE PLAZA TIMES SQUARE MANHATTAN
◆ **D** C2
1605 Broadway
(at 49th St)
Tel. (212) 977-4000
or 1-800-243-NYNY
Fax (212) 333-7393
www.ichotels.com
Traditional rooms, some with an unbeatable view of Times Square.
⊞

THE HUDSON
◆ **C** B2
356 West 58th Street
(between 8th and
9th aves)
Tel. (212) 554-6000
Fax (212) 554-6001
Reservations
(800) 606-6090
www.hudsonhotel.com
A raucous yet affordable hotel designed within an inch of its life by Philippe Starck. Small rooms and spotty service, but the hotel has beautiful public areas, its own park and a restaurant. The bar alone is worth a visit for the glowing glass floor that illuminates the amazing ceiling painting by Francesco Clemente.
⊞

MILLENNIUM BROADWAY
◆ **D** D2
145 W. 44th St
(between 6th and
7th aves)
Tel. (212) 768-4400
or 1-866-858-9973
www.millennium
hotels.com
A huge hotel complex with 625 rooms, conference center, theater, fitness center, boutique, and restaurant of repute.

Small but stylish and well-equipped rooms.
⊞

MODERNE
◆ **D** B1
243 W. 55th St
(between Broadway
and 8th Ave.)
Tel. (212) 397-6767 or
1-888-66-HOTEL
Fax (212) 397-8787
www.nychotels.com
Small, new hotel, pleasantly decorated, located in an old building. Room rate includes breakfast.
⊞

NOVOTEL NEW YORK
◆ **D** B1-2
226 W. 52nd St
(between 8th Ave.
and Broadway)
Tel. (212) 315-0100
or 1 800-668-6835
Fax (212) 765-5365
www.novotel.com
Ideal location for theatergoers. Large, clean rooms, some with a view over the Hudson River.
⊡

PARAMOUNT
◆ **D** C1-2
235 W. 46 St
(between 8th Ave.
and Broadway)
Tel. (212) 764-5500
or 1-800-225-7474
Fax (212) 354-5237
www.solmelia.com
A Renaissance-style building from the early 1900's cleverly redesigned by Philippe Starck. Discount rates in this high style make the Paramount a singular hotel in the city. There's a restaurant on the mezzanine level and the popular Whiskey Bar.
⊞

PARKER MÉRIDIEN
▲ 302 ◆ **D** A2
118 W. 57th St
(between 6th
and 7th aves)
Tel. (212) 245-5000
or 1-800-543-4300
www.parkermeridien.
com
This well-located

■ < $20
■ $21 to $34
■ $35 to $49
⊞ > $50

midtown hotel has modern rooms that were refurbished in 2001. There is a fitness center, a swimming pool on the top floor, and three restaurants.
⊞

PENINSULA
◆ **D** B3
700 5th Ave.
(at 55th St)
Tel. (212) 956-2888 or 1-800-262-946
Fax (212) 903-3949
www.peninsula.com/choice
This luxurious hotel, in the heart of of the 5th Avenue shopping district and very near MoMA, dates from the turn of the 20th century. Small rooms decorated in the Beaux-Arts style, some of which look out onto St Patrick's Cathedral. Fitness center and rooftop swimming pool. Fantastic views of the midtown skyscrapers from the bar.
⊞

RENAISSANCE NEW YORK HOTEL
◆ **D** C2
714 7th Ave.
(at 48th St)
Tel. (212) 765-7676 or 1-800-628-5222
www.renaissance hotels.com
In the middle of the theatre district, there are unbeatable views of Times Square from some of the rooms of this tower of gleaming black glass. The huge bay windows of the dining room also offer stunning views. Quiet, spacious and elegant rooms.
⊞

RIHGA ROYAL HOTEL
◆ **D** B2
151 W. 54th St
(between 6th and 7th aves)
Tel. (212) 307-5000 or 1-866-656-1777
Fax (212) 765-6530
www.rihgaroyalny.com

Luxury, comfort and service are the trademarks of this all-suite hotel. Fitness and business centers, round-the-clock room-service, multilingual staff and superb restaurant. There are panoramic views from most of the rooms and the hotel is popular with the hip-hop set.
⊞

ROYALTON
▲ 252 ◆ **D** D2-3
44 W. 44th St
(between 5th and 6th aves)
Tel. (212) 869 4400 or 1-800-606-6090
www.royalton.com
Philippe Starck used cobalt-blue carpeting, polished green granite and steel to create a cutting-edge look for this hotel. Rooms are small but efficient and the restaurant stays open late.
⊞

SHERATON NEW YORK and **SHERATON MANHATTAN**
◆ **D** B2
811 and 790 7th Ave.
(between 51st and 53rd sts)
Sheraton New York:
Tel. (212) 581-1000
Fax (212) 262-4410
Sheraton Manhattan:
Tel. (212) 581-3300
Fax (212) 541-9219
Reservations:
1-800-598-1753
www.starwood.com/sheraton
There is nothing special about these hotels, sited opposite one another, sharing the same management. They have comfortable, spacious rooms, but the look is ordinary. Fitness center, swimming pool and three restaurants.
■

THE WARWICK
◆ **D** B2
65 W. 54th St
(at 6th Ave.)

Tel. (212) 247-2700 or 1-800-203-3232
Fax (212) 247-2725
www.warwick hotelny.com
Comfortable hotel in a good location. Large but rather gloomy rooms. The restaurant, Murals on 54, serves traditional food, but has murals by Dean Cornwell (restored in 2004) that depict Sir Walter Raleigh's travails. One was covered for 40 years as it was considered obscene.
⊞

WOLCOTT HOTEL
◆ **C** D3
4 West 31st St
(between 5th and 6th aves)
Tel. (212) 268-2900
Fax (212) 563-0008
www.wolcott.com
This bargain just a few blocks from the Empire State Building has surprisingly large rooms for the price as well as a fitness and business center.
■

BECCO
◆ **D** C1
355 W. 46th St
(between 8th and 9th aves)
Tel. (212) 397-7597
A trattoria where the pastas change daily, there is a bargain fixed-price menu with wine, making this a popular pre-theater stand-by.
■

LE BERNARDIN
◆ **D** C2
155 W. 51st St
(between 6th and 7th aves)
Tel. (212) 489-1515
Closed Sat. lunch and Sun.
This superb, rather corporate-looking but comfortable French restaurant specializes in fish and seafood dishes—some raw—now under the direction of its expert

chef Éric Ripert. Perfect service. Jacket required.
⊞

BISTRO DU VENT
◆ **C** C2
411 W. 42nd St
(between 9th and 10th aves)
Tel. (212) 239-3060
A reasonably priced French-style bistro from Mario Batali that packs in the pre-and post-theater crowds.
■

BRYANT PARK GRILL & CAFÉ
◆ **C** D3
Bryant Park,
(25 W. 40th St)
Tel. (212) 840-6500
An oasis in the heart of midtown Manhattan. The café, only open in the summer and cheaper than the grill, is a restaurant-terrace overlooking the park.
■

CARNEGIE DELI
◆ **D** B2
854 7th Ave.
(between 54th and 55th sts)
Tel. (212) 757-2245
Open daily until 4am
If you can ignore the offhand service, the noise and crowds, then you'll enjoy the enormous sandwiches, frankfurters, hamburgers and fries. No credit cards.
■

DB BISTRO MODERNE
◆ **C** C3
55 W. 44th St
(between 5th and 6th aves)
Tel. (212) 391-2400
Perfect for before or after theater and known for its extravagant $30 hamburger – that includes braised short ribs, foie gras, and black truffles – this attractive bistro is Daniel Boulud's (see also Daniel, page 387) newest outpost.
■

385

ESCA
◆ **C** C2
402 W. 43rd St
(at 9th Ave.)
Tel. (212) 564-7272
Closed Sun. lunch
This serious Italian
restaurant, the
brainchild of chef
owner Mario Batali,
offers exquisite fish
dishes in a simple
modern setting.
Reservations
necessary.
⬛

ESTIATORIO MILOS
◆ **C** B3
125 W. 55th St
(between 5th and 6th
aves)
Tel. (212) 245-7400
In this modern take
on a Greek
restaurant, you may
see a few famous
faces at dinner in
this beautiful, airy,
loft like space which
offers exceptional
fish and meats.
▦

GALLAGHER'S
STEAK HOUSE
◆ **D** B1-2
228 W. 52nd St
(between Broadway
and 8th Ave.)
Tel. (212) 245-5336
Authentic rustic
décor with sawdust
on the floor, red-and-
white check
tablecloths and a
huge mahogany bar.
▦

IPANEMA
◆ **D** C2-3
13 W. 46th St
(between 5th
and 6th aves)
Tel. (212) 730-5848
Delicious Brazilian
cuisine at reasonable
prices. The best of a
number of Brazilian
places along 46th St.
⬛

JEKYLL & HYDE
◆ **D** A2
1409 Ave. of the
Americas (between
57th and 58th sts)
Tel. (212) 541-9505
A multi-floor
funhouse of a
restaurant with an
animated décor of
smoke machines and
coffins hanging from
the ceiling, low
lighting and sound
effects. There are
over 250 types of
beer.
⬛

JOE ALLEN
◆ **D** C1
326 W. 46th St
(between 8th
and 9th aves)
Tel. (212) 581-6464
For a quick bite
before or after a
show. Hamburgers
and spare ribs of
pork often served
by aspiring actors
in this cozy, simple
classic.
⬛

KOI
◆ **C** D3
40 W. 40th St
(between 5th and
6th aves)
Tel. (212) 921-3330
Trendy Japanese
eatery in the Bryant
Park Hotel, above a
nightclub. Fresh
sushi, black cod, and
delicious soft shell
crab in season are
excellent lunch-time
choices. Dinner is
crowded and loud.
▦

MCHALE'S
◆ **C** C2
750 8th Ave.
(at 46th St)
Tel. (212) 997-8885
Hell's Kitchen's place
of choice for a burger
and a beer. Eat at the
bar and watch the
ball game, or sit in
the back dining room
and... watch the ball
game.
⬛

MICHAELS
◆ **C** B3
24 W. 55th St
(between 5th and 6th
aves)
Tel. 212) 767-0555
At least as well
known for the high
wattage media mogul
lunchtime clientele as
it's menu, this "new
American" is really
quite good. You must
reserve.
▦

MOLYVOS
◆ **C** B2
871 7th Ave. (between
55th and 56th sts)
Tel. (212) 582-7500
A popular and not
cheap Greek
restaurant right near
Carnegie Hall with a
traditional menu with
– flaming saganaki,
grilled octopus – and
more adventurous
options, like crab
kefte and lamb ravioli.
▦

ORSO
◆ **D** C1
322 W. 46th St
(between 8th
and 9th aves)
Tel. (212) 489-7212
Delicious pasta,
pizza, salads and
game in a cozy room
make this the most
popular restaurant in
the Theater District.
Book in advance.
▦

PLANET HOLLYWOOD
◆ **C** C2
1540 Broadway
(at 45th St)
Tel. (212) 840-8326
The food is certainly
not the major
attraction here, but
the décor – movie
memorabilia – and
the atmosphere are
what makes this
place so popular.
⬛

SEA GRILL
◆ **C** C3
19 W. 49th St
(between 5th
and 6th aves)
Tel. (212) 332-7610
The Sea Grill is a very
attractive restaurant
that looks out onto
the ice-skating rink at
Rockefeller Center.
Seafood is the
specialty, and the
wine list is splendid.
▦

TRATTORIA DELL'ARTE
▲ 301 ◆ **D** A-B2
900 7th Ave.
(between 56th
and 57th sts)
Tel. (212) 245-9800
A perfect place to go
before or after a
concert at Carnegie
Hall. Burnt plaster
body parts hang on
the wall and there's a
fabulous antipasti
buffet.
▦

21 CLUB
▲ 287 ◆ **D** B2-3
21 W. 52nd St
(between 5th and 6th
aves)
Tel. (212) 582-7200
Closed Sat. lunch
and Sun.
Amusing décor of old
toys – planes, trains,
cars, trucks among
them – hang from the
ceiling of the Bar
Room in this former
speak easy beloved
by society and
celebrities alike.
Delicious game, fish
and pasta.
▦

UPPER EAST SIDE
HOTELS

CARLYLE
▲ 312 ◆ **C** A3
35 E. 76th St
(at Madison Ave.)
Tel. (212) 744-1600
or 1-888-ROSEWOOD
www.thecarlyle.com
One of the best
hotels in New York.
All rooms are in
exquisite taste.
Renowned for its
afternoon tea and the
evening cabaret
singing. The
Bemelman Bar is
charming and there
is an excellent
restaurant, Dumonet.
▦

LOWELL
◆ **C** B3
28 E. 63 St
(at Madison Ave.)
Tel. (212) 838-1400
or 1-800-745-8883
www.lhw.com
An extremely
romantic, small hotel
in a quiet residential
area near all the
Madison Avenue
shops. Many rooms
come with books,

and many have a wood-burning fireplace. All are done in great taste.
⊞

MARK
◆ **C** A3
25 E. 77th St
(at Madison Ave.)
Tel. (212) 744-4300
or 1-800-THE-MARK
Fax (212) 744-2749
www.mandarin
oriental.com/themark
Outside, Art Deco elements. Inside, antiques, paintings, architectural drawings. Elegant and comfortable rooms, impeccable service and a very good restaurant make this hotel one of the best in New York.
⊞

PIERRE
▲ 132 ◆ **D** A3
2 E. 61st St
(at 5th Ave.)
Tel. (212) 838-8000
or 1-800-PIERRE-4
www.fourseasons.
com/pierre
A high tower dating back to 1930, it has been restored in traditional style. Inlaid furniture, antiques and duvets in each room. One of the great New York classics for 70 years running.
⊞

HOTEL PLAZA ATHÉNÉE
◆ **C** B3
37 E. 64th St
(between Madison and Park aves)
Tel. (212) 734-9100
or 1-800-447-8800
www.plaza-
athenee.com
This small hotel on a residential street has a style similar to that of the Carlyle. Rooms are done with French furniture. There is excellent French gourmet cuisine in the stylish restaurant, Arabelle. Possibly the most elegant of New York's small hotels.
⊞

REGENCY HOTEL
◆ **D** A4
540 Park Ave. (at 61st St)
Tel. (212) 759-4100
or 1-800-235-6397
www.loewshotels.
com/hotels/newyork
Redone in 1999, this hotel is walking distance from midtown. It has comfortable rooms and is ideal for business breakfasts or cocktails.
⊞

SURREY HOTEL
◆ **E** D3
20 E. 76th St
(between 5th and Madison aves)
Tel. (212) 288-3700
or 1-800-ME-SUITE
Fax (212) 628-1549
www.mesuite.com
Mainly suites with self-catering facilities. There are secretarial services, fax and modems for use by guests on business and sofa-beds for families. Negotiable weekly rates.
⊞

HOTEL WALES
◆ **E** C3
1295 Madison Ave.
(between 92nd and 93rd sts)
Tel. (212) 876-6000 or 1-866-WALES-HOTEL
www.waleshotel.com
Restored to its original Edwardian style. This hotel has a friendly, relaxed atmosphere. It has two popular restaurants and one, Sarabeth's, is perfect for brunches and for lunch or dinner.
⊞

RESTAURANTS

AURÉOLE
◆ **D** A3-4
34 E. 61st St
(between Madison and Park aves)
Tel. (212) 319-1660
Closed Sat. lunch and Sun.
Gastronomic treat in a townhouse duplex. Splendid floral arrangements and an equally magnificent menu devised by Charlie Palmer. Impeccable service.
⊞

BISTRO DU NORD
◆ **E** C3
1312 Madison Ave.
(at 93rd St)
Tel. (212) 289-0997
Bustling, congenial atmosphere in a cozy space. Highly inventive brasserie dishes.
✿

DANIEL
◆ **C** B3
60 E. 65th St
(between Madison and Park aves)
Tel. (212) 288-0033
Closed Sun.
You can drink great wines with your guinea hen terrine with pickled chanterelles or Peeky Toe crab salad and fricassee of Dover sole at this sanctuary of Lyonnais French chef Daniel Boulud. The talented chef also runs Café Boulud (20 E. 76th St, tel. (212) 772 2600), which is not as expensive, and DB Moderne (see page 385).
⊞

DAVID BURKE & DONATELLA
◆ **D** A4 or **C** B3
133 E. 61st St
(between Park and Lexington aves)
Tel. (212) 813-2121
Home of the "angry lobster" and a pretzel-coated crab cake at this new upscale American also offers an idling limousine in winter for its guests in need of a cigarette.
⊞

EAT GOURMET CAFÉ
◆ **E** D3
1064 Madison Ave.
(at 80th St)
Tel. (212) 772-0022
At this east-side outpost of Zabar's (◆ 394), a selection of salads and delicious bread to take out or eat in. Ideal for lunch or brunch.
✿

HARRY CIPRIANI
◆ **D** A3
781 5th Ave.
(between 59th and 60th sts) at the Sherry Netherland Hotel
Tel. (212) 753-5566
This branch of Venice's legendary Harry's Bar is a true institution in fashionable New York circles. The dishes are simple and delicious but expensive.
⊞

JO JO
◆ **C** B3
160 E. 64th St
(between Lexington and 3rd aves)
Tel. (212) 223-5656
Closed Sat. lunch and Sun.
Located on two floors in a beautiful townhouse, this was Jean-Georges Vongerichten's first restaurant in New York. The chef continues to offer delicious French-inspired dishes with dazzling flavor.
⊞

MISS SAIGON
◆ **E** D3
1425 3rd Ave.
(at 81st St)
Tel. (212) 988-8828
Good Vietnamese cuisine in a simple setting.
✿

PAPAYA KING
◆ **E** D3
179 E. 86th St
(at 3rd Ave.)
Tel. (212) 369-0648
The strange combination of hot dogs, washed down with papaya juice, invented in the 1930's, has become a real New York tradition. Note that credit cards are not accepted. Other

branches of Papaya King are at 225 W. 43rd St and 121 W. 125th St.
🖰

PARK AVENUE CAFÉ
◆ C B3
100 E 63rd St
(at Park Ave.)
Tel. (212) 644-1900
Highly imaginative vertical nouvelle cuisine in a pretty room.
🎴

SERAFINA
◆ C B3
29 E. 61st St
(between Madison and Park aves)
Tel. (212) 702-9898
A lively, young and popular place for standard spot Italian fare, known as much for its fun rooftop terrace dining as for its pizza and pasta.
🃏

SETTE MEZZO
◆ C A3
969 Lexington Ave.
(between 70th and 71st sts)
Tel. (212) 472-0400
This neighborhood spot has quick service and a delicious menu with many specials. No credit cards.
🎴

VIA QUADRONNO
◆ C A3
25 E. 73rd St
(between Madison and 5th aves)
Tel. 212 650-9880
This tiny, authentic Milanese restaurant has what many people claim to be the best espresso in New York, as well as delicious, made-to-order Italian paninis and, in the summer, a stand outside selling homemade sorbet. The Via Quadronno is always lively and full of locals – and is open seven days a week.
🃏

ZÓCALO
◆ E D3
174 E. 82nd St
(between Lexington and 3rd aves)
Tel. (212) 717-7772
An upscale Mexican eatery, the Zócalo will surprise you with almost every dish – especially after two margaritas.
♻

UPPER WEST SIDE
HOTELS

BEACON HOTEL
◆ C A1
2130 Broadway
(at 75th St)
Tel. (212) 787-1100
or 1-800-572-4969
www.beaconhotel.com
This inexpensive hotel in the residential section of the Upper West Side has views over the Hudson River or Central Park from the upper floors. Spacious rooms with kitchenettes.
♻

HOTEL BELLECLAIRE
◆ C A1
250 W. 77th St
(at Broadway)
Tel. (212) 362-7700 or
1-877-HOTELBC
www.hotelbelleclaire newyork.com
Built in 1903 in the heart of the Upper West Side, this hotel had Russian novelist Maxim Gorky as a guest in 1906. Located in a lively residential neighborhood near Central Park, Riverside Park and Lincoln Center, it has moderately priced, comfortable rooms.
🃏/🎴

COUNTRY INN THE CITY
◆ E D1
270 W. 77th St
(between Broadway and West End Ave.)
Tel. (212) 580-4183
www.countryinn thecity.com
This small hotel consists of several

apartments with kitchenettes in a limestone townhouse on a quiet street; three nights minimum. No children under 12, no credit cards, and no smoking. Maximum occupancy of two people per apartment.
♻

MANDARIN ORIENTAL
◆ D A1 or C B2
80 Columbus Circle
(at 60th St)
Tel. (212) 805-8800 or
1-866-801-8880
www.mandarin-oriental.com
This hotel between the 35th and 54th floors of the Time Warner Center on Columbus Circle is every bit as luxurious as its Hong Kong branch and has unparalleled views of Central Park as does its high-style fusion restaurant Asiate and the bar next to the lobby. Rooms are the ultimate in style and comfort. Great sevice and a spectacular pool and spa on the 36th floor.
🎴

MILBURN HOTEL
◆ C A1
242 W. 76th St
(between Broadway and West End Ave.)
Tel. (212) 362-1006
or 1-800-833-9622
www.milburnhotel.com
This is a comfortable hotel on a small, quiet street. Reasonably-priced rooms with suites and kitchenettes.
♻

TRUMP INTERNATIONAL HOTEL AND TOWER
◆ D A1
1 Central Park West
(at Columbus Circle)
Tel. (212) 299-1000
or 888-448-7867
www.trumpintl.com
This hotel is situated between the 4th and 18th floors and offers luxury rooms and

suites that are surprisingly restrained in style, consider who owns the hotel. Ask for a room on one of the upper floors with a view over Central Park. The famous restaurant Jean Georges is on the main floor.*
🎴

WEST SIDE YMCA
◆ C B2
5 W. 63rd St
(at Central Park West)
Tel. (212) 875-4273
www.ymcanyc.org
The best value in New York if you're not picky about thread counts.
🖰

RESTAURANTS

BARNEY GREENGRASS
◆ E D1
541 Amsterdam Ave.
(at 86th St)
Tel. (212) 724-4707
Closed Mon.
Barney Greengrass is an institution in the neighborhood, famous for its scrambled eggs, lox and sturgeon. A good place for brunch.
🃏

CAFÉ DES ARTISTES
▲ 344 ◆ C A-B2
1 W. 67th St (between Columbus Ave. and Central Park West)
Tel. (212) 877-3500
Howard Chandler Christy's murals of frolicking naked ladies are an amusing background to a menu that includes marinated salmon, pot-au-feu, chicken pie, cassoulet and tarte Ilona.
🎴

CAFÉ GRAY
◆ D A1 or C B2
10 Columbus Circle
(at 60th St)
Tel. (212) 823-6338
Overlooking Central Park, Gray Kunz's first restaurant after the close of the 4-

star Lespinasse has a French menu with a whiff of Austria and Asia. The Skate Schnitzel is as close as you're going to come to the Ringstrasse. This is one of New York's most coveted reservations, so book well in advance. ⊞

THE CENTRAL PARK WEST BOATHOUSE
◆ **C** A2
Central Park Lake (at 72nd St and East Park Drive)
Tel. (212) 517-2233
The most bucolic of cafés-restaurants in Manhattan, by the lake in Central Park. The place has recently acquired a new name and gone up in the world. American cuisine.
▣

JEAN-GEORGES
◆ **D** A1
1 Central Park West (between 60th and 61st sts)
Tel. (212) 299-3900
Closed lunch Sun. Try the more casual (and inexpensive) front Nougatine Room of this restaurant of celebrated owner Jean-Georges Vongerichten (see also Vong ◆ 383 and JoJo ◆ 386). Adam Tihany's minimalist design is the perfect setting in which to enjoy sea scallops in a caper-raisin sauce, or loin of lamb dusted with black trumpet mushroom and a leek purée.
▣ (lunch);
⊞ (dinner)

OUEST
◆ **E** D1
2315 Broadway (at W. 84th St)
Open dinner daily, brunch Sun.
Theater people, locals and writers love chef-owner Tom Valenti's hard-

to-get-into restaurant. The long, narrow bar opens up into a glorious dining room with red leather banquettes and an open kitchen. The food is spectacular. Don't miss Valenti's signature dish, lamb shank, or the braised short ribs.

PICHOLINE
◆ **C** B2
35 W. 64th St (between Broadway and Central Park West)
Tel. (212) 724-8585
Very conveniently located close to the Lincoln Center, Picholine combines an elegant dining room and the delicious cuisine of Chef-owner Terrence Brennan.The spiced loin of lamb with vegetable couscous, the sea scallops done in a Basque style are two reasons to come here. The poached fillot of beef is divine and the cheese course is among the best in the city. An oasis of gourmet food on the West Side. Jackets are required for dinner.
⊞

TAVERN ON THE GREEN
▲ 044 ◆ **C** A-B2
Central Park West and 67th St
Tel. (212) 873-3200
This very kitsch restaurant situated in Central Park caters mostly to tourists. The dishes are nevertheless delicious and there are some very reasonable fixed-priced menus.
⊞

THE TERRACE IN THE SKY
◆ **E** A1
400 W. 119th St (between Amsterdam Ave. and Morningside Dr.)
Tel. (212) 666-9490

Closed Sat. lunch and Sun.–Mon.
This restaurant, setup on the roof of a building, offers unusual food and an equally unusual view.
⊞

HARLEM
RESTAURANTS

MISS MAMIE'S SPOONBREAD TOO
◆ **E** B2
366 W 110th St (between Manhattan and Columbus aves)
Tel. (212) 865 6744
You might see college students, locals, Oprah Winfrey and Bill Clinton at this old-fashioned spot for soul food, famous for its fried chicken and banana bread pudding. Live music on Mondays at 9pm.
▣

SYLVIA'S RESTAURANT
▲ 358 ◆ **E** A2
328 Lenox Ave. (between 126th and 127th sts)
Tel. (212) 996 0660
People come here in droves to sample the best authentic Southern cooking and soul food in the city. Desserts are a must. Brunch on Sunday with gospel music is very popular. Order a taxi to get back.
▣

BROOKLYN
RESTAURANTS

GROCERY
288 Smith St (between Sackett and Union sts)
Tel. (718) 596-3335
This New American restaurant draws foodies to Brooklyn from Manhattan. Ingredients are from local farmers' markets, so the menu changes seasonally, the garden is lovely in the summertime, and the service is impeccable, but not

at all pretentious.
▣

GRIMALDI'S
19 Old Fulton St (between Front and Water sts)
Tel. (718) 858-4300
Stop for the coal oven pizza after checking out the galleries of DUMBO. Expect a long wait as the place is incredibly popular, but well-worth it.
▣

MISS WILLIAMSBURG DINER
206 Kent Ave. (between Metropolitan Ave. and N. 3rd St)
Tel. (718) 963-0802
Popular with the locals, this "diner" actually serves fontina bruschetta with nutmeg-laced zucchini puree, octopus-fava salad, pork chops with brown butter and sage, and homemade pastas. The chef is from Bologna and the décor is bohemian kitsch.
▣

PETER LUGER STEAK HOUSE
178 Broadway (between Driggs and Bedford aves)
Tel. (718) 387-7400
This well-liked establishment has served the best steaks in New York since 1887. Note that credit cards are not accepted. Order a taxi to get back to Manhattan.
⊞

RIVER CAFÉ
Brooklyn Heights 1 Water St
Tel. (718) 522-5200
Some dishes can be disappointing, but the views of Manhattan are unbeatable. Desserts are always delectable. Order a taxi to get back.
⊞

◆ CAFÉS AND BARS

The ◆ symbol indicates a mention in the Itineraries section
The letter and number (e.g. B A2) indicates the place's
location on the maps at the end of this boopk.

CAFÉS AND BARS
FINANCIAL DISTRICT

BUBBLE LOUNGE
◆ **B** D2
228 West Broadway
(at North Moore)
Tel. (212) 431-3433
Open 5pm–4am (till
2am Mon, Tue)
*Baroque, cozy
champagne-bar.
A favorite with
Wall Street yuppies.
Live jazz Mondays
and Tuesdays.*

SOHO

DOUBLE HAPPINESS
◆ **B** C–D3
173 Mott St.
(between Broome
and Grand sts.)
Tel. (212) 941-5542
*Former Prohibition
bar, now a vaulted
cellar with Chinese
decorations where
you can sip a green
tea martini while
listening to DJ music.*

SWEET & VICIOUS
◆ **B** C3
5 Spring St.
(at Bowery St)
Tel. (212) 334 7915
*Undeniably stylish
thanks to the wooden
benches, wall lamps
and the long, candle-
lit bar counter, and
patronized by a lively
crowd of regulars.*

LOWER EAST SIDE

KUSH
◆ **B** C3
191 Chrystie St.
(between Stanton
and Rivington sts)
Tel. (212) 677-7328
*Daily from 7pm
Enjoy the plush,
comfortable
Moroccan cushions
and the unusual
cocktails in this
intimate, candle-
lit lounge. Free jazz
concerts and theme
musical evenings.*

TONIC
◆ **B** C3
107 Norfolk St.
(between Delancey
and Rivington sts)
Tel. (212) 358 7504

*This is the meeting
place of local artists,
independent film-
makers and late-night
revelers. Live
music is performed in
the first floor-bar. In
the basement of this
former distillery, the
huge barrels
in which alcohol used
to be stored, have
been chopped into
intimate spaces.*

EAST VILLAGE

B-BAR
◆ **B** C3
40 E. 4th St.
(at Bowery)
Tel. (212) 475-2220
*A very mixed crowd
comes here. In
summer, a charming
garden offers shade.
Popular theme and
private parties are
held here many
evenings, but B-Bar
is a great spot for a
relaxing brunch.*

KGB
◆ **B** C3
85 E. 4th St.
(between 2nd Ave
and Bowery St.)
Tel. (212) 505-3360
*Red walls, soft
lighting and fans are
part of the interior
décor, along with rare
posters, pamphlets
and photographs
with an ex-Soviet
Union and
Communist Party
theme. The drinks are
strong and the music
loud (mostly rock).
KGB often holds
readings by up-and-
coming novelists.*

**MCSORLEY'S OLD
ALE HOUSE** ◆ **B** B3
15 E 7th St.
(at 3rd Ave.)
Tel. (212) 254-2570
*Open daily till 1am
One of the oldest
bars in New York
(dating from 1854).
Wide range of beers.*

GREENWICH VILLAGE

**S.O.B.'S (SOUNDS OF
BRAZIL)** ◆ **B** C2
204 Varick St.

(at W. Houston St.)
Tel. (212) 243-4940
www.sobs.com
*Brazilian and
Caribbean bar-
restaurant. A must
for those who love
reggae, world and
Brazilian music.
Often has big-name
artists with reserve
only tables. Check in
advance.*

CAFFE REGGIO
◆ **B** C2
119 MacDougal St.
(at W. 3rd St.)
Tel. (212) 475-9557
*Daily 9am–2am
The most famous
café in the Village.
It boasts the oldest
coffee percolator in
New York and still
has the original Italian
décor from its
opening in 1927.*

CHUMLEY'S
▲ 213 ◆ **B** C1
86 Bedford St.
(Barrow St.)
Tel. (212) 675-4449
*Open til 2am on
weekends
This unmarked
former speakeasy,
through an interior
courtyard, is now a
bar-restaurant
packed on weekends.
Brunch served
weekends.*

FIGARO CAFÉ
◆ **B** C2
184 Bleecker St.
(at MacDougal St.)
Tel. (212) 677-1100
*Daily till 2am
The haunt of Beat
Generation artists
and Café Society
back in the 1950's,
this café has now
recovered its original
décor.*

HOGS & HEIFERS
◆ **B** B1
859 Washington St.
(at 13th St.)
Tel. (212) 929-0655
*Daily till 4am
Raucous country
music bar known for
impromptu strip
shows by drunken
celebrities.*

WHITE HORSE TAVERN
▲ 215 ◆ **B** B1
567 Hudson St
(at 11th St)
Tel. (212) 243-9260
*Open daily till 2am
Bar-restaurant with
a terrace in the
summer. A former
favorite of Dylan
Thomas.*

GRAMERCY AREA

PETE'S TAVERN
▲ 229 ◆ **B** A2
129 E. 18th St.
(at Irving Place)
Tel. (212) 473-7676
*Daily 11am–
12.45am (bar 3am)
The famous writer
0. Henry apparently
wrote The Gift of the
Magi sitting at the
second booth on
the right of this old
restaurant, which is
still a nice place to
have a beer and a
burger.*

THEATER DISTRICT

COCO PAZZO TEATRO
◆ **C** C2
Time Hotel
224 W. 49th St.
(between 6th and
7th aves.)
Tel. (212) 320-2929
*Relax with a drink in
the cozy lounge, or
order a meal from the
menu at this calm,
modern room
removed from the
bustle of Broadway.*

CONCERT HALLS AND NIGHTCLUBS
TRIBECA

KNITTING FACTORY
◆ **B** D2
74 Leonard St
(between Broadway
and Church St)
Tel. (212) 219-3006
www.knittingfactory.com
*Open every evening
A tiny place where
you can watch
musicians who were
once household
names as well as a
new generation of
rising stars.
Enthusiastic audience
and welcoming
atmosphere. A must.*

LOWER EAST SIDE

BOWERY BALLROOM
◆ **B** B3
6 Delancey St
(at Bowery St)
Tel. (212) 533-2111
www.boweryhallroom.
com
*PJ Harvey and
Peaches are only two
of the famous
contemporary rock
and electro music
names to appear in
this former theater.
Pleasant bar in the
entrance.*

THE DELANCEY
◆ **B** C3
168 Delancey St
(at Clinton St)
Tel. (212) 254-9920
www.thedelancey.com
*Punk rockers playing
in the basement, a
spacious bar on the
first floor, and a
surprisingly lovely
roof deck make this
the new hassle-free
hotspot in the
neighborhood.*

MERCURY LOUNGE
◆ **B** C3
217 E. Houston St
(at Essex St)
Tel. (212) 260-4700
www.mercurylounge
nyc.com
*A popular concert
spot that packs in
crowds for emerging
rock groups and
intimate shows by
superstars. Buy
tickets in advance or
miss out.*

PIANO'S
◆ **B** C3
158 Ludlow St (at
Stanton St)
Tel. (212) 505-3733
www.pianosnyc.com
*An intimate spot to
see up-and-coming
singer-songwriters
and Broadway stars
trying to stretch their
legs a bit. Call to
reserve a table.*

EAST VILLAGE

BOTANICA
◆ **B** C3
47 E. Houston St.
(between Mott and
Mulberry sts)

Tel. (212) 343-7251
*In the original Knitting
Factory space,
Botanica is basically
a bar popular with
models from around
the world, who then
dance the night away
upstairs.*

NUYORICAN POETS CAFÉ
◆ **B** C3-4
236 E. 3rd St
(between avenues B
and C)
Tel. (212) 505-8183
www.nuyorican.org
*Nuyorican is the
nickname given to
Puerto Ricans born
or living in New York.
Would-be poets,
rappers and
musicians mix with
the public. Jam
sessions on
Wednesdays and
Fridays.*

GREENWICH VILLAGE

BACK FENCE
◆ **B** C2
155 Bleecker St.
(at Thompson St.)
Tel. (212) 475-9221
*Open daily 4pm–4am
Live music every
night from 8.30pm
(country, rock, folk).*

BIRDLAND
◆ **D** D1
315 W 44th St.
(between 8th
and 9th aves.)
Tel. (212) 581-3080
*Open daily 5pm–2am
www.birdlandjazz.com
This legendary
concert hall offers
jazz concerts every
night (9pm, 11pm).*

BITTER END
◆ **B** C2
147 Bleecker St.
(at Thompson St.)
Tel. (212) 673-7030
*Daily 7.30pm–2am
www.bitterend.com
Bob Dylan, Joan
Baez and Neil Young
started out in this
bar-restaurant, as did
Woody Allen.
One of the best jazz
clubs in town.*

BLUE NOTE
◆ **B** C2
131 W 3rd St.
(at 6th Ave.)
Tel. (212) 475-8592
*Daily 6pm–3.30am
www.bluenote.net
This bar-restaurant is
a jazz mecca.
The music is of a
consistently high
standard, with great
classic performers
such as Ray Charles,
Dave Brubeck, Lionel
Hampton and George
Benson. Brunch.*

CBGB OMFUG
▲ 224 ◆ **B** C3
315 Bowery
(at Bleecker St.)
Tel. (212) 982-4052
*Daily 7pm–3am
www.cbgb.com
From Ramones
to Talking Heads,
many now-famous
bands started out in
this long and narrow
little club. In danger
of going out of
business since it
opened in 1974.*

CIELO
◆ **B** B1
18 Little West 12th St
(between 9th Ave.
and Washington St)
Tel. (212) 645-5700
*A nice little dance
club in the
Meatpacking District
popular with
Europeans living in
and visiting New
York.*

THE DUPLEX
◆ **B** B1
61 Christopher St
(at 7th Ave. South)
Tel. (212) 255-5438
*A two-story affair
with a piano bar and
a show room
upstairs. There might
be anything from a
drag revue to a
famous comedian
performing, so call
ahead.*

JOE'S PUB
◆ **B** B2
425 Lafayette St.
(at Astor Place)
Tel. (212) 539-8770
*Daily 6pm–4am
Small restaurant-bar-*

*concert venue
situated in the former
Astor Library, the
current Public
Theater. An eclectic
mix of musicians,
from rock to jazz or
showtunes in a
popular, low-key
environment. Book a
table in advance for
most shows.*

LOTUS
◆ **B** B1
409 W. 14th St
(between 9th and
10th aves)
Tel. (212) 243-4420
*A hot-spot where
you'll see people
eating (spring rolls,
caviar) as you dance
by with champagne.*

VILLAGE VANGUARD
◆ **B** B1
178 7th Ave. South
(at W. 11th St)
Tel. (212) 255-4037
www.villagevanguard.
com
*A favorite. The spirit
of John Coltrane is
kept very much alive
at this club, where
the old guard of jazz
still come. Shows
9pm, 11pm.*

CHELSEA

BARRACUDA
◆ **B** A1
275 W. 22nd St.
(between 7th and
8th aves)
Tel. (212) 645-8613
*A space-age bar
that caters to the gay
men of the
neighborhood, but
that is welcoming
to all. Hilarious live
performances and
'drag bingo'.*

THE ROXY
◆ **B** A1
515 W 18th St.
(between 10th
and 11th aves.)
Tel. (212) 645-5156
*The biggest and
longest-lasting
gay dance club in
New York. They offer
with flair: New York's
only roller-disco (with
rental for those
without their own*

skates) on Wednesdays, and on the weekends concerts and dancing often carry on, literally, until dawn.

CAJUN
◆ **B** B1
129 8th Ave.
(at 16th St.)
Tel. (212) 691-6174
Daily 11.30am–midnight
Restaurant offering live New Orleans jazz and Cajun music every evening.

IRVING PLAZA
◆ **B** B2
17 Irving Place (at 15th St)
Tel. (212) 777-6800
A human-scaled hall geared for rock and roll and reggae concerts. Check in advance as many shows sell out early.

MARQUEE
◆ **B** A1
289 10th Ave.
(at 26th St)
Tel. (646) 473-0202
If you can get past the doorman – it will help if you arrive with Paris Hilton or Jay-Z – this intimate nightclub is well-designed with good service. You're sure to see a model or three dancing on a banquette, if that's your thing.

MIDTOWN

BIRDLAND
◆ **C** C2
315 W 44th St
(between 8th and 9th aves)
Tel. (212) 581-3080
Daily 9pm–2am
This legendary concert hall offers jazz concerts every night (9pm, 11pm).

DON'T TELL MAMA
◆ **D** C1
343 W. 46th St
(between 8th and 9th aves)
Tel. (212) 757-0788
www.donttellmama.com

Cabaret where amateur musicians, comedians and magicians are as welcome as professionals.

SWING 46 JAZZ AND SUPPER CLUB
◆ **D** C1
349 W. 46th St
(between 8th and 9th aves)
Tel. (212) 262-9554
Open daily
This restaurant-club is one of New York's most popular centers for swing, lindy-hop, and 1930's dance styles. Free dance classes most nights at 9.15pm (beginners welcome). Big band live from 10pm.

IRIDIUM JAZZ CLUB
◆ **C** B2
1650 Broadway
(at 51st St)
Tel. (212) 582-2121
Daily 6.30pm–1am
(11pm on Sun)
www.iridiumjazzclub.com
One of the best jazz clubs in Manhattan. Show every night.

UPPER EAST SIDE

FEINSTEIN'S AT THE REGENCY
◆ **D** A4
540 Park Ave.
(at 61st St)
Tel. (212) 339-4095
A revolving cast of cabaret and other singing stars. Expensive (usually $60 with a $40 minimum per person) but worth the good service and location.
HOTEL CARLYLE
◆ **C** A3
35 E 76th St.
(at Madison Ave.)
Tel. (212) 744 1600
BEMELMANS BAR
5pm–1am, piano music from 9.30pm
CAFÉ CARLYLE
Mon.–Sat. 6pm–1am
Closed summer
Elegant, intimate room with well-known cabaret singers.

MILES DAVIS

UPPER WEST SIDE

DIZZY'S CLUB COCA-COLA
◆ **C** B2
Broadway at 60th St
Tel. (212) 258-9595
www.jalc.org
The city's newest Jazz club, located in the Time Warner Center and part of Jazz at Lincoln Center. Shows often begin at 7.30pm and 9.30pm, and often at 11.30pm, so call ahead and reserve. There are only 140 seats and the setting is incomparable.

LE MONDE
◆ **E** B1
2885 Broadway
(at W. 112th St.)
Tel. (212) 531-3939
Large, traditional French brasserie: a spacious bar area, many wines by the glass, and some 50 different beers. Frequented by a mix of professors from Columbia University and local residents.

HARLEM

APOLLO THEATER
◆ **E** B2
253 W. 125th St
(between 7th and 8th aves.)
Tel. (212) 531-5305
www.apollotheater.com
Legendary venue famous for its amateur nights and big-name comedy shows.

COTTON CLUB
◆ **E** A1
656 W. 125th St
(at Riverside Drive)
Tel. (212) 663-7980
www.cottonclub-newyork.com
Live jazz every night except Tuesday and Wednesday. Booking essential.

LENOX LOUNGE
◆ **E** A2
288 Malcolm X Blvd
(between 124th and 125th sts)
Tel. (212) 427-0253
www.lenoxlounge.com
A jazz landmark, with superb 1930's décor and live jazz bands.

SAINT NICK'S PUB
◆ **F** C2
773 St Nicholas Ave.
(at 149th St)
Tel. (212) 283-9728
Harlem bar offering live jazz every night from from 9.30pm, except on Tuesdays.

BROOKLYN

GALAPAGOS
70 N. 6th Ave.
(between Kent and Wythes aves.)
Tel. (718) 782-5188
Set in a former factory, this is one of the first bars to have opened in the trendy Williamsburg area. Superb water display at the entrance. DJ music, shows and concerts.

The ▲ symbol indicates a mention in the Itineraries section.
The letter and number (e.g. **B** A2) following a placename indicates
its location on the maps at the end of this book.

ACCESSORIES

JAMIN PUECH
◆ **B** C3
SOHO
247 Elizabeth St
(at Houston St)
Tel. (212) 334-9730
*Original and elegant
beaded bags at high
prices.*

KATE SPADE
◆ **B** C2
SOHO
454 Broome St
(Mercer St)
Tel. (212) 274-1991
*Local handbag
designer. Trendy
styles.*

KIEHL'S
◆ **B** B3
EAST VILLAGE
109 3rd Ave.
(between 13th
and 14th sts)
Tel. (212) 677-3171
*The New Yorkers'
favorite cosmetics
store is set in an old
19th-century
pharmacy. It sells
hundreds of products
packaged the old-
fashioned way –
wonderful handmade
perfumes, beauty and
bath items for men
and women.
Well-informed staff.*

L'OCCITANE
◆ **C** A2
UPPER WEST SIDE
198 Columbus Ave.
(at 69th St)
Tel. (212) 362-5146
*This whiff of
Provence in New
York has the
traditional stone
floors and pale yellow
walls and an aromatic
assortment of herbal
oils, candles,
perfumes, creams
and soaps.*

ANTIQUES

**JACQUES
CARCANAGUES**
◆ **B** C2
SOHO
21 Green St (between
Grand and Canal sts)
Tel. (212) 925-8110
*This store rivals most
ethnographic
museums, with a
peerless collection of
southeast Asian
sculpture, fine
furniture and jewelry.*

LAURA FISHER
◆ **C** B4
MIDTOWN EAST
1050 Second Ave.
(at 55th St.)
Tel. (212) 838-2596
*Antique Americana
specializing in
beautiful quilts from
the 18th and 19th
century.*

LOST CITY ARTS
◆ **B** C2 NOHO
18 Cooper Sq. (at
5th St)
Tel. (212) 375-0500
*Take a trip into the
world of American
Art Deco, with
furniture from the
1930s to the 1960s,
ephemera and
publicity material,
industrial art (Coca-
Cola machines, gas
pumps), architectural
details (friezes,
gargoyles) and home
accessories (lamps,
fans, chandeliers).*

SECOND HAND ROSE
◆ **B** D2
TRIBECA
138 Duane St (at
Church St)
Tel. (212) 393-9002
*One of the boutiques
in the new antique
corner at Duane and
Franklin streets. Here
you will find an odd
mix of 19th-century
Moorish furniture and
antique wallpaper.*

URBAN ARCHAEOLOGY
◆ **B** D2
TRIBECA
143 Franklin St.
(between Varick and
Hudson sts.)
Tel. (212) 343-9312
*Sells rehabilitated
fixtures from the
19th century to the
mid-20th century.*

BOOKSTORES

BARNES & NOBLE
◆ **C** B2
UPPER WEST SIDE
1972 Broadway
(at 66th St)
Tel. (212) 595-6859
*One of a dozen
outlets of this famous
bookstore in
Manhattan. You can
browse or have a
coffee. Open until
midnight.*

**BORDERS BOOKS &
MUSIC**
◆ **D** A4
MIDTOWN EAST
461 Park Ave.
(at 57th St)
Tel. (212) 980-6785
*Four floors of books,
records, videotapes
and CD ROMs.*

COLISEUM BOOKS
◆ **C** C3
MIDTOWN WEST
11 W. 42nd St
(between 5th and
6th aves)
Tel. (212) 803-5890
*A well stocked
independent
bookstore and cozy
café across the street
from the New York
Public Library and
Bryant Park.*

GOTHAM BOOK MART
▲ 299 ◆ **D** C3
MIDTOWN EAST
16 E. 46th St
(between 5th
and Madison aves)
Tel. (212) 719-4448
*The recently
reopened classic
New York City
bookstore.*

**HAGSTROM MAP
AND TRAVEL CENTER**
◆ **D** D2
MIDTOWN WEST
51 W. 43rd St
(at 6th Ave.)
Tel. (212) 398-1222
*Map and guidebook
specialists.*

**LENOX HILL
BOOKSTORE**
◆ **C** A3
UPPER EAST SIDE
1018 Lexington Ave.
(between 72nd and
73rd sts)
Tel. (212) 472-7170
*First-rate
neighborhood
bookstore. Lots of
signed first editions
and poetry.*

POSMAN BOOKS
◆ **C** C3
MIDTOWN EAST
9 Grand Central
Terminal (at 42nd St
and Vanderbilt)
Tel. (212) 983-1111
*One of the finest
academic and literary
bookstores in the
city.*

RIZZOLI
▲ 288 ◆ **D** A3
MIDTOWN EAST
31 W. 57th St
(between 5th and
6th aves)
Tel. (212) 759-2424
*A wood-paneled New
York bookstore with
the air of a university
library It sells the best
books on art,
photography and
fashion published in
the U.S. and Europe.*

SHAKESPEARE AND CO.
◆ **C** A3
MIDTOWN EAST
939 Lexington Ave.
(at 69th St)
Tel. (212) 570-0201
*This New York
favorite has a wide
selection, helpful staff
and stores in three
other locations.*

STRAND BOOK STORE
◆ **B** B2
GREENWICH VILLAGE
828 Broadway
(at 12th St)
Tel. (212) 473-1452
*First and second-
hand books and
limited editions.*

THREE LIVES & CO.
◆ **B** B2
GREENWICH VILLAGE
154 W. 10th St
(between Waverly
Place and 7th Ave.)
Tel. (212) 741-2069
*A first-rate
neighborhood
bookshop with very
knowledgeable staff.
The fiction section is
particularly strong.*

ELECTROVISUAL
PRODUCTS

B. & H. PHOTO-VIDEO
◆ **C** D2
CHELSEA
420 9th Ave. (at 34th
St)

Tel. (212) 444-6615
One of the largest photo and electronic specialists: photographic, video and computer goods at very reasonable prices. Excellent range of digital cameras.

J & R MUSIC & COMPUTER WORLD
◆ **A** A3
FINANCIAL DISTRICT
Park Row (across from City Hall)
Tel. (212) 238-9000
New York's largest selection of personal computer equipment at reasonable prices. Very knowledgeable staff.

UNCLE STEVE'S
◆ **B** D2
SOHO
343 Canal St
(between Broadway and Church)
Tel. (212) 226-4010
Electronic goods at reduced prices.

DELICATESSENS PATISSERIES

CITARELLA
◆ **B** B2
GREENWICH VILLAGE
424 6th Ave.
(at 9th St)
Tel. (212) 874-0383
Downtown outpost of the gourmet Italian grocery store, fishmonger and butcher which opened its first store in Harlem in 1912.

ZABAR'S
◆ **E** D1
UPPER WEST SIDE
2245 Broadway
(at 80th St)
Tel. (212) 787-2000
A former deli, Zabar's is today a renowned food store which is excellent value. The atmosphere and the tempting smells make it an absolute must.

DEPARTMENT STORES

BERGDORF GOODMAN
▲ 297 ◆ **D** A3
MIDTOWN EAST

754 5th Ave.
(at 58th St)
Tel. (212) 753-7300
The most prestigious department store in New York selling the best of American and international design for women. The men's store is opposite.

BLOOMINGDALE'S
▲ 311 ◆ **D** A4
MIDTOWN EAST

1000 3rd Ave.
(at 59th St)
Tel. (212) 705-2000
'Bloomie's' sells everything: clothes for men and women, perfume, cosmetics, furniture and household goods. Particularly good for linens, day and evening wear and accessories

CENTURY 21 DEPARTMENT STORE
◆ **A** B2 DOWNTOWN
22 Cortland St
Tel. (212) 227-9092
Three floors of 'end-of-line' and marked-down goods.

HENRI BENDEL
◆ **D** B3
MIDTOWN EAST
712 5th Ave. (between 55th and 56th sts)
Tel. (212) 247-1100

Collections by young avant-garde designers.

MACY'S
▲ 249 ◆ **C** D2
MIDTOWN WEST
151 W 34th St
(at Herald Square)
Tel. (212) 695-4400
A New York institution and the world's largest store.

SAKS FIFTH AVENUE

▲ 282 ◆ **D** C3
MIDTOWN EAST
611 5th Ave.
(at 49th St)
Tel. (212) 753-4000
This old-fashioned and elegant department store is one of the most luxurious places to shop in the whole city.

TAKASHIMAYA
◆ **C** B-C3
MIDTOWN EAST
693 5th Ave.
(between 54th and 55th sts)
Tel. (212) 350-0100
Chic and expensive Japanese department store. Five floors of clothes, furniture, and Asian table settings, exquisite flowers, linens and cosmetics. In the basement is a

Japanese café and tea store.

FLEA MARKETS

THE ANNEX / HELL'S KITCHEN FLEA MARKET
◆ **C** D1
HELL'S KITCHEN
W. 39th St. (between 9th and 10th aves.)
Tel. (212) 234-5343
Open Sat.-Sun.
By far, the most extensive and famous flea market in town.

HATS

AMY DOWNS HATS
◆ **B** C3
LOWER EAST SIDE
151 Ludlow St
(at Stanton St)
Tel. (212) 358-8756
Fun, excentric, retro handmade hats.

J. J. HAT CENTER
◆ **C** D3
GRAMERCY AREA
310 5th Ave.
(at 32nd St)
Tel. (212) 239-4368
From stetsons to top hats. For both men and women.

WORTH & WORTH
◆ **D** D3
MIDTOWN EAST
101 W. 55th St
(at 6th Ave.)
Tel. 1 800-HAT-SHOP
The number one men's hat supplier since 1918.

INTERIOR DECORATION

ABC CARPET & HOME
◆ **A** A2
GRAMERCY AREA
881 & 888 Broadway
(at 19th St)
Tel. (212) 473-3000
Incredible bric-à-brac of household objects and furniture. Do not miss the Parlor Café and its fine delicatessen.

ANTHROPOLOGIE
◆ **B** C2
SOHO
375 W. Broadway
(at Spring St)
Tel. (212) 343-7070
All kinds of simple, rustic accessories for the home.

SHOPPING ◆

BED, BATH & BEYOND
◆ **B** A2
CHELSEA AREA
620 Ave. of the
Americas (at 18th St)
Tel. (212) 255-3550
*Wide range of
household items in a
magnificent building.*

HOUSING WORKS
◆ **E** D3
UPPER EAST SIDE
202 E. 77th St.
(between 2nd
and 3rd aves.)
Tel. (212) 772-8461
*One of four locations
in Manhattan that sell
fantastic second-
hand furniture (and
clothes) donated to
raise money
for AIDS patients.*

JEWELRY
ME & RO
◆ **B** C3
LOWER EAST SIDE
241 Elizabeth St
(at Prince St)
Tel. (917) 237-9215
*Stylish and hip men's
and women's jewelry.*

TIFFANY & CO.
▲ 296 ◆ **D** A3
MIDTOWN EAST
727 5th Ave.
(at 57th St)
Tel. (212) 755-8000
*World-famous store
that is in a class of
its own for jewelry.
Also has a small
souvenir department.*

MEN'S CLOTHING
BROOKS BROTHERS
◆ **D** B3
MIDTOWN
666 5th Ave.
(at 52nd St)
Tel. (212) 261-9440
*The place to go in
New York for classic
and stylish mens'
shirts.*

MARC
BY MARC JACOBS
◆ **B** C2
GREENWICH VILLAGE
403-405 Bleecker St
Tel. (212) 924-0026
*Marc Jacobs' less
expensive lines are
in these two stores.
The men's collection*

connects to the
women's, where
there are clothes,
shoes, jewelry and
bags. A collection of
high-end women's
accessories and
shoes is down the
street at 385 Bleeker,
tel. (212) 924-6126.
Marc Jacobs, the
more expensive line
of clothing (for both
men and women)
is located at 163
Mercer, tel. (212)
343-1490.

MUSIC STORES
A1
◆ **B** B3
EAST VILLAGE
439 E 6th St
(between 1st Ave.
and Ave. A)
Tel. (212) 473-2870
*Funk and electronic
music specialist
store. Patronized
by Fatboy Slim.*

BLEECKER BOB'S
GOLDEN OLDIES
◆ **B** C2
GREENWICH VILLAGE
118 W 3rd St
(at 6th Ave.)
Tel. (212) 475-9677
*All the pop and rock
classics are here.
There are also many
rare collectors' items
to be found.*

COLONY RECORDS
◆ **D** C2
MIDTOWN WEST
1619 Broadway
(at 49th St)
Tel. (212) 265-2050
*This store has LPs,
CDs, cassettes and
music scores.
Competent staff are
on hand to help you
with any requests.*

FAT BEATS
◆ **B** B2
GREENWICH VILLAGE
406 6th Ave.
(at 8th St)
Tel. (212) 673-3883
*The number-one rap
store in New York for
all independent hip-
hop labels. Do not
miss, but ignore the
service, which is not
what one would
hope for.*

JAZZ RECORD CENTER
◆ **B** A1-2
CHELSEA
236 W. 26th St
(between 7th and 8th
aves), 8th floor
Tel. (212) 675-4480
*Rare, new or
imported numbers,
collectors' items, and
staff that can answer
all your questions.*

OTHER MUSIC
◆ **B** C2
EAST VILLAGE
15 E. 4th St
(at Lafayette St)
Tel. (212) 477-8150
*Where rock, pop and
electronic music
purists go. Small but
specialist selection
and friendly, attentive
service.*

SATELLITE
◆ **B** B3
LOWER EAST SIDE
259 Bowery
(between Houston
and Prince sts.)
Tel. (212) 995-1744
*The city's best shop
for up-to-the-minute
vinyl and DJ
equipment.
Dancetracks (91 E
3rd St in the East
Village) is a rather
similar store.*

TOWER RECORDS
◆ **B** C2
GREENWICH VILLAGE
692 Broadway
(at 4th St)
Tel. (212) 505-1500
*Open until midnight
Large store where
you can find all the
great names at
reasonable prices.
Helpful staff.*

VIRGIN
MEGASTORE
◆ **D** C-D2
MIDTOWN WEST
1540 Broadway
(between 45th
and 46th sts)
Tel. (212) 921-1020
*Open until midnight
This megastore is
right on Times
Square. Branch at
52 E. 14th St, off
Union Square.*

SHOES
COLE HAAN
◆ **D** A3
UPPER EAST SIDE
667 Madison Ave.
(at 61st St)
Tel. (212) 421-8440
*Shoes and fancy
leather goods.*

HARRY'S SHOES
◆ **E** D1
UPPER WEST SIDE
2299 Broadway
(at 83rd St)
Tel. (212) 874-2035
*All the leading makes
of shoe (Timberland,
Sebago, etc.).*

MANOLO BLAHNIK
◆ **C** C3
MIDTOWN
31 W. 54th St
(between 5th and 6th
aves)
Tel. (212) 582-3007
*A favorite of Upper
East Side fashion
victims and Sex and
the City heroines.*

OTTO TOOTSI
PLOHOUND
◆ **B** C2
SOHO
413 West Broadway
(at Prince St)
Tel. (212) 925-8931
*The number-one
store for trendy
shoes. Other
locations at 38 E.
57th St and 137 5th
Avenue at 20th St.*

SIGERSON MORRISON
◆ **B** C3
LOWER EAST SIDE
28 Prince St.
(between Elizabeth
and Mott sts.)
Tel. (212) 219-3893
*Popular (and
expensive)
hand-made women's
shoes and bags.*

SOUVENIRS / PRESENTS
METROPOLITAN
MUSEUM OF ART SHOP
◆ **D** C2-3
MIDTOWN WEST
15 W 49th St
(between 5th
and 6th aves)
Tel. (212) 332-1360
*Reproductions of the
museum's exhibits at
reasonable prices.*

395

THE NEW YORK FIREFIGHTERS' FRIEND STORE
◆ **B** C2
NOLITA
263 Lafayette St (between Prince and Spring sts)
Tel. (212) 226-3142
Tee-shirts, badges, gadgets, raincoats, etc. based on the equipment used by firefighters from New York and other large American cities.

SPORTS

BLADES BOARD AND SKATE
◆ **E** D3
UPPER EAST SIDE
120 W. 72nd St (at Columbus Ave.)
Tel. (212) 996-1644
Roller blades to buy or rent. Very close to Central Park.

FOOT LOCKER
◆ **C** D2
MIDTOWN WEST
120 W. 34th St (between 6th and 7th aves)
Tel. (212) 629-4419
Sports goods. Many other branches.

NBA STORE
◆ **D** B3
MIDTOWN
5th Ave. (at 52nd St)
Tel. (212) 515-NBA1
The National Basketball Association's showroom. You can even shoot a few baskets.

NIKETOWN
◆ **D** A3
UPPER EAST SIDE
6 E. 57th St (between 5th and Madison aves)
Tel. (212) 891-6453
The number-one store for all Nike products. Interesting décor and activities.

PARAGON
◆ **B** A2
GRAMERCY AREA
867 Broadway (at 18th St)
Tel. 212 255 8036
Three floors

dedicated to all kinds of sports goods.

REEBOK CONCEPT STORE
◆ **C** A2
UPPER WEST SIDE
160 Columbus Ave. (between 67th and 68th sts)
Tel. (212) 595-1480
The flagship branch of Reebok sportsgear. Several floors of clothing and footwear.

SPORTS AUTHORITY
◆ **C** C3
MIDTOWN EAST
51st St and 3rd Ave.
Tel. (212) 355-9725
Sports equipment and clothing. Also has stores in other locations in Manhattan.

YANKEE'S CLUBHOUSE SHOP
◆ **D** A4
MIDTOWN EAST
110 E 59th St (between Park and Lexington aves)
Tel. (212) 758-7844
Store dedicated to the famous New York baseball team. Tee-shirts and caps of other teams available. Tickets can also be purchased for forthcoming games.

TOBACCO

NAT SHERMAN
◆ **D** D3
MIDTOWN
500 5th Ave. (between 42nd and 43rd sts)
Tel. (212) 764-4175
The most famous tobacconist in New York. Renowned for its traditional American tobacco mixes, its smoker's accessories and rows of cigar boxes.

TOYS

THE COMPLETE STRATEGIST
◆ **C** D3
MIDTOWN EAST
11 E. 33rd St (at 5th Ave.)
Tel. (212) 685-3880
All kinds of games.

DISNEY STORE
◆ **D** B3
MIDTOWN
711 5th Ave. (at 55th St)
Tel. (212) 702-0702
Gadgets, accessories, toys and clothes inspired by the various Disney characters.

F.A.O. SCHWARZ
◆ **D** A3
MIDTOWN EAST
767 5th Ave. (at 58th St)
Tel. (212) 644-9400
The most stylish toy store in New York.

HAMMACHER SCHLEMMER
◆ **C** B3
MIDTOWN EAST
147 E. 57th St (between Lexington and 3rd aves)
Tel. (212) 421-9000
All sorts of gadgets, from the large to the small.

LOUIS TANNEN
◆ **B** A2
CHELSEA
45 W. 34th St (at Broadway)
Tel. (212) 929-4500
For 70 years this has been the largest store for magicians' supplies for professionals, enthusiasts and children.

LOVE SAVES THE DAY
◆ **B** B3
EAST VILLAGE
119 2nd Ave. (at 7th St)
Tel. (212) 228-3802
Second-hand clothing and unusual gadgets.

THE SHARPER IMAGE
◆ **D** A3
MIDTOWN WEST
4 W 57th St (at 5th Ave.)
Tel. (212) 265-2550
Gadgets.

TOYS "R" US
◆ **C** D2
CHELSEA
24–32 Union Square E. (at 16th St)

Tel. (212) 674-8697
Toy and video game supermarket. Stores in other locations.

ZITOMER
◆ **C** A3
UPPER EAST SIDE
969 Madison Ave. (between 75th and 76th sts.)
Tel. (212) 737-2016
This pharmacy has a great selection of toys and children's clothing.

UNISEX CLOTHING

ALEXANDER MCQUEEN
◆ **B** BI
GREENWICH VILLAGE
417 W. 14th St (between 9th and 10th aves)
Tel. (212) 645-1797
Celebrated British designer Alexander McQueen has joined Stella McCartney and Jeffrey in the Meatpacking District, with an amazing 3,600 square-foot space done up by English designer William Russell. You will find not only accessories – shoes, belts, jewelry, handbags – but suits, evening gowns, leather as well as a new menswear line, Despoke, from Huntsman.

BANANA REPUBLIC
◆ **D** B3
MIDTOWN
626 5th Ave. (at 50th St)
Tel. (212) 974-2350
One of the casual fashion chains.

CALVIN KLEIN
◆ **D** A3
UPPER EAST SIDE
654 Madison Ave. (at 60th St)
Tel. (212) 292-9000
Clothes and accessories from the designer's top-of-the-range collections.

CENTURY 21
◆ **A** A2
DOWNTOWN
22 Cortlandt St. (at Church St.)

Tel. (212) 227-9092
This vast store is a mecca for designer clothing often reduced by 70%.

CLUB MONACO
◆ **B** A2
CHELSEA
160 5th Ave.
(at 21st St)
Tel. (212) 352-0936
New Canadian clothing chain.

DIESEL
◆ **D** A4
UPPER EAST SIDE
-770 Lexington Ave.
(at 60th St)
Tel. (212) 308-0055
-1 Union Sq. W
(at 14th St)
Tel. 646-336-8552
Trendy store with original clothing.

GAP
◆ **C** D2
MIDTOWN
34th St and Broadway
(at Herald Square)
Tel. (212) 643-8960
The largest Gap store in Manhattan. Includes a Gap Kids and a Baby Gap

H&M
◆ **C** C3
MIDTOWN
640 Fifth Avenue
(at 51st St)
Tel. (212) 489-0390
European sportswear at startlingly low prices. Four other stores in the city.

J. CREW
◆ **B** C2 SOHO
99 Prince St
(at Mercer St)
Tel. (212) 966-2739
Well-known American brand of chic, casual clothing.

ORIGINAL LEVI'S STORE
◆ **D** A4
UPPER EAST SIDE
750 Lexington Ave.
(between 59th and 60th sts)
Tel. (212) 826-5957
Levi's products from floor to ceiling.

PAUL STUART
◆ **D** D3
MIDTOWN

Madison Ave.
and 45th St
Tel. (212) 682-0320
Clothes and accessories for men and women.

RALPH LAUREN
▲ 300 ◆ **C** A3
UPPER EAST SIDE
867 Madison Ave.
(at 72nd St)
Tel. (212) 606-2100
Casual wear and stylish clothing in a splendid building.

REPLAY STORE
◆ **B** C2
SOHO
109 Prince St
(at Greene St)
Tel. (212) 673-6300
'Western'-style clothing and Jeans.

SCREAMING MIMI'S
◆ **B** C2
NOHO
382 Lafayette St (at E. 4th St)
Tel. (212) 677-6464
High-quality second-hand clothing from the 1940s to the 1970s. The interior decoration is well worth a visit.

TIMBERLAND
◆ **C** B3
UPPER EAST SIDE
709 Madison Ave.
(at 63rd St)
Tel. (212) 754-0434
Footwear, clothing and accessories.

URBAN OUTFITTERS
◆ **B** C2
SOHO
628 Broadway
(at Houston St)
Tel. (212) 475-0009
Half-grunge, half-New Age clothing and accessories chainstore. There are eight store locations in New York.

UNISEX CLOTHING (REDUCED)

DAFFY'S
◆ **C** D2
CHELSEA AREA
1311 Broadway
(at 34th St)
Tel. (212) 736-4477
Several outlets in the

city. Wide selection of Italian labels.

OLD NAVY
◆ **B** A2
CHELSEA
610 6th Ave. (at 18th St)
Tel. (212) 645-0663
Young casual clothing at very reasonable prices.

SSS SALES CO.
◆ **C** D2
MIDTOWN WEST
261 W. 36th St, 2nd floor (between 7th and 8th aves)
Tel. (212) 947-8748
Sample sale store in the Garment District.

WOMEN'S CLOTHING

ALPANA BAWA
◆ **B** C4
EAST VILLAGE
70 E. 1st St.
(between 1st and 2nd aves.)
Tel. 212-254-1249
Embroidered fabrics with hippie flair, a new men's line and a home collection.

ANNA SUI
◆ **B** C2
SOHO
113 Greene St
(between Prince and Spring sts)
Tel. (212) 941-8406
Women's retro-style clothing by American designer.

BETSEY JOHNSON
◆ **C** A2
UPPER WEST SIDE
248 Columbus Ave.
(between 71st and 72nd sts)
Tel. (212) 362-3364
Young fashion inspired by the 1960s in a pink-walled, neon-lit showroom.

CALYPSO CHRISTIANE CELLE
◆ **B** C2
NOLITA
280 Mott St
(between Prince and E. Houston sts)
Tel. (212) 965-0990
424 Broome St
Tel. (212) 274-0449

935 Madison Ave.
Tel. (212) 535-4100
French, hip and young resort clothing.

MICHAEL KORS
◆ **E** D3
UPPER EAST SIDE
974 Madison Ave.
(between 76th and 77th sts)
Tel. (212) 452-4658
Popular with socialites and preppies alike, Kors designs tennis skirts as well as evening gowns.

PRADA
◆ **B** C2
SOHO
575 Broadway
(at Prince St)
Tel. (212) 334-8888
An architectural marvel in the former SoHo Guggenheim is the base for this leading luxury Italian designer store selling ultra expensive clothes and accessories for men and women. Three additional locations on the Upper East Side.

SCOOP
◆ **B** C3
-532 Broadway
(between Prince and Spring sts)
Tel. (212) 925-2886
-1275 3rd Ave.
(between 73rd and 74th sts)
Tel. (212) 535-5577
-873 Washington St
(between W. 13 and W. 14th sts)
Tel. (212) 929-1244
Stylish and pricey clothes arranged by color.

VICTORIA'S SECRET
◆ **D** A3-4
MIDTOWN EAST
34 E. 57th St
(between Madison and Park aves)
Tel. (212) 758-5592
Attractive lingerie, including silk underwear, at reasonable prices. Nearly 20 New York locations.

◆ PLACES TO VISIT

Many museums are closed on Monday. Some may be closed on Tuesday or Wednesday as well.
Closures on public holidays may also vary from one place to another. It is therefore recommended you
check opening days and times by phone first. We have used the American floor numbering system
throughout this list, that is to say 1st floor instead of groundfloor, 2nd floor instead of 1st, etc.

MANHATTAN

A/D GALLERY 560 Broadway (Prince St.) Tel. (212) 966-5154	*Open Tue.-Sat. 10am–6pm.* *A/D explores the intersection of object and art,* *commissioning such artists as Robert Gober,* *Andrea Zittel, and Rosmarie Trockel.*	◆ B C3
ALLAN STONE GALLERY 113 E. 90th St. (between Park and Lexington aves.) Tel. (212) 987-4997	*Open Tue.-Fri. 10am–6pm, Sat. 10am–5pm.* *Closed in Aug.* *Expositions and retrospectives of modern* *art masters.*	◆ E C3
AMERICAN ACADEMY AND INSTITUTE **OF ARTS AND LETTERS** 633 W. 155th St. (Audubon Terrace) Tel. (212) 368-5900	*Opens only for the three annual exhibitions, or* *by arrangement if you want to use the library.*	◆ F B1 ▲ 361
AMERICAN CRAFT MUSEUM 40 W. 53rd St. (between 5th and 6th aves.) Tel. (212) 956-3535	*Open daily 10am–6pm (until 8pm Thu.).* *Arts and crafts from 1900 to the present day.*	◆ D B3
AMERICAN MUSEUM OF NATURAL **HISTORY** Central Park W. and 79th St. Tel. (212) 769-5100	*Open daily 10am–5.45pm (until 8.45pm Fri.)* *Closed Thanksgiving and Christmas.* *Rose Center for Earth and Space: same opening* *times as above; Hayden Planetarium: shows Sun.-* *Thu. and Sat. 10.30am–4.30pm, Fri. 10.30–7.30pm*	◆ E D2 ▲ 347
AMERICAN NUMISMATIC SOCIETY 96 Fulton St. Tel. (212) 571-4470	*Open Tue.-Fri. 9.30am–4.30pm. and public hols.* *Museum of coins and medals.*	◆ F B2 ▲ 361
APPELLATE DIVISION COURTHOUSE 27 Madison Ave. (Madison Square) Tel. (212) 340-0400	*Open Mon.-Fri. 9am–5pm.* *New York's Magistrates' Court. The lobby and the* *courts are open to the public.*	◆ B A2 ▲ 234
ARTISTS' SPACE 38 Greene St. (3rd fl.) Tel. (212) 226-3970	*Open Tue.-Sat. 11am–6pm.* *Voluntary organization exhibiting avant-* *garde works. Thematic exhibitions are also* *organized.*	◆ B C2
THE ASIA SOCIETY 725 Park Ave. (70th St.) Tel. (212) 288-6400	*Open Tue.-Sun. 11am–6pm (9pm Fri.) except July 4* *through Labor Day.* *Shows, conferences, lectures and Asian art* *exhibitions.*	◆ E D3 ▲ 311
BARBARA GLADSTONE GALLERY 515 W. 24th St. (between 10th and 11th aves.) Tel. (212) 206-9300	*Open Tue.-Sat. 10am–6pm* *(summer hours Mon-Fri 10am–6pm).* *The most radical masterpieces of conceptualist* *masters (Acconci, Faigenbaum, Holzer, Mullican,* *Trockel, etc.).*	◆ B A1
BUDDHIST CHURCH OF NEW YORK 332 Riverside Drive (106th St.) Tel. (212) 678-0305	*Open Sun. 11.30am–1pm for services.*	◆ E B1
CARNEGIE HALL **AND ROSE MUSEUM** 152 W. 57th St. (7th Ave.) Tel. (212) 247-7800	*Museum open daily 11am–4.30pm and in the* *evening for shows. Guided tours Mon-Fri. at* *11.30am, 2pm and 3pm.*	◆ C B2 ▲ 301
CASTLE CLINTON **NATIONAL MONUMENT** Battery Park Tel. (212) 344-7220	*Open daily 8am–5.30pm. Closed public hols.* *Former fort, where tickets for the Statue of Liberty* *and the Ellis Island Immigration Museum can be* *purchased.*	◆ A D2 ▲ 143
CATHEDRAL CHURCH **OF ST JOHN THE DIVINE** Amsterdam Ave. (112th St.) Tel. (212) 316-7540	*Open 7am–6pm. Sung masses on Sun. at 11am* *and 6pm. Public tours Tue.-Sat. at 11am and on* *Sun. at 1pm.*	◆ E B1 ▲ 354

The letter and number (e.g. **B** A2) following a placename indicates its location on the maps at the end of this book, the symbol ▲ refers to the page in the Itineraries section.

CENTRAL PARK

BOAT HOUSE Near 72nd St., Shuttle from 5th Ave. Tel. (212) 517-2233	*Bicycle, boat and gondola rental (March–Nov.).*	◆ C A3 ▲ 314
BELVEDERE CASTLE Near 79th St. Tel. (212) 772-0210	*Open Wed.-Mon. 11am–4pm.*	◆ E D2 ▲ 314
CENTRAL PARK HOTLINE Tel. (212) 360-3444	*For information on events taking place in the park.*	▲ 314
CENTRAL PARK ZOO WILDLIFE CENTER 5th Ave. (E. 64th St.) Tel. (212) 861-6030	*Open daily 10am–5pm.*	◆ C B3 ▲ 314
THE DAIRY Near 65th St. Tel. (212) 794-6554	*Open Tue.-Sun. 10am–5pm.*	◆ C B3 ▲ 314
DANA DISCOVERY CENTER Near 110th St. Tel. (212) 860-1370	*Open Tue.-Sun. 10am–5pm.*	◆ E B2 ▲ 314
HORSE-DRAWN CARRIAGES 5th Ave. and Central Park South	*Trips around the park.*	◆ C B3 ▲ 314
URBAN PARK RANGERS Tel. (212) 427-4040	*Guided tours of Central Park and other parks in the five New York boroughs.*	▲ 314 ◆ C B3 ▲ 314
WOLLMAN RINK (Near 59th St.) Tel. (212) 982-2229 (summer) Tel. (212) 439-6900 (winter)	*Ice-skating rink (Nov.–March) and roller-skating rink (April–Oct.). Rental of rollerskates and rollerblades for skating through the park.* *Summer hours: Mon.-Fri. 11am–7pm,* *Sat.-Sun. 10am-8pm.* *Winter hours: Mon.-Tue. 10am–2:30pm,* *Wed.-Sat. 10am-11pm, Sun. 10am–9pm.*	

CENTRAL SYNAGOGUE 123 E. 55th St. (between Park and Lexington aves) Tel. (212) 838-5122	*Open only for services.*	◆ D B4
CHILDREN'S MUSEUM OF MANHATTAN 212 W. 83rd St. (between Broadway and Amsterdam aves) Tel. (212) 721-1234	*Open Tue.-Sun. 10am–5pm. Closed public hols.* *Interactive exhibitions for children who are allowed to touch anything they like, enjoy themselves and learn at the same time.*	◆ E D1
CHURCH OF OUR LADY OF THE ROSARY Shrine of St. Elizabeth Seton 7–8 State St. Tel. (212) 269-6865	*Open Mon.-Fri. 10am–2pm. Weekday services at 8.05am, 12.15pm and 1.05pm. Sunday service at 11am.*	◆ A D3 ▲ 157
CHURCH OF SAINT LUKE IN THE FIELDS 487 Hudson St. Tel. (212) 924-0562	*Open for services.* *Garden open Mon.-Fri. 9am until dusk.*	◆ B C1 ▲ 214
CHURCH OF THE ASCENSION 5th Ave. and 10th St. Tel. (212) 254-8620	*Open Mon.-Sat. noon–2pm, Sun. for services at 9am, 11am and 6pm.*	◆ B B2 ▲ 218
CITY HALL City Hall Park (between Broadway and Park Row) Tel. (212) 788-3000	*Call ahead to check details of visiting days and times.*	◆ A A3 ▲ 168
COLUMBIA UNIVERSITY 114th St. to 120th St., (Broadway and Amsterdam Ave.) Tel. (212) 854-4900	*Guided tours: Mon.-Fri. 11am and 2pm, starting from the Visitor Center at 213 Low Library.*	◆ E A-B1 ▲ 352
CONGREGATION SHEARITH ISRAEL 8 W. 70th St. (Central Park West) Tel. (212) 873-0300	*Guided tours by appointment.*	◆ C A2 ▲ 344
COOPER-HEWITT NATIONAL DESIGN MUSEUM 2 E. 91st St. (between Madison and 5th aves.) Tel. (212) 849-8400	*Open Tue.-Thu. 10am–5pm, Fri. 10am–9pm,* *Sat. 10am–6pm, Sun. noon–6pm.* *Closed public hols.* *Decorative and applied arts.*	◆ E C3 ▲ 320

◆ PLACES TO VISIT

DAHESH MUSEUM 580 Madison Ave. (between 48th and 49th sts.) Tel. (212) 759-0606	*Open Tue.-Sat. 11am–6pm.* *19th- and 20th-century European academic arts* *museum.*	◆ D C3 ▲ 282
D. C. MOORE GALLERY 724 5th Ave. (between 56th and 57th sts.) Tel. (212) 247-2111	*Open Tue.-Sat. 10am–5.30pm.* *Large gallery displaying the works of major* *20th-century artists.*	◆ D B3
DIA CENTER FOR THE ARTS	*Closed for renovations.*	▲ 220
ELDRIDGE ST PROJECT 12 Eldridge St. Tel. (212) 219-0888	*Open Sun., Tue.-Thu. 11am–4pm. Guided tours* *11am, noon, 1pm, 2 pm, 3pm. Restored 19th-* *century synagogue.*	◆ B C3 ▲ 194
EL MUSEO DEL BARRIO 1230 5th Ave. (104th St.) Tel. (212) 831-7272	*Open Wed.-Sun. 11am–5pm.* *Closed public hols.*	◆ E B3 ▲ 321
ELLIS ISLAND IMMIGRATION MUSEUM New York Harbor Tel. (212) 363-3200 Ferry leaves every 30 mins from Battery Park (till 5pm) Tel. (212) 269-5755	*Open daily 9.30am–5pm. Closed Christmas.* *Extraordinary museum of immigration.* *The tour lasts approximately three hours.* *See also p. 369.*	▲ A D1 ▲ 148
EMPIRE STATE BUILDING **OBSERVATORIES** 350 5th Ave. (34th St.) Tel. (212) 736-3100	*Open 9.30am–midnight (last elevator ride at* *11.15pm). Magnificent views of New York from* *the 86th and 102nd floors.*	◆ C D3 ▲ 242
EXIT ART, THE FIRST WORLD 475 10th Ave. (corner of 36th St.) Tel. (212) 966-7745	*Open Tue.-Thu. 10am–6pm, Fri. 10am–8pm,* *Sat. noon–8pm.* *Huge contemporary art center that presents works* *by young artists. Boutique and tapas bar.*	◆ B C2
FEATURE GALLERY 530 W. 25th St. (between 10th and 11th aves.) Tel. (212) 675-7772	*Open Tue.-Sat. 11am–6pm.* *A highly distinctive group of artists whose works* *run the gamut from conceptual installations to* *expressive drawing. A gallery where you are most* *likely to discover new creative talent.*	◆ B C-D2
FEDERAL HALL NATIONAL MEMORIAL 26 Wall St. (Nassau St.) Tel. (212) 825 6888	*Closed for renovations.* *Museum of 18th-century New York, presenting the* *history and the formation of the United States.*	
FEDERAL RESERVE BANK **OF NEW YORK** 33 Liberty St. Tel. (212) 720-6130	*Guided tours (around 1 hour): Mon.-Fri. 9.30am,* *10.30am, 11.30am, 1.30pm, 2.30pm.* *Limited number of places. Reserve at least one* *week before by telephone or in writing to the* *Public Information Division.*	▲ A B3 ▲ 158
THE FORBES MAGAZINE GALLERY 62 5th Ave. (12th St.) Tel. (212) 206-5549	*Open Tue.-Wed., Fri.-Sat. 10am–4pm.* *Guided tours Thu. by appointment (book one* *month in advance). Malcolm Forbes's collection* *(Fabergé eggs, 12,000 toy soldiers, etc.).*	◆ B B2 ▲ 218
FORD FOUNDATION ATRIUM 320 E. 43rd St. (between 1st and 2nd aves.) Tel. (212) 573-5000	*Open Mon.-Fri. 9am–5pm.* *Atrium with winter garden.*	◆ C C4 ▲ 265
FRAUNCES TAVERN MUSEUM 54 Pearl St. Tel. (212) 425-1778	*Open Tue.-Fri. noon–5pm, Sat.10am–5pm.* *Closed public hols.* *18th- and 19th-century American history, with* *reconstructions of period interiors.*	◆ A C3 ▲ 166
FRENCH EMBASSY CULTURAL SERVICES 972 5th Ave. (78th St.) Tel. (212) 439-1400	*Lobby open to visitors Mon.-Fri. 9am–5.30pm.* *Former townhouse. Guided tour of the Venetian* *room Fri. 12.30–2.30pm.*	◆ C A3 ▲ 320
FRICK COLLECTION (THE) 1 E. 70th St. (5th Ave.) Tel. (212) 288-0700	*Open Tue.-Sat. 10am–6pm, Sun. 1–6pm.* *Closed public hols. No children under 10.* *Henry Clay Frick's house and art collection.*	◆ C A3 ▲ 322

GAGOSIAN GALLERY – 980 Madison Ave. (76th St.) Tel. (212) 744-2313 – 555 W. 24th St. Tel. (212) 741-9692	*Open Tue.-Sat. 10am–6pm.* *With two annexes (one in the Upper East Side* *and the other in Chelsea), this gallery exhibits* *established contemporary artists, as well as* *masters such as Beckmann or Giacometti.*	◆ **E** D3
GALERIE ST. ETIENNE 24 W. 57th St. (8th floor) (between 5th and 6th aves.) Tel. (212) 245-6734	*Open Tue.-Sat. 11am–5pm.* *Closed Sat. June–Sep.* *Gallery specializing in German and Austrian* *Expressionism as well as American folk art.*	◆ **D** A2-3
GENERAL THEOLOGICAL SEMINARY 175 9th Ave. (between 20th and 21st sts.) Tel. (212) 243-5150	*Open Mon.-Sat. noon–3pm.* *Exhibition in the lobby. Garden.*	◆ **B** A1 ▲ **220**
GOETHE INSTITUTE NEW YORK 1014 5th Ave. and 83rd St. Tel. (212) 439-8700	*Open Mon.-Fri. 10am–5pm.* *German cultural center. Exhibitions, conferences,* *library. Telephone for programs.*	◆ **E** D3 ▲ **320**
GRACIE MANSION 88th St. and East End (in Carl Schurz Park) Tel. (212) 570-0985	*Guided tours March 15–Nov. 15. Wed. at 10am,* *11am, 1pm and 2pm by appointment.* *The residence of the Mayor of New York.*	◆ **E** C4 ▲ **313**
GRAND CENTRAL TERMINAL 42nd St. (between Park and Lexington aves.) Tel. 212 935-3960	*Guided tour organized by the Municipal Arts* *Society every Wed. at 12.30pm. Meeting point* *under the central clock in the Main Concourse.*	◆ **D** D4 ▲ **236**
GREENE NAFTALI GALLERY 526 W 26th St. (8th floor) (between 10th and 11th aves.) Tel. (212) 463-7770	*Open Tue.-Sat. 10am–6pm.* *Huge premises and superb views. Young avant-* *garde artists from New York, London and* *Los Angeles are represented here.*	◆ **B** A1
GREY ART GALLERY 100 Washington Square East Tel (212) 998-6780	*Open Tue., Thu.-Fri. 11am–6pm; Wed. 11am–8pm* *and Sat. 11am–5pm.* *Contemporary art gallery located in the main* *building of New York University.*	◆ **B** C2
INTERNATIONAL CENTER **OF PHOTOGRAPHY MIDTOWN** 1133 6th Ave. (43rd St.) Tel. (212) 857-0000	*Open Tue.-Thu. 10am–6pm, Fri. 10am–8pm,* *Sat.-Sun. 10am–6pm.*	◆ **E** C3 ▲ **321**
INTREPID SEA-AIR-SPACE MUSEUM Pier 86 12th Ave. and W. 46th St. (Hudson River) Tel. (212) 245-0072	*Open Mon.-Fri. 10am–5pm, Sat.-Sun. 10am–7pm.* *Closed Mon in winter.* *The chance to see one of the famous aircraft* *carriers of World War II, a submarine, a lightship* *and a destroyer.*	◆ **C** C1 ▲ **257**
ISLAMIC CULTURAL CENTER **OF NEW YORK** 1711 3rd Ave. (97th St.) Tel. (212) 722-5234	*New York's mosque.* *Open daily 9am–5pm.* *Call to visit.*	◆ **E** C3
JACOB K. JAVITS CONVENTION CENTER 655 W 34th St. Tel. (212) 216-2000	*Opening times depend on the exhibitions.*	◆ **C** D1 ▲ **248**
JEFFERSON MARKET COURTHOUSE **LIBRARY – NEW YORK PUBLIC LIBRARY** 425 6th Ave. (10th St.) Tel. (212) 243-4334	*Open Mon., Wed. noon–8pm, Tue. 10am–6pm,* *Thu. noon–6pm, Fri. 1–6pm, Sat. 10am–5pm.* *Former courthouse converted into a public library.*	◆ **B** B2 ▲ **211**
THE JEWISH MUSEUM 1109 5th Ave. (92nd St.) Tel. (212) 423-3200	*Open Sun.-Wed. 11am–5:45pm, Thu. 11am–9pm,* *Fri. 11am–3pm. Closed public hols.*	◆ **E** C3 ▲ **321**
JOHN STREET METHODIST CHURCH 44 John St. Tel. (212) 269-0014	*Museum open Mon., Wed., Fri. noon–4pm.*	◆ **A** B3 ▲ **158**
JUDSON MEMORIAL BAPTIST CHURCH 55 Washington Square South Tel. (212) 477-0351	*Visits by arrangement.*	◆ **B** C2 ▲ **200**

◆ PLACES TO VISIT

KNOEDLER AND COMPANY GALLERY 19 E. 70th St. (between 5th and Madison aves.) Tel. (212) 794-0550	*Open Tue.-Fri. 9.30am–5.30pm.* *Specializes in post-war works, such as those by artists like Milton Avery, Helen Fraukenthaler, Donald Sultan.*	◆ **B** A1
LEO CASTELLI GALLERY 18 E. 77th St. (between 5th and Madison Aves) Tel. (212) 249-4470	*Open Tue.-Sat. 10am–6pm.* *Leo Castelli is the man who introduced Johns, Rauschenberg, Lichtenstein, Warhol, Rosenquist, Stella, Judd and Nauman, and who continues to exhibit their works. His influence has shaped the world of contemporary art for the past 30 years.*	◆ **E** D3
LINCOLN CENTER Broadway and 65th St. Tel. (212) 875-5456 *www.lincolncenter.org* Guided tours: call (212) 875-5350 for an appointment.	*An enormous cultural center which houses a library as well as more than 20 auditoria for dance performances, opera, concerts and drama.* *Alice Tully Hall: Tel. (212) 875-5050;* *Avery Fischer Hall: Tel. (212) 875-5030;* *Jazz at Lincoln Center Tel. (212) 721 6500;* *Juilliard Theater: Tel. (212) 799-5000;* *Metropolitan Opera: Tel. (212) 365-6000;* *Library of the performing Arts: 40 Lincoln Center Plaza, Tel. (212) 870-1630;* *Backstage tour Oct.-June: Mon.-Fri. 3.30pm, Sun. 10.30am. Call for reservations: Tel. (212) 769-7020.*	◆ **C** B1 ▲ *305*
THE LOCK COLLECTION **– GENERAL SOCIETY OF MECHANICS AND TRADESMEN** 20 W. 44th St. (5th and 6th aves.) Tel. (212) 840-1840	*Open Mon.–Fri. 10am–4pm.* *Small museum of locksmithing.*	◆ **D** D2-3 ▲ *250*
LOWER EAST SIDE TENEMENT MUSEUM 90 Orchard St. Tel. (212) 431-0233	*Open Tue.-Fri. 11am–6pm, Mon. 11am–5.30pm, Sat.-Sun. 10.45am–6pm. Closed public hols.* *Guided tours of a restored Lower East Side tenement. Reservations recommended.*	◆ **B** C3 ▲ *194*
THE LOWER EAST SIDE VISITOR CENTER 261 Broome St. (between Orchard and Allen sts.) Tel. (212) 226-9010	*Open daily 10am–4pm.* *Complete information on the neighborhood. Free tour of the Lower East Side Sun. at 11am, April–Dec. Meeting point outside Katz Deli at 205 E. Houston St.*	◆ **B** C3
MADISON SQUARE GARDEN 7th Ave. (between 31st and 33rd sts.) Tel. (212) 465-6741	*Vast sports and entertainment complex. New York's basketball and hockey stadiums. Guided tours of the locker rooms. Also a forum for other sports venues, shows and concerts.*	◆ **C** D2 ▲ *249*
MARIAN GOODMAN GALLERY 24 W. 57th St. (4th floor) (between 5th and 6th aves.) Tel. (212) 977-7160	*Open Mon.-Sat. 10am–6pm.* *All the key figures in the American and European conceptual movement.*	◆ **D** A2-3
MARINERS' TEMPLE 3 Henry St. Tel. (212) 233-0423	*Open Tue.-Thu. 10am–6pm.* *Service with gospel choir Sun. at 11am.*	◆ **B** D3 ▲ *193*
MARLBOROUGH GALLERY – 40 W. 57th St. (2nd floor) (between 5th and 6th aves.) Tel. (212) 541-4900 – 211 W. 19th St. (between 7th and 8th aves., Chelsea) Tel. (212) 463-8634	*Open Mon.-Sat. 10am–5.30pm (Tue.-Sat for the Chelsea location). Closed Sat. in summer.* *Works by famous painters, photographers and sculptors such as Henry Moore or Brassai are displayed in both annexes of this gallery (one in Midtown Manhattan, the other in Chelsea). The space and the terrace on 57th St. also have sculptures on display.*	◆ **D** A2-3 ◆ **B** A1
MARY BOONE GALLERY – 745 5th Ave. (58th St.) – 541 W. 24th St. Tel. (212) 752 2929 (for both galleries)	*Open Tue.-Fri. 10am–6pm and Sat. 10am–5pm. 24th St. location open Tue.-Sat. 10am–6pm. Mary Boone launched some of the most important artists of the 1980's: Eric Fischl, Ross Bleckner, Barbara Kruger, David Salle, Julian Schnabel.*	◆ **C** B3

MATTHEW MARKS GALLERY
– 522 W. 22nd St.
– 523 W. 24th St.
– 521 W. 21st St
(all between 10th and 11th aves.)
Tel. (212) 243-0200
(for all three galleries)

Open Tue.-Sat 10am–6pm (closed some Sat. in summer). 21st St gallery open Thu.-Fri.1–6pm, Sat. 11am–6pm.
Two of the largest galleries in Chelsea and a brand-new annex. The largest of the three, on 22nd St., has been set up in a former garage. Works by artists such as Willem de Kooning, Lucian Freud, Brice Marden, Nan Goldin and Terry Winters are introduced.

◆ **B** A1

◆ **B** A1

MAX PROTECH GALLERY
511 W. 22nd St.
(between 10th and 11th aves.)
Tel. (212) 633-6999

Open Tue.-Sat. 10am–6pm. Mon.-Fri. 10am–6pm in July and Aug. Contemporary art: paintings, videos, sculptures, photographs, potteries, prints and architectural elements.

◆ **B** A1

MERCHANT'S HOUSE MUSEUM
29 E. 4th Street (between Lafayette St. and the Bowery)
Tel. (212) 777-1089

Open Thu.-Mon. noon–5pm.
Upper middle-class house dating back from 1832 with original furniture and private garden.

◆ **B** C2-3
▲ **227**

METROPOLITAN MUSEUM OF ART
5th Ave. (82nd St.)
Tel. (212) 535-7710

Open Sun.-Thu. 9.30am–5.30pm,
Fri.-Sat. 9.30am–9pm.

◆ **E** D3
▲ **328**

MICHAEL WERNER
4 E. 77th St. (2nd floor)
(5th Ave.)
Tel. (212) 988-1623

Open Mon.-Sat. 10am–6pm.
Contemporary artists from Europe, especially from Germany (Michael Werner also has a gallery in Cologne), and older works by 20th-century masters such as Joseph Roës, Kunt Witters, etc.

◆ **E** D3

MOST HOLY CRUCIFIX CHURCH
378 Broome St.
Tel. (212) 226-8075

Open Mon.-Fri. 11am–3pm and Sun. but visits are not allowed during services.

◆ **B** C2
▲ **196**

MOUNT VERNON HOTEL MUSEUM AND GARDENS
421 61st St. (First Ave.)
Tel. (212) 838-6878

Open Tue.-Sun. 11am–4pm (9pm Tue in June-July). Closed Aug.

◆ **C** B4
▲ **311**

MUSEUM OF AMERICAN FINANCIAL HISTORY
28 Broadway
Tel. (212) 908 4519

Open Tue.-Sat. 10am–4pm. Closed public hols.
Temporary exhibitions on the financial history of the US.

◆ **A** C2
▲ **156**

MUSEUM OF AMERICAN FOLK ART
– 45 W. 53rd St. (5th and 6th aves.)
Tel. (212) 265-1040
– 2 Lincoln Square
(Columbus Ave. and 65th St.)
Tel. (212) 595-9533

Open Tue.-Sun. 10.30am–5.30pm, Fri. 10.30am–7.30pm. Closed public hols.
Popular American art museum.
Lincoln Square annex (Eva & Morris Feld Gallery); open Tue.-Sat. noon–7.30pm, Sun. noon–5pm.

◆ **D** B3

◆ **C** B2

MUSEUM OF CHINESE IN THE AMERICAS
70 Mulberry St. (2nd floor)
Tel. (212) 619-4785

Open Tue.-Sat. noon–5pm. Closed public hols.
History of the Chinese community in the US.

◆ **B** D3
▲ **191**

MUSEUM OF JEWISH HERITAGE: A LIVING MEMORIAL TO THE HOLOCAUST
36 Battery Place,
Battery Park City
Tel. (646) 437-4200

Open Sun.-Tue. and Thu. 10am–5.45pm, Wed. 10am–8pm, Fri. and eve of Jewish hols. 10am–5pm. Closed Sat., Jewish hols and Thanksgiving.
Retraces the history of Jewish people in the 1900s.

◆ **A** D1
▲ **142**

MUSEUM OF MODERN ART (MOMA)
11 W. 53rd St.
Tel. (212) 708-9400
www.moma.org

Open Sat.-Thu. 10.30am–5.30pm,
Fri. 10.30am–8pm.
One of the largest post-impressionist modern art collections in the world. Permanent and temporary exhibitions.

◆ **C** C3
▲ **290**

MUSEUM OF TELEVISION AND RADIO
25 W. 52nd St.
(between 5th and 6th aves.)
Tel. (212) 621 6600

Open Tue.-Sun. noon–6pm, Thu. noon–8pm.
Extensive archives containing recordings of television and radio broadcasts.

◆ **D** B2-3
▲ **288**

MUSEUM OF THE CITY OF NEW YORK
1220 5th Ave. (103rd St.)
Tel. (212) 534 1672

Open Tue.-Sun. 10am–5pm.
Records and mementos of the city's history.

◆ **E** B3
▲ **321**

NATIONAL ACADEMY OF DESIGN 1083 5th Ave. (between 88th and 89th sts.) Tel. (212) 369-4880	*Open Wed.-Thu. noon–5pm, Fri.-Sun. 11am–6pm.* *Closed public hols.*	◆ E C3 ▲ 320
NATIONAL MUSEUM OF THE AMERICAN INDIAN Smithsonian Institute 1 Bowling Green Tel. (212) 514-3700	*Open daily 10am–5pm (8pm Thu.).* *Closed Christmas.* *Large collection of American-Indian objects, crafts and photographs.*	◆ A C2 ▲ 157
NEUE GALERIE 1048 5th Ave. (86th St.) Tel. (212) 628-6200	*Open Sat.-Mon. 11am–6pm, Fri. 11am–9pm.* *Sabarky Viennese café: open Mon., Wed. 9am–6pm, Thu.-Sun. 9am–9pm.*	◆ E D3 ▲ 320
NEW MUSEUM OF CONTEMPORARY ART 556 W. 22nd (at 11th Ave.) Tel. (212) 219-1222 *www.newmuseum.org*	*Open Tue.-Sat. noon–6pm (8pm Thu.).* *Closed public hols.* *Contemporary artists.*	◆ C B1 ▲ 220
NEW YORK CITY FIRE MUSEUM 278 Spring St. Tel. (212) 691-1303	*Open Tue.-Sat. 10am–5pm, Sun. 10am–4pm.* *History of the New York fire department.*	◆ B C2-3 ▲ 205
NEW YORK CITY POLICE MUSEUM 100 Old Slip St. (between Water and South sts.) Tel. (212) 480-3100	*Open Tue.-Sat. 10am–5pm, Sun. 11am–5pm.* *History and mementos of the New York police force from its origins until today.*	◆ A C2-3 ▲ 155
NEW YORK HISTORICAL SOCIFTY 170 Central Park West Tel. (212) 873-3400	*Museum: open Tue.-Sun 11am–6pm.* *Closed public hols.* *Library: open Tue.-Fri. 10am–5pm.* *Closed public hols.* *Archives and photographs of the city.*	◆ E D2 ▲ 346
NEW YORK PUBLIC LIBRARY – HUMANITIES AND SOCIAL SCIENCES 5th Ave. and 42nd St. Tel. (212) 930-0830	*Open Tue.-Wed. 11am–7.30pm, Thu.-Sat. 10am–6pm.* *New York City's main reference library.*	◆ D D3 ▲ 252
NEW YORK SKYRIDE In the Empire State Building Tel. (212) 279-9777	*Open 10am–10pm.* *Experience a hair-raising flight over New York City thanks to flight simulators.*	◆ C D3
NEW YORK STOCK EXCHANGE 20 Broad St. Tel. (212) 656-3000	*Currently closed to the public.*	▲ 163
OLD SAINT PATRICK'S CATHEDRAL Corner of Mott and Prince sts Tel. (212) 226-8075	*Open daily 8am–1pm and 3–6pm.*	◆ B C3 ▲ 196
PACE WILDENSTEIN GALLERY – 32 E. 57th St. (2nd floor) Tel. (212) 421-3292 – 534 W. 25th St. (Chelsea) Tel. (212) 929-7000	*57th St. location: open Mon.-Fri 9.30am–6pm (4pm Fri.). Chelsea location: open Mon.-Fri. 10am–6pm (4pm Fri.).* *Do not miss the exhibition on the contemporary art market. After presenting artists such as Picasso, Noguchi and Joseph Cornell, Pace made inroads into the contemporary art world of Martin, Richard Serra and Louise Nevelson.*	◆ D A3
PAULA COOPER GALLERY – 534 W. 21st St. (between 10th and 11th aves.) – 521 W. 21st St. (between 10th and 11th aves.) Tel. (212) 255-1105	*Open Mon.-Fri. 10am–5pm.* *Gallery specialized in conceptual and minimalist art, presenting the works of Donald Judd, Tony Smith, Jonathan Borofsky, Dan Walsh and Zeo Leonard.*	◆ B C2 ◆ B A1
PEN & BRUSH CLUB 16 E. 10th St. (University Place and 5th Ave.) Tel. (212) 685-0610	*Exhibitions of works by the club's members.* *Call for event listings.*	◆ B B2 ▲ 218
PIERPONT MORGAN LIBRARY 29 E. 36th St. (Madison Ave.) Tel. (212) 685-0610	*Rare books (including one of Gutenberg's bibles), manuscripts from the Middle Ages and the Renaissance, drawings, paintings, etc. Temporary exhibitions. New Renzo Piano addition.*	◆ C D3 ▲ 241

RADIO CITY MUSIC HALL 1260 6th Ave. (50th St.) Tel. 212 247-4041	*Call for information on tours.*	◆ **D** C3 ▲ *277*
ROBERT MILLER GALLERY 524 W. 26th St. (between 10th and 11th aves.) Tel. (212) 366-4774	*Open Tue.-Sat. 10am–6pm.* *Downtown-style gallery, despite its location.* *Contemporary American painters, sculptors and* *photographers.*	◆ **B** A1
ROCKEFELLER CENTER 5th and 6th Aves., 48th and 51st Sts. Tel. (212) 332-6868	*Guided tours by the Municipal Arts Society leaving* *every hour from the NBC Experience Store.* *Tours available daily10am–5pm (4pm Sun.).* *Call (212) 664-7174 to reserve.*	◆ **D** C2 ▲ *274*
ROOSEVELT ISLAND TRAMWAY 2nd Ave. and 59th St. Tel. (212) 832-4543	*Open daily 6am–2.30am (3.30am Sat.-Sun.).* *Leaves every 15 minutes. Buy return tokens before* *departure from Manhattan.*	◆ **C** B-C4 ▲ *311*
RUBIN MUSEUM OF ART 150 W 17th St. (7th Ave.) Tel. (212) 620 5000 *www.rmanyc.org*	*Tue and Sat. 11am–7pm, Wed. 11am–5pm,* *Thu–Fri 11am–9pm, Sun 11am–6pm.*	▲ *220* ◆ **B** B1
ST. BARTHOLOMEW'S CHURCH 109 E. 50th St. (Park Ave.) Tel. (212) 378-0200	*Open Mon.-Wed. 8.45am–6pm, Thu. 8.45am–7pm,* *Sun. 8.45am–8.30pm. Sunday services at 8am, 9am,* *11am, 5pm, and 7pm.*	◆ **D** B4 ▲ *285*
ST. JAMES' CHURCH 23 Oliver St. Tel. (212) 233-0161	*Open only for services.*	◆ **A** A4 ▲ *193*
ST. JAMES' EPISCOPAL CHURCH 865 Madison Ave. (71st St.) Tel. (212) 774-4200	*Open daily 9am–5pm.*	◆ **C** A3 ▲ *309*
ST. MALACHY ROMAN CATHOLIC **CHURCH** 239–245 W. 49th St. (between Broadway and 8th Ave.) Tel. (212) 489-1340	*Open daily 7am–5pm.*	◆ **D** C1-2 ▲ *300*
ST. MARK'S CHURCH IN THE BOWERY 10th St. and 2nd Ave. Tel. (212) 674-6377	*Open for services. The church is used for special* *venues, such as the Poetry Project: tel. (212) 674-* *0910, and the Dance Space Project: tel. (212) 674-* *8112.*	◆ **B** B3 ▲ *224*
ST. PATRICK'S CATHEDRAL 460 Madison Ave. Tel. (212) 753-2261	*Open daily 7am–8.45pm.* *New York's Roman Catholic cathedral.* *Superb sung mass on Sun.*	◆ **D** C3 ▲ *283*
ST. PAUL'S CHAPEL Broadway and Fulton St. Tel. (212) 233-4164	*Open Mon.-Fri. 9am–3pm, Sun. 7am–3pm.* *Concerts and operas every Mon. at noon,* *tel. (212) 602-0747.*	◆ **A** B2 ▲ *176*
ST. PETER'S CHURCH 16 Barclay St. Tel. (212) 233-8355	*Open daily 6am–6pm.*	◆ **A** A2 ▲ *178*
ST. THOMAS CHURCH 1 W. 53rd St. (5th Ave.) Tel. (212) 757-7013	*Open daily 9am–5.30pm.*	◆ **D** B3 ▲ *288*
SALMAGUNDI CLUB 47 5th Ave. (12th St.) Tel. (212) 255-7740	*Open Mon.-Sat. 1–5pm and Sun. noon–5pm.* *Exhibitions of works by the club's members.*	◆ **B** B2 ▲ *218*
SCULPTURE CENTER GALLERY 167 E. 69th St. (between 3rd and Lexington aves.) Tel. (212) 966-5790	*Open Tue.-Sat. 11am–3pm.* *Exhibitions of contemporary sculptures.*	◆ **C** A3
THE SEAMEN'S CHURCH INSTITUTE 241 Water St. (between Peck Slip and Beekman St.) Tel. (212) 349-9090	*Open Mon.-Fri. 8am–4pm. In summer closes at* *12.30pm on Fri.* *Models of boats and ships. Maritime art.*	◆ **A** A4
SEVENTH REGIMENT ARMORY 643 Park Ave. (between 67th and 66th sts.) Tel. (212) 744-2968	*Barracks used as exhibition halls. Guided tours* *by appointment.*	◆ **C** B3 ▲ *310*

THE SKYSCRAPER MUSEUM 39 Battery Place Tel. (212) 968-1961 www.skyscraper.org	*Open Wed.-Sun. noon–6pm.* *Devoted to the study of the high-rise building.*	◆ A C3 ▲ *163*
SOLOMON R. GUGGENHEIM MUSEUM 1071 5th Ave. (89th St.) Tel. (212) 423-3500	*Open Sat.-Wed. 10am–5.45pm, Fri. 10am–8pm.* *One of the finest collections of modern art in* *the world.*	◆ E C3 ▲ *338*
SONNABEND GALLERY 536 W. 22nd St. Tel. (212) 627-1018	*Open Tue.-Sat. 10am–6pm.* *One of SoHo's historic galleries, relocated to* *Chelsea.*	◆ B D2
SONY PLAZA 550 Madison Ave. (between 55th and 56th sts.) Tel. (212) 833-8830	*Atrium: open 7am–11pm.* *Sony boutique: Mon.-Sat. 10am–7pm and* *Sun. noon–6pm.* *Sony Wonder Technology Lab: free entrance.* *Open Tue.-Sat. 10am–5pm (8pm Thu.) and* *Sun. noon–5pm.*	◆ D B3
SONY THEATER 1998 Broadway (68th St.) Tel. (212) 336-5000	*Exhibition on the latest technologies.* *Seven movie theaters with superb decoration.* *IMAX giant screen and 3-D movies.*	◆ C A2
SOUTH STREET SEAPORT MUSEUM 207 Front St. Tel. (212) 748-8600	*Open April-Oct.: Tue.-Sun. 10am–6pm.* *Open Nov.-March: Fri-Sun. 10am–5pm.* *Maritime museum. Ship tours. Boat trips.* *Tour of the fish market, April–Oct., duration:* *six hours, reservations: Tel. (212) 748-8590.*	◆ A B4 ▲ *172*
SPERONE WESTWATER GALLERY 415 W. 13th St. Tel. (212) 999-7337	*Open Tue.-Sat. 10am–6pm.* *Summer hours: Mon.-Fri. 10am–6pm.* *Exhibitions of works by renowned American as* *well as international artists such as Bruce Nauman,* *Susan Rothenberg, Richard Tuttle and Guillerma* *Knitka.*	◆ B B2
STATUE OF LIBERTY Liberty Island, New York Harbor Tel. (212) 363-3200 Ferry leaves every 30 mins from Battery Park (until 3.30pm)	*Tickets available from Castle Clinton, in Battery* *Park. The tour lasts a total of four hours. Extremely* *popular in summer and at weekends.* *See also p. 369.*	▲ *144*
TEMPLE EMANU-EL 1 E. 65th St. (5th Ave.) Tel. (212) 744-1400	*Open Sun.-Fri. 10am–4pm.* *Closed to non-members during Jewish hols.*	◆ C B3 ▲ *311*
THEODORE ROOSEVELT'S BIRTHPLACE 28 E. 20th St. (between Broadway and Park Ave.) Tel. (212) 260-1616	*Open Wed.-Sun. 9am–5pm.*	◆ B A2 ▲ *233*
TONY SHAFRAZI GALLERY 544 W. 26th St. Tel. (212) 274-9300	*Open Tue.-Sat. 10am–6pm.* *Tony Shafrazi achieved notoriety for defacing* *Picasso's Guernica at the Museum of Modern* *Art. He now exhibits contemporary artists, some of* *whom (Basquiat, Keith Haring and Scharf), started* *out as graffitists.*	◆ B C-D2
TRANSFIGURATION CATHOLIC CHURCH 29 Mott St. Tel. (212) 962-5265	*Open daily 8am–4pm.*	◆ B D3 ▲ *191*
TRINITY CHURCH Broadway and Wall St. Tel. (212) 602-0700	*Church: guided tours daily at 2pm.* *Concert and recital Thu. at 1pm. Museum: open* *Mon.-Fri. 9–11.45am and 1–3.45pm.*	◆ A C2 ▲ *154*
UNITARIAN CHURCH OF ALL SOULS Lexington Ave. and 80th Street Tel. (212) 535-5530	*Open daily 8am–9.30pm.*	◆ E D3 ▲ *312*
UKRAINIAN INSTITUTE 203 2nd Ave. (12th St.) Tel. (212) 288-0110	*Visits by appointment or for exhibitions.* *Call ahead for details of programs.*	◆ C A3 ▲ *312*
UKRAINIAN MUSEUM 222 E. 6th St. (between 2nd and 3rd aves.) Tel. (212) 228-0110	*Open Wed.-Sun. 11.30am–5pm.* *Museum retracing the history of the* *neighborhood's Ukrainian community.*	◆ B B3 ▲ *224*

UNITED NATIONS 1st Ave. and 46th St. Tel. (212) 963-7713	*Headquarters of the United Nations* *Organization. Guided tours every half hour* *Mon.-Fri. 9.30am– 4.45pm and Sat.-Sun. 10am-* *–4.30pm. Tel. (212) 963-TOUR for information* *and reservations.*	◆ **C** C4 ▲ *264*
URBAN CENTER GALLERIES 457 Madison Ave. and 51st St. Tel. (212) 935-3960	*Open Mon.-Wed., Fri.-Sat. 11am–5pm.* *Headquarters of the Municipal Arts Society* *which organizes thematic visits of the city* *(history, architecture). Its bookstore stocks* *many works on New York: Tel. (212) 935-3595.*	◆ **D** C3
WHITNEY MIDTOWN: **MUSEUM OF ART AT ALTIRA** 120 Park Ave. (42nd St.) Tel. (212) 663-2453	*Open Mon.-Fri. 11am–6pm (Thu. until 7.30pm).* *Branch of the Whitney Museum of American* *Art.*	◆ **D** D4 ▲ *240*
WHITNEY MUSEUM **OF AMERICAN ART** 945 Madison Ave. (75th St.) Tel. 1-877-WHITNEY	*Open Wed., Fri.-Sun. 11am–6pm, Thu. 1–9pm.* *In the basement of the museum is Sarabeth's,* *a very pleasant café, open Wed.-Thu.* *11am–6pm, Fri. 1–9pm, Sat.-Sun. 11am–6pm.*	◆ **E** D3 ▲ *326*

BRONX

BARTOW-PELL MANSION Shore Road, Pelham Bay Park Tel. (718) 885-1461 *Subway: Line 6, Pelham Bay* *Park station, then bus Bx45* *to Bartow-Pell.*	*Open Wed., Sat., Sun. noon–4pm and first* *Friday of month from 5.30–9.30pm.* *One of the few 19th-century manor houses* *(1842) in New York open to the public. The* *country residence of a wealthy New York* *family. Beautiful terrace garden.*
BRONX ZOO, NEW YORK **ZOOLOGICAL PARK** 2300 Southern Blvd Tel. (718) 220-5100 *Take to $5 BXM bus up Madison Ave.,* *first stop in the Bronx, or 2 or 5 subway* *to E. Tremont Ave./ West Farm Sq., then* *walk 2.5 blocks.*	Nov.-March: open daily 10am–4.30pm. April-Oct.: open Mon.-Fri. 10am–5pm, Sat.-Sun. 10am–5.30pm. Wednesday is pay-what-you-wish admission.
NEW YORK BOTANICAL GARDEN Bronx River Parkway (Fordham Rd) Tel. (718) 817-8700 *Take MTA train from Grand Central to* *Botanical Garden stop, or subway D or* *4 to Bedford Park Blvd stop, then* *BX-26 bus to Garden.*	*Open April-Oct.: 10am–6pm.* *Nov.-March: 10am–5pm.* *Closed public hols.* *Daily docent-led tours; bird walks on Sat.*
POE COTTAGE – **BRONX HISTORICAL SOCIETY** Poe Park, Grand Concourse & Kingsbridge Road Tel. (718) 881-8900 *Subway: Line D or 4 to Kingsbridge* *Road station;* *Bus: Bx12 to Grand Concourse;* *Bx34, Bx26 or Bx9 to 194th St.*	*Open Sat. 10am–4pm and Sun. 1–5pm.* *Open weekdays for groups by appointment.* *Small country house where Edgar Allan Poe* *ended his days.*
WAVE HILL W. 249th St. and Independence Ave. Tel. (718) 549-3200 *Subway: Line 1 or 9 231st St. station* *then bus 7 or 10 to 252nd St.* *Train: Metro North to Riverdale* *station.*	*Open April 14–Oct. 14: Tue.-Sun. 9am–5.30pm* *(Wed. until 9pm in June and July).* *Open Oct. 15-April 13: Tue.-Sun. 9am–4.30pm.* *A park and cultural center located on an* *exceptional site, by the Hudson River. Pleasant* *open-air cafeteria in summer.*
YANKEE STADIUM E. 161st St. and River Ave. Tel. (718) 293-6000 (info) Tel (718) 293-4300 (tickets) *Subway: Line 3, D or 4 to 161st* *station/Yankee Stadium.*	*The Yankees baseball team's stadium.* *The season runs from April until the beginning* *of October.* *Guided tours daily at noon and 1pm.* *Call (212) 307-1212 for tour tickets.*

HARLEM AND BROOKLYN

ABYSSINIAN BAPTIST CHURCH 132 Odell Clark Place (between Adam Clayton Powell Jr. and Malcom X blvds.) Tel. (212) 862-7474	*Services on Sun. at 9am and 11am with gospel choir.* *Memorial Room in memory of Adam Clayton Powell, Jr.*	◆ F C2 ▲ 359
BROOKLYN ACADEMY OF MUSIC 30 Lafayette Ave. Tel. (718) 636-4100 *Shuttle from Manhattan (from 120 Park Ave. and 42nd St.).*	*Organizes musical and theatrical shows, as well as some of the best dance events.*	
BROOKLYN BOTANIC GARDEN 1000 Washington Ave. (Prospect Park) Tel. (718) 623-7200 *Subway: Line 2 or 3 to Grand Army Plaza station*	*Open Tue.-Fri. 8am–4.30pm (6pm in summer), Sat.-Sun. 10am–4.30pm (6pm in summer).* *Closed public hols.* *Botanical garden within an enormous park. Greenhouses, cafeteria.*	
BROOKLYN CHILDREN'S MUSEUM 145 Brooklyn Ave. (St. Mark's Ave.) Tel. (718) 735-4400	*Open Tue.-Fri. 1–6pm (closed Tue. Sep.–June), Sat.-Sun. 11am–6pm.* *Free movies and shows for children interested in natural sciences.*	
BROOKLYN HISTORICAL SOCIETY 128 Pierrepont St. Tel. (718) 624-0890 *Subway: Line 2, 3, 4 or 5 to Brooklyn Museum station*	*Open Fri.-Sun. noon–5pm.* *Call for schedule of events and tours.*	▲ 366
BROOKLYN MUSEUM OF ART 200 Eastern Parkway Tel. (718) 638-5000 *Subway: Line 2, 3, 4 or 5 to Brooklyn Museum station*	*Open Wed.-Fri. 10am–5pm, Sat.-Sun. 11am–6pm.* *Closed Thanksgiving, Christmas and New Year's Day.* *The second-largest museum in New York. Renowned for its department of Egyptian antiquities. Permanent collections include works by Rodin, Toulouse Lautrec, Modigliani and Chagall.*	▲ 366
THE CLOISTERS MUSEUM Fort Tryon Park Tel. (212) 923-3700 *Easily reached by bus M4 on Madison Ave.*	*Open March-Oct.: Tue.–Sun. 9.30am–5.15pm.* *Nov.-Feb.: Tue.-Sun. 9.30am–4.45pm.* *Closed public hols.* *Museum of medieval art housed in former cloisters brought over from Europe. Part of the Metropolitan Museum. Free admission if you use the Metropolitan badge on the same day of purchase.*	◆ F B3 ▲ 362
CONEY ISLAND AMUSEMENT PARK 1000 Surf Ave. Tel. (718) 265-2100 *Subway: Line F or D to W. 8th St. station; Lines B or N, or Q to Stillwell Ave. station*	*Open daily noon–midnight in June-Aug., Sat.-Sun. noon–midnight in April-May and Sep.-Oct. Closed Nov.–April.* *Amusement park by the water.*	
DYCKMAN FARMHOUSE MUSEUM 4881 Broadway (204th St.) Tel. (212) 304-9422	*Closed for renovations* *17th-century Dutch colonial house.*	▲ 361
GENERAL GRANT NATIONAL MEMORIAL – GRANT'S TOMB Riverside Drive (122nd St.) Tel. 212 666-1640	*Open daily 9am–5pm.* *The tomb of President Grant and his wife.*	◆ E A1 ▲ 357
HAMILTON GRANGE NATIONAL MEMORIAL 287 Convent Ave. (141st St.) Tel. (212) 283-5154	*Open Wed.-Sun. 9am–5pm.* *A country house dating back from the time when Harlem was still a village.*	◆ F C2 ▲ 360
HISPANIC SOCIETY OF AMERICA Broadway and 155th St. (Audubon Terrace) Tel. (212) 926-2234	*Open Tue.-Sat. 10am–4.30pm, Sun. 1–4pm.* *Closed public hols.* *Hispanic art, literature and culture.*	◆ F B2 ▲ 361
MORRIS-JUMEL MANSION MUSEUM 65 Jumel Terrace (corner 160th and Edgecombe aves.) Tel. (212) 923-8008	*Open Wed.-Sun. 10am–4pm.* *Closed public hols. Guided tours by appointment.*	◆ F B2 ▲ 361

NEW YORK AQUARIUM W 8th St. and Surf Ave. Coney Island, Brooklyn Tel. (718) 265-FISH *Subway: Line F or Q to W. 8th St.* *station*	*Open daily 10am–5pm, closing slightly later in* *the summer and earlier in the winter.* *Aquatic museum leading to the famous Coney* *Island boardwalk. Sharks, beluga whales and* *dolphin shows every day.*
NEW YORK TRANSIT MUSEUM Boerum Place and Schermerhorn St. (Brooklyn Heights) Tel. (718) 694-1600	*Open Tue.-Fri. 10am–4pm, Sat.-Sun. noon–5pm.* *History of public transportation in New York.* *Gallery-boutique, annex of the museum at* *Grand Central. Terminal open Mon.-Fri.* *8am–8pm, Sat. 10am–6pm. Tel. (212) 878-0106.*
PROSPECT PARK Flatbush Ave. and Grand Army Plaza *Subway: Line 2 or 3 to* *Grand Army Plaza station.*	*Hotline (programs): Tel. (718) 965-8999.*
RIVERSIDE CHURCH Riverside Drive and 122th St. Tel. (212) 870-6700	*Tower closed and recitals suspended during* *renovations.* ✦ E A1 ▲ 356
SCHOMBERG CENTER **FOR RESEARCH IN BLACK CULTURE** 515 Malcom X Boulevard (135th St.) Tel. (212) 491-2200	*Open Tue.-Wed. noon–8pm, Thu.–Sat.* ✦ F D2 *noon–6pm.* ▲ 359 *Annex of the New York Public Library* *specializing in African-American culture.*
STUDIO MUSEUM IN HARLEM 144 W. 125th St. (between Lenox and 7th aves.) Tel. (212) 864-4500	*Open Wed.-Fri. and Sun. noon–6pm, Sat. 10am–* ✦ E A2 *6pm. Closed public hols.* ▲ 351 *Exhibitions of African, African-American and* *Caribbean art.*

QUEENS

AMERICAN MUSEUM **OF THE MOVING IMAGE** 35th Ave. and 36th St., Astoria Tel. (718) 784-0077 *Subway: Line N to Steinway St.* *station; Bus Q101 to Steinway St.*	*Open Wed.-Thu. 11am–5pm, Fri. 11am–9pm* *(free after 4pm), Sat.-Sun. 11am–6pm.* *Closed Thanksgiving and Christmas.* *Fascinating museum retracing the history and* *techniques of the movie and television world.*
THE ISAMU NOGUCHI **GARDEN MUSEUM** 9-01 33rd Rd. (at Vernon Blvd.), Long Island City Tel. (718) 204-7088 *Take the N or W subway to* *Broadway, in Queens, walk 10+* *blocks along waterfront to museum.* *Weekend shuttle leaving from* *Manhattan (Park Ave. and 70th St.)*	*250 works by the Japanese American sculptor.*
JAMAICA BAY WILDLIFE REFUGE Cross Bay Boulevard Tel. (718) 318-4340 *Subway: Line A to Broad Channel* *station, then bus Q21 to Wildlife* *Refuge.*	*Open daily 8.30am–5pm.* *A natural sanctuary by the ocean. Walking and* *nature trails.*
MUSEUM FOR AFRICAN ART 36–01 43rd Ave. (36th St.) Long Island City Tel. (718) 784-7700 *Subway: Line 7, 33rd St station;* *Bus: Q32 to 35th St. and Queens Blvd.*	*Open Mon., Thu.-Fri. 10am–5pm, Sat.-Sun.* *11am– 5pm.* *One of only two American museums specializing* *in traditional and contemporary African art (the* *other being the Smithsonian's National Museum* *of African Art in Washington, D.C.)*
NEW YORK HALL OF SCIENCE 47-01 111th St., Flushing Meadows Corona Park Tel. (718) 699-0005 *Subway: Line 7 to 111th St. station.*	*Open Mon.-Thu. 9.30am–2pm, Fri. 9.30am–5pm* *(free after 2pm), Sat.-Sun. 10am–6pm.* *Science museum located in a pavilion built for* *the 1964 World Fair in Corona Park.*

P.S. 1 CONTEMPORARY ART CENTER Jackson Ave. and 46th Ave., Long Island City Tel (718) 784-2084 *Subway: Line E or V to 23rd / Ely St. station; Line 7 to Courthouse Sq. / 45th Rd station.*	*Open Thu.-Mon. noon–6pm.* *Set up in a former school (Public School no.1), this contemporary art center, opened in 1976 and linked up with MoMa since 1999, houses artist studios and exhibition rooms.*
SCULPTURE CENTER 44-19 Purves St., Long Island City Tel. (718) 361-1750 *Take the E or V train to 23rd/Ely, in Queen walk two blocks toward 43rd St., turn right.*	*Open Thu.-Mon. 11am–6pm.* *Exhibitions of contemporary sculptures.*
SHEA STADIUM 123–01 Roosevelt Ave. (126th St.), Flushing Meadows, Corona Park Tel. (718) 507-METS *Subway: Line 7 to Willets Pt-Shea Stadium station.*	*The New York Mets baseball team's stadium. Season April–Oct. Call (718) 507-TIXX for tickets.*
SOCRATES SCULPTURE PARK Broadway and Vernon Blvd, Long Island City Tel. (718) 956-1819 *Subway: Line N or W to Broadway station, then walk towards the East River (approx. 8 blocks)*	*Open daily from 10am until dusk.* *Situated next to the Isamu Noguchi Garden Museum, this gigantic-sculpture park presents works by New York as well as international artists. Exhibitions are renewed twice a year (spring and fall).*
STATEN ISLAND	
ALICE AUSTEN HOUSE MUSEUM 2 Hylan Blvd. Tel. 718 816-4506 *Staten Island Ferry, then bus S51 to Hylan Blvd.*	*Open Thu.-Sun. noon–5pm. Closed Jan.-Feb.* *Victorian cottage that belonged to photographer Alice Austen. Permanent exhibition of her work on New York. The house looks out onto the beach and affords a splendid view over the New York straits.*
HISTORIC RICHMOND TOWN 441 Clarke Ave. Tel. (718) 351-1611 *Staten Island Ferry, then bus S74 to Richmond Road/ St Patrick's Place.*	*Open Sep.-June: Wed.-Sun. 1–5pm.* *June-Aug.: Mon., Wed.-Sat. 10am–5pm, Sun. 1–5pm.* *The only historic village in New York with 28 houses built between the 17th century and the beginning of the 20th century. Actors in period dress re-enact life as it was then.*
STATEN ISLAND BOTANICAL GARDEN 1000 Richmond Terrace Tel. (718) 273-8200 *Staten Island Ferry, then bus S40 to Snug Harbor*	*Open daily during daylight hours.* *Botanical garden belonging to the Snug Harbor Cultural Center, Tel. (718) 448-2500, a large center set up in a sailors' hospice founded in 1801. The center houses the Staten Island Children's Museum, Tel. (718) 273-2060).*
TIBETAN MUSEUM **(JACQUES MARCHAIS MUSEUM OF TIBETAN ARTS)** 338 Lighthouse Ave. Tel. (718) 987-3500 *Staten Island Ferry, then bus S74 to Lighthouse Ave.*	*Open Wed.-Sun. 1–5pm.* *Unusual museum dedicated to Tibetan art and ethnography.*

BIBLIOGRAPHY ◆

ESSENTIAL READING

◆ ALLEN (Oliver E.): *New York, New York*, Atheneum, NY, 1990
◆ CARO (Robert): *Power Broker, Colin Robert Moses and the Fall of New York*, Alfred A. Knopf, NY, 1974
◆ PERL (Jed): *New Art City*, Alfred A. Knopf, NY, 2005
◆ WHITE (E. B.): *This is New York*, Warner Books, NY, 1988
◆ WILLENSKY (Elliot) and WHITE (Norval) eds., *AIA Guide to New York City*, Harcourt Brace Jovanovich, Publishers, NY, 1988

GENERAL READING

◆ ALLEN (Irving Lewis): *The City in Slang: New York Life and Popular Speech*, Oxford University Press, NY, 1993
◆ BOORSTIN (Daniel): *The Americans*, 3 vols, Random House, NY, 1975
◆ CHARYN (Jerome): *Metropolis: New York as Myth, Marketplace, and Magical Land*, Avon, NY, 1987
◆ COHN (Nik): *Heart of the World*, Alfred A. Knopf, NY, 1992
◆ DIAMONSTEIN (Barbaralee): *Landmarks: Eighteen Wonders of the New York World*, Harry Abrams, NY, 1992
◆ FONER (Nancy): *New Immigrants in New York*, Columbia University Press, NY, 1987
◆ GOLD (Joyce): *From Windmills to the World Trade Center: A Walking Guide to Lower Manhattan History*, Old Warren Road Press, NY, 1988
◆ GLUECK (Grace) and GARDNER (Paul): *Brooklyn: People, Places, Past and Present*, Harry Abrams, NY, 1991
◆ GRAFTON (John): *New York in the Nineteenth Century*, Dover, NY, 1992
◆ HORNUNG (Clarence P.): *The Way It Was, New York, 1850–1890*, Schocken Books, NY, 1977
◆ JOHNSON (Harry) and LIGHTFOOT (Frederick S.): *Maritime New York in Nineteenth Century Photographs*, Dover, NY, 1980
◆ KINKEAD (Gwen.): *Chinatown: A Portrait of a Closed Society*, Harper Collins, NY, 1992
◆ KOUWENHOVEN (John A.): *The Columbia Historical Portrait of New York*, Harper & Row, NY, 1972
◆ MANGIONE (Jerre) and MORREALE (Ben): *La Storia: Five Centuries of the Italian American Experience*, Harper Collins, NY, 1992
◆ PLOTCH (Batia) ed. with MORSE (John) et al.: *New York walks*, Henry Holt, 1992
◆ SANTE (Luc): *Low Life: Lures and Snares of Old New York*, Random House, NY, 1992
◆ SALWEIN (Peter): *Upper West Side Story*, Abbeville Press, NY 1989
◆ SHEPARD (Richard F.): *Broadway from Battery to the Bronx*, Harry Abrams, NY, 1987
◆ STARR (Roger): *The Rise and Fall of New York City*, Basic Books, NY, 1985
◆ TRACHTENBERG (Alan): *Brooklyn Bridge: Fact and Symbol*, Univ. of Chicago Press, Chicago, 1979
◆ TRAGER (James): *Park Avenue: Street of Dreams*, Atheneum, NY, 1990
◆ WALLOCK (Leonard) ed.: *New York: Culture Capital of the World, 1940–1965*, Rizzoli, NY, 1988

ARCHITECTURE

◆ ALPERN (Andrew): *Luxury Apartment Houses of Manhattan*, Dover, NY, 1993
◆ BADGER (Daniel D.): *Badger's Illustrated Catalogue of Cast-Iron Architecture*, Dover, NY, 1982
◆ BOYER (M. Christine): *Manhattan Manners, Architecture and Style 1850–1900*, Rizzoli, NY, 1985
◆ BREEZE (Carla): *New York Deco*, Rizzoli, NY 1993
◆ CROMLEY (Elizabeth Collins): *Alone Together: A History of New York's Early Apartments*, Cornell Univ. Press, Ithaca, 1990
◆ DOLKART (Andrew S.): *A Guide to New York City Landmarks*, Preservation Press, NY, 1992
◆ DUNLAP (David W.): *On Broadway, A Journey Uptown over Time*, Rizzoli, NY, 1990
◆ FRIEDMAN (Joe) and BERENHOLTS (Richard): *Inside New York: Discovering New York's Classic Interiors*, Harper Collins, NY, 1992
◆ GILLON (Edmund V.), REED (Henry. H.): *Beaux-Arts Architecture in New York*, Dover, NY, 1988
◆ GOLDBERGER (Paul): *The Skyscraper*, Alfred A. Knopf, NY, 1983
◆ HAWES (Elizabeth): *New York, New York*, Alfred A. Knopf, NY, 1993

◆ HOOD (Clifton): *722 Miles: The Building of the Subways and How They Transformed New York*, Simon & Schuster, NY, 1993
◆ IRACE (Fulvio): *Emerging Skylines: The New American Skyscrapers*, Whitney Library of Design, NY, 1990
◆ KLOTZ (Heinrich): *New York Architecture, 1970–1990*, Rizzoli, NY, 1989
◆ MACKAY (Donald A.): *The Building of Manhattan*, Harper Collins, NY, 1989
◆ ROSEN (Laura): *Top of the City*, Thames and Hudson, London, 1983
◆ ROTHSCHILD (Nan): *New York City Neighborhoods: The 18th Century*, Academic Press, NY, 1990
◆ SHAPIRO (Mary J.): *A Picture History of the Brooklyn Bridge*, Dover, NY, 1983
◆ SILVER (Nathan): *Lost New York*, Schocken Books, NY, 1967
◆ STERN (Robert. A.), GILMARTIN (G.), MELLINS (T.): *New York Nineteen Thirty*, Rizzoli, NY, 1987
◆ WHYTE (William H.): *City: Rediscovering the Center*, Doubleday, NY, 1990
◆ WOLFE (Gerard R.): *New York: A Guide to the Metropolis*, McGraw-Hill, NY, 1994

ARTS

◆ ABBOTT (Berenice): *New York in the Thirties*, Dover, NY, 1973
◆ AVEDON (Richard): *Autobiography*, Random House, NY, 1993
◆ CHWAST (Seymour) and HELLER (Steven) ed.: *The Art of New York*, Harry Abrams, NY, 1983
◆ COHEN (Barbara) CHWAST (Seymour) and HELLER (Steven) ed.: *New York Observed: Artists and Writers Look at the City*, Harry Abrams, NY, 1987
◆ FIELDS (Armond and Marc L.): *From the Bowery to Broadway: Lew Fields and the Roots of the American Popular Theatre*, Oxford University Press, NY, 1993
◆ HINE (Lewis): *Men at Work*, Dover, NY, 1977
◆ KIRSTEIN (Lincoln): *Mosaic*, Farrar, Straus & Giroux NY, 1994
◆ WILLIS-BRAITHWAITE (Deborah): *Van Der Zee, Photographer*, Harry Abrams, NY, 1993

LITERATURE

◆ AUSTER (Paul): *New York Trilogy: City of Glass, Ghosts, The Locked Room*, Viking

Penguin, NY, 1990
◆ BELLOW (Saul): *Seize the Day*, Viking Penguin, 1984
◆ CAPOTE (Truman): *Breakfast at Tiffany's*, Random House, NY, 1994
◆ CARR (Caleb): *The Alienist*, Random House, NY, 1994
◆ DOCTOROW (E. L.): *The Waterworks*, Random House, NY, 1994
◆ DONLEAVY (J. P.): *A Fairy Tale of New York*, Atlantic Monthly, NY, 1989
◆ DOS PASSOS (John): *Manhattan Transfer*, Houghton-Mifflin, NY, 1991
◆ EDMISTON (Susan) and CIRINO (Linda D.): *Literary New York*, Gibbs Smith Pubs., Indianapolis, 1991
◆ ELLISON (Ralph): *The Invisible Man*, Random House, NY, 1989
◆ FITZGERALD (F. Scott): *Tender is the Night*, Macmillan, NY, 1977
◆ GOOCH (Brad): *City Poet: The Life and Times of Frank O'Hara*, Alfred A. Knopf, NY, 1993
◆ HALEY (Alex): *The Autobiography of Malcolm X*, Ballantine, NY, 1992
◆ LIMEG (Charles): *A Rage of Harlem*, Random House, NY, 1989
◆ JAMES (Henry): *The American Scene*, St. Martin's Press, NY, 1987
◆ LORCA (Federico García): *Poet in New York*, W. W. Norton, NY, 1940
◆ MITCHELL (Joseph): *Up in the Old Hotel*, Pantheon, NY, 1992
◆ WAKEFIELD (Dan): *New York in the '50s*, Houghton-Mifflin, NY, 1992
◆ WHARTON (Edith): *The Age of Innocence*, Alfred A. Knopf NY, 1993
◆ WHITMAN (Walt): *Leaves of Grass*, Random House, NY, 1993
◆ WOLFE (Thomas): *Bonfire of the Vanities*, Farrar, Straus & Giroux, NY 1987

PAINTING

◆ COOPER (Martha), CHALFANT (Henry): *Subway Art*, Henry Holt and Co., NY, 1988
◆ GLUECK (Grace): *New York: The Painted City*, Gibbs Smith Pubs., Indianapolis, 1992
◆ MAJOR (Mike): *Drawings & Paintings of New York*, Main Graphics, 1990
◆ WALDMAN (Diane): *Roy Lichtenstein*, Guggenheim Museum, NY, 1993
◆ WATSON (Steven): *Strange Bedfellows*, Abbeville Press, NY, 1991

411

List of abbreviations used in the picture credits:
MCNY = Museum of The City of NY;
MMA = The Metropolitan Museum of Art;
MOMA = Museum of Modern Art;
MP = Magnum, Paris;
TO = United States Tourist Office in Paris;
RB = Richard Berenholtz;
Sch C = Schomberg Center for Research in Black Culture, The NY Public Library;
SC = Steven L. Cohen;
SD = Seymour Durst Old York Library;
TH = Ted Hardin.

Front cover (US edition): Painting by Charles Sheeler, *Canyons*, 1932 (detail) © Art Resource, NY. Fundacion Coleccion Thyssen-Bornemisza, Madrid, Spain. Courtesy Spanierman Gallery LLC, New York. **Back Cover (US edition):** Top photograph of Brooklyn Bridge © Robert Essel NYC/Corbis.
Endpaper1 : *World Trade Center*. Cl. RB. *WTC Observatory Deck. View of Manhattan from Brooklyn*. Explorer, Paris. *White Horse Tavern*. Cl. TH. NYCVB and Battman (top). *Times Square*. Cl. B.Lévy/N. Christitch. *Broadway Boogie Woogie*, Piet Mondrian, 1942-43 (127 X 127), detail © SPADEM. *Central Park*. Cl. É. Courtade. Metropolitan Museum of Art. *Salomon R. Guggenheim Foundation*-D. M. Heald. *Street in Harlem*. MP. *Carte infographique*, Édigraphie/Gallimard Nouveaux Loisirs. **10** *"Theoline", Pier 11, East River*, photo 1936. Berenice Abbott/Commerce Graphics. **12** *The Bowery, beneath the 3rd Ave El*, photo c. 1940, Andreas Feininger. **14** *Interior of the El station (Columbus Ave/72nd Street)*, photo 1936. Berenice Abbott/Commerce Graphics. **16** *Snowstorm*, 19th-century engraving, all rights reserved. Ill. P. Biard, all rights reserved. **16–17** Map, P. Coulbois, all rights reserved. Drawings T. Sarg. SD. **17** *The Ice-bound Hudson*, photo L. Freed. MP. *Midtown Garment District, in the Rain*, photo T. Hoepker. MP. *Dog Days in Manhattan*, photo R. Keystone, Paris. *Woolworth Building in the Fog*, photo, all rights reserved. *Upper West Side in the snow*, photo, all rights reserved. *Depression over the East Coast*, satellite photo, NASA. **18** *North bank of Manhattan*, photo S. Horenstein. **18–19** Ill. J. Torton and G. Houbre, all rights reserved. **19** *Marble outcrop in Isham Park*, photo S. Horenstein. **20** *Leaping sturgeon in Hudson Bay*, 19th-century engraving. SD. *Hudson River - pier*, photo Joseph Olmstead Holmes, all rights reserved. Ill. F. Desbordes, all rights reserved. **22** Ill. F. Desbordes and P. Merienne, all rights reserved. **23** *Red Cardinal*, photo P. Dubois, all rights reserved. **24** Ill. J. Chevallier, B. Duhem, J. Wilkinson and F. Desbordes, all rights reserved. **25** *Centennial of the evacuation of New York by the British*, poster by Joseph Koehler, 1883. Coll. of the NY Historical Society. **26** *Algonquin Natives*, engraving, by Théodore de Bry, all rights reserved. *Bernardo da Verrazano*, engraving 1767, all rights reserved. *Peter Minuit buys the island of Manhattan from the natives*, engraving. Library of Congress. **27** *City of New York's coat of arms*, engraving. SD. *Washington's arrival in New York, 1783*, lithograph. Federal Hall Archives, NY. *Federal sugar refinery*, engraving. Old Print Shop. **28** *Leaving for the Civil War*, engraving. New York Bound. *"Wanted" notice for William Tweed*, December 6,1875, all rights reserved. *Flatiron Building*, all rights reserved. **29** *Panic in Wall Street*, engraving. SD. *Einstein and La Guardia in 1936*, the Bettmann Archive/UPI, NY. **30** *New Holland*, engraving by Joost Hartgers, 1651. Coll. of the NY Historical Society. *Barry Faulkner, detail from a mural (Fur Trade)*. Washington Irving High School, reproduced with kind permission of the NYC Art Commission. *King's College, 1790*, engraving. SD. **30–31** *View of Fort George in New York*, engraving, 1731–6. SD. **31** *New Amsterdam*, engraving, Nicholas Visscher, 1651–5. SD. *Peter Stuyvesant's army arriving in New Amsterdam*, oil painting by W. Mulready, in *Valentine's Manual*, 1859. SD. *Trinity Church in 1737*, engraving G. Hayward, in *Valentine's Manual*, 1859. SD. **32** *Map showing the Dutch East India Company's allocation of original plots of land in New Amsterdam to its inhabitants*, engraving, in *Valentine's Manual*, 1857. **32–33** *Map of New York City*, 19th century. *Commissioners' Map of New York City*. SD. **33** *Boulevard lining the Hudson River*, all rights reserved. *Plan of south Manhattan*, all rights reserved. *Plan of Central Park*, 19th century. SD. **34** *New York cop*. In *Fortune*, July 1939. *Croton Reservoir*, 19th-century photo, Mary Black, all rights reserved. *Mounted metropolitan police officer*, engraving. In *Harper's Weekly*, May 31, 1884. *Lamp lighter*, lithograph. SD. **34–35** *Laying underground telephone cables and electric wiring*. In *Frank Leslie's Illustrated Newspaper*, January 29, 1887. **35**

Underground section of New York. In *Fortune*, July 1939. *Interior of an ambulance*, engraving in *Harper's Weekly*, May 24, 1884. *Public School in New York*, engraving, end 19th century, all rights reserved. **36** *Disembarking from the ferry on the East River, at 26th St*, lithograph. SD. *Carriage*, 19th-cen. print, Publicité DR. *The first yellow taxis in New York in the 1970's*. Photo TH. **36–37** *Yellow cab*, ©Bertrand Rieger/Hémisphères. **37** *Bend of the El over 110th St*, all rights reserved. *The Bowery and its El*, all rights reserved. *City Hall subway station*, all rights reserved. *Hackney Carriage*, 19th-century engraving, advertisement, all rights reserved. **38** *Detail from the façade of a New York fire house*, all rights reserved. *Triangle shirtwaist Company Fire*, painting by Victor J. Gatto. MCNY. **38–39** *Fire Department fire engine*, all rights reserved. **39** *Fire at Crystal Palace*, engraving. SD. *Fire at the headquarters of the Equitable Insurance Company, on Broadway, in March 1908*, all rights reserved. *Fire Escapes*. Photo R. Arroche, all rights reserved. **40** *Lucky Luciano*. NY City Municipal Archives. *W 47th Street Police Station*, by Robert Riggs. In *Fortune*, July 1939, all rights reserved. *Poster for the movie "Mean Streets"*. Ciné plus. *Arrest of "Boss Tweed"*, engraving. NY Bound. *Destruction of 10,000 gallons of liquor and alcohol by the New York police, in 1937*, photo. Coll. Roger Viollet, Paris. **40–41** *The weapon of crime*, photo by Weegee. Shirmer Mosel, Munich. **41** *Gotti's Trial*, drawing. AP/Wide World Photos. *Front Headline from the "Times" of July 25, 1977. Headline from the "Times" of December 1980. Police inquiry in the Oriental community*. Photo F. Dannen. **42** *Barges in Coenties Slip*, engraving. In *Harper's Weekly*, February 16,1884. **42–43** *The southern tip of Manhattan*. Ill. in *King's Views of New York. Passengers disembarking from a ship*, engraving. In *Harper's Weekly*, July 14, 1877. **43** *View of New York Harbor over the East River*, and *The construction of the Brooklyn Bridge*, late 19th-century photo, all rights reserved. *Satellite view of Manhattan*. NASA Archives and photo. *Cruiser in New York Harbor*. SD. *Queen Mary 2*, photo Joseph Olmstead Holmes, all rights reserved. **44** *Postcard of Saint Patrick's Day*. Coll. Gallimard. *Sweatshop in the Jewish Quarter*, photograph by Jacob Riis, all rights reserved. *Jewish shoe seller*. SD. *Street scene in Chinatown*, all rights reserved. **45** *German brasserie in the Bowery district*, 19th-century engraving, by J. R. Brown. In *The London Graphic*, February 10, 1877. *The Vesuvio Bakery, 160 Prince Street*. Photo RB. *Street scene in Harlem*. Sch C. **46** *Attack* © Seth Maccallister–STR/AFP. *Pedestrians running down Church Street* © Susan Meiselass/Magnum photos. **47** *Firefighters in front of the ruins*. © Doug Kanter-STR/AFP. *A survivor* © Stan Honda-STR/AFP. *Father Nychal Judge's funeral* © Paul Fusco/Magnum Photos. **48** *"We speak French, etc."*, photo. SD. *"Big Apple" logo. Street in Chinatown*, all rights reserved. **49** *Fashion ill.*, watercolor by Benegni, for *Femina*, Christmas 1928. Bibliothèque des Arts décoratifs, Charmet, Paris. **50** *Saint Elizabeth Seton*, 19th-century engraving, all rights reserved. *Saint Patrick's Cathedral*, photo. OT. *Jehovah's Witness magazines*, all rights reserved. *Protestant anti-Catholic engraving*, in *Harper's Weekly*, September 30, 1871, all rights reserved. **50** *Two Chassidic Jews, diamond dealers on 47th St/5th Ave*, photo R. Burri. MP. **51** *Mosque in Manhattan*. US Kuwait Embassy Archives. *Moonie Wedding*, photo. AP/Wide World Photos. *Statue of Shinran-Shonin*, photo, all rights reserved. *96th Street mosque*, photo Joseph Olmstead Holmes, all rights reserved. **52** *Thanksgiving Greetings*, all rights reserved. *Marquis de Lafayette*, engraving, all rights reserved. *Hanging out the flags at the end of the Civil War*, detail from engraving. In *Harper's Weekly* of March 25, 1865. **52–53** *Ticker-tape Parade*, 1991. AP/Wide World Photos. **53** *Fourth of July celebrations in New York*, photo J. Lukas, taken from Brooklyn Heights. Explorer. *Macy's Thanksgiving Day*, photo by John F. Nugent. Kind permission of Macy's. *Chinese New Year*. AP/Wide World Photos. *Halloween celebrations in Greenwich Village*, 1990. AP/Wide World Photos. **54** *Newspaper seller*, Nicolino Calyo, watercolor c. 1840–44. MCNY. *Hamilton defends Zenger*, 18th-century engraving, all rights reserved. *The Yellow Dugan Kid*, watercolor, all rights reserved. **54–55** *Headline from the "New York Times"*, December 8, 1941. **55** *Interiors from "Frank Leslie's Newspaper" publishing house: editorial office, typesetting office, printing press*, all rights reserved. *Covers of The New Yorker, including one by Sempé*, all rights reserved. **56** *Lee De Forest, inventor of the triode lamp*, photo. Roger Viollet. *David Sarnoff, champion of the Morse code*, photo. AP/Wide World Photos. *Broadcast with George Burns and Gracie Allen*. FPG International, Explorer. *Felix the Cat*, ill. P. Sullivan, all rights reserved. *Television broadcast*, engraving. *Walter Cronkite*. Library of Congress. **56–57** *Radio City Music Hall sign*, all rights reserved. **57** *Big Bird*, all rights reserved. *Televised*

◆ LIST OF ILLUSTRATIONS

◆ LIST OF ILLUSTRATIONS

We would like to thank the following for their kind assistance:

Seymour Durst, *Old New York Foundation* • Gordon MacCollum, *American Architecture Archives* • Luis Cancel, *former commissioner of the New York City Department of Cultural Affairs* • Deborah Bershad, Margaret Hammerle, *Art Commission of the City of New York* • Idilio Gracia-Peña, *commissioner of the New York City* • *Department of Records and Information Services* • Kenneth Cobb, *NYC Municipal Archives* • Jane Harris, *Manhattan Sites* • Jane Hausen, *The NYC Landmarks Preservation Commission* • Sherrill Wilson, Tuesday Brooks, *The Office of Public Education and Interpretation* • Cathy del Priori, Betsy Becker, *Madison Square Garden* • Robert M. Browning, *National Baseball Hall of Fame and Museum* • Anne Marie Gilmartin, *N. Y. Rangers* • Paul Spinelli, Lisa Shulman, Frank Ramos, *Jets NFL Properties* • Ro Lohin, *The New York Studio School* • Nancy Cricco, *New York University* • Kathleen Goncharov, *The New School for Social Research* • Janet Parks, *Avery Library, Columbia University* • Robert MacDonald, Leslie Nolan, Marguerite Lavin, Tony Piasani, Terry, Ariano, Peter Simmons, Billie Heller, Marty Jacobs, *Museum of the City of New York* • Alison Whiting, Mary Beth Betts, *The New York Historical Society* • Diana Pardue, Jeffrey S. Dosik, Geraldine Santoro, Kevin Daley, *Ellis Island Immigration Museum* • Amy Hines, Neil Calvanese, Sarah Cedar Miller, *Central Park Conservancy* • Tom Ching, *Parks Horticulture* • Barbara Treitel, *The Jewish Museum* • *The Jewish Forward* • Lori Duggan Gold, *Brooklyn Botanic Garden* • Karen L. Saber, *New York Botanical Garden* • Linda Corcoran, *NYZS The Wildlife Conservation Society* • Harry Hunter, *National Museum of American History, Smithsonian Institution* • Mary Ison, *Prints and Photographs Division, Library of Congress* • Michelle Saffir, *Asia Society* • Susan George, *Fraunces Tavern* • Charles Juno, *Empire State Building* • Patty Schickram, *Macy's* • James Reed, Celeste Torello, *Rockefeller Group* • Joe Grabowski, Ken Walmsley, *The Woolworth Corporation* • Geraldine Barnett, *US Post Office Bowling Green Station* • Lisa Berlin, *US Post Office* • Steve Gilkenson, *McAuley Mission* • Mons. Anthony Dalla Villa, Thomas Young, *Saint Patrick's Cathedral* • The Very Rev. James P. Morton, William Logan, *The Cathedral Church of Saint John the Divine* • Rebecca Carlisle Blind, *Saint James Episcopal Church* • Joan Baachus-Patterson, *Riverside Church* • Eric Hilton, *First Presbyterian Church* • Sister Rita King • Sister Margarita Smith • Anthony Bellov, *Abigail Adams Smith Museum* • Paul Glassman, *Morris-Jumel Mansion* • Kathy Stocking, *New York State Historical Association* • Aldon James, Carol Lowrey, *The National Arts Club* • Tom Gilbert, *AP/Wide World Photos-Inc.* • Helaine Pardo, *Commerce Graphics* • Dan May, Karl Nemchek, *Met Life* • Barbara Cohen, Judith Stonehill, Francis Morrone, *New York Bound Bookshop* • Mike Regan, *World Trade Center* • Leon Haft, *Marshall Chelsa Club* • Ian Ginsberg, *Bigelow Pharmacy* • Major Waddington, *Salvation Army* • Melissa L. Burian, *US Dept. of Commerce* • Lloyd Morgan, *Morgan Press* • Don Luck, Ester Smith, *Institute of Jazz Studies* • Donna Walker Collins, *Dance Theater of Harlem* • Nancy Lassale, Steve Miller, *New York City Ballet* • James Johnson, Martha Graham • Yee Chan, *Alvin Ailey* • Ellen Jacobs, *Merce Cunningham* • Nicole Vandestienne, *Paul Taylor Dance Company* • *RCA Archives* • Azita Corton, *CBS* • Scott Fain, Carol Brokaw, *ABC* • Betty Hudson, *NBC* • Lida Lauffer, *HBO* • Richard Betz, *La Verne* • J. Carter, Stacey Friedman, *MTV Networks* • Mark Magner, Kingson Chou, Richard Termini, *Children's Television Workshop* • William L. Noble • Walter Gasnick • Rev. Stephen S. Garney •

We would like to thank the following for permission to reproduce the extracts on pages 114 to 128:

◆ DONADIO & ASHWORTH, INC: Excerpt from *Good As Gold* by Joseph Heller, copyright © 1979 by Joseph Heller. Reprinted by permission of Donadio & Ashworth, Inc. (UK) Excerpt from *Good As Gold* by Joseph Heller, published by Jonathan Cape Ltd, reprinted by permission of Jonathan Cape Ltd, London.

◆ ELIZABETH H. DOS PASSOS: Excerpt from *Manhattan Transfer* by John Dos Passos (Harper and Brothers, 1925). Reprinted by permission of Elizabeth H. Dos Passos, Co-Executor, the Estate of John Dos Passos.

◆ THE DREISER TRUST: Excerpt from *The Color of a Great City* by Theodore Dreiser, copyright © 1923 by Boni & Liveright, Inc. copyright renewed 1951 by Mrs Theodore Dreiser, as widow of the author. Reprinted by permission of The Dreiser Trust, Harold J. Dies, Trustee.

◆ FABER AND FABER LIMITED: "Broadway" by Vladimir Mayakovsky, translated by Peter Jukes from *A Shout in the Street* by Peter Jukes (1990). Reprinted by permission of Faber and Faber Ltd. Also reprinted in the U.K. by permission of Faber and Faber Ltd.

◆ FARRAR, STRAUS & GIROUX, INC.: Excerpt from *I Thought of Daisy* by Edmund Wilson, copyright © 1953 by Edmund Wilson, copyright renewed 1981 by Helen Miranda Wilson. Reprinted by permission of Farrar, Straus & Giroux, Inc. Also reprinted in the U.K. by permission of Farrar, Straus & Giroux, Inc.

– Excerpt from "Harlem Literati" from *The Big Sea* by Langston Hughes. Copyright © 1940 by Langston Hughes. Copyright renewed 1968 by Arna Bontemps and George Houston Press. Reprinted by permission of Hill and Wang, a division of Farrar, Straus & Giroux, Inc.

◆ HARPERCOLLINS PUBLISHERS, INC.: Excerpt from 'Here is New York' from *Essays of E. B. White* by E. B. White, copyright © 1949 by E. B. White, copyright renewed 1977 by E. B. White. Reprinted by permission of HarperCollins Publishers, Inc.

◆ ALFRED A. KNOPF, INC: Excerpt from *Souvenir and Prophecies* by Holly Stevens, copyright © 1966, 1976 by Holly Stevens. Also reprinted in the U.K. by permission of Alfred A. Knopf, Inc.

– Excerpt from *Odd Jobs*, by John Updike, copyright © 1991 by John Updike. Reprinted by permission of Alfred A. Knopf, Inc.

(UK) Excerpt from *Odd Jobs*, by John Updike (Penguin Books) 1992, first published in the U.K. by André Deutsch) copyright © 1991 by John Updike. Reprinted by permission of Hamilton Ltd.

◆ LITTLE, BROWN AND COMPANY: "A Brief Guide to New York" from *Verses from 1929 On*, by Ogden Nash, copyright © 1940 by Ogden Nash. Reprinted by permission of Little, Brown and Company. (UK) "A Brief Guide to New York" poem published in *Many Long Years Ago*, Little, Brown 1945 © 1945 by Ogden Nash. Reprinted in the UK by permission of Curtis Brown Ltd.

◆ MACMILLAN PUBLISHING COMPANY: Excerpt from *The Diary of George Templeton Strong* by Allan Nevins and Milton Halsey Thomas, copyright © 1952 by Macmillan Publishing Company, copyright renewed 1980 by Milton Halsey Thomas. Reprinted by permission of Macmillan Publishing Company.

◆ NEW DIRECTIONS PUBLISHING CORP.: Excerpt from *The Crack-Up* by F. Scott Fitzgerald, copyright © 1945 by New Directions Publishing Corp. Reprinted by permission of New Directions Publishing Corp. (UK) Excerpt from *The Crack-Up* by F. Scott Fitzgerald, published by the Bodley Head, reprinted by permission of the Fitzgerald Estate and the Bodley Head, London.

◆ PANTHEON BOOKS: Excerpt from *Up in the Old Hotel* by Joseph Mitchell, copyright © 1992 by Joseph Mitchell. Reprinted by permission of Pantheon Books, a division of Random House, Inc.

◆ THE WALLACE LITERARY AGENCY, INC : Excerpt from *Great Jones Street* by Don DeLillo, copyright © 1973 by Don DeLillo (Penguin Books). Reprinted by permission of The Wallace Literary Agency, Inc. Also reprinted in the U.K. (published there by Picador Books) by permission of The Wallace Literary Agency, Inc.

◆ A. P. WATT LTD: Excerpt from *What I Saw in America* by G. K. Chesterton (Hodder & Stoughton, London, 1922). Reprinted by permission of A. P. Watt Ltd on behalf of the Royal Literary Fund.

◆ INDEX

◆ INDEX

THEATERS

RELIGIOUS BUILDINGS

MUSEUMS

PARKS AND GARDENS

Map section

Key

95	Freeway
	Main road
	Railroad
	State boundary
	Borough boundary
✈	Airport
Ⓜ	Subway station
✚	Hospital

◆ STREET INDEX

◆ STREET INDEX

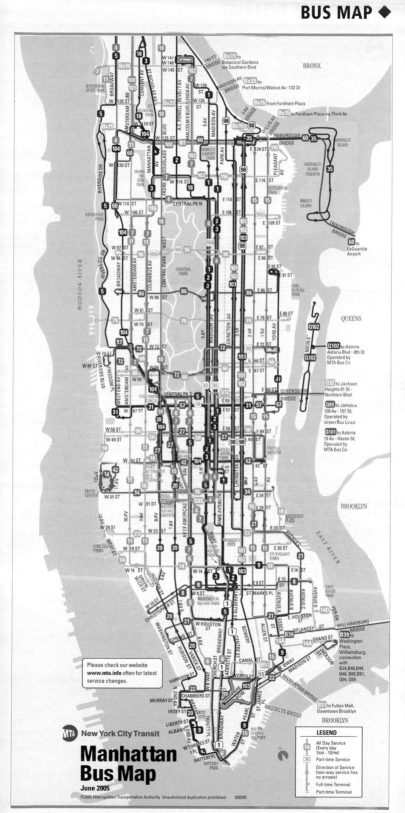

Please check our website
www.mta.info often for latest
service changes.

MTA New York City Transit

Manhattan Bus Map

June 2005

©2005 Metropolitan Transportation Authority. Unauthorized duplication prohibited   050305

LEGEND

14	All Day Service (Every day 7AM - 10PM)
30	Part-time Service
	Direction of Service (two-way service has no arrows)
■	Full-time Terminal
□	Part-time Terminal

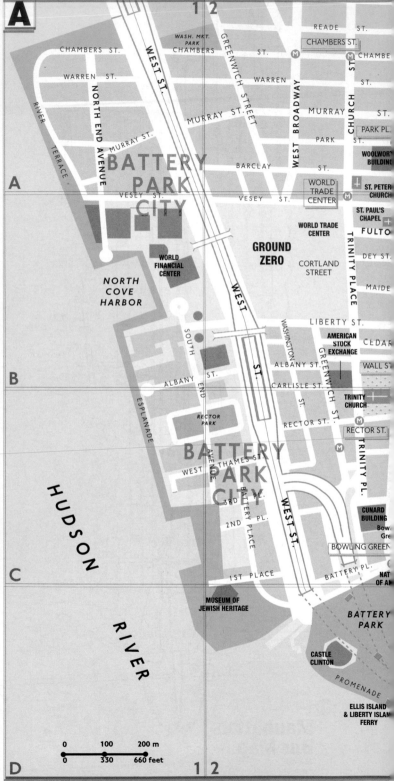

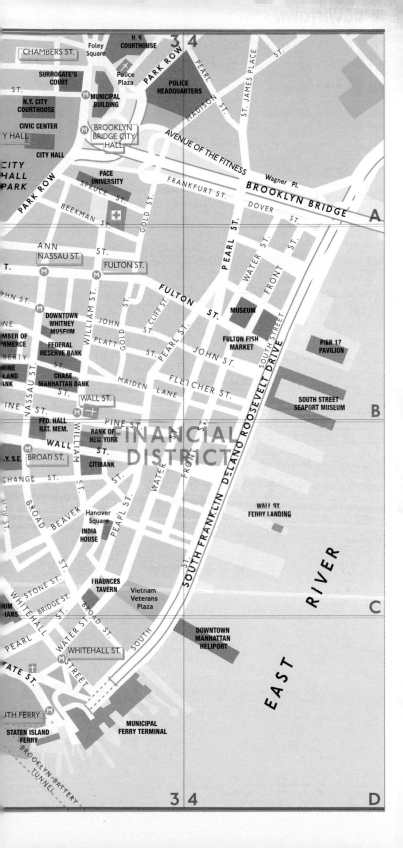

CHAMBERS ST.

Foley
Square

U.S.
COURTHOUSE

3   4

PARK ROW

SURROGATE'S
COURT

Police
Plaza

POLICE
HEADQUARTERS

PEARL ST.

ST. JAMES PLACE

ST.

ST.

N.Y. CITY
COURTHOUSE

MADISON ST.

ST.

MUNICIPAL
BUILDING

CIVIC CENTER

Y HALL

BROOKLYN
BRIDGE CITY
HALL

AVENUE OF THE FITNESS

CITY HALL

Wagner Pl.

CITY
HALL
PARK

PARK ROW

PACE
UNIVERSITY

SPRUCE ST.

FRANKFURT ST.

GOLD ST.

DOVER ST.

BROOKLYN BRIDGE

A

BEEKMAN ST.

ANN
NASSAU ST.

ST.

FULTON ST.

PEARL ST.

WATER ST.

FRONT ST.

T.

FULTON ST.

HN ST.

NE

DOWNTOWN
WHITNEY
MUSEUM

WILLIAM ST.

JOHN
ST.

CLIFF ST.

ST.

PEARL ST.

MUSEUM

SOUTH STREET

PIER 17
PAVILION

MBER OF
MMERCE

FEDERAL
RESERVE BANK

PLATT
ST.

GOLD
ST.

JOHN ST.

FULTON FISH
MARKET

BERTY

RINE
LAND
ANK

CHASE
MANHATTAN BANK

VASSAU ST.

MAIDEN LANE

FLETCHER ST.

SOUTH STREET
SEAPORT MUSEUM

B

INE ST.

WALL ST.

FED. HALL
NAT. MEM.

PINE ST.

WILLIAM ST.

WALL
ST.

BANK OF
NEW YORK

FINANCIAL
DISTRICT

N.Y.S.E.

BROAD ST.

CITIBANK

WATER ST.

FRONT ST.

WALL ST.
FERRY LANDING

CHANGE ST.

BROAD ST.

BEAVER ST.

Hanover
Square

PEARL ST.

SOUTH FRANKLIN DELANO ROOSEVELT DRIVE

RIVER

C

NW ST.

INDIA
HOUSE

UM
IANS

STONE ST.

BRIDGE ST.

FRAUNCES
TAVERN

BROAD ST.

Vietnam
Veterans
Plaza

WHITEHALL ST.

PEARL ST.

WATER ST.

WHITEHALL ST.

SOUTH ST.

DOWNTOWN
MANHATTAN
HELIPORT

EAST

ATE ST.

STREET

UTH FERRY

STATEN ISLAND
FERRY

MUNICIPAL
FERRY TERMINAL

RIVER

D

BROOKLYN-BATTERY
TUNNEL

3   4

◆ DOWNTOWN

B

1 2

WEST 30TH ST.
WEST 29TH ST.
WEST 28TH ST.
CHELSEA PARK
WEST 26TH ST.
WEST 25TH ST.
WEST 24TH ST.
WEST 23RD ST.

28TH STREET
28TH STREET
28TH STREE

BROADWAY

NEW YORK LIFE INSURANCE BUILDING
APPELLATE COURT
MADISON SQUARE PARK
METROPOLI TAN
LIFE TOWER

23RD STREET
23RD STREET
23RD STREET
23RD STRE

GENERAL THEOLOGICAL SEMINARY
CHELSEA HOTEL

FLATIRON BUILDING

GRAM PAR

WEST 20TH ST.
WEST 19TH S

CHELSEA

T. ROOSEVELT BIRTHPLACE

WEST 17TH ST.

TENTH AVE
NINTH AVE
EIGHTH AVE
SEVENTH AVE
(SIXTH AVE)
FIFTH AVE
PARK AVE SOUTH

PORT AUTHORITY UNION ISLAND TERMINAL

14TH ST.
6TH AVE.
WEST 14TH ST.
14TH ST.
14TH ST.

UNION SQUARE PARK
CONSOLIN EDISO BUILD

8TH AVENUE

WEST 13TH ST.
WEST 12TH ST.
WEST 11TH ST.
WEST 10TH ST.
WEST 9TH ST.
WEST 8TH ST.

GREENWICH AVE

ST. JOHN'S CHURCH

EIGHTH AVE
GREENWICH AVE
WEST 11TH ST.
SEVENTH

GREENWICH VILLAGE

University Place

ASTOR PLAC

CHRISTOPHER ST.

8TH ST.

COLONNAD ROW

CHRISTOPHER ST.
BLEECKER

WEST 4TH ST.

WASHINGTON ARCH
WASHINGTON SQUARE PARK
NEW YORK UNIVERSITY

B

WEST STREET

GANSEVOORT ST.
HORATIO ST.
JANE ST.
WASHINGTON ST.
BANK ST.
PERRY ST.
CHARLES ST.
WEST 10TH ST.
CHRISTOPHER
BARROW ST.
MORTON ST.
LEROY ST.

GREENWICH ST.
HUDSON STREET
BLEECKER ST.
BEDFORD ST.
SOUTH

WEST 4TH ST.

ST. LUKE'S CHAPEL

HOUSTON ST.

BLEECKER ST.

LA GUARDIA PL.

BROADWAY

BLEECKER

HUDSON

WEST ST.

WEST

AMERICAS
McDOUGAL
SULLIVAN ST.
THOMPSON ST.
WEST BROADWAY
GREENE ST.
MERCER ST.

HOUSTON ST.

THE NEW MUSEUM OF CONTEMPORARY ART

PRINCE

B'W

PRINCE

KING ST.
CHARLTON ST.
VANDAM ST.
VARICK
SPRING

SPRING ST.

SPRING

SPRING S

SPRING ST.

HAUGHWO BUILDING

C

HUDSON

BROOME ST.

SOHO

GRAND

CROSBY S

CANAL
WATTS
HUDSON STREET
STREET
AVENUE
OF
THE
ST.

MUSEUM OF HOLOGRAPHY

RIVER

HOLLAND TUNNEL

CANAL ST.

CANAL ST.

LAIGHT
HUBERT ST.
GREENWICH ST.
NORTHMORE ST.
HARRISON ST.
WEST ST.

CIVIC CENTER SYNAGOGUE

FRANKLIN ST.

LEONARD ST.
WORTH ST.
THOMAS ST.
DUANE ST.
READE ST.

CHURCH
BROADWAY

CIVIC
CENTER S
U.S.
COURTHOU
MUNICIPA
BUILDING

0   210   420 m
0   690   1380 feet

CHAMBERS
CHAMBERS ST.

1 2

CHAMBERS ST.

D

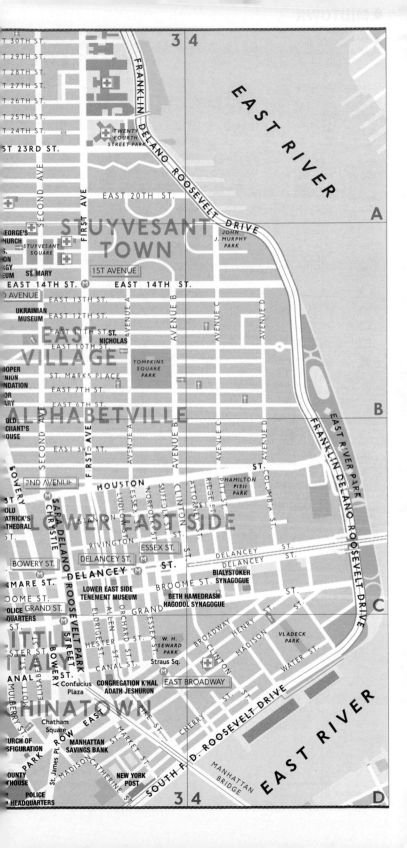

C

BOAT BASIN

79TH STREET

WEST 77TH ST.
WEST 76TH ST.
WEST 75TH ST.
WEST 74TH ST.

ANSONIA HOUSE

72ND STREET

WEST 70TH ST.

WEST 69TH ST.
WEST 68TH ST.
WEST 67TH ST.

LINCOLN CENTER

FORDHAM UNIVERSITY

WEST 60TH ST.
WEST 59TH ST.
WEST 58TH ST.

WEST 57TH ST.

WEST 56TH ST.
WEST 55TH ST.
WEST 54TH ST.
WEST 53RD ST.
WEST 52ND ST.
WEST 51ST ST.
WEST 50TH ST.
WEST 49TH ST.
WEST 48TH ST.
WEST 47TH ST.
WEST 46TH ST.
WEST 45TH ST.
WEST 44TH ST.
WEST 43RD ST.

WEST 42ND ST.

WEST 41ST ST.
WEST 40TH ST.
WEST 39TH ST.
WEST 38TH ST.

WEST 34TH ST.
WEST 33RD ST.

AMERICAN MUSEUM OF NATURAL HISTORY

NEW YORK HISTORICAL SOCIETY

DAKOTA BUILDING

UPPER WEST SIDE

72ND STREET

Lincoln Square

Columbus Circle

NEW YORK COLISEUM

59TH STREET COLUMBUS CIRCLE

MAINE MEMORIAL

CLINTON

DE WITT CLINTON PARK

PASSENGER SHIP TERMINAL

NEW YORK SCHOOL OF PRINTING

50TH ST.

49TH ST.

INTREPID SEA-AIR-SPACE MUSEUM

THEATER DISTRICT

MARRIOTT MARQUIS HOTEL

Duffy Square

Times Square

42ND ST.

HUDSON RIVER DAY LINE

WEST 42ND ST.

PORT AUTHORITY BUS TERMINAL

TIMES SQUARE 42ND STREET

GARMENT DISTRICT

JACOB K. JAVITS CONVENTION CENTER

34TH ST.

GENERAL POST OFFICE

MADISON SQUARE GARDEN

PENNSYLVANIA STATION

34TH ST.

Herald Square

0   200   400 m

HELIPORT

CENTRAL PARK

TRANSVERSE ROAD

THE RAMBLE

THE LAKE

BOW BRIDGE

CHERRY HILL

BETHESDA FOUNTAIN

Bandshell

BOWLING GREENS

WEST DRIVE

TRANSVERSE ROAD

SHEEP MEADOW

HECKSCHER PLAYGROUND

VISITOR INFORMATION CENTER

WOLLMAN SKATING RINK

CENTRAL PARK

57TH ST.

CARNEGIE HALL

7TH AVE

ROCKEFELLER

50TH ST.

47TH-50TH ST ROCKEFELLER CENTER

BROADWAY

42ND

BROADWAY

HUDSON RIVER

RIVERSIDE PARK

H. HUDSON PKW

RIVERSIDE DRIVE

MILLER HWY J. DIMAGGIO HWY

WEST END AVE

AMSTERDAM AVE

BROADWAY

COLUMBUS AVE

CENTRAL PARK WEST

WEST DRIVE

ELEVENTH AVE

EIGHTH AVE

SEVENTH AVE

TWELFTH AVE

ELEVENTH AVE

TENTH AVE

DYER AVE

NINTH AVE

EIGHTH AVE

SEVENTH AVE

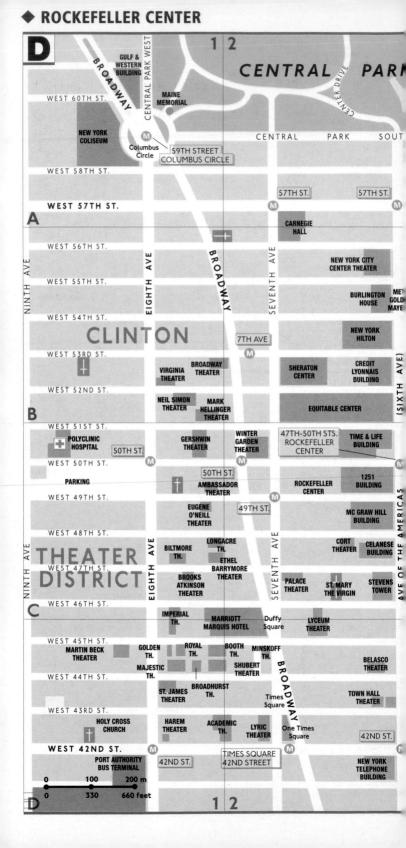

◆ ROCKEFELLER CENTER

D

1 2

BROADWAY

GULF &
WESTERN
BUILDING

CENTRAL PARK WEST

MAINE MEMORIAL

WEST 60TH ST.

CENTRAL PARK

CENTER DRIVE

NEW YORK COLISEUM

Columbus Circle

59TH STREET COLUMBUS CIRCLE

CENTRAL PARK SOUTH

WEST 58TH ST.

WEST 57TH ST.

57TH ST.

57TH ST.

A

CARNEGIE HALL

WEST 56TH ST.

NINTH AVE

EIGHTH AVE

BROADWAY

SEVENTH AVE

NEW YORK CITY CENTER THEATER

WEST 55TH ST.

BURLINGTON HOUSE

MET
GOLD
MAYE

WEST 54TH ST.

CLINTON

7TH AVE

NEW YORK HILTON

WEST 53RD ST.

VIRGINIA THEATER

BROADWAY THEATER

SHERATON CENTER

CREDIT LYONNAIS BUILDING

(SIXTH AVE)

WEST 52ND ST.

NEIL SIMON THEATER

MARK HELLINGER THEATER

EQUITABLE CENTER

B

WEST 51ST ST.

POLYCLINIC HOSPITAL

50TH ST.

GERSHWIN THEATER

WINTER GARDEN THEATER

47TH–50TH STS. ROCKEFELLER CENTER

TIME & LIFE BUILDING

WEST 50TH ST.

PARKING

50TH ST.

AMBASSADOR THEATER

ROCKEFELLER CENTER

1251 BUILDING

AVE OF THE AMERICAS

WEST 49TH ST.

EUGENE O'NEILL THEATER

49TH ST.

MC GRAW HILL BUILDING

WEST 48TH ST.

THEATER

BILTMORE TH.

LONGACRE TH.

CORT THEATER

CELANESE BUILDING

WEST 47TH ST.

DISTRICT

ETHEL BARRYMORE THEATER

NINTH AVE

EIGHTH AVE

SEVENTH AVE

BROOKS ATKINSON THEATER

PALACE THEATER

ST. MARY THE VIRGIN

STEVENS TOWER

WEST 46TH ST.

C

IMPERIAL TH.

MARRIOTT MARQUIS HOTEL

Duffy Square

LYCEUM THEATER

WEST 45TH ST.

MARTIN BECK THEATER

GOLDEN TH.

ROYAL TH.

BOOTH TH.

MINSKOFF TH.

BELASCO THEATER

MAJESTIC TH.

SHUBERT THEATER

WEST 44TH ST.

ST. JAMES THEATER

BROADHURST TH.

Times Square

BROADWAY

TOWN HALL THEATER

WEST 43RD ST.

HOLY CROSS CHURCH

HAREM THEATER

ACADEMIC TH.

LYRIC THEATER

One Times Square

42ND ST.

WEST 42ND ST.

PORT AUTHORITY BUS TERMINAL

42ND ST.

TIMES SQUARE 42ND STREET

NEW YORK TELEPHONE BUILDING

0   100   200 m
0   330   660 feet

D

1 2

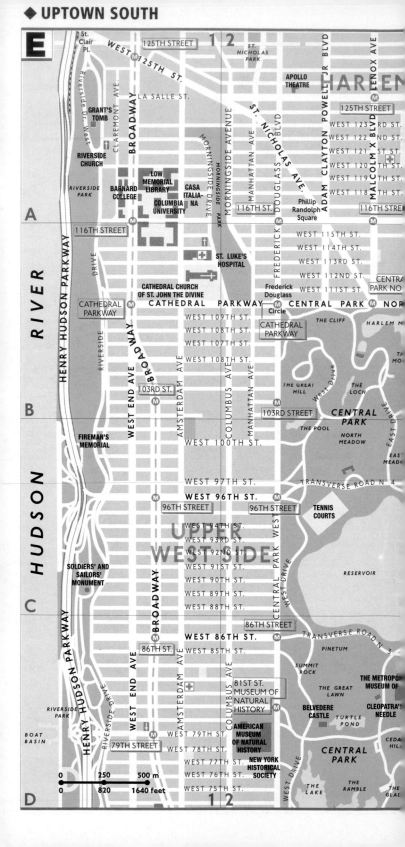

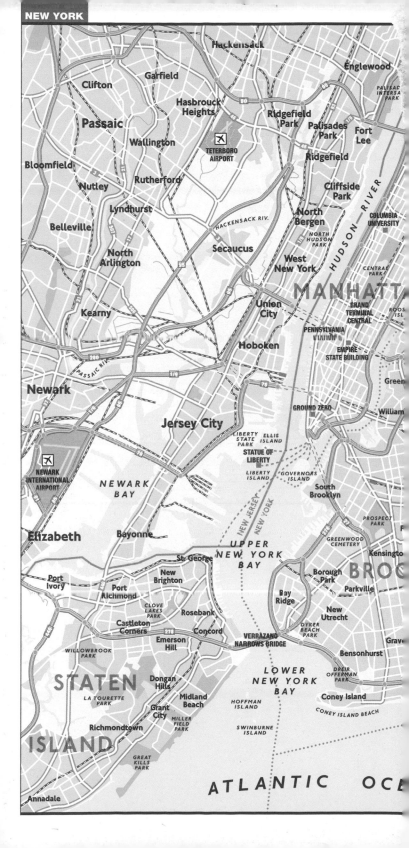

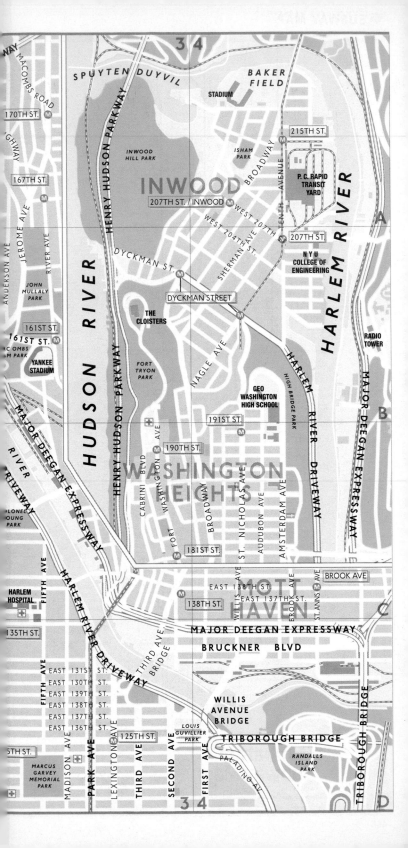

MUSEUM OF MODERN ART ▲ 290

CENTRAL PARK ▲ 314

METROPOLITAN MUSEUM ▲ 328

GUGGENHEIM MUSEUM ▲ 339

HARLEM ▲ 350

WILLIAMSBURG ▲ 366

STATUE OF LIBERTY
The symbol of America.

BROOKLYN BRIDGE
A breathtaking stroll over the East River on New York's oldest bridge.

CHINATOWN
An oriental journey through hundred-year-old Chinatown: buildings converted into pagodas, street signs written in Chinese characters, performances of Tai Chi in the squares, mouthwatering smells from stalls and restaurants.

GREENWICH VILLAGE
A complete change of scenery in narrow streets lined with small houses and trees. Greenwich has retained the relaxed atmosphere of its Bohemian years at the turn of the 20th century.

EMPIRE STATE BUILDING
A "cathedral in the sky", and another symbol of New York.

TIMES SQUARE
By day or night, Times Square buzzes with life in the heart of the Broadway Theater District. Welcome to the bright lights of Broadway, with its musicals, media and advertising signs.

MUSEUM OF MODERN ART
A unique collection of 20th-century masterpieces. Ten thousand works from the Post-Impressionists to the present day.

CENTRAL PARK
A vast oasis in the center of Manhattan.

METROPOLITAN MUSEUM
One of the largest museums of art in the world, with collections covering all civilizations and all periods, from pre-history to the present.

GUGGENHEIM MUSEUM
A unique building for a unique collection. Five thousand works, from the Impressionists to contemporary art.

HARLEM
The cultural and political hub of Black America. Harlem is undergoing a rehabilitation program and is no longer closed to other neighborhoods in the city.

WILLIAMSBURG
This Brooklyn neighborhood is going through a remarkable renaissance, and has a lively nightlife and artistic community.

BRONX

LEM
3

RK

M

N

RANDALLS
ISLAND

WARDS
ISLAND

SEVELT ISLAND

QUEENS

MOMA QNS

G

N

0	1	2 km
0	0.6	1.2 miles